THE TRAGEDY OF
U.S. FOREIGN POLICY

THE
TRAGEDY OF
U.S. FOREIGN
POLICY

How America's Civil Religion
Betrayed the National Interest

WALTER A. McDOUGALL

Yale

UNIVERSITY PRESS

New Haven and London

Published with assistance from the foundation established in memory of Calvin Chapin of the Class of 1788, Yale College.

Yale University Press books may be purchased in quantity for educational, business, or promotional use. For information, please e-mail sales.press@yale.edu (U.S. office) or sales@yaleup.co.uk (U.K. office).

Set in Janson type by IDS Infotech Ltd.
Printed in the United States of America.

ISBN: 978-0-300-21145-0 (hardcover : alk. paper)

Library of Congress Control Number: 2016939152

A catalogue record for this book is available from the British Library.

This paper meets the requirements of ANSI/NISO Z39.48-1992 (Permanence of Paper).

10 9 8 7 6 5 4 3 2 1

To all who have prayed for me
and to the Spirit that moved them

A nation ought to know itself. It ought to form a just estimate of its own situation, both with respect to itself and to its neighbors. It ought to learn the excellencies, and the blemishes likewise of its own constitution. . . . Without a discriminating sagacity of this kind, the principles of imitation, intended for the wisest purposes in states as well as in individuals, would be always an uncertain, sometimes a dangerous guide. A measure extremely salutary to one state, might be extremely injurious to another. What, in one situation, would be productive of peace and happiness, might, in another, be the unfortunate cause of infelicity and war. . . . This duty of self-knowledge is of vast extent and of vast importance, in nations as well as in men.

—*The Works of the Honourable James Wilson*,1804

A half-century ago [1901] people in this country had a sense of security vis-à-vis their world environment such as I suppose no people had ever since the days of the Roman Empire. Today that pattern is almost reversed. . . . What has caused this metamorphosis? How did a country so secure become so insecure?

—george f. kennan, *American Diplomacy,* 1951

Everything begins in mysticism and ends in politics. . . . Politics laughs at mysticism; nevertheless it is still mysticism which feeds these same politics.

—charles péguy, *Notre Jeunesse,* 1910

Contents

Introduction: 9/11 in Parallax Vision

Four political cartoons framed the whole sorry story. The first served as cover art for the final 2001 issue of *The American Spectator*. It reproduced a Victorian lithograph of fierce Afghan warriors firing muskets from a rocky redoubt. The added caption, however, was entirely up to date. "They've got Avanex Powermuxes!" shouts one tribesman. "We're toast," his comrade replies. As that issue went to press, Operation Enduring Freedom, the post-9/11 assault on Al Qaeda and the Taliban, had barely begun. Yet the cover story by Victor Davis Hanson, "Why the West Has Won . . . and Will," anticipated the swift campaign that apotheosized the high-tech "new American way of war," which in turn persuaded the administration of George W. Bush that an Iraqi invasion would be equally antiseptic. That righteous confidence was captured in a second cartoon on the cover of the February 18, 2002, issue of *Der Spiegel*. Above the title, "Die Bush Krieger: Amerikas Feldzug gegen das Böse" (The Bush warriors: America's campaign against evil), the artist caricatured the architects of the Global War on Terror as superheroes. Secretary of State Colin Powell was Batman; Secretary of Defense Donald Rumsfeld, Conan the Barbarian; President George W. Bush, Rambo; Vice President Richard Cheney, the Terminator; and National Security Adviser Condoleezza Rice, Xena the Warrior Princess.

Operation Iraqi Freedom in spring 2003 seemed to unfold according to script. But soon both blitzkriegs degenerated into protracted occupations whose costs in blood, money, and prestige mocked the boasts of American "benevolent hegemony." Hence a third cartoon on *Der Spiegel*'s cover of October 27, 2008, displayed "Die Bush Krieger: Ende der Vorstellung" (End of the performance). Powell is long gone, his Batman suit discarded. A wounded Rumsfeld limps offstage. Bush is exhausted, his bandolier now a sling for his arm. Cheney and Rice are stunned and bedraggled. The show's over.

Only it wasn't. To be sure, Barack Obama seemed and sounded like Bush's opposite to the degree American politics will permit. But presidential transitions are always blurrier than remembered or depicted in textbooks, and in any case the conflict with Islamic terrorism appears indeed to be generational. So Obama confounded his friends (including the Nobel Peace Prize committee) by continuing to wage the Global War on Terror, albeit on a limited-liability basis, and did not repeal the Bush Doctrine. Accordingly, a fourth withering cartoon, this one sketched by the *Philadelphia Inquirer*'s Tony Auth, appeared on August 1, 2010. It depicted a dilapidated, garbage-strewn urban neighborhood devoid of people. In the foreground a federal building displayed the American flag, but it, too, was decrepit and empty. A sign on the wall explained why: "GONE NATION-BUILDING."

In 1997 a certain Cassandra published *Promised Land, Crusader State: The American Encounter with the World since 1776*, which questioned the conventional lexicon of U.S. diplomatic history and warned against imperial overstretch in pursuit of utopian goals. Walter Russell Mead, whose own erudite histories have explored the cultural roots of American foreign policy, later credited the book for having "challenged two generations of received historical wisdom" and "changing the way the history of American foreign policy is taught." That certainly seemed the case given the subsequent spate of titles containing such phrases as "Messianic Nation," "Redeemer Nation," "Crusader Nation," and Mead's own "Special Providence." What is more, the themes and issues raised by that 1997 book have only grown in immediacy. Suffice to say the book was translated into Arabic.

Promised Land, Crusader State defined eight traditions in foreign affairs inspired by two centuries of U.S. engagement with the world.

A first set of four traditions—those born of the image of the United States as a Promised Land—constituted a sort of Old Testament that informed U.S. foreign relations from George Washington's Farewell Address (1796) to the end of Grover Cleveland's second term (1896). Those nineteenth-century traditions included (1) Liberty, or Exceptionalism (so-called), which sanctified unity, sovereignty, and freedom at home as the highest purpose of statecraft while shunning aggressive export of American ideology; (2) Unilateralism or Isolationism (so-called), which sanctified peace, friendship, and commerce with all nations but entangling alliances with none; (3) the American System, or Monroe Doctrine (so-called), which declared the New and Old Worlds to be separate spheres; and (4) Expansionism, or Manifest Destiny (so-called), which blessed territorial growth in North America but only commercial and cultural outreach overseas.

A second set of four traditions—those born of the image of the United States as a Crusader State—constituted a sort of New Testament that informed U.S. foreign relations from William McKinley's inauguration (1897) to the end of Bill Clinton's first term (1997). Those twentieth-century traditions included (5) Progressive Imperialism, through which Americans embraced navalism, overseas empire, and Open Door economics; (6) Wilsonianism, or Liberal Internationalism (so-called), under whose banner Americans waged two world wars for new world orders; (7) Containment of communism throughout the Cold War; and (8) Global Meliorism, the conflation of American policies designed to assist other countries (especially Third World ones) through foreign aid, humanitarian intervention, nation-building, and democracy promotion.

The four Promised Land traditions were "all about Being and Becoming, and were designed by the Founding Fathers to deny the outside world the chance to shape America's future." The four Crusader State traditions were "all about Doing and Relating, and were designed to give America the chance to shape the outside world's future." All eight traditions were authentically American, but whereas the first four were complementary parts of a single grand strategy, the second four often clashed with each other as well as with the older traditions. Thus, while it was true the United States played an indispensable role in ridding the world of Fascist

and Communist threats, it is also true that American strategic confusion inflated those threats and the human, financial, and moral
costs of combating them.

At length the Soviet Union went "poof" like the Wicked Witch
in *The Wizard of Oz* or Sauron in *The Lord of the Rings*, and the
fifty-year emergency dating from Pearl Harbor came to an end. It
seemed only logical that the militarism, propaganda, and imperial
presidency, not to mention the federal regulations, direct taxes, and
welfare state needed to sustain public support for the warfare state,
would also now come to an end. American politics in the 1990s re-
volved around such long-deferred domestic issues as the national
debt, trade deficit, decaying infrastructure, social security reform,
health care, education, illegal immigration, de-industrialization,
drugs, crime, and the collapse of families. Even formerly hawkish
neo-conservatives such as Irving Kristol and Jeane Kirkpatrick bade
the United States become a normal nation again. Hence *Promised
Land, Crusader State* posed the following query:

> Does our blessed heritage as a land of liberty require us to
> crusade abroad on behalf of others, as our New Testament
> in foreign policy commands? Or does giving in to the
> temptation to impose our will abroad, however virtuous
> our intent, violate the Old Testament principles that made
> America great in the first place? In short, can the United
> States be a Crusader State and still remain a Promised
> Land? That question hangs over our third century.

When that century began on September 11, 2001, the answers
came quickly. America the Crusader State not only could not remain
a Promised Land, it could not even remain a Crusader State because
the financial and political costs of war had become prohibitive. In just
over a decade—without even engaging some new peer competitor—
the United States nearly exhausted its armed forces, good faith and
credit, bipartisanship and patience at home, and prestige among
friends and foes abroad. Perhaps, later in the century, positive global
trends will inspire revisionist histories with an alternate interpretation of the post–Cold War era. But as of 2016 the direct costs of the
Global War on Terror will soon surpass $2 trillion and indirect costs,

$5 trillion, while the butcher's bill to the U.S. military numbers about six thousand killed, over forty thousand wounded, an estimated three hundred thousand subject to post-traumatic stress disorder, a suicide rate among veterans triple that of U.S. civilians, and at least one hundred thousand non-combatant deaths in Iraq and Afghanistan alone, let alone the rest of the Muslim world. The Arab Spring, with the exception of Tunisia, aborted, and Al Qaeda gave way to the even more fanatical Islamic State in Syria and Iraq. Fifteen years on, it appears the only powers to gain from the U.S. crusades of the twenty-first century have been Iran, China, and Russia.

No wonder the question *Promised Land, Crusader State* posed back in 1997 already sounds "so twentieth century." How could American power and prestige have fallen so far and so fast? Did the Al Qaeda attacks trigger a self-destructive overreaction? Has it indeed always been so that foreign enemies cannot harm Americans more than they harm themselves, through strategic malpractice and financial malfeasance, over and over again? Or did 9/11 simply provide the occasion for Americans to indulge some deeply embedded imperial urges of their own? Those are the riddles that inspired this book.

Maybe it was just a matter of chances and choices, beginning with the dead-heat election of November 2000. What might Al Gore have done were he the president after 9/11? Perhaps he would have continued Bill Clinton's (and the world's) practice of treating terrorism as a crime rather than an act of war. Perhaps he would have confined the U.S. response to a Department of Homeland Security, a global coalition of intelligence and law enforcement agencies, and severe U.N. sanctions against Afghanistan. But Bush might also have chosen differently, even after declaring a War on Terror. He might have made the Afghan campaign a brief, violent, punitive expedition rather than committing halfheartedly to building a modern nation where none had ever existed before. He might have waited to topple Saddam Hussein until U.N. inspections had run their course and U.S. diplomacy had forged the sort of grand coalition Bush's father fashioned for the First Gulf War in 1991. He might have postponed an invasion until a viable, internationally sanctioned regime was ready to take over in Baghdad. He might have heeded the military advisers who said that

140,000 troops were only a fraction of the number needed for an occupation (not to mention a counter-insurgency). He might not have attacked Iraq at all. The fact that he chose to initiate two protracted conflicts whose carnage and ruin dwarfed that of 9/11 itself almost lends credence to the theory that messianic republics must engage in periodic blood sacrifice as a sort of totem worship.

Such mysticism, however, is not required. Three historical telescopes can serve to bring into focus (1) the immediate post-9/11 decisions that launched a Global War on Terror; (2) the intermediate post–Cold War decisions that established the pretense of U.S. hegemony; and (3) the perennial impulses that have always tempted Americans to meet discriminate challenges through indiscriminate crusades. The first two chapters of this book describe what the first two telescopes reveal. The rest of the book explores what that third telescope reveals, which is nothing less than the progress and regress of American civil religion over 240 years. Call it U.S. diplomatic history in the metaphysical mode.

CHAPTER ONE

Why the Bush Blunders?

THE FIRST TELESCOPE REVEALS kaleidoscopic confusion because no less than nine plausible theories compete to explain the 2003 invasion of Iraq. Nor are the testimonies of the principals any help. President Bush's memoirs admit to no mistakes and blame no one. Those of Vice President Cheney, Secretary of Defense Rumsfeld, Secretary of State Powell, National Security Adviser Rice, Pentagon official Douglas Feith, White House aide Scott McClellan, CIA chief George Tenet, Iraq proconsul L. Paul "Jerry" Bremer III, and General Tommy Franks belong to what Feith called the "I-was-surrounded-by-idiots school of memoir writing." So what was the Iraqi invasion about?

Was it all about terrorism, which is to say fear? If so, that made it the president's overwhelming priority to prevent a recurrence. But that in itself says a great deal about the privileged history of the United States. For millions of people terrorism has been a daily danger and war a periodic one. Indeed, to Europeans or Japanese during World War II the loss of two buildings, four aircraft, and three thousand people in an air raid would have been considered light damage. But 9/11 was sufficiently traumatic to justify, even require, that Americans invoke a preventive war doctrine that they had previously spurned. On September 20, 2001, Bush issued an ultimatum to every government in the world:

"Either you are with us, or you are with the terrorists. From this day forward, any nation that continues to harbor or support terrorism will be regarded by the United States as a hostile regime." The Bush Doctrine has since been roundly criticized for naming terror the enemy rather than specific terrorist movements and obliterating national sovereignty. But its vague universality kept U.S. options open and left the government free to pursue Cheney's goal of reducing to nearly zero the chance of another homeland attack. The political cost of anything else was simply too awful to contemplate. That brought Iraq into play because Saddam Hussein's contemptible regime was suspected of being in cahoots with Al Qaeda. What more is needed to explain the Iraq invasion than that? Well, something more, because the Bush administration evidently considered "regime change" in Iraq well before 9/11.

Was it all about weapons of mass destruction (WMD)? After all, every Western intelligence agency suspected that Saddam possessed some. He had used chemical weapons in his wars against Iran and his own Kurdish minority, while U.N. inspectors after 1991 had been shocked by Iraqis' nuclear progress since Israel had bombed their Osirak reactor ten years before. In the post-9/11 environment Bush and Cheney dared not risk even a small chance that Saddam might provide terrorists with WMD. But this explanation runs up against three objections. First, the Bush administration clearly assumed its conclusion because it ruled out of hand the ten thousand pages of documentation Iraq provided in compliance with the U.N. resolution. Second, Bush refrained from attacking North Korea or Iran, whose nuclear programs were far more advanced. Third, Deputy Secretary of Defense Paul Wolfowitz confessed: "For bureaucratic reasons, we settled on one issue, weapons of mass destruction, because it was the one reason everyone could agree on." What other reasons were there on which they could not agree?

Was it all about neo-conservatism? That was a favorite theory in the early going. It was widely believed that an aggressive cabal had captured the Bush administration because 9/11 seemed to vindicate its members' worldview. Rejecting the lessons of Vietnam to the effect that the United States lacked the power, patience, institutions, knowledge, wisdom, and right to treat alien cultures like potter's clay, they blithely imagined American occupiers could conjure democracy in a country devoid of democrats. That is why numerous books and articles initially explained Operation Iraqi Freedom as a pure expression of the neo-cons' Leo Straussian philosophy. But a second wave of scholars in the 2010s examined the growing body of evidence and found that no important decisions could be traced exclusively to neo-con influence and that the Iraq invasion in particular happened because strategic realists and oil lobbyists were also on board. Indeed, when Rumsfeld was later asked about neo-con manipulation, he scoffed, "I suppose the implication is that the president and the vice-president and myself and Colin Powell just fell off a turnip truck to take these jobs."

Was it all about Israel? As early as 1996 a neo-con delegation led by Richard Perle had presented the Likud party's leader, Binyamin Netanyahu, with its plan to overthrow Saddam Hussein. Moreover, the Evangelical President Bush was unabashedly pro-Israeli, while the American Israel Public Affairs Committee (AIPAC) exercised influence with both parties on Capitol Hill. But the fact remained that the Israel lobby did not get its way on regime change in Iraq until 9/11. Nor did it follow that if the invasion of Iraq was not in the U.S. national interest, it must have served some other interest. More likely the administration's realist and neo-con wings alike blundered in their calculation of the risks and benefits of shaking up the Middle East. Suffice to say Israelis themselves were divided over the Iraq invasion and have received little but bad news ever since.

Was it all about oil? The major oil companies wanted predictable supplies and prices, but the Saudis had ceased to be reliable partners. As early as 1999 Cheney told the London Petroleum Institute that control of the Iraqi spigot would be an excellent substitute. Moreover, it was imperative that the United States close its military bases in Saudi Arabia since the presence of infidels on holy soil fed jihadi propaganda. Finally, Wolfowitz promised Iraqi oil exports would pay for the war and nation-building to follow. But the truth was more complicated. State Department officials and oil executives alike knew that they could not coerce a post-Saddam Iraqi regime into granting U.S. companies the requisite concessions, that Iraq would remain in the OPEC cartel, and that war damage and sabotage might severely cut production. As it happened, the loss of

Iraqi supplies combined with soaring demand, led by China and India, meant the price of crude oil did not fall under Bush but quintupled by 2008.

Was it all about Bush family dynamics? Books ranging from sympathetic to lurid have purported to reveal the inner workings of the dynasty. Did George W. Bush exploit the War on Terror to rub out the Iraqi dictator who had tried to assassinate his father, or finish the job his father had left undone, or prove himself tougher than the old man? Such psycho-historical flights are tempting but moot in the presence of so many other material factors.

Was it all about the reelection calendar of Bush's political "architect," Karl Rove? That is another tempting explanation because of what happened after the First Gulf War. Bush 41 enjoyed the highest approval ratings in history after Operation Desert Storm, only to lose reelection over domestic issues. Bush 43 was especially vulnerable given his contested victory in 2000. Did the White House contrive the Iraq invasion just to keep the War on Terror on voters' minds through 2004? Not surprisingly, Rove scorned the accusation, adding that Bush's popularity might have "cratered" had the war gone badly. It did, but only because another ticking clock ran out on Bush by 2006. After shocks like Pearl Harbor or the Kennedy assassination Americans give their presidents emergency powers to deal with the crisis—but only for about five years, after which time their patience evaporates.

Was it all about Rumsfeld's New American Way of War? Perhaps the administration was so mesmerized by the Pentagon's high-tech wizardry that it dispensed with postwar planning or even a serious internal debate over the costs and consequences of regime change in Iraq. As former chief of counter-terrorism Richard Clarke recalled, "All along it seemed inevitable that we would invade [Iraq]. . . . It was an idée fixe, a rigid belief, received wisdom, a decision already made and one that no fact or event could derail." Rumsfeld confirms that judgment by recording that Bush never discussed with him privately or in the National Security Council (NSC) whether to invade Iraq. But if that were so, then Rumsfeld himself must have sold the White House on the notion that the "revolution in military affairs" had matured to the point that the Powell Doctrine could be repealed. That cautious post-Vietnam doctrine made U.S. interventions contingent on overwhelming force, clear political goals, and an exit strategy. The heavy, expensive, and limited 1991 campaign to expel Iraqi forces from Kuwait was conducted on that basis. But Rumsfeld believed that lean, lethal U.S. forces equipped with satellite-linked cybernetic systems for command, control, and intelligence could now decapitate target regimes at minimal cost.

Rumsfeld signed the 1998 petition calling for the overthrow of Saddam Hussein and discussed Iraq as soon as Bush took office. He began planning an Iraq invasion before the Afghan campaign even ended. His protégé Kenneth Adelman believed that "liberating Iraq would be a cakewalk." But Rumsfeld's insistence on a light footprint ignored the possibility that a long occupation might be required in a land scarred by dictatorship, sanctions, and ethnic and sectarian strife. When Air Force Secretary James Roche gently warned, "Don, you do realize Iraq could be another Vietnam?" Rumsfeld barked, "Of course it won't be another Vietnam! We are going to go in, overthrow Saddam, and get out. That's it." In short, Rumsfeld did not want to do nation-building. But his bullish determination that no one even draft a Plan B all but ensured that his battle plan to win the war must inevitably lose the peace.

Was it all about democratizing the Middle East? Rumsfeld's memoirs criticize the administration's "mission creep," noting that Bush's Freedom Agenda was a late development and one sure to alarm the Saudis, Gulf emirates, and Egyptians. Even (or especially) Israel had cause to blanch at talk of empowering the Arab masses. Yet no sooner did Saddam's WMD turn out to be imaginary than Bush shifted into high moral gear. He now declared it America's purpose to "end tyranny in our world." Where, Rumsfeld wondered, did the democracy talk come from: Condi Rice? Tony Blair? Bush's own Evangelical faith? If from the last, then the fanaticism in his second inaugural address was at least sincere. But whatever the case, democratizing the Middle East could not have been what the wars were primarily about because Bush's defensive preemption morphed into offensive prescription only after Osama bin Laden eluded capture in Afghanistan, after no WMD turned up in Iraq, and after the U.S. occupations provoked more of the terrorism they were meant to suppress.

Historians will long debate the origins of the 9/11 attacks and the causes of the U.S. riposte. But two judgments seem incontestable: (1) the Bush administration did not know what it was doing when a new Pearl Harbor hurled the United States into a maelstrom of fear; (2) the Bush administration knew exactly what it is doing when a new Pearl Harbor freed the United States from all constraints.

Those judgments are not mutually exclusive. But let us begin with the notion that the White House, Pentagon, CIA, and other agencies displayed confusion and ignorance after 9/11. Indeed, perhaps the only official who was neither confused nor ignorant was Clarke, the counter-terrorism chief who could never get anyone's attention. Otherwise, the evidence of interagency rivalries over intelligence, policy, tactics, and turf mocks the unity displayed by common citizens. Even persons and agencies that agreed on a given assessment or course of action often did so for contrary reasons, none of which had anything to do with that American fetish, democracy. Yet the fact that nation-building (more accurately state-building) ended up as the default mission in Iraq is especially damning because confusion and ignorance were doubly characteristic of the Phase Four (post-conflict) planning. Did anyone other than the State Department's distrusted Arabists bother to study the history of Iraq and the religious, ethnic, and tribal rivalries that Saddam had repressed? Did gullible Pentagon officials assume they need only install the slippery exile Ahmed Chalabi as the George Washington of Iraq because that gave them an excuse not to do their own homework?

Whatever the reasons, neither the White House nor Pentagon deliberated about the consequences of invading two forbidding countries. Maybe Cheney and Rumsfeld, who both had witnessed the evisceration of the presidency during Gerald Ford's administration, saw a golden opportunity to pay back Congressional Democrats. Maybe they were what the Germans call *Fachmänner*, experts in their own specialties but incompetent outside of them. Such men need a leader who will tap their talents but not permit them to strategize. Bush was not that sort of leader.

The War on Terror started well. The Afghan campaign was supported by NATO and benefitted from the fact that the tribes of the

Northern Alliance provided ground troops for an offensive that routed the Pashtun Taliban. A *loya jirga*, or tribal council, promptly agreed on a political transition. An allied conference in Bonn pledged security and development aid for the new regime of Hamid Karzai. That only emboldened the hawkish civilians in the Pentagon to imagine that Iraq—a modern state by contrast to Afghanistan— could be fixed even more easily. The State Department, by contrast, did due diligence, warning in January 2003 that democratic change in Iraq "would be a long, difficult, and probably turbulent process in a deeply divided society." The CIA likewise anticipated that former Ba'ath regime elements and Islamic terrorists might resort to guerilla war. Neither agency believed that Iraqi externals (exiles) were a magical means to avoid risky nation-building. But the Cabinet and NSC never debated whether this was a war of necessity and, if not, whether the likely rewards justified the costs and risks. Congress, fearful of seeming soft on terrorism, deferred to the executive branch as it had ritually done since the 1950 Korean conflict. The vice president's staff functioned like a shadow White House. The Departments of State and Defense blamed each other for every mishap. The CIA politicized intelligence in order to sell the president's war. No one but Rice thinks the NSC did its duty to mediate disputes and knock heads together. Rumsfeld's shorthand for it all was "Too Many Hands on the Steering Wheel," but in retrospect it seems far too few people had meaningful input on the questions of whether, why, and how.

In the blinding fog of war generals can never be sure where the "bridge too far" is located until their armies have already crossed it. In the event, the Bush administration launched the war in Iraq under the worst possible circumstances, without U.N. authorization or expected Turkish support, without a Plan B in case regime change got messy, without consideration of the secondary and tertiary effects of removing a big piece from the Middle East jigsaw, and without foresight that another "Christian Zionist Crusade" might inflame terrorism rather than snuff it out. So the Pentagon's surgically precise military triumphs were wasted. In Afghanistan it soon became evident that Karzai's writ barely extended beyond Kabul and that his army and police were incompetent, corrupt, and porous. A tangle of international agencies pursued ignorant and contradictory programs for human rights and economic development while Afghan officials wasted and stole billions of dollars in foreign aid. The Taliban sprang back to life. In Iraq Rumsfeld's prediction that political stabilization would happen so fast that all but thirty thousand U.S. troops could be withdrawn by August 1, 2003, proved risible. The Coalition Provisional Authority (CPA), headed by Bremer, was uniquely ill-equipped to do nation-building. Chalabi, spirited back to Iraq by Wolfowitz, turned out to have no support even among fellow Shi'ites. Instead, he encouraged Bremer to issue decrees that only completed Iraq's slide into anarchy. He summarily fired all Ba'athist state employees, even though party membership was mandatory under Saddam, and disbanded the Iraqi Army without pay despite CIA assurances to the contrary. He ended government subsidies and sold off state enterprises, including utilities and petroleum. As a result the economy seized up, public services collapsed, and security became a do-it-yourself obligation for rural tribes and urban militias. The decrees also made half a million people plus their dependents idle, angry, and desperate in a country bristling with weapons, long-suppressed feuds, and factions jockeying for advantage in anticipation of the Americans' departure.

The predictable results included a multi-sided civil war characterized by demoralizing guerilla tactics (including improvised explosive devices, or IEDs); bloody battles for objectives soon abandoned (Fallujah, Sammara, Sadr City); inevitable U.S. atrocities (Abu Ghraib, waterboarding); infiltration across porous borders (Iran and Syria); indigent, infiltrated "allies" (Iraqi regime and security forces); soaring costs ($80 billion supplementals every six months); massive American aid ($53 billion), which mostly fueled waste and corruption ($8.8 billion "lost" by the CPA in its first year alone); mounting casualties (1,487 American dead and wounded just by November 2004, the month Bush barely won reelection); and fruitless tactics ("whack-a-mole"). General Anthony C. Zinni, who had warned Bush he would rue the day he lit a fuse in the Middle East, sighed, "I have seen this movie, it was called Vietnam." Bremer confessed, "We've become the worst of all things—an ineffective occupier." The invasion of Iraq, testified General William Odom, was "the greatest strategic disaster in our history."

It might have been even worse had Bush not changed course after his party's thumping in the 2006 elections. He persuaded Rumsfeld to retire; approved a counter-insurgency strategy of Clear, Hold, and Build; appointed General David Petraeus; and sent thirty thousand more troops to support a surge. Thanks also to a revolt against Al Qaeda by desert sheikhs (the Anbar Awakening) and Prime Minister Nouri al-Maliki's belated crackdown on Shi'ite militias, Iraq gained a modicum of security by the time Bush left office. But the country he imagined the vanguard of a broader Freedom Agenda was far from democratic, prosperous, law-abiding, or pro-American. Petraeus's more realistic goal was just a peaceful, defensible Iraq cleansed of terrorists. But even that slipped beyond America's reach when negotiations deadlocked over a residual U.S. military presence in Iraq. The last U.S. forces withdrew in December 2011, after which violence and chaos spread to the far reaches of the Muslim world, which only gave neo-conservatives a pretext to blame the lost peace on Obama.

Aged baby boomers recall growing up in an era when Americans boasted of never having lost a war. That was before they began to wage unwinnable wars against abstractions such as poverty, drugs, and tyranny, not to mention third-rate countries they were too foolish to leave alone and too rule-bound to defeat. British philosopher G. K. Chesterton was premature but prophesied a century ago:

> It may be said with rough accuracy that there are three stages in the life of a strong people. First, it is a small power, and fights small powers. Then it is a great power, and fights great powers. Then it is a great power, and fights small powers, but pretends that they are great powers, in order to rekindle the ashes of its ancient emotion and vanity. After that, the next step is to become a small power itself. ... America added to all her other late Roman or Byzantine elements the element of the Caracallan triumph, the triumph over nobody.

The U.S. homeland has so far been spared another catastrophic attack. But it is dubious how much the Afghan and Iraqi wars contributed to homeland security, while any victories have been pyrrhic and have added $5 trillion to the national debt. To be sure, the Obama administration rang up even higher deficits during the Great Recession, but Republicans must shoulder the blame for setting a terrible precedent. It was Vice President Cheney who smugly observed in 2002, "Reagan proved deficits don't matter."

The only excuse to be made for the strategic insolvency bequeathed by the Bush 43 administration is that it gave the public what it demanded. For Americans at large behaved the way they always do when demonic foreigners dare to interfere with their pursuit of happiness. They demanded disproportionate vengeance and perfect security, while pretending their government's wars were part of a universal crusade. Far from being sui generis, the administration's response to 9/11 and the public's response to that response were altogether predictable. As Adam Garfinkle concluded, "At its core, the 9/11 decade has not been about what others have done to America; it has been about what we Americans have done to ourselves, here in our transcontinental, open-air church we call a country."

CHAPTER TWO

Why the Imperial Overstretch?

"WE ARE GOING TO do something terrible to you—we are going to deprive you of an enemy," said Georgy Arbatov, the founder of the Soviet Institute of USA and Canada. The collapse of the USSR was the "greatest geopolitical disaster of the twentieth century," said Russian president Vladimir Putin. They did—and it was—because the death of the Soviet Union endowed the United States with too much power for its own good. As Henry Adams observed, "Power is poison. Its effect on Presidents had always been tragic."

The second telescope, focused on the post–Cold War era as a whole, reveals the opposite of kaleidoscope confusion and in fact reveals remarkable coherence. For fifty years—1941 to 1991—Americans had lived in a permanent state of emergency that turned their nation into a welfare-warfare state with a vast array of global commitments. Could Americans even remember what life was like in a world without existential threats? In the 1990s some tried. Traditional foreign policy realists hoped that the nation would lower its profile abroad and concentrate on long-deferred domestic problems, while structural realists in political science predicted that other great powers would soon counterbalance the United States. But "naive realists" (in political scientist Richard Betts's cutting phrase) were let down by American and world leaders alike, neither of whom constrained or contained U.S. power. In the case of foreigners this might have been due in part to the relatively benign character of the hegemon or their own disorientation. But it meant that the rest of the world inadvertently behaved in the worst possible way from the standpoint of America's true national interest: it did nothing. That lack of resistance made it hard to resist calls that the United States wield a universal police power on behalf of the human rights agenda they themselves had sponsored to good propaganda effect throughout the Cold War. Following 9/11, when exigency reinforced temptation and America was accused of being a rogue superpower, some international resistance at last arose but too late to save Americans from their zeal.

All three post–Cold War administrations aimed for a paradigm amounting to one or another form of U.S. preponderance. All were based on dubious assumptions of American exceptionalism, a unipolar world, and democratic peace theory. It was, therefore, hard to escape the conclusion that in cases involving rogue regimes, failed states, aggressors, and tyrants Americans bore responsibility to engage in regime change whenever necessary and possible. Suffice to say that the United States conducted large-scale military interventions more, not less, often than during the Cold War, averaging one every eighteen months prior to 9/11. The three administrations differed only in their styles of governance. George H. W. Bush's New World Order was administrative, cautious, and responsible. His foreign policy motto was the Hippocratic adage to do no harm, and he surmounted one crisis after another through multilateral institutions. His focus was always on security and stability, at least until the very end of his term. Bill Clinton's approach was casual and confident that all good things go together in a world defined by the so-called Washington Consensus. Originally a ten-point program for neo-liberal capitalist reforms in Latin America, the consensus quickly broadened to include liberal political and international norms and to encompass the entire rapidly globalizing world. In other words, the collapse of communism unleashed free flows of capital, goods, labor, and ideas such that economic growth would naturally foster strong middle classes, which would naturally foster transparent democratic regimes, which would naturally live in peace with each other. The Information Technology (IT) revolution reinforced globalization by empowering common people with instantaneous communications and social media. Stubborn authoritarian holdouts—China, North Korea, Iran—might cause mischief for a season, but engagement, not containment, was the best way to handle them. In sum, the Clinton administration dispensed with grand strategy because it was no longer needed: the clash of ideologies was over and won and history had come to an end.

Harvard political scientist Samuel Huntington challenged the Washington Consensus by predicting that international affairs after the Cold War would be driven by a clash of civilizations already evident, for instance, in the Balkans. But what really mocked the conceits of the 1990s was the reaction to the 9/11 attacks because it demonstrated how little the United States itself had transcended history. Rather than stoically but confidently absorbing the attack as a virulent, but ultimately futile, protest against globalization, Americans apparently went berserk. Thus did the posture of sole superpower evolve over a single decade from Bush 41's cautious assertion to Clinton's casual assumption to Bush 43's caustic aggression.

Brent Scowcroft, George H. W. Bush's national security adviser, put the matter succinctly: "The Cold War struggle had shaped our assumptions about international and domestic politics, our institutions and processes, our armed forces and military strategy. In a blink of an eye, these were gone. We were suddenly in a unique position, without experience, without precedent, and standing alone at the height of power." Yet Bush 41 was a Point-A-to-Point-B executor who disparaged the so-called "vision thing." From 1989 to 1991 he slow-pedaled the collapse of the Soviet Union in hopes of saving Mikhail Gorbachev. He even warned Ukrainians against secession in the Chicken Kiev speech made at Gorbachev's behest. Still, he had no choice but to take the initiative in post–Cold War global security after Saddam Hussein invaded oil-rich Kuwait. Bush promised the invasion "will not stand," brushed aside forlorn Soviet objections, and assembled two extensive coalitions—an inner one comprised of Middle Eastern states and an outer one comprised of NATO, Japan, and other contributors. He then requested U.N. authorization to use military force to expel the Iraqis. "We thought that we were perhaps at a watershed in history," Scowcroft recorded. "Compared to the period we had just come through, the era seemed like a new world order."

The U.S. military designed to fight the Red Army in the heart of Europe made quick work of the Iraqis with very few casualties, despite some dire warnings and Saddam's own boasts. Operation Desert Storm purged the lingering Vietnam Syndrome and made the United States seem invincible. In retrospect, that was due as much to Bush's prudent decision not to march into Baghdad. Instead, he settled for U.N. sanctions, no-fly zones, and dual containment of Iraq and Iran in the Persian Gulf pending the overthrow of Saddam from within. It now seemed no power on earth could challenge the high-tech U.S. military. Even after the 1990s peace dividend sharply reduced the U.S. defense budget, it still exceeded those of the next dozen countries combined. U.S. hegemony was so complete that analogies to the Roman and British empires even fell short of reality. Certainly few Americans, drunk on power and righteousness, imagined the unipolar moment ending any time soon, while Pentagon planners determined to turn the moment into an era. The Defense Policy Guidance issued in 1992 stated bluntly: "Our first objective is to prevent the re-emergence of a new rival, either on the territory of the former Soviet Union or elsewhere, that poses a threat on the order of that posed formerly by the Soviet Union." Its corollary objective was to prevent any regional domination in Western Europe, East Asia, and Southwest Asia. The implication was that the United States would even take preemptive or preventive action to ensure against such domination, which sounds shocking in retrospect, but was taken for granted in those heady days. Defense Secretary Cheney just edited out of the document impolitic references to specific regions and signed off on it in January 1993.

American voters hire their presidents to perform certain tasks and sometimes fire them when they perform those tasks too well or too quickly. Bush managed the endgame of the Cold War and First Gulf War so adroitly that the nation was freed to refocus attention on domestic tasks. That allowed Clinton (with critical assistance from third-party candidate Ross Perot) to defeat Bush on the slogan "It's the Economy, Stupid!"

Clinton's 1990s are doubtless remembered by older Americans as the best years of their lives. The United States was secure, democracy spread, the dot-com economy boomed, and even the federal budget was in surplus. But though peaceful and prosperous, those years were rife with contention over the very identity and purpose of America. The decade was poisoned by paranoia over U.N. black helicopters and domestic militias, the Waco massacre, and the Oklahoma City bombing. The decade was embittered by the climactic phase of a "culture war" over education and public mores that dated from the 1960s. Not least, the decade contained harbingers of disturbing new trends such as ethnic cleansing and greedy nationalism in the post-Communist world, proliferation of WMD, failed states, terrorist movements, and protests against globalization. Indeed, the first bombing of the World Trade Center in 1993 and the attack on the *U.S.S. Cole* in 2000 might be considered the bookends of the Clinton era and Osama bin Laden's 1996 declaration of war on the United States its midpoint.

That such events might be harbingers of worse to come was scarcely evident when the Clinton administration took office, which helps to explain why its foreign policy transition was unusually relaxed. When at last National Security Adviser Tony Lake, Secretary of State Warren Christopher, Clinton himself, and U.N. Ambassador Madeleine Albright made a series of speeches on foreign policy, they articulated an entirely new vision. The administration replaced the Cold War doctrine of Containment with Engagement (of not-yet democratic powers such as China), Enlargement (of the zones of democracy and free enterprise), and Assertive Multilateralism (when dealing with rogue regimes and failed states). These doctrines, according to Lake, were based on the premises that "America's core concepts—democracy and market economics—are more broadly accepted than ever" and that "we are [this era's] dominant power." But Democrats and Republicans fell to debating between and among themselves over whether, when, and how to deploy military and economic power, especially for nation-building. The Weinberger and Powell Doctrines that distilled the lessons of the Vietnam War required that the United

States commit its armed forces only when vital national interests were at stake; the cost, risk, and consequences were all frankly assessed; the commitment had broad support from the American people and international community; and a clear exit strategy was in place. But was such restraint, such self-containment, still relevant in an era of U.S. hegemony? Realists might insist that superpowers don't do windows, excoriate foreign policy as social work, and oppose military deployments when vital national interests were not engaged. But anxious neo-conservatives believed the Clinton administration was wasting the unipolar moment. They called for national greatness and benevolent hegemony, founded the Project for a New American Century in 1997, and raised alarms about cuts in defense. Finally, liberal internationalists insisted the United States had a duty to engage in humanitarian interventions on behalf of universal human rights, an ethic soon formalized by the United Nations as R2P (Responsibility to Protect). The U.S. armed forces jumped on board, if only to justify their budgets, and began to plan for Operations Other Than War.

Real-world crises, however, revealed the frustrating contradictions in all such operations. By definition humanitarian interventions were responses to disasters; hence they usually occurred only after the worst killing had been done. By definition their targets were failed states or rogue regimes; hence they predictably triggered open-ended nation-building projects. By definition they occurred not in great powers but only in weak ones unable to resist. Hence they appeared to recolonize countries by using the same law-and-order pretext as Theodore Roosevelt's 1904 Corollary to the Monroe Doctrine. Albright might insist the United States was the indispensable nation, but Tony Lake objected: "Neither we nor the international community has either the responsibility or the means to do whatever it takes for as long as it takes to rebuild nations."

In the event, the Clinton administration botched the nation-building missions it declared for Somalia and Haiti, ignored a genocide in Rwanda, and intervened in Bosnia only after the European Union proved impotent to prevent ethnic cleansing in the former Yugoslavia. But Clinton was content to surf through the 1990s with limited commitments that gave minimal offense and triggered no hostile coalitions. The European Union was busy widening and deepening itself among former Soviet satellites. Russia drifted under the bibulous rule of Boris Yeltsin. China exploited globalization to achieve stormy economic growth, which prompted Japan to cling more tightly to its U.S. alliance. Moreover, Clinton gratified the international community by signing the Kyoto Protocol on global warming, the Rome Statute on an International Criminal Court, and the U.N. Convention on the Law of the Sea, even though he never expected Senate ratification.

Clinton's record was mixed. Though he solved no problems and exacerbated some others, he made no costly blunders of the sort that squandered U.S. hegemony. However, four omens and anticipations occurred on his watch: the 1995 presidential directive (PDD-39) naming terrorists with WMD the top national-security priority; the 1998 embassy bombings in Africa and retaliatory cruise missile strikes against Al Qaeda bases in Afghanistan and Sudan; the 1998 Iraqi Liberation Act; and the 1999 Kosovo war. The first one foreshadowed the consensus excuse for Bush 43's later invasion of Iraq. The second foreshadowed the Bush Doctrine's unilateral disregard for national sovereignty. The third called for regime change in Iraq even though Clinton realized it could not be accomplished without military force. The fourth seemed to demonstrate the efficacy of air power alone to break determined enemy resistance, encourage the Serbs themselves to oust Slobodan Milošević, and prepare the ground for an international peacekeeping mission. Indeed, a straight line runs from Kosovo to Iraq, however much they seem separated by a millennium.

Ample precursors to the Bush Doctrine were already on display in the post–Cold War decade. The untoward shock of 9/11 gave Bush a window to express as principles what Clinton had implied were contingencies. That is why Bush's rhetoric seemed for a time like noble candor by contrast, for instance, to the apparent cynicism of the Germans and French. But its fanatical streak was evident from the start. On September 12, 2001, work began on a National Security Presidential Directive (NSPD) that called for "the elimination of terrorism as a threat to our way of life." On September 14, 2001, Bush said, "Our responsibility to history is already clear, to answer these attacks and rid the world of evil." On September 20, 2001, the president insisted, "You are either with us or with the terrorists" and declared the war "will not stop until every terrorist group of global reach has been found, stopped, and defeated." In 2002 Bush's State of the Union address, West Point graduation speech, and new National Security Strategy fleshed out the new agenda. Since the United States now possessed unprecedented and unequaled strength and influence, it was time to "translate this moment of influence into decades of peace, prosperity, and liberty"; to pledge preemptive and unilateral strikes to confront threats before they reached America's shores; to confront the Axis of Evil, comprising Iraq, Iran, and North Korea. In January 2003 Bush proclaimed, "Americans are a free people, who know that freedom is the right of every person and the future of every nation. The liberty we prize is not America's gift to the world, it is God's gift to humanity." The utopian rhetoric peaked in Bush's second inaugural address, which referred forty-seven times to liberty and freedom and committed America to "the ultimate goal of ending tyranny in our world."

Oscar Wilde observed that the fanatic's worst vice is sincerity. But the only ones possibly fooled were Americans themselves, who were persuaded to compromise personal freedoms, rights, and protections in the apparent belief that terrorists posed a greater threat than had the Soviet Union's thirty-five thousand nuclear warheads. To name terror the enemy rather than terrorist organizations, to claim jihadis hate the West only for its liberty, and to speak of a contest between freedom and tyranny were simplifications at best. To speak of draining the swamps of Islamo-fascism through democratization of the whole Muslim crescent was mad.

Power corrupts, said Lord Acton, and absolute power corrupts absolutely. But the forms and fashions of corruption and power vary widely among states and cultures. It is not really surprising that the United States threw away many of its strategic advantages in just fifteen years through the escalating pursuit of hegemony. But the form and fashion of that self-negation were distinctive and intimately connected to G. K. Chesterton's modern heresy, wherein not only the human vices are loosed, but "the virtues are let loose also; and the virtues wander more wildly, and the virtues do more terrible damage." What was it that made Americans, especially in the post–Cold War era, peculiarly susceptible to the terrible power of wandering virtues?

CHAPTER THREE

Why the American Heresies?

I N 1967 sociologist Robert Bellah discovered a previously unspoken truth. The United States was not only what Chesterton had called a nation with the soul of a church, but was also the living embodiment of American Civil Religion (ACR). Curiously, what inspired him to think about the matter was the presidential inauguration of John F. Kennedy. Prior to that all the God talk permeating public life seemed a relic of the nation's Puritan culture or else cant targeting Bible Belt voters. But in 1961 Bellah observed a hip, young, liberal, rich, Harvard-trained Catholic president intoning "the belief that the rights of man come not from the generosity of the state but from the hand of God" and that "here on earth God's work must truly be our own." Fascinated by the non- or poly-sectarian cast of this rhetoric, Bellah recalled how Dwight D. Eisenhower had said, "Our government has no sense unless it is founded in a deeply felt religious faith—and I don't care what it is." Clearly there was more to this than political pandering or false piety. So Bellah turned to history and discovered ample evidence that above and beyond familiar biblical denominations wafted an invisible civil creed that united Americans and called them to realize the destiny God had in store for them.

The most surprising feature of Bellah's article and the scholarship it inspired is that there was anything surprising about it at all.

Jean-Jacques Rousseau, meditating on civil religion in his *Social Contract*, observed that republics—having dispensed with monarchy and an established church—required some transcendental glue to cement their citizens together and give their polity purpose. But Americans' civil religion did not stem from Rousseau because his civil faith was explicitly anticlerical. Rather, it derived from the God-affirming English civil religion that was painfully crafted over 175 years of Tudor-Stuart history. First the English tamed the church by placing their own monarch instead of the pope at its head; then they tamed the monarch by asserting parliamentary supremacy in 1688. Their Protestantism in fact protested all authorities that inhibited mobilization of Britons for secular goals. In other words, their kingdom—the United Kingdom—*was* of this world, and to render unto Caesar *was* to render under God. Their patron saints included Richard Hakluyt, Francis Drake, Walter Raleigh, Francis Bacon, Isaac Newton, and John Locke. They baptized themselves a new chosen people in the vanguard of human progress. With supreme confidence that God was on England's side and England on God's, they embarked on a stunning career in navigation, commerce, colonization, science, and industry, imbued with the four spirits of English expansion. Generations of mostly Anglo-Protestant migrants carried those spirits to America.

The first spirit of English expansion was economic: a hustling rural and commercial capitalism that broke down feudalism, infused all classes with an ethic of self-improvement, and ultimately inspired the Scottish Enlightenment's free-market and pursuit-of-happiness moral philosophies. The second spirit was political: the Elizabethan compromise that mobilized a broad Protestant church behind the crown. To be sure, the absolutist ambitions of the Anglo-Catholic Stuart dynasty sparked civil war, which led to Oliver Cromwell's Puritan dictatorship in the mid-seventeenth century, but the Glorious Revolution of 1688 established the Protestant Whig ascendancy. Great Britain quickly rose to power and glory on the strength of parliamentary supremacy and the Bill of Rights, the 1707 Acts of Union with Scotland, and the maturation of a fiscal-military state and floating national debt. The third spirit was strategic: pursuit of New World empire in defiance of the monopolistic claims of Catholic Spain and France. The growth of the English colonies, combined with the ambitions of the Whig war party, sparked a conflict for control of North America that lasted on and off from 1689 to 1763. The fourth spirit was legal: the Common Law judgment that only occupation and improvement of land confer ownership; hence hustling British colonists had every right to dispossess indigent Irish or American Indians.

This fantastic outpouring of energy was always a national project, a British project, and a Protestant project under a latitudinarian Anglican God. The Calvinist nonconformists who peopled New England after 1630, far from being some kind of proto-Americans, were in fact uncomfortable participants in that British imperial project, at least until spiritual Puritans devolved over several generations into material Yankees. The other colonists, with the partial exception of pacifist Quakers, embodied the four spirits of English expansion from the get-go. All thirteen colonies flourished under the Whigs' policy of benign neglect, which in turn inspired Benjamin Franklin to predict the seat of empire must eventually gravitate to America.

Instead, the climactic triumph of the Anglo-American Atlantic world—the conquest of Canada in the Seven Years' War—provoked controversy over the very nature of the empire. The crown and Parliament enacted reforms meant to appease their new French and Indian subjects while belatedly exerting authority over the thirteen colonies. The policies included the imposition of new taxes and commercial restrictions, the concession to Catholic Spain of the Louisiana Territory, the prohibition of white settlements beyond the Alleghenies, and the toleration of the Catholic Church in Québec. In so doing, the crown and Parliament traduced all four spirits of English expansion in ways that choked the colonists' otherwise unstoppable rise to power and wealth. It seemed the British had become apostates in their own church. So just twelve years after toasting King George III, a critical mass of colonists damned his eyes and reached for their muskets. Many were Presbyterians, Congregationalists, and Methodists whose individualism had been quickened by the eighteenth-century revival called the First Great Awakening. Others were Quakers, Baptists, and low-church Anglicans. Still others were Unitarians, Deists, and/or Freemasons drawn to the philosophies of the Enlightenment. But whether awakened, enlightened, or both, the

Patriots' lives, fortunes, and sacred honor were truly at stake because insofar as they believed their spirits of civil and religious liberty, free enterprise, self-government, and empire—that is, their ideals and interests alike—were sanctioned by the laws of nature and nature's God, then the American struggle for independence must be a species of holy war. The Continental Congress called colonists to repentance, prayer, and fasting, resolving in March 1776 that "it may please the Lord of Hosts, the God of America, to animate our officers and soldiers with invincible fortitude, earnestly beseeching him to ... grant that a spirit of incorruptible patriotism and undefiled religion may universally prevail."

Eloquent preachers from Jonathan Edwards to George Whitefield had prepared Americans to imagine themselves a new chosen people in a new promised land with a millenarian destiny. Tom Paine's *Common Sense* closed the deal. He quoted the Bible to prove that God "hath rendered his protest against monarchical government" and named it "the most prosperous invention the Devil ever set on foot for the promotion of idolatry." Citing the book of 1 Samuel, Paine lamented that the Israelites rejected God and demanded an earthly king to be as all other nations. But now Americans had the chance to begin the world over again. Paine's warning that "Ye that oppose independence now, ye know not what ye do!" made independence the messiah and faint-hearted colonists the Roman soldiers on Calvary. In sum, Christians reading *Common Sense* found in it the God of the Bible and a politics derived from religion. Deists just as readily found in it the God of nature and a religion derived from politics. The Continental Congress, trusting God's blessing, declared independence from Britain.

Now, according to the Bible, the Jews did not invent the Lord; rather the Lord raised up children to Abraham, who gradually made sense of the divine intercessions they experienced over 1,500 years. Nor did Jesus's disciples invent Christianity; rather God formed the church as the Holy Spirit revealed to them the meaning of the miraculous events they had witnessed. Likewise no one invented American Civil Religion; rather the Patriots deduced divine patronage from their collective exodus to a New World richly blessed with milk and honey, not to mention the seemingly miraculous events that allowed the ragtag colonies to defeat the world's mightiest empire.

So while historians are correct to trace the intellectual origins of the American Creed to James Harrington's neoclassical republicanism, John Locke's theory of natural rights, the Scottish Enlightenment's common-sense philosophy, English common law, Whig ideology, and the First Great Awakening, the fact remains that Patriots imagined themselves under a special Providence. Indeed, it is impossible to imagine the Continental Congress, comprised mostly of wealthy, well-connected men, ever making the leap into treason without faith that they, their forbears, and their descendants were actors in a play scripted by the Author of History.

Who was that Author? To be sure, most churched Americans were Protestant Christians and readily assumed the God looking out for their country was the same one they worshiped on Sunday. But the civil God was not strictly Jehovah or the Holy Trinity. The American God had no name and a hundred names. Franklin called him Father of Lights and Supreme Architect; Washington, the Almighty Being, Invisible Hand, and Parent of the Human Race; John Adams, the Patron of Order, Fountain of Justice, and Protector; Thomas Jefferson, the Infinite Power; James Madison, the Being who Regulates the Destiny of Nations; James Monroe, the Almighty and Providence; John Quincy Adams, the Ark of our Salvation and Heaven; Andrew Jackson, that Power and Almighty Being Who mercifully protected our national infancy. For Washington, Monroe, Jackson, Henry Clay, and a surprising percentage of early national statesmen he was also the Freemasons' *G*, that Geometry above all theologies whose watchful, protective Eye oversaw the Unfinished Pyramid on the Great Seal of the United States. If Americans had ever fallen to quarreling over the identity of their national God, the Union could not have survived. So the Articles of Confederation and Constitution were silent about religion, not because the American Revolution was secular, but because it was too religious. Therein lay the secret of the First Amendment. By prohibiting Congress from establishing any particular religion, it silently established a civil religion to which all sectarian believers must bow.

Political scientist Ellis West has coined as neat and neutral a definition as anyone: "A civil religion is a set of beliefs and attitudes that explain the meaning and purpose of any given political society in terms of its relationship to a transcendent, spiritual reality, that are held by the people generally of that society, and that are expressed in public rituals, myths, and symbols." That "transcendent, spiritual reality" is what distinguishes civil religion from nationalism and ideologies of state worship. Americans did not worship their government, a fact made palpable by the checks and balances of their Constitution. They worshiped a deity who made them one out of many *(e pluribus unum)* and a new order for the ages *(novus ordo seclorum)* and who has blessed their undertakings *(annuit coeptis)*.

What does that divine-right republicanism, if you will, have to do with the history of U.S. foreign relations? Did God's covenant with the American Founders oblige them to practice some new diplomacy based on idealism or ideology? Not at all, because America would be defined not by anything its government did abroad but by what it was supposed to be at home: a land of civil and religious liberty under law, united, consensual, and utterly sovereign—which is what the word "empire" meant to Britons ever since Henry VIII. George Washington gave eloquent voice to that in his last general orders to the Continental Army on April 18, 1783: "For, happy, thrice happy, shall they be pronounced hereafter, who have contributed anything, who have performed the meanest office; in erecting this stupendous fabric of freedom and empire on the broad basis of independency; who have assisted in protecting the rights of human nature, and establishing an asylum for the poor and oppressed of all nations and religions." So long as they were devoted to those qualities ("seek ye first the kingdom of God"), the United States would flourish and prosper ("and all this shall be added unto you"). The only ones who could thwart the nation's destiny were Americans themselves by falling into disunion or by provoking foreign hostility. No wonder Americans imagined their foreign policy principles—unity, liberty, sovereignty, neutrality, expansion, peace, friendship, and commerce with all nations—to be derivatives of the laws of nature and nature's God.

That is not to say Americans were never split-minded. Thomas Jefferson, Henry Clay, James K. Polk, and Ulysses S. Grant, to name a representative few, could at times be susceptible to a utopian temptation that led them to imagine vain things. But fanaticism rarely seized even temporary control over foreign policy because the United States in the nineteenth century was both contained and self-contained by four powerful checks against zealotry. The first was relative weakness in the dangerous world at large, which inspired Monroe's doctrine that the New and Old Worlds must be separate spheres. The second was westward expansion because no sane American wanted to risk the nation's Manifest Destiny by picking ideological quarrels with overseas monarchies. The third were the lessons of history to be learned from the collapse of republics ancient and modern. American statesmen lived in fear of an Alcibiades, Caesar, or Cromwell in their midst and were on guard against hubris. The fourth was residual Christian anthropology because nearly all the Founders believed in the incorrigible imperfection of human nature (original sin) or its philosophical equivalent, the universal tendency toward selfishness and faction. That is why Federalists were anxious to check the powers of the general government and why Anti-Federalists feared any general government at all. Indeed, a major check on foreign policy adventurism was the Constitution itself. Finally, standing above all foreign policy principles was the invisible ACR, whose gospels included the Declaration of Independence, the Constitution, and Washington's Farewell Address, and whose accumulating epistles included the presidential inaugural addresses and state papers.

Historians have long disputed whether U.S. foreign policy is primarily driven by ideology or economic interest. (What a fortunate country to have such luxury; most countries are slaves to geopolitics.) But the ACR brooks no divergence between ideology and interest because the American Dream that venerates life and liberty also venerates opportunity, prosperity, and the pursuit of happiness. To freedom-loving Americans God's material blessings are simply a birthright. In other words, Americans want to feel good about doing well. So historians distort reality whenever they pit idealism against realism or ideology against economics because civil religion is omnivorous and digests any antimony. But civil religion is always in more or less flux because each generation must re-imagine the national God who blesses whatever foreign policy posture Americans, or at least their elites, believe the times demand. Behind all the tectonic shifts in rhetoric, economics, and strategy, therefore, lurks a mystical, magical, shape-shifting civil religion whose orthodoxies

can turn into heresies and whose heresies can turn into new orthodoxies.

Civil religious dogma with regard to foreign relations has
passed through three distinct eras since the founding of constitutional government in 1789. It is interesting that all have their roots
in the last decade of a century, as if Americans anticipated their
world was about to change. The Classical ACR, the original orthodoxy, was conceived in the 1790s, the Progressive ACR in the
1890s, and the Millennial ACR in the 1990s. The Classical ACR
underwent wrenching revisions, especially during the Civil War,
but its foreign policy tenets survived intact. Under that post-1865
neo-Classical ACR the United States became a world power. The
Progressive ACR suffered wrenching setbacks throughout its for-
mative half-century, but after World War II it captured the country
and much of the world. Under the post-1945 neo-Progressive ACR
the United States became a dominant global power. The Millennial
ACR has so far led to a series of wrenching false starts and mistakes
that have confused and frightened Americans. But if the pattern repeats, they will eventually convert to a neo-Millennial ACR that
will style itself a global civil religion for all humankind.

Washington's World: The
Civil Church Expectant

In 1817 John Quincy Adams, the U.S. minister to Great Britain, wrote to his friend William Plumer, the governor of New Hampshire, about the reputation of the United States following the Napoleonic wars: "The universal feeling of Europe in witnessing the gigantic growth of our population and power is that we shall, if united, become a very dangerous member of the society of nations. They therefore hope what they confidently expect, that we shall not long remain united. That before we shall have attained the strength of national manhood our Union will be dissolved, and that we shall break up into two or more nations in opposition against one another."

An interesting choice of phrases: "dangerous member of the society of nations." What could Adams have meant? The United States certainly posed no military threat to Old World powers. The recently concluded War of 1812 had been fought entirely in North American lands and waters, rendering silly the intemperate threats of American war hawks about setting London aflame. They had intended to endanger British Ontario, but their invasions aborted. The United States was a clear and present danger to Spain but only because that derelict empire still laid claim to a third of North America. Nor did the United States threaten the domestic security of European regimes. Those monarchies had just emerged from twenty-three years of total war against the truly dangerous French

Revolution without the Americans lifting a finger except to wage
an undeclared naval war against the French Republic from 1798 to
1800. What is more, Washington and Jefferson had sent loud signals, soon to be echoed by John Quincy Adams himself, foreswear-
ing any U.S. intention of meddling in Europe's affairs.

Nor could the rapid growth of the United States endanger
the Old World balance of power, regardless of its intentions. On
the contrary, Britannia's naval hegemony was never more secure
than over the following seventy-five years, while France, Russia,
and the German powers pursued their own ambitions with barely
a thought for the United States until the twentieth century.
No, Adams's (somewhat self-satisfied) missive to his like-minded
Yankee colleague referred to the dangerous example the American
experiment in popular sovereignty might pose if it were seen to bestow stability, freedom, and prosperity upon the general population. That neither Adams nor Europeans imagined the United
States behaving as a revolutionary threat is evident in his reference
to American membership in the society of nations and warning
that the Union might prove dangerous only to itself. Adams's letter
was no spread-eagled threat against ideological opponents. It was a
plea for *e pluribus unum* three years after Redcoats had burned
Washington City and Plumer's Yankees had convened in Hartford
to ponder secession.

The principal goal of the American War of Independence was
precisely membership in the club of Christian sovereignties because Americans could not isolate themselves from the Atlantic
world even if they had wished. Nobody knew that better than John
Quincy Adams, the most accomplished diplomat of the generation
that grew up in Washington's World.

When George Washington was inaugurated president on April
30, 1789, the United States of America were bounded by British colonies later called Canada to the north, the Spanish colonies called the
Floridas to the south, the Spanish colonies of Tejas and Louisiana to
the southwest and west, and the Atlantic Ocean to the east, bristling
with hostile navies. U.S. territory extended only to the Mississippi
River; its settled portions, just beyond the spine of the Appalachians.
The Ohio Territory and Gulf Coast were still Indian country.
Technically there were only eleven states since North Carolina and

Rhode Island had not yet ratified the Constitution, while quirky Vermont toyed with independence before joining the Union in 1791. The first census of the United States counted 3,199,355 free citizens and 694,280 slaves for a total of 3,893,635 people in 1790. By contrast, Spain numbered 10 million, Britain 15 million, and France 28 million. The United States had a federal government but no army or navy and a diplomatic corps one could count on two hands. For the next sixty years the largest federal agency—and the only one most citizens encountered—was the post office.

In Washington's World men might agree to stand for office, but they did not run for it because public service was a duty, not a prize. Men both high- and low-born demanded respect and courted honor, if necessary with dueling pistols. Yet no one believed in democracy, and the white male voters who were enfranchised still deferred to those whom Jefferson called the "natural aristocracy." In many cases those gentlemen from New England, the mid-Atlantic, and Virginia knew Latin and Greek or else the classics in translation, plus British history and law, and the philosophies of the Enlightenment. All knew the Bible intimately, whether or not they strictly adhered to a creed. But contrary to modern myth, a large majority of the American Founders and constitutional Framers were confessing Protestants to whom human imperfection was a matter of common sense. They might have rejected the Catholic doctrine of original sin and the Calvinist doctrine of total depravity, but they readily granted James Madison's maxim that men were not angels. That is why Federalists checked and balanced the strictly enumerated powers of the branches of the general government, reserved all other powers to the states, then ratified a Bill of Rights for safety's sake. All the Framers believed the citizenry must embody sufficient republican virtue to sustain self-government, and most believed in the possibility of moral progress, but very few were utopian. Indeed, the genius of the Constitution derived in good part from its ability to harness selfish private ambition for the collective good.

In Washington's World a motley coalition of Patriots scattered among the seaboard colonies had made a revolution that abolished monarchy and legal privileges based on birth. Yet many of the most enlightened and religious Patriots owned slaves. Indeed, Edmund Burke instructed Parliament that the Virginians' status as slaveholders was what made them so fiercely jealous of their own liberty. In time the domestic dispute over the extension of slavery would tear the Union apart, but that did not mean the Southern planters who played such prominent roles in the American founding were snakes in the garden or cancerous cells whom true Americans would have to exterminate to realize their national destiny. Southern planters belonged to the early modern Atlantic world just as much as the Hancocks of Boston. George Washington belonged to Washington's World.

It is necessary to state such commonplace facts because some twenty-first-century historians have asserted in teleological fashion that right-minded northern Founders believed from the start that the United States must transform the world through active engagement, not just passive example. But the false-hearted Southern Founders clung to slavery, which soon spread westward with the cotton gin. Like a moral and political anchor, slavery kept the American ship of state tethered until the Civil War cut the cord. At last the United States, now a singular noun, was free to project its power and ideals worldwide, fulfilling its destiny. That account might seem credible if "American Founder" were an archetype in the thought experiment of a political philosopher. But the Founders were people chiseled by the past they inherited and the history that happened to them. They were not disembodied neo-Platonists, Kantians, or proto-Straussians. The Founders were just what a historian would expect them to be: late-eighteenth-century Anglo-American exponents of Whiggish country-party philosophy who protested capricious rule in the name of their ancient rights as Englishmen. The idea that the colonies-turned-states were now called to purify each other in the manner of Cromwell's Puritan Commonwealth, not to mention reform foreign countries, would have struck them as a howling contradiction in terms. The pragmatic, liberty-loving Framers accordingly drafted a Constitution friendly to the horizontal expansion of hustling pioneers, not the vertical expansion of grasping officials.

As for the ultimate destiny of the United States, the citizens of Washington's World were content to leave that in the hands of a Providence in which they almost all fervently believed. Washington made that civil religious assumption explicit in his first inaugural address:

Such being the impressions under which I have, in obedience to the public summons, repaired to the present station, it would be peculiarly improper to omit in this first official act my fervent supplications to that Almighty Being who rules over the universe, who presides in the councils of nations, and whose providential aids can supply every human defect, that His benediction may consecrate to the liberties and happiness of the people of the United States a Government instituted by themselves for these essential purposes, and may enable every instrument employed in its administration to execute with success the functions allotted to his charge. In tendering this homage to the Great Author of every public and private good, I assure myself that it expresses your sentiments not less than my own, nor those of my fellow-citizens at large less than either. No people can be bound to acknowledge and adore the Invisible Hand which conducts the affairs of men more than those of the United States. Every step by which they have advanced to the character of an independent nation seems to have been distinguished by some token of providential agency; and in the important revolution just accomplished in the system of their united government the tranquil deliberations and voluntary consent of so many distinct communities from which the event has resulted can not be compared with the means by which most governments have been established without some return of pious gratitude, along with an humble anticipation of the future blessings which the past seem to presage.

That "humble anticipation" behooved Americans to cherish the liberty, unity, and sovereignty they had won for themselves in a dangerous world and articulate principles for the defense of that trinity. The process of articulation and trials by fire took some sixty years from the inauguration of Washington (and outbreak of the French Revolution) in 1789 to the death of John Quincy Adams (and end of the Mexican War) in 1848. But the principles themselves, including reciprocity, neutrality, a separate American system of states, and expansion across the continent, were all present at the creation of the republic, implicit in Washington's Farewell Address, and so obviously successful that they inspired U.S. grand strategy for a century, even as democratization and industrialization swept away most other features of Washington's World.

CHAPTER FOUR

A Divine-Right Republic in the Family of Nations

P OLITICAL LIBERTY, ECONOMIC PROSPERITY, cultural creativity, and all other human aspirations are impossible without order or what world historian William H. McNeill called predictability of behavior. For philosopher and historian Russell Kirk order was the first need of the soul and the first need of any commonwealth aspiring to the good. Kirk traced the roots of American ideas of order through London, Rome, and Athens back to Jerusalem, noting that the first line of the first book printed in the thirteen colonies, the Puritans' *New England Primer*, read "In Adam's fall we sinned all." A fallen world was the prerequisite for the Mosaic Law—"the precious gift of Jehovah by which Israel might exist in justice"—which established a divine standard above all human government. That, according to Britain's former chief rabbi, Jonathan Henry Sacks, is what made it possible, for the first time in history, even to conceive of human liberty and equality. But the first need of all was order. That was the postulate the Founders of the United States applied to their domestic institutions. It was also the postulate they applied to their foreign relations. They were not firebrands yearning to remake world order. They just wanted to establish their place in that order without compromising the liberty they enjoyed at home.

This statement by historian Robert Smith sparkles with clarity: "The story of early American diplomacy is therefore the search for a republican realpolitik, a diplomacy compatible with republican institutions at home that recognized the realities of world politics." When Tom Paine called for Americans to begin the world again, he meant to return to the pristine condition of the twelve tribes of Israel prior to their apostate request for a human king. In his preamble to the Declaration of Independence Jefferson justified republican rebellion against royal authority on the self-evident truth that all men were endowed by their Creator with unalienable rights. New England militias marched to a new anthem that shouted "No king but God." The idea was not original. The Dutch republic and English Commonwealth had made similar claims. But the "Hebraic republicanism" of American Patriots had unprecedented appeal due to its fusion of Protestant biblical and Enlightened rational authority. Belief that Providence blessed their glorious cause emboldened the signers of the Declaration to pledge their lives, fortunes, and sacred honor. But how did Heaven intend for a free republic to behave in a fallen world ruled by predatory monarchies? Could Americans maintain their independence through war and diplomacy without subverting liberty at home?

To make a long story short, the hopes of Congressmen that independence might be won without protracted conflict were dashed. Their winter 1775–76 invasion of Canada—the only feint made toward exporting revolution—was a fiasco. Their putative friends in Parliament failed to dissuade the king and cabinet, backed by a strong majority in public opinion, from trying to crush the revolt. Their Model Treaty of 1776, in which Congress offered all nations friendship and commerce, was insufficient to pry recognition and aid from Britain's rivals in Europe. So the Patriots had no choice, if they wished to cheat the gallows, but to trust in espionage and secret diplomacy to procure clandestine, mostly French, arms and money. That timely foreign assistance kept the Continental Army extant until victory at Saratoga, and the wily blandishments of Benjamin Franklin persuaded Louis XVI to make not only a treaty of amity and commerce, but also a military alliance with the self-styled United States of America. Their basis was "the most perfect equality and reciprocity," which (John Quincy Adams later boasted) expressed the "spirit of liberty and equal rights" of the American Revolution. Hence, the fundamental quality of American diplomacy from its inception was precisely not to be dangerous or endangered but to display mutual respect.

France declared war on Britain in 1778; its Bourbon ally, Spain, did likewise the following year. In 1781 Washington's army won the climactic victory at Yorktown, thanks to the Spanish governor in Havana (who conceived the campaign), one and a half French armies, and a French fleet offshore. Thus, two Catholic monarchies midwived the birth of the divine-right republic. Negotiations ensued in Paris, where the American delegates Franklin, Adams, and John Jay violated their pledge not to break ranks with the French and instead played them off against the British. The resulting 1783 Peace of Paris, the international birth certificate of the United States, was a stunning triumph. But one more act was needed before the republic could congratulate itself on playing power politics without losing its soul. Its own commander-in-chief had to resign his commission in deference to civil authority, persuade his (unpaid) army to disband, and return every man to his farm, which of course is exactly what Washington did.

The consequences of American independence were enormous. From 1492 until 1783 the Atlantic Ocean was *res nullius*, a no-man's-land, which in turn meant it was by definition an imperial zone governed only by ships and cannon, forts and soldiers. To be sure, Spain once claimed a monopoly, but the buccaneers, merchants, colonists, and regular armed forces of the English, Dutch, and French punctured all pretensions to paper claims over lands, seas, and commerce. Even the solemn treaties meant to regulate relations among the colonial empires, such as the Treaty of Utrecht in 1713, were habitually abused by anyone who could get away with it. But an independent United States—a New World sovereignty—changed the legal status of the Atlantic into *res communis*, a commons belonging to everyone and thus potentially subject to legal norms and free trade. Americans, anything but isolationist, yearned to be treated as equal members of that community. "Such sentiments," historians Eliga Gould and Peter Onuf have written, "formed the *fons et origo* of an American patriotism." But from a

European perspective that was going to take some getting used to if it did not provoke outright resistance. Americans would have to keep struggling to win respect for their sovereignty on the high seas and even on their own borders. After the peace treaty the British continued to occupy Great Lakes forts, the Spaniards closed the Mississippi River, both encouraged Native Americans to resist U.S. authority, and all Europeans exploited the state governments' rivalries to win commercial advantage. Since the Articles of Confederation provided for a feeble legislature and no executive branch at all, a Federalist movement called for a convention, allegedly to fix the Articles but really to draft an entirely new constitution. Everyone knows that one of the principal tasks of the delegates at Philadelphia in 1787 was to design a government strong enough to defend the republic against foreign powers without threatening the liberty of its own citizens. A less appreciated corollary, however, was the need to design into the machinery a bias toward *peace* rather than war lest a fractious, passionate public or a capricious, ambitious president foment conflicts dangerous to Americans or to foreigners.

Why then did the Framers draft a constitution that had little to say about war, peace, and diplomacy and contained no specific instructions or warnings? Were the delegates who gathered in Philadelphia in 1787 naive, absentminded, or oblivious to the importance of sound politics? Certainly not. The first twenty-nine articles in *The Federalist* papers comprise an extended defense of the Constitution on foreign policy grounds. Yet the document itself contains only those few, familiar clauses in Article I, Section 8, which grant Congress power to regulate foreign commerce; define and punish piracy on the high seas; declare war; raise and support armies for no more than two years at a time; provide for a navy; and call up state militias in need. Article II, Section 2, is sparer still, simply granting the president power to serve as commander-in-chief, appoint ambassadors with advice and consent of the Senate, and make treaties with consent of two-thirds of senators present.

That is all. No one is delegated authority to make or execute foreign policy. No mention is made of a power to recognize or de-recognize foreign regimes, terminate treaties as opposed to make them, make peace as opposed to war, declare neutrality in the wars of others, annex or cede territory, bestow or deny foreign aid, impose sanctions, regulate immigration and the status of aliens, proclaim great doctrines like Monroe's, or for that matter prescribe or proscribe any specific behavior at all. What were the Framers thinking? Forrest McDonald's great book on the subject says it in the very first sentence: "The Framers of the Constitution were, for the most part, intensely practical men who were skeptical, even contemptuous, of abstract schemes of political theory." They meant to fashion a government able to defend the United States whatever that may require; hence they left its foreign policy powers vague and elastic while carefully separating the powers to raise and command armies and declare and wage war.

History and experience, not least the War of Independence itself, persuaded Federalists of the need for a single robust executive to execute foreign relations and command the military. Sound philosophy supported that judgment. John Locke considered executive prerogative to include "the power of war and peace, leagues and alliances, and all the transactions with all persons and communities without the Commonwealth." The alternative, he warned, must be disorder and ruin. Montesquieu praised the unwritten British constitution that deemed domestic policy primarily the business of the legislature and foreign policy that of the executive. Sir William Blackstone's voluminous commentaries on the Common Law found ample precedent for the Crown's exclusive authority over war and diplomacy so long as it was exercised for the public good in a constitutional manner. That was the ideal so eloquently expressed in Viscount Bolingbroke's 1738 treatise *The Idea of the Patriot King*. But American Patriots, needless to say, also identified strongly with Country Party or Whig philosophy, which damned executive caprice and upheld Parliamentary supremacy and cabinet government. Even Alexander Hamilton, who insisted that foreign affairs be executive altogether in the interest of unity, secrecy, decisiveness, dispatch, and intelligence, conceded in Federalist No. 75 that the "history of human conduct does not warrant that exalted opinion of human virtue which would make it wise to commit interests of so delicate and momentous a kind, as those which concern its intercourse with the rest of the world, to the sole disposal of . . . a President of the United States." James Madison was sufficiently worried about executive malfeasance that he wanted all residual or implied constitutional powers to rest with Congress.

To be sure, the office of American president was a novelty, and the expectations of the Framers regarding its evolution cannot be fully guessed. We can be sure, however, that nobody wanted to court executive tyranny, be it that of a monarch like George III or a demagogue like Oliver Cromwell. Consider, too, the very different provisions made for the raising of armies and navies. Article I, Section 8, grants to Congress the power to raise armies, but "no Appropriation of Money to that Use shall be for a longer Term than two Years." It then grants to Congress the power "To provide and maintain a Navy"—period, no restrictions. The distinction derived from the obvious fact that ships are big capital investments that take a long time to build and are expected to do lengthy service. But it also derived from the Framers' conviction that standing armies potentially threatened the liberties of people at home whereas navies could only defend them. (Thus did Britain's monarchs deploy a Royal Navy but not an army, which belonged to Parliament.) Moreover, the automatic expiration of military spending after two years meant that Congress could disband an army misused by a rogue commander-in-chief, while the voters could oust a rogue Congress that leapt into foolish or unjust war.

References to peace, both foreign and domestic, abound in *The Federalist* papers. Peace was the immediate purpose of the Union itself and whatever military establishments deemed prudent. Peace was the prerequisite for the preservation of the liberty and prosperity of the states and citizens, which is why Madison assured them in Federalist No. 45 that interruptions of peace would be rare: "The operations of the federal government will be most extensive and important in times of war and danger; those of the State governments, in times of peace and security. As the former periods will probably bear a small proportion to the latter, the State governments will here enjoy another advantage over the federal government." In fact, the Framers went to such "extraordinary lengths to prevent the central government from initiating war on its own accord" that political scientist Daniel Deudney has argued the federal government was not a state at all in terms understood by Europeans but a peace pact that, being neither anarchy nor hierarchy, amounted to negarchy. It preserved liberty through divided jurisdictions empowered to negate each other if a clear national interest was not being served. Indeed, High Federalists such as the first two presidents would have faced far more resistance to their military and financial establishments had the various checks and balances not reassured Jeffersonian skeptics.

The debate over the enumerated powers of the Constitution really concerned how best to preserve peace. Jefferson might be said to have embodied the wisdom of *Sic semper tyrannis*, the defiance to military dictators that became the motto of the Commonwealth of Virginia. Washington embodied the wisdom of *Si vis pacem para bellum*—If you wish for peace, prepare for war. As early as May 1783, in response to a request from Hamilton, Washington drafted the United States' first national security strategy. He began with the new nation's geopolitics, including the potential threats posed by the British and Spanish empires and hostile Indians on the frontier. Thanks to the Atlantic, America was distant from Europe, but the ocean also served as an avenue for attack against America's lengthy, exposed coastline. Accordingly, Washington proposed that Congress provide for a standing army to garrison forts on the frontiers and coasts, well-trained citizen militias required of every state, arsenals stocked with weapons and ammunition in case of sudden emergency, a military academy for the training of officers, and a permanent navy. Washington titled his document Sentiments on a Peace Establishment.

CHAPTER FIVE

Washington's Farewell Address

NATIONAL DIGNITY REQUIRED A balance of military strength and diplomatic tact so as not to tempt or provoke other nations. President Washington repeatedly asked Congress to vote military and naval funds even as he pursued irenic foreign relations. The French Revolution that erupted in 1789 vastly complicated that pursuit not only because it sparked a frighteningly ideological war, but also because it revealed the split-mindedness of some Americans in high places. As U.S. minister in Paris, Thomas Jefferson observed the French Revolution's violent but hopeful beginnings and flattered himself to think the French Declaration of the Rights of Man and the Citizen was inspired by his Declaration of Independence. Upon returning home to serve as Washington's secretary of state, Jefferson orchestrated a press campaign insinuating that Americans skeptical of the French Revolution were blasphemers of the true God, liberty. If so, then Washington was among them. As early as October 1789 Washington shared with Gouverneur Morris his view that while the "wonderful" revolution had survived its "first paroxysm," it would not be the last, and "the licentiousness of the People on one hand and sanguinary punishment on the other might drive events from one extreme to another." Thus did Washington anticipate Edmund Burke's *Reflections on the Revolution in France* (1790), with its closely argued distinctions between the historical, moderate rights that Americans invoked to justify independence and the anti-historical, abstract ideology invoked by the French revolutionaries. But during his first term Washington maintained a prudent silence about events in Europe in deference to the public's wish to believe that 1789 was an echo of 1776.

What forced the president to take a stand was the second French Revolution in 1792. The National Assembly declared war against monarchy, arrested Louis XVI, and proclaimed a republic. Would the United States honor the Franco-American alliance of 1778 in some overt fashion, especially now that France was a sister republic? Had that issue dominated the 1792 presidential campaign, it might have torn the Union asunder. That is why the Hamiltonian and Jeffersonian camps alike prevailed on the reluctant Washington to serve another term. But Jefferson's fanatical streak was on full display in his infamous letter of January 3, 1793, in which he expressed his belief that the "liberty of the whole earth was depending on the issue of the contest, and was ever such a prize won with so little innocent blood? My own affections have been deeply wounded by some of the martyrs to this cause, but rather than it should have failed, I would have seen half of the earth desolated. Were there but an Adam and an Eve left in every country, and left free, it would be better than it now is." Three weeks later the Jacobin party in Paris condemned the king to the guillotine and launched the Reign of Terror. That demonstrated the wisdom of Washington's proclamation of U.S. neutrality in April 1793: "The duty and interest of United States require, that they should with sincerity and good faith adopt and pursue a conduct friendly and impartial" toward all. He also warned Americans they would forfeit their government's protection "by committing, aiding, or abetting hostilities." In short, the president exerted peace powers equivalent to his war powers and made them stick even though James Madison challenged his action in Congress and Secretary of State Jefferson resigned.

Following Washington's proclamation the Democratic-Republican and Federalist factions turned into political parties that immediately resorted to mudslinging. The former accused the latter of opposing the French out of a secret wish to transplant British institutions (perhaps even monarchy) in America, while the latter accused the former of opposing the British out of a secret wish to transplant French institutions (perhaps even terror) in America. In fact, Jeffersonians were trying to exploit foreign policy in their campaign to abort Hamilton's program for an energetic executive branch, standing armed forces, a national bank, and promotion of manufactures. In the short run they were thwarted because the French Republic's envoy to the United States, Citizen Edmund Genêt, had secret instructions to manipulate politics, outfit pirate ships, and recruit a private army to seize New Orleans. Evidently, the arrogant French ideologues expected the United States to be as subservient as the European republics they established through propaganda and force. Genêt's contempt for American sovereignty was so egregious that Washington insisted he be recalled. But it is important to note that the 1793–94 Reign of Terror, in which some forty thousand people were slain, did not poison Franco-American relations. On the contrary, Washington restored full diplomatic relations to Paris. Nevertheless, the obvious perils of foreign influence over American politics during the infancy of the federal republic were much on Washington's mind as he prepared to set another patriotic precedent by retiring after two terms.

The specific context of Washington's Farewell Address, published on September 19, 1796, has led some recent historians to claim that his intentions were narrow and his precepts ephemeral, as if he were speaking out just to help John Adams get elected. That crabbed interpretation ignores Washington's character and the provenance of the principles he and his co-author, Hamilton, recommended to posterity. Washington spoke for his times but quite consciously for the ages as well. From the moment he took command of the army in 1775 and again upon assuming the office of president, Washington knew everything he did and said, or did not do or say, created a precedent. Moreover, he worked hard on the draft of a political testament back in 1792 in anticipation of retiring after one term, so the eventual text was not just a gloss on current events. His chief aide in 1792 had been James Madison, who shared Washington's bias toward peace and never grew tired of warning that war was the most dreadful enemy of liberty. Finally, as political scientist David Hendrickson has stressed, the crises of the 1790s were not atypical but prototypical, likely to recur throughout the future, and thus parables to illustrate principles that appeared again and again in Washington's papers over decades. Perhaps his imminent retirement explains the timing of his remarks, but we may take Washington at his word when he states his motive was "zeal for your future interest."

Washington's Farewell Address became dogma not only because of his prestige, but also because his rejection of missionary idealism suited American values and interests so well for so long. Indeed, its "oracular quality" (in biographer Ron Chernow's words) only increased to the point that the Senate, beginning in 1862 and then annually since 1893, recited the Farewell Address in liturgical fashion at the start of each session.

The tone of the political testament was suitably grave and explicitly civil religious. Washington knew Americans loved liberty with every ligament of their hearts. But he urged on them reverence for the qualities that preserved liberty, including patriotism, wisdom, virtue, prudence, and unity. The Constitution must be "sacredly maintained" and "sacredly obligatory" because unity of government was the "main pillar in the edifice of your real independence, the support of your tranquillity at home, your peace abroad, of your safety, of your prosperity, or that very liberty which you so highly prize." The economies of the northern, southern, eastern, and western portions of the United States were interdependent and complementary. So long as the sections cultivated domestic harmony and combined their strengths, there would be "less frequent interruption of their peace by foreign nations" and less necessity for an "overgrown military establishment which, under any form of government, are inauspicious to liberty." Washington also warned against the worst enemy of republics, a spirit of faction and party, and against the danger of one branch of government encroaching upon the powers of another.

The survival of even the sturdiest constitution, however, ultimately rested on the people's character: "It is substantially true that virtue or morality is a necessary spring of popular government." Washington therefore admonished Americans to cultivate six healthy habits.

(1) "Of all the dispositions and habits which lead to political prosperity, religion and morality are indispensable supports. In vain would that man claim the tribute of patriotism, who should labor to subvert these great pillars of human happiness, these firmest props of the duties of men and citizens. ... And let us with caution indulge the supposition that morality can be maintained without religion. Whatever may be conceded to the influence of refined education on minds of peculiar structure, reason and experience both forbid us to expect that national morality can prevail in exclusion of religious principle."

(2) "As a very important source of strength and security, cherish public credit. One method of preserving it is to use it as sparingly as possible, avoiding occasions of expense by cultivating peace, but remembering also that timely disbursements to prepare for danger frequently prevent much greater disbursements to repel it, avoiding likewise the accumulation of debt, not only by shunning occasions of expense, but by vigorous exertion in time of peace to discharge the debts which unavoidable wars may have occasioned, not ungenerously throwing upon posterity the burden which we ourselves ought to bear."

(3) "Observe good faith and justice toward all nations; cultivate peace and harmony with all. Religion and morality enjoin this conduct; and can it be, that good policy does not equally enjoin it? It will be worthy of a free, enlightened, and at no distant period, a great nation, to give to mankind the magnanimous and too novel example of a people always guided by an exalted justice and benevolence."

(4) "In the execution of such a plan, nothing is more essential than that permanent, inveterate antipathies against particular nations, and passionate attachments for others, should be excluded; and that, in place of them, just and amicable feelings towards all should be cultivated. The nation which indulges towards another a habitual

hatred or a habitual fondness is in some degree a slave.
... Against the insidious wiles of foreign influence (I
conjure you to believe me, fellow-citizens) the jealousy
of a free people ought to be constantly awake, since history and experience prove that foreign influence is one
of the most baneful foes of republican government."

(5) "The great rule of conduct for us in regard to foreign
nations is in extending our commercial relations,
to have with them as little political connection as possible. ... Why, by interweaving our destiny with that of
any part of Europe, entangle our peace and prosperity
in the toils of European ambition, rivalship, interest,
humor or caprice? It is our true policy to steer clear of
permanent alliances with any portion of the foreign
world. ... Taking care always to keep ourselves by suitable establishments on a respectable defensive posture,
we may safely trust to temporary alliances for extraordinary emergencies."

(6) "Harmony, liberal intercourse with all nations, are
recommended by policy, humanity, and interest. But
even our commercial policy should hold an equal and
impartial hand; neither seeking nor granting exclusive
favors or preferences. ... There can be no greater error
than to expect or calculate upon real favors from nation
to nation. It is an illusion, which experience must cure,
which a just pride ought to discard."

Washington doubted his counsels would make a strong and
lasting impression but flattered himself to think they might do
some good "to moderate the fury of party spirit, to warn against
the mischiefs of foreign intrigue, to guard against the impostures
of pretended patriotism." He then reminded his countrymen one
last time "to maintain inviolate the relations of peace and amity towards other nations" and closed with a prayer that the effects of
any mistakes he had made over forty-five years of service would be
consigned by the Almighty "to oblivion, as myself must soon be to
the mansions of rest." Three and a quarter years later Washington
went to the mansions of rest.

The Farewell Address codified the precepts of the Classical American Civil Religion. In domestic policy the United States were defined by unity, sovereignty, and liberty. In foreign policy they were defined by peace, neutrality, and reciprocity. Washington declared Europe a separate sphere with a foreign set of interests, anticipating the Monroe Doctrine, and prophesied rapid expansion if the nation kept these commandments. He devised a coherent, self-reinforcing grand strategy from a commonsense notion of human nature; warned Americans not to indulge their own character flaws; and allowed for temporary suspension of his rules during emergencies caused by the bad faith of foreigners. But the precepts themselves were eternally valid, so if the United States had an idealistic mission in world politics, it was precisely "to give to mankind the magnanimous and too novel example of a people always guided by an exalted justice and benevolence."

A few months before Washington had written Charles Carroll of Carrollton: "Twenty years peace with such an increase of population and resources as we have a right to expect; added to our remote situation from the jarring power, will in all probability enable us in a just cause, to bid defiance to any power on earth." That quotation has prompted the fantastic claim to the effect that Washington imagined his precepts mere expedients that America soon could discard. But the "novel example" that Washington hoped Americans would give to the world was categorically not the one from Thucydides' Melian Dialogue ("The strong do what they can and the weak suffer what they must"). Washington expressed his own sylvan vision of national greatness in a letter to Lafayette: "I wish to see the sons and daughters of the world in Peace, and busily employed in fulfilling the first and great commandment, Increase and Multiply: as an encouragement to which we have opened the fertile plains of the Ohio to the poor, the needy and the oppressed of the Earth; and one therefore who is heavily laden, or who wants to cultivate, may repair to thither and abound, as in the Land of promise with milk and honey."

Well and truly spoken by a gentleman farmer, surveyor, soldier, statesman, and patriot.

CHAPTER SIX

Thomas Jefferson and the
Utopian Temptation

A MERICAN STATESMEN OF THE founding and early national eras sought neither to transform nor to hide from the world because they aspired to equal membership in the international community. Indeed, nothing disproves the myths known as isolationism (a term not even coined until the 1890s) and exceptionalism (a term not even coined until the 1930s) more than the United States' proud, petulant, and sometimes paranoid quest for respect. In his 1797 inaugural address John Adams condemned foreign influence as "the angel of destruction to elective governments" and bade "that Being who is supreme over all, the Patron of Order, the Fountain of Justice, and the Protector in all ages of the world of virtuous liberty to continue His providential blessing on America." Still, his administration was consumed by disrespect on the part of the rueful French Republic, which demanded Americans pay tribute (the XYZ Affair), then waged a so-called Quasi-War against American shipping. But Congress had authorized construction of a navy, whose sturdy frigates retaliated so sharply against the French that Adams was prompted to boast: "The trident of Neptune is the scepter of the world." But he and his secretary of state, John Marshall, maintained the Washingtonian bias for peace. In the Convention of Mortefontaine (1800) France agreed to cease hostilities, make reparation, and terminate the 1778 alliance.

Thomas Jefferson then won the presidency by a slender margin over Adams and by an act of Congress over his own running mate, Aaron Burr. Would Jefferson try to turn what he called the Revolution of 1800 to genuinely revolutionary purposes? On the contrary, he enunciated all of Washington's civil religious precepts and became a magnificent high priest, subtle in theology and skilled in evangelism. Jefferson's inaugural address swept aside the bitter election and simply *announced* the unity of the nation: "We have called by different names brethren of the same principle. We are all Republicans, we are all Federalists." He described America as a chosen country and congratulated the people for "acknowledging and adoring an overruling Providence." He instructed Americans in "the creed of our political faith" through a long litany of domestic and foreign policy virtues and goals, including "peace, commerce, and friendship with all nations, entangling alliances with none." Finally, like Washington and Adams before him, he made polite confessions of humility, bade the people's support, and prayed "that Infinite Power which rules the destinies of the universe" might "lead our councils to what is best, and give them a favorable issue for your peace and prosperity."

That is not to say serious differences did not remain between the parties. Federalists considered foreign policy the shield that defended liberty. Hence it would be courting disaster to forgo the sorts of institutions European monarchies employed to maximize military, economic, and financial power. Republicans considered foreign policy a mirror that reflected liberty. Hence it would be courting disaster to replicate monarchical institutions that only invited war, the *ultima ratio regum* and hangman of liberty. Jefferson was no pacifist when it came to defending civilization against Barbary pirates or hostile Indians. But he distrusted armaments and opposed foreign engagements lest they spawn militarism and oppression at home. Jefferson was also very expansionist, but his preferred means (observed a French diplomat in 1805) was to "conquer without war." He might wax romantic about the French Revolution but had no desire to fight on its behalf. "Certainly," scholars Robert

Tucker and David Hendrickson conclude, "Jefferson never consciously contemplated the role of crusader for the nation."

So Jefferson might have been split-minded in theory and temperament, but his non-interventionist policies showed surprising consistency over decades. In 1787 he wrote, "I know, too, that it is a maxim with us, and I think it a wise one, not to entangle ourselves with the affairs of Europe." In 1793 he repeated that even (or especially) as ideological warfare spread across the continent: "We wish not to meddle with the internal affairs of any country, nor with the general affairs of Europe." In 1797 he wrote, "We shall never give up our Union, the last anchor of our hope, and that alone which is to prevent this heavenly country from becoming an arena of gladiators." In 1799, during the Quasi-War, he wrote, "I am for free commerce with all nations, political connection with none, and little or no diplomatic establishment," and "I cordially wish well to the progress of liberty in all nations, and would forever give it the weight of our countenance, yet they are not to be touched without contamination from their other bad principles." In 1801, President Jefferson wrote, "We have a perfect horror at everything like connecting ourselves with the politics of Europe," and again in 1804, "On the subject of treaties, our system is to have none with any nation, as far as can be avoided." During the War of 1812 he looked forward to the time when "our strength will permit us to give the law of our hemisphere, it should be that the meridian of the mid-Atlantic should be the line of demarcation between war and peace, on this side of which no act of hostility should be committed, and the lion and the lamb lie down in peace together." In 1823, during the formulation of the Monroe Doctrine, he wrote, "I have ever deemed it fundamental for the United States never to take active part in the quarrels of Europe. Their political interests are entirely distinct from ours. . . . They are nations of eternal war."

In a subsequent book on the Founders Hendrickson concluded that the American leitmotif was a practical idealism to promote reciprocity, freedom of the seas, free trade, and international law. "Did, then, the appearance of the United States in the community of nations represent a new diplomacy? In vital respects, it did. So far as Europe was concerned, however, it was not so much how America was to act as what it was to be that excited optimistic

visions of the structural transformation of the European system."
In other words, the United States were different because of their
identity. Just as Josef Stalin would later insist the Soviet Union had
to adjust to the reality of Socialism in One Country, so did the
United States have to adjust to the reality of Republicanism in One
Country. That made the American calling in foreign affairs a civil
religious equivalent of the biblical exhortation to the church to be
in the world but not of it.

Four episodes in Jefferson's presidency demonstrated how hard it
was to put that holy aspiration into practice. The first was the cor-
sair system on the Barbary Coast of North Africa, which obliged
him to choose between his Virginia planter's contempt for money-
grubbing, navy-loving merchants and his Virginia gentleman's
commitment to honor. As minister to France he had felt so helpless
to defend U.S. citizens in the Mediterranean that he wrote: "The
motives for war rather than tribute are numerous and honorable,
those opposing them mean and short-sighted." Yet the Federalists'
Naval Act of 1794 passed Congress over the unanimous opposition
of Jefferson's faction. It was deeply ironic that President Jefferson
was able to launch the first campaign of a fourteen-year war
against the Barbary pirates thanks to John Adams's navy and thanks
to the peace Adams bequeathed with both Britain and France. But
Jefferson's war aims, needless to say, did not include permanent occupation or nation-building on distant Muslim littorals. His sole
purpose was to compel respect for the American flag.

A second conundrum obliged a choice between Jefferson's categorical views on revolution and race. In 1791 enslaved Africans in
the sugar colony of Saint-Domingue (Haiti) got wind of the
French Revolution and rebelled in the name of the Rights of Man.
Atrocities, reprisals, and pitched battles dragged on for a decade.
Imagine how that compromised Jefferson. Where whites were con-
cerned, his rhetorical endorsement of rebellion was limitless.
Where blacks were concerned, he at least pretended to endorse
emancipation. But the prospect of slave revolts spreading to the
American South made Jefferson's blood run cold, especially as the
Federalist administrations encouraged commerce with Toussaint
l'Ouverture's regime. Indeed, during the Quasi-War Toussaint, the

so-called black Talleyrand, practiced deft diplomacy in hopes of recognition and help from Britain and/or the United States. But the Treaty of Mortefontaine, the accessions to power of Napoleon and Jefferson, and the short-lived Anglo-French Peace of Amiens in 1802 changed everything, for a few months at least. U.S. relations with Haiti chilled, then ceased altogether when Napoleon launched an expedition to reconquer Saint-Domingue in anticipation of rebuilding the French empire in Louisiana.

Napoleon's New World ambitions posed a third dilemma because they obliged Jefferson to consider the limits of no entangling alliances. If the French fortified New Orleans, he wrote, "we must marry ourselves to the British fleet and nation." Luckily, the French army deployed to crush the Haitian rebellion perished from yellow fever, war resumed in Europe, and Napoleon liquidated the Louisiana affair by selling out to the United States. The 1803 purchase was a coup for the Jefferson administration and too good a real estate deal for the Senate to reject. But it belied the president's vision of an Empire of Liberty since nobody asked the Creoles, Africans, and Indians beyond the Mississippi River whether they wanted to live under U.S. authority. Constitutionally dubious, the Louisiana Purchase had ominous implications for the expansion of slavery and dispossession of Native Americans.

The fourth episode that challenged Jefferson's split-mindedness was the economic warfare to which both sides resorted in the Napoleonic wars. In 1806 the French and British declared reciprocal blockades that harmed the commerce of neutrals such as the United States. If Congress had funded just half the frigates and ships-of-the-line authorized in the 1790s, they might have intimidated the Royal Navy's modest North American squadron based in Nova Scotia. But the Democratic-Republican majority had cut naval construction in the midst of a world at war! Unable to oblige belligerents to change their behavior, Jefferson could only try to change Americans' behavior. In 1808 he ordered his majority in Congress to pass an Embargo Act prohibiting citizens from engaging in foreign trade altogether. The embargo wrecked whole sectors of the economy from Boston to Charleston. It also encouraged wholesale smuggling, which the stubborn president tried to suppress through the exercise of coercive executive powers. It seemed as if the worst Federalist nightmares of the 1790s were now coming true. Jeffersonians, like Jacobins, were imposing tyranny in the name of liberty while ruining American prosperity. They were sinning against the civil religion.

Upon the inauguration of James Madison the Congress repealed the embargo in favor of "peaceable coercions" that eventually worked. In June 1812 the British Parliament suspended its Orders in Council targeting neutral trade. But the news came too late to prevent a declaration of war by the Democratic-Republican majority, whipped to a frenzy by a youthful, self-styled caucus of war hawks. American belligerence had nothing directly to do with freedom of the seas because all the Federalists and some northeastern Republicans voted nay. Western war hawks like Henry Clay and Andrew Jackson, however, itched for a pretext to expel British monarchy from North America, extirpate Indian resistance, and open the north and west to unlimited white settlement. South Carolinian John C. Calhoun added the argument that it was time for Americans to stop being on the defensive. He called for a second war of independence that (he predicted) would unify all Americans, rekindle the Spirit of '76, and lay the foundations of national greatness. Did no one besides Federalists cling to Washington's bias for peace? Indeed, a few Southern Republicans sniffed the odor of imperial pomposity. They accused the war hawks of betraying republican principles and formed a third force *(tertium quid)* to defend them. Their leader, Congressman John Randolph of Roanoke, cried, "Go to war without money, without men, without a navy! . . . The people will not believe it!"

War hawks, by contrast, expected a walkover, and their confidence evidently infected Jefferson. In August 1812 he wrote in a letter to William Duane: "The acquisition of Canada, this year, as far as the neighbourhood of Quebec, will be a mere matter of marching; & will give us experience for the attack of Halifax the next, & the final expulsion of England from the American continent." In retrospect the United States was fortunate that the invasions of Canada failed. If instead Americans had conquered it, they would have suffered the ordeal of nation-building fifty years prior even to Reconstruction, in a vast country populated by Tories, Québecois, and Native Americans who had no love for the United

States and were beginning to display a nationalism of their own. To be sure, the U.S. Navy won some historic victories, while Jackson's militias broke the Creeks' resistance in Alabama and the British invasion at New Orleans. So when the 1815 Treaty of Ghent restored the status quo ante bellum, Americans could brag how they fought the British to a draw and broke down the barriers to westward expansion. But Americans were suitably chastened so as not seriously to contemplate war against a European power for eighty years.

CHAPTER SEVEN

John Quincy Adams and the
Problem of Neighborhood

P EACE BROKE OUT IN Europe after the defeat of Napoleon in 1814–15. At the Congress of Vienna delegations from Britain, the Austrian and Russian empires, the kingdom of Prussia, and the restored Bourbon kingdom of France upheld the principle of dynastic legitimacy, compromised on territorial issues, calibrated a balance of power, and pledged to concert their diplomacy to prevent future wars. Far less significant was the so-called Holy Alliance, whereby the monarchs of Russia, Austria, and Prussia pledged to suppress the radical ideologies of democracy and nationalism in the name of Christian fraternity. This Restoration or Metternichian System, named for the Austrian foreign minister, proved too reactionary for the liberal British, who distanced themselves from the continent after just seven years. But to suggest, as some fanciful historians have done, that the Vienna system was a foretaste of twentieth-century totalitarianism is absurd. The real foretaste had been the Jacobin and Bonapartist regimes, whose recurrence the Vienna system was designed to prevent. Americans, in their ignorance and republican pride, nevertheless used "Holy Alliance" as shorthand for the entire Vienna system while ignoring the magnificent blessing it bestowed on the United

States. The relative peace and balance of power established in Europe in 1815 would endure for a hundred years, thereby liberating Americans to focus their energies on their own neighborhood of continental proportions.

No modern nation save maybe Brazil has enjoyed such geopolitical advantage as the United States in the century after 1815. Only Americans themselves could have spoiled it through gratuitous aggravation of foreign powers; hence the wise course was to practice a strategy of self-containment as regards the Old World. Likewise, the only power that might hope to pursue a containment strategy against the United States was Great Britain. Accordingly, the first problem of neighborhood was how to expand the mere truce made at Ghent into a permanent Anglo-American peace pact founded on the demarcation and demilitarization of the U.S.-Canadian border. That task was accomplished in the Rush-Bagot Accords of 1817–18. A second problem of neighborhood was how to relate to whatever regimes emerged from the wreckage of the Spanish American empire. That task preoccupied the Monroe administration, not least its incomparable secretary of state, John Quincy Adams.

Imagine being home-schooled by John and Abigail Adams, and the brilliance, erudition, integrity, precocity, and piety of John Quincy Adams will come as no surprise. The parents collaborated on a curriculum that amounted to six foreign languages, the classics, history, political theory, and the Bible, which John Quincy believed to be the font of all principles required for wise statecraft. His education also included seventeen years of residence in European capitals starting in 1778, when he accompanied his father to Paris. By the age of twelve he was clerking for the highest-ranking U.S. emissaries. Back home he took two degrees from Harvard and began a law practice. But his 1793 Marcellus and Columbus letters defending U.S. neutrality so impressed Washington that he persuaded his vice president's twenty-seven-year-old son to accept a diplomatic post. He devoted the rest of his life to public service.

John Quincy's mother drilled into him Horace's motto about Roman mothers despising war *(bella matronis detestata)* and the trinity of doctrines on which all morality rested: God's existence, the soul's immortality, and certain judgment to come. Remove any of these, he instructed his own children, and man's conscience would have "no other law than that of the tiger or the shark." His father in-sisted he derive moral philosophy—"a compound of Christian faith and classical virtue"—from Plato, Aristotle, Thucydides, Machiavelli, Francis Bacon, James Harrington, Algernon Sydney, Alexander Pope, Montesquieu, and David Hume. Protestant to the core, John Quincy grew up believing in human progress; Yankee to the core, he grew up believing in America's destiny. But he understood fully that the flawed nature of man and amoral nature of politics imposed lim-its on a nation's moral authority. Hence the wise statesman must sto-ically accept Pope's depiction of man as "Plac'd in this isthmus of a middle state, / A being darkly wise and rudely great. . . . Sole judge of truth, in endless error hurl'd; / The glory, jest and riddle of the world!" There was nothing for it but to cultivate a "tragic sense of politics," which alone granted immunity to the twin temptations of delusory messianism or hypocritical pretense. As his father put it in 1814: "We may boast that we are the chosen people; we may even thank God that we are not like other men; but, after all, it will be but flattery, and the delusion, the self-deceit of the Pharisee."

Scrupulous analysis and self-examination enabled John Quincy to discern the character of a democratic foreign policy and the re-lationship between ends and means in a fallen world. He reflected upon such questions as whether internal or external affairs should enjoy primacy in calculations of national interest, whether foreign engagements were compatible with republican principles, and whether popular governments could pursue wise foreign policies and still win support from voters driven by faction, emotion, and impatience. In every case he came down on the side of a principled realism that placed American values "upon the adamantine rock of human rights" but insisted "the purpose of our foreign policy is not to bring enlightenment or happiness to the rest of the world but to ensure the life, liberty, and happiness of the American people." He believed the United States had a calling but must shun tempting crusades. The fanatical cry "Let justice be done though the world perish" (*fiat justitia pereat mundus*) might occasionally have ap-pealed to Jefferson but abominated John Quincy Adams.

In 1776, when the thirteen British colonies declared themselves a novel alternative to European imperial rule, the long, languid retreat of Spanish power in the Americas was well advanced. But the spark that ignited armed revolts among colonial elites was Napoleon's invasion of Spain itself in 1808. By 1815 various juntas were achieving de facto independence although their boundaries and regimes were up for grabs, while liberty under law was rarely in evidence. What was the destiny of these other Americans? Should the United States court the Latin American revolutionaries, perhaps even invite them into the North American union? Or were they unfit for self-government? John Adams spoke that smug conventional wisdom when he called the Latin Americans "the most ignorant, the most bigoted, the most superstitious of all the Roman Catholics in Christendom" and thought state-building efforts there "as absurd as similar plans would be to establish democracies among the birds, beast, and fishes." No doubt the Latin Americans were disadvantaged by comparison to the colonists of British heritage, but U.S. citizens were mistaken if they saw only violence and chaos in Venezuela, Colombia, or Peru. What they chose to ignore was the distinctive fact that the Latin juntas abolished slavery and empowered Indians (at least in theory) during their multiracial wars for independence.

Only the fact that the thirteen North American colonies managed to keep Africans and Indians largely offstage during their revolution made their war and state founding seem more civilized. It also meant that fear of importing racial revolts discouraged the early dreams nurtured by some U.S. citizens of a single republican empire in the Americas. But if the United States did not annex or absorb Latin America, then it risked having to live with hostile countries or, what was worse, European clients in its neighborhood.

The most immediate crisis arose in the province that bordered the United States, derelict Florida. The sandy spit 360 miles wide was virtually unoccupied by Spain save for St. Augustine and a few motley garrisons. Otherwise, it was a refuge for marauding Seminole Indians, fugitive slaves, and pirates. Georgians and Alabamians complained ever more loudly until John C. Calhoun's War Department authorized Tennessee militia commander Andrew Jackson to deal with the problem. Old Hickory proceeded to invade Spanish Florida and declare martial law, prompting diplomatic protests from Spain and Great Britain, two of whose subjects were summarily executed for gunrunning. Secretary of State John Quincy Adams wrote a long, blistering defense that demanded Spain either police its province or sell it to the United States. The beleaguered Spanish crown elected to bargain.

Back in the 2000s some neo-conservatives tried to argue that Jackson's invasion of Florida was evidence that the Bush Doctrine's unilateral preemption was not a departure but an old American tradition. It is a very thin reed to bear such weight. Jackson's mission was retaliatory, not preemptive, punitive not permanent, and used to excellent diplomatic effect. In 1819 John Quincy Adams and Spanish minister Luis de Onís signed the Transcontinental Treaty, in which Spain sold Florida, ceded its claims to the northwest coast (Oregon), and fixed a boundary between Mexico, the Louisiana Purchase, and points west to the Pacific Ocean. Obviously it would have been impolitic for the United States to aid and abet the Latin American revolutionaries until this favorable treaty was ratified, and, as it happened, a revolution in Spain itself delayed ratification. Is that fact sufficient to explain another important event later that year, John Quincy Adams's July 4, 1821, address in which he proclaimed "America goes not abroad in search of monsters to destroy"? The answer is no; the Transcontinental Treaty had nothing to do with Adams's speech because by then it had been ratified, as James Monroe celebrated in his second inaugural address.

How about the general issue of timing with regard to U.S. recognition of Latin independence? That was a matter of some controversy. In 1818 Clay had spoken for four days in hopes of persuading Congress to pass a resolution in favor of seizing Florida, treaty or no treaty, while recognizing the Latin states. He even likened Simón Bolívar to George Washington.

The resolution, which would have amounted to a de facto declaration of war against Spain, was voted down 45 to 115. But it testified to the youthful Clay's ignorance of the cultural divide between North and South America. Bolívar had pledged to wage a "war to the death" and countenanced the summary beheading of a thousand Spanish prisoners. Bolívar proclaimed that "Our people are nothing like Europeans or North Americans; indeed, we are more a mixture of Africa and America than we are the children of

Europe." Bolívar rejected federalism in the belief that governing his people required strong central authority and a standing army. Bolívar dreamed of a United States of South America, the better to resist imperial pretensions from the north. Given those deep differences, John Quincy Adams saw no advantage whatever in premature recognition of Venezuela, Colombia, Peru, La Plata, or, for that matter, Mexico. He lectured Clay: "That the final issue of their present struggle would be their entire independence of Spain I had never doubted. That it was our true policy and duty to take no part in the contest I was equally clear. The principle of neutrality to *all* foreign wars was, in my opinion, fundamental to the continuance of our liberties and our Union."

Add to that principle the domestic contingencies raised by the financial Panic of 1819 and the scary debate over Missouri statehood with slavery (Jefferson's fire bell in the night), and the caution exhibited in Adams's July 4, 1821, speech seems overdetermined. But to dismiss it as merely tactical is dumb, if not dishonest. The self-described purpose of the speech—which Adams delivered in an academic gown from the podium of the House of Representatives—was "to reply to Edinburgh as well as Lexington." The former referred to the *Edinburgh Review*, which had launched the first salvo in what became known as the War of the Quarterlies by posing the question, "What Has America Done for Mankind?" The latter referred to Clay's pronouncements from his Kentucky plantation. Most of Adams's long address amounted to a lecture on the Whig interpretation of British history. Once upon a time Anglo-Saxon yeomen had enjoyed primordial freedom based on self-government, private property, and the Common Law. But they lost it all in the Norman invasion of 1066 and spent the rest of the Middle Ages struggling to regain their liberties. They also suffered reverses, most recently under King George III. That emboldened American colonists to replace Britain in the vanguard of the history of liberty and base their constitution on principles that made the United States a glorious contrast to martial, imperial Britain. But what did the *Edinburgh Review* now propose? It proposed—nay insisted—that America unite with the "liberal and enlightened part of the English nation" to crusade on behalf of reform movements in Germany, France, Spain, and Italy, as well as Latin America. That set the stage for John

Quincy Adams's stirring climax, for which the rarely quoted introductory paragraphs provide crucial context:

> AND NOW, FRIENDS AND COUNTRYMEN, if the wise and
> learned philosophers of the elder world, the first observers
> of nutation and aberration, the discoverers of maddening
> ether and invisible planets, the inventors of Congreve rock-
> ets and Shrapnel shells, should find their hearts disposed to
> enquire what has America done for the benefit of mankind?
> Let our answer be this: America, with the same voice which
> spoke herself into existence as a nation, proclaimed to
> mankind the inextinguishable rights of human nature, and
> the only lawful foundations of government. America, in the
> assembly of nations, since her admission among them, has
> invariably, though often fruitlessly, held forth to them the
> hand of honest friendship, of equal freedom, of generous
> reciprocity.
>
> She has uniformly spoken among them, though often
> to heedless and often to disdainful ears, the language of
> equal liberty, of equal justice, and of equal rights. She has,
> in the lapse of nearly half a century, without a single excep-
> tion, respected the independence of other nations while as-
> serting and maintaining her own. She has abstained from
> interference in the concerns of others, even when conflict
> has been for principles to which she clings, as to the last vi-
> tal drop that visits the heart. She has seen that probably for
> centuries to come, all the contests of that Aceldama [the
> potter's field bought with Judas's thirty pieces of silver] the
> European world, will be contests of inveterate power, and
> emerging right.
>
> Wherever the standard of freedom and Independence
> has been or shall be unfurled, there will her heart, her
> benedictions and her prayers be. But she goes not abroad,
> in search of monsters to destroy. She is the well-wisher to
> the freedom and independence of all. She is the champion
> and vindicator only of her own. She will commend the
> general cause by the countenance of her voice, and the be-
> nignant sympathy of her example. She well knows that by

once enlisting under other banners than her own, were they even the banners of foreign independence, she would involve herself beyond the power of extrication, in all the wars of interest and intrigue, of individual avarice, envy, and ambition, which assume the colors and usurp the standard of freedom. The fundamental maxims of her policy would insensibly change from liberty to force. The frontlet on her brows would no longer beam with ineffable splendor of freedom and independence; but instead would soon be substituted an imperial diadem, flashing in false and tarnished lustre the murky radiance of dominion and power. She might become the dictatress of the world. She would be no longer the ruler of her own spirit.

Adams concluded by hurling the question back at the British: "What have you done for mankind?" Material inventions aplenty, and engines of war and empire. But "[America's] glory is not dominion, but liberty. Her march is the march of the mind. She has a spear and a shield: but the motto upon her shield is, Freedom, Independence, Peace."

Like Washington, Adams self-consciously spoke for the ages and in deadly earnest. Several months later he confided as much in a letter to Edward Everett. He condemned colonialism of all kinds and foresaw its abolition in British India and throughout the world. But he explicitly condemned what would later be called wars of national liberation or interference in the domestic affairs of other countries because of the "inevitable tendency of a direct interference in foreign wars, even wars for freedom, to change the very foundations of our own government from liberty to power." It was imperative that Adams blow this "trumpet upon Zion" because "Erroneous moral principle is the most fruitful of all the sources of human calamity and vice. The leaders of nations . . . are generally but accomplished sophists, trained to make the worse appear the better reason."

Neo-conservative historians have claimed John Quincy Adams cannot be considered the spokesman for twentieth-century realism. Far more egregious it is to consider him the spokesman for what parades as twenty-first century idealism. Adams, in the words of historian Greg Russell, was a man of his era who understood, no less than Burke, that "universal norms cannot be applied to the action of states in their abstract formulation, but that they must be filtered through the concrete circumstance of time and place." John Quincy Adams meant what he said.

In 1822 the Monroe administration recognized five Latin American regimes. The new policy simply acknowledged faits accomplis that the British also recognized and the liberal Spanish Cortes was prepared to accept. Far more momentous was the train of events triggered by the European Congress's decision to permit a royal French army to cross the Pyrenees and crush the revolution in Spain. Beyond those events, which came to pass in spring 1823, were rumors that France might help King Ferdinand VII reconquer Spain's overseas empire. Adams did not credit them for a moment. The Bourbons would not be so mad as to try it and the Royal Navy so lax as to permit it. Why then did British foreign secretary George Canning flatter U.S. minister Richard Rush by offering to collaborate in defense of the independence of Latin America? Adams suspected a trap because Canning added that Britain and America would of course forswear any territorial ambitions of their own. It seemed the British were adopting a containment policy toward the growing, grasping United States. But even more dangerous was the temptation dangled by the *Edinburgh Review* for Americans to entangle themselves in the affairs of Europe. So Adams stubbornly insisted before President Monroe's entire Cabinet that the United States must reject the British offer on the grounds that it invited them to meddle in the New World and invited Americans to meddle in the Old World. Earlier that year Adams had drafted instructions for his minister to Spain describing the high stakes involved:

> Two of the principal causes of the wars between the nations of Europe since that of our own Revolution, have been, indeed, the same as those in which that originated—civil liberty and national independence. To these principles, and to the cause of those who contend for them, the people of the United States can never be indifferent. A feeling of sympathy and of partiality for every nation struggling to secure

or to defend these great interests, has been and will be manifested by the Union; and it is among the most difficult and delicate duties of the general government, in all its branches, to indulge this feeling so far as it may be compatible with the duties of neutrality, and to withhold and restrain from encroaching upon them. So far as it is indulged, its tendency is to involve us in foreign wars, while the first and paramount duty of the government is to maintain *peace* [emphasis in original] amidst all the convulsions of foreign wars, and to enter the lists as parties to no cause, other than our own.

Adams wanted the United States to issue a unilateral declaration to this effect and prepared a draft for the president's annual message to Congress. But Monroe was thick-headed. He repeatedly inserted into Adams's text expressions of support for European revolutions such as the Greek revolt against the Ottoman Empire. Adams patiently explained that the principle of reciprocity required Americans to forswear involvement in the Old World if they expected Europeans to forswear involvement in the New World. He won his point, which made the Monroe Doctrine, declared in December 1823, a great exercise in *self*-containment and an eloquent condemnation of the fanatical streak that was heresy in the Classical American Civil Religion. As Adams explained to the Russian minister, "The first paragraph of my paper stated the fact that the Government of the United States was republican; the second, what the fundamental principles of this Government were— referring them all to Liberty, Independence, Peace. . . . I added, by way of apology for the solicitude that I felt on this subject, that I considered this as the most important paper that ever went from my hands."

Adams used the Monroe Doctrine to put Spain and France, but above all Britain and tsarist Russia (which claimed the Pacific Northwest) on notice that any new colonization in the Americas, or transfer of existing colonies, or attempt to reconquer ex-colonies would be evidence of an unfriendly disposition toward the United States. The doctrine did not threaten monarchy and empire where it existed—for instance, in Canada, the Caribbean colonies, and Brazil. But it grandfathered those institutions and prevented their spread. It had immense implications for the United States' own continental expansion even as it mandated scrupulously correct relations toward governments in Europe and Asia. In short, the Monroe Doctrine solved, as best as circumstances allowed, the problem of neighborhood.

John Quincy Adams matters deeply because everyone wants to claim him. He was certainly complicated and expressed many viewpoints over his lifelong career. He was a peaceful diplomat, yet an avid expansionist, yet an opponent of territorial growth that might also extend slavery. But to suggest that Adams, upon becoming president in 1825, moved in Clay's direction regarding ideological missions abroad is an exaggeration. He dispatched a single secret agent to report on the Greek revolution and did not follow up when the agent died at sea. It was hardly a precedent for militant interventions.

Nor did Adams move in Clay's direction regarding Latin America. When Simón Bolívar convened the Congress of Panama in 1826 to promote his Federation of the Andes, U.S. politicians argued at length over whether to send delegates. Those representing southern slave states were mostly opposed, and those representing northern commercial interests were mostly in favor. At length Adams appointed two observers, one of whom died en route and the other arrived too late. But it did not matter a whit. Bolívar did not want U.S. participation and had no interest in replicating U.S. institutions. Clay, thoroughly disillusioned, wrote him a condescending letter expressing "the hope that South America would add a new triumph to the cause of human liberty, and that Providence would bless her as he had her northern sister, with the genius of some great and virtuous man." But it seemed instead that Bolívar had taken the "bloody road" chosen by "the vulgar crowd of tyrants and military despots." The Venezuelan Liberator returned the insult, warning of "American hucksters" and observing that the "United States seems destined by Providence to plague America with torments in the name of freedom."

CHAPTER EIGHT

Manifest Destiny

I N FEBRUARY 1848 THE Treaty of Guadalupe Hidalgo ended the Mexican War and transferred to the United States its entire southwest from the mouth of the Rio Grande on the Gulf of Mexico to the Pacific Ocean north of San Francisco Bay. Most Americans were relieved that President James K. Polk pulled it off (thanks to his professional military and naval officers plus a great deal of luck). But a large minority of mostly northern Americans were ashamed of a war of conquest that also increased the prospects for an expansion of slavery. The Mexican treaty even prompted an anonymous author in the *North American Review* to call the nation to account like the prophet Amos. "This is criminal, but it was the besetting sin of the stock from whom, in the pride of our hearts, we claim to be descended;—the sin of the Saxons, the Danes, and the Normans [who] upon various self-satisfying pretences, have appropriated to themselves a large share of all the territory inhabited or inhabitable by the human family. Of these Englishmen we are the true children." The Patriots of 1776 might have loved liberty, but they "were by no means exempt from the lust of dominion. Several of them were among the most noted land-speculators of their time. . . . Avarice and rapacity were as common then as now. The stock-jobbing, the extortion, the forestalling, the low arts and devices to amass wealth, that were practised during the war for independence, seem almost incredible." Yet avarice had grown worse over the decades since. "In developing our resources, and in increasing our wealth, we have done more than any nation of modern times. Our territory is vastly more than sufficient for the subsistence of those who now inhabit it, but is still deemed by many quite too small to meet our future growth. If, then, we have made, and are making, no progress in virtue, the fault is all our own, and the consequences of it will be upon our heads and upon those of our children."

That, to be sure, was a high-minded Yankee writing for a highbrow journal founded in Boston in 1815. The sour message would not have shocked Emerson or Thoreau. But it almost thoroughly contradicted the message of Jacksonian Democrats, who wanted to believe the gospel preached by the likes of John O'Sullivan. His 1839 editorial, "The Great Nation of Futurity," in New York's *United States Magazine and Democratic Review* chanted American Civil Religion so brazenly that it made the Union the church against which the gates of hell could not prevail:

> The expansive future is our arena, and for our history. We are entering on its untrodden space, with the truths of God in our minds, beneficent objects in our hearts, and with a clear conscience unsullied by the past. We are the nation of human progress, and who will, what can, set limits to our onward march? Providence is with us, and no earthly power can. We point to the everlasting truth on the first page of our national declaration, and we proclaim to the millions of other lands, that "the gates of hell"—the powers of aristocracy and monarchy—"shall not prevail against it." The far-reaching, the boundless future will be the era of American greatness. In its magnificent domain of time and space, the nation of many nations is destined to manifest to mankind the excellence of divine principles.

Six years later O'Sullivan tightened that phrase while warning of Anglo-French plots to thwart America's "manifest destiny to overspread the continent allotted by Providence." He urged the immediate annexation of Texas, Oregon, and California so that the peaceful march of free pioneers might spread American civilization coast to coast. That was the sentiment romantically expressed by John Gast's 1872 painting, *American Progress*, in which Indians and wild animals retreat before Conestoga wagons and railroads pressing westward under the goddess of liberty clutching her book of law.

O'Sullivan surely knew that the westward spread of civilization could never be peaceful. By 1839 Andrew Jackson's Indian Removal Act had already condemned the Five Civilized Tribes to the Trail of Tears, while the U.S. Army was waging a bitter counter-insurgency against the Seminoles in Florida. On the other hand, that anonymous Yankee's reduction of the American Dream to a gigantic land grab went to the other extreme. Yes, there is truth in William Appleman Williams's Wisconsin School of history that names Open Door economic expansion the wellspring of U.S. foreign policy. American history can be made to appear like a great Ponzi scheme in which a constantly growing pie of resources at home or abroad is needed to accommodate a growing and grasping population. During the nineteenth century, when most people made a living from agriculture, the pie that had to increase was land. But to reduce the American experience to naked avarice cloaked by a pious fig leaf is to miss the spirituality in the original civil religion. Historian Walter Russell Mead got it right when he discerned how Americans "read themselves into the covenantal patterns of Old Testament history. . . . We have our Ark of the Covenant. If we stick with the commandments, we prosper."

Could Americans live up to the commandments of their religion any better than the people of Israel and Judah? Americans believed (or pretended to believe) that they were a new chosen people in a new promised land. They believed (or pretended to believe) that their destiny was to spawn the freest, happiest, richest commonwealth in the world. They believed (or pretended to believe) that their history was a continuing revelation of God's purpose. O'Sullivan's prose and his colleague Walt Whitman's poetry said so explicitly. But none of that would happen—which is to say God's plan would be thwarted—if the Union did not survive. Hence, secession was the unforgivable sin against the Holy Ghost in the American Civil Religion. That explains why Andrew (Old Hickory) Jackson, a frontier chieftain, lawyer, and slave-owning planter, was also a nationalist fiercely jealous of the Union. That is also what makes James K. (Young Hickory) Polk so perplexing because the expansionist destiny he was impatient to manifest only exacerbated the sectional crisis between the slave and free states. So what was Polk thinking when he manufactured the war against Mexico?

Why ask? Objectively Polk would seem to be one of the greatest U.S. presidents. He accomplished his entire domestic and foreign agendas in one term, then retired as promised. He avoided another war against Britain by climbing down from his "54° 40′ or Fight!" motto and partitioning the Oregon Territory. He completed the process of Texas statehood and dispatched multiple clandestine expeditions to plant the U.S. flag in California in case Mexico refused to sell the province. When diplomacy failed, Polk fomented a conflict in 1846 by claiming the Rio Grande boundary for Texas and sending General Zachary Taylor to patrol it. When the Mexican Army attacked the invaders, Polk claimed American blood had been shed on American soil and asked Congress for a declaration of war. The war was very successful and lasted just twenty-one months, but that was long enough in those dear, dead days to try the American people's patience. Thanks to General Winfield Scott's brilliant campaign, the U.S. Army occupied Mexico City, but only weeks had passed before resistance flared up and threatened Scott with guerilla war. That in turn made a mockery of a so-called All-Mexico Movement that had sprung up among zealous Democrats. They imagined the war might be redeemed if the United States annexed the whole of Mexico and dispatched teachers, lawyers, businessmen, engineers, and Protestant preachers to uplift the benighted Catholic country. When instead diplomat Nicholas Trist found Mexican authorities willing to cede Texas, California, and the land in between, Polk and the Senate jumped at the chance.

That account, so far as it goes, has survived recent scholarship. No evidence has emerged to revive the old canard that the Mexican War was a slaveholders' plot. Texas was already admitted, the southwestern deserts were unlikely terrain for slavery, and some of Polk's sharpest opponents were Southerners. What is more, Polk mistakenly believed that territorial expansion—in Oregon as well as in the southwest—was a nationalist policy that would reduce rather than exacerbate sectional strife. Finally, Polk's otherwise measured calibration of U.S. national interest included two provinces he failed to acquire: the densely populated Yucatán peninsula and Spain's Cuban colony. Perhaps historian William Dusinberre was too harsh when he labeled Polk a provincial entrepreneur who "brought to the national stage the constricted views of a Tennessee slavemaster," but it is probably not too harsh to conclude that Polk, like Jefferson, sometimes betrayed a split-mindedness about foreign policy.

None of those critical historical issues, however, speak to contemporary Americans so much as two others raised by the Mexican War. The first is the question of presidential war powers, which Polk vastly expanded and (in the minds of Whig critics) sorely abused when he maneuvered the enemy into firing the first shot and providing a *casus belli*. The fact is that Polk's Cabinet had decided on war even before news of the Rio Grande skirmish arrived. But the bloodshed permitted the president to ask for a declaration of war as a matter of urgency, which gave the Democratic majority the excuse to close off debate after a day. In 1812 Madison had laid out his grounds for believing a state of war already existed, but he deferred to the Congress, which debated at length. In 1846, the Philadelphia *North American* accused the Polk administration of violating the Constitution by making war without Congressional sanction and leaving the people no room for consideration. The Boston *Daily Atlas* quoted Senator Calhoun to the effect that the United States could not legally be at war until Congress declared it so, yet the president's fait accompli gave it no choice. The Albany *Evening Journal* warned, "The Evil we apprehend concerns our form of Government. When we cease to be a quiet, peaceful, unambitious People, our Republican form of Government will slide from under us." Whigs hotly protested, but only fourteen dared to vote nay lest their party seem unpatriotic and suffer the same extinction that befell the Federalists after the War of 1812.

The constitutional implications were ominous. The president had used his powers as commander-in-chief to send a military force into harm's way. When the harm happened, the president made it the pretext for war. Congress felt it could not turn its back on the nation's soldiers, so it resigned itself to carping after the fact. John Quincy Adams mourned, "It is now established as an ir-reversible precedent that the President of the United States has but to declare that War exists, with any Nation upon Earth, by the act of that Nation's Government, and the War is essentially declared." The most famous protest was lodged by a one-term Congressman from Illinois. Abraham Lincoln theatrically intro-duced "spot resolutions," demanding to know the precise spot on which American blood had been shed on American soil. As Lincoln explained to his law partner, William Herndon, "Allow the President to invade a neighboring nation whenever he shall deem it necessary to repel an invasion, and you allow him to do so when-ever he may choose to say he deems it necessary for such purpose, and you allow him to make war at pleasure. . . . If to-day he should choose to say he thinks it necessary to invade Canada to prevent the British from invading us, how could you stop him? You may say to him, 'I see no probability of the British invading us'; but he will say to you, 'Be silent. I see it, if you don't.'" Thus did Lincoln espy how a bold chief executive might employ his enumerated powers to trump the enumerated powers of Congress. Ironically, Lincoln would use the same ploy at Fort Sumter in 1861 to fix blame for the Civil War on the Confederacy.

The second issue raised by Manifest Destiny is the historicity of the alleged U.S. tradition of nation-building based on three hy-potheses. First, it has been argued that Americans have always been magnificent nation-builders, as proven by their own pioneer his-tory. Second, it has been argued that nation-building was always the work of a vigorous public-private partnership. Third, it has been ar-gued that the U.S. military has always been actively engaged in nation-building. Those postulates appear to support assertions such as historian Jeremi Suri's: "Nothing could be more American than to pursue global peace through the spread of American-style insti-tutions. Nothing could be more American than to expect ready sup-port for this process from a mix of local populations, international allies, and, of course, the United States government. Between the presidencies of Washington and Obama, nation-building became the dominant template for political change among Americans."

One scarcely knows where to begin—and not because the pos-tulates are mistaken. On the contrary, they are substantially right.

A large and authoritative literature describes the roles played by the federal government and especially the military in the exploration, pacification, and development of the United States' land and water frontiers. Rather, one scarcely knows where to begin because these postulates are all derived from experience on America's own, mostly open, frontier, in which "nation-building" was done by America's own dominant race, with the assistance of America's own military and civil authorities. The U.S. experience of nation-building at home has obviously been successful (albeit bloody). But that experience has no relevance for military occupations and bureaucratic nation-building among foreign peoples with alien cultures halfway around the world.

It might have been possible to draw some valid analogies between U.S. nation-building at home and abroad if the army, federal authorities, territorial governments, and settlers on the frontier had accommodated Indians and Mexicans instead of killing, expelling, and expropriating them. The earnest efforts of a few philanthropists and Catholic prelates notwithstanding, the American attitude was pretty much one of assimilate or else perish. Virtually all Hispanic and sympathetic Anglo literature attests to that forlorn choice, beginning with Helen Hunt Jackson's *Ramona* (1884). That is no cause for guilt—it was probably inevitable—but it is certainly no cause to celebrate an alleged American talent for civilizing other cultures. No one knew better than Herman Melville, whose early novels *Omoo* and *Typee* (1846) questioned who is more civilized or more savage: the Yankee or the South Sea Islander? Melville's *The Confidence Man* (1858) explained in "The Metaphysics of Indian-hating" why the red man's only choice was between physical extinction and cultural suicide. In *White Jacket, or the World in a Man-of-War* (1850), Melville's sailor boasts, "And we Americans are the peculiar, chosen people—the Israel of our time; we bear the ark of the liberties of the world." But only an ignoramus could miss the irony drenching a passage in which Melville is saying in effect, "America, since you boast of bearing the ark of the liberties, the least you can do is abolish flogging in your Navy (not to mention slavery, as the monarchical British have already done)."

The conquest of the American West is so far from being a model of orderly nation-building that it was only a matter of time before someone compared it to the Nazi pursuit of *Lebensraum* in Eastern Europe. The author granted that sharp distinctions must be drawn between the Native American die-off and the carnage in World War II but was disturbed by the similarities between the national projects of space and race. Suffice to say the Great Plains, Rocky Mountains, southwestern deserts, and Pacific slope were far more peaceful—even among peoples of mixed races—before the U.S. federal government arrived. Almost all the wars, massacres, famines, epidemics, environmental catastrophes (think: buffalo), and systematic discrimination followed the flag westward. That is why Western historian Anne Hyde summed up the Manifest Destiny era as follows: "In our imagination and national mythology, the state brings order and peace. But in these years in this place it brought mayhem and massacre."

It is certainly so that the U.S. Constitution followed the flag in the nineteenth century and thereby gave genuine content to Jefferson's empire of liberty. From the Appalachian Mountains to the Pacific Ocean the Congress organized territories, not to exploit them as colonies but to prepare them for statehood (usually premature statehood at that). But sadly the progress of American law and institutions made nuisances of indigenous peoples unable or unwilling to get with the program. With regard to overseas peoples, however, the United States adhered to its Classical ACR principle of strict reciprocity. Merchants were active in the Pacific, East Asia, the Muslim world, and the Mediterranean from 1783 and missionaries from 1819. But those private citizens offered their wares and their faith to the heathen in the hope that they would embrace the twin gospels of Christ and commerce peacefully and reform their civilizations from within. Of course, such activity provoked occasional conflicts with foreign officials and pirates, which in turn obligated the federal government to mount punitive naval expeditions.

By far the largest and most momentous naval expedition was Commodore Matthew Perry's 1853–54 embassy to Japan. It was meant to be a show of force because the truly isolationist Japanese tortured and killed shipwrecked Yankee sailors (mostly whalers) washed up on the shores of the Land of the Gods. But President Millard Fillmore also hoped the Tokugawa Shogunate would establish a coaling station for steamships and open the country to foreign trade, as China had recently done under British coercion. Still, the decision to open Japan was made, however reluctantly, by the Shogun's bureaucracy, as was the decision made by the leaders of the 1868 Meiji Restoration to recruit foreign experts to teach Japanese how to modernize. In sum, the U.S. government in the nineteenth century consistently defended its flag and the lives and property of its people abroad, sometimes fiercely. But it never presumed to design the futures of overseas countries. Manifest Destiny remained a blessing (or curse) exclusive to North America.

CHAPTER NINE

European Revolutions and American Civil War

ISTORIAN DANIEL WALKER HOWE summed up the Whig party's reaction to the Mexican War and All-Mexico Movement as follows: "American imperialism did not represent an American consensus; it provoked bitter dissent within the national polity. . . . Whigs saw America's moral mission as one of democratic example rather than one of conquest." For instance, the aged Henry Clay judged at the time that "War, pestilence, and famine are the three greatest calamities which can befall our species; and war, as the most direful, justly stands in front." Clay thought it absurd to think "that two such immense countries, with territories of nearly equal extent, with populations so incongruous, so different in race, in language, in religion, and in laws, could be blended together in one harmonious mass, and happily governed by one common authority." Daniel Dewey Bernard, editor of the *American Whig Review*, called the All-Mexico Movement a folly and injustice, fearing the Anglo-Saxon notion of destiny would pervert the United States into "a rapacious, a warlike, a conquering nation." John Quincy Adams despaired: "The Constitution is a menstruous rag, and the Union is sinking into a military monarchy, to be rent asunder like the empire of Alexander or the kingdoms of Ephraim and Judah."

After Adams died on the floor of Congress in February 1848, William H. Seward asked in his eulogy: "Does freedom own and accept our profuse oblations of blood, or does she reject the sacrifice? Will these conquests extend her domain, or will they be usurped by ever-grasping slavery? What effect will this new-born ambition have upon ourselves? Will it leave us the virtue to continue the career of social progress? How shall we govern the conquered people? Shall we incorporate their mingled races with ourselves, or shall we rule them with the despotism of pro-consular power? Can we preserve these remote and hostile possessions, in any way, without forfeiting our own blood-bought heritage of freedom?" Aged Albert Gallatin, who had served as Thomas Jefferson's secretary of the treasury, scolded Americans for departing from the founding principles. "Your mission was to be a model for all other governments and for all other less-favored nations, to adhere to the most elevated principles of political morality, to apply all your faculties to the gradual improvement of your own institutions and social state, and by your example to exert a moral influence most beneficial to mankind at large."

Given this chorus of recrimination regarding the threat posed by American militarism on its own continent, what is one to make of the apparent enthusiasm of both Whigs and Democrats for interventions of some sort in Central Europe? For in February 1848— the same month as the Treaty of Guadalupe Hidalgo—popular revolutions began to spread quickly from Paris to Milan, Vienna, Budapest, Berlin, and throughout the German Confederation. The revolutionary mobs and assemblies displayed a confused and ultimately self-defeating admixture of democratic, nationalist, and socialist impulses, but Americans flattered themselves that the peoples of the Old World were at last demanding what they already enjoyed: nationhood and liberty. Late in 1851 Lajos Kossuth, leader of the erstwhile Hungarian rebellion against Austria's Habsburg monarchy, arrived in the United States hoping to garner support. New York gave him a reception third in scale only to those given Washington and Lafayette. He dined with President Fillmore and delivered six hundred speeches on a national tour. Whig senators such as Seward and Charles Sumner lauded Kossuth and proclaimed American support for national self-determination. Illinois lawyer Abraham Lincoln is said to have introduced a resolution calling for U.S. intervention on Hungary's behalf. Democrats founded a Young America Movement emulating the Young Italy and Young Germany movements. Its spokesmen included John O'Sullivan and Senator Stephen Douglas, who suggested Americans consider discarding the Monroe Doctrine's prohibition against political involvement in Europe.

Given such enthusiasm for the Revolutions of 1848, would it be accurate to conclude that public opinion in the American North wanted to help European freedom fighters only to be thwarted by what Robert Kagan has called "realist Southerners" who were in fact "proto-totalitarians"? Not a smidgen of evidence exists to suggest the answers are yes.

First, the men who made a fuss over Kossuth did not favor U.S. intervention. Webster gave him "all personal and individual respect, but if he shall speak to me of the policy of 'intervention' I shall 'have ears more deaf than adders.'" Clay looked up from his deathbed to tell Kossuth that if the United States once abandoned "our ancient policy of amity and non-intervention in the affairs of other nations," then others would be justified in "abandoning the terms of forbearance and non-interference which they have hitherto preserved toward us." Far better for the cause of liberty "that we should keep our lamp burning brightly on this western shore as a light to all nations, than to hazard its utter extinction amid the ruins of fallen or falling republics in Europe." Seward believed it imperative that Americans voice their "mission of republicanism" but was scrupulous about reciprocity: "We shall best execute [the republican mission] by maintaining peace at home and peace with all mankind."

Second, it goes without saying that U.S. diplomacy under Presidents Polk, Taylor, and Fillmore remained strictly aloof from Europe's internal affairs except to join all other nations in recognizing the new Second French Republic.

Third, the question posed by the Hungarian Revolution was thoroughly moot by the time of Kossuth's visit. The Hungarian Army fought bravely but had suffered decisive defeat at the hands of the Habsburg Austrian and tsarist Russian armies in August 1849. Kossuth went into exile, only to be interned by the Ottoman Turks. By the time he reached the United States in 1852, he was pleading a long-lost cause.

Fourth, even if the Hungarian fires had still been flickering, the United States possessed no means whatsoever of influencing events in a landlocked Central European country. The most Daniel Webster, now secretary of state, could do was to petition the Ottomans for Kossuth's release and dispatch the *U.S.S. Mississippi* to carry him into asylum.

Fifth, Kossuth proved nearly as obnoxious as Citizen Genêt. He took sides in the U.S. political campaign, encouraged Protestant bias against Catholics, offended slaveholders and abolitionists alike, and flirted with filibusters in a plot to overthrow black rule in Haiti.

Sixth, that Illinois resolution supposedly introduced by Lincoln was in fact drafted by a committee, and Lincoln's role was to pour cold water on the idea when ardent petitioners moved another resolution to condemn British rule in Ireland. Accordingly, the *Illinois Journal* reported on January 12, 1852: "Lincoln spoke to the meeting on the 8th in favor of sympathy but non-intervention."

Seventh, the comparison of antebellum Southerners to twentieth-century totalitarians or realists is an outrageous anachronism. Southern planters might have rammed a gag rule through Congress and controlled the mails to suppress abolitionist propaganda, but otherwise they were proud-to-a-fault Jeffersonians devoted to states' rights. Moreover, Southern planters, so far from acting like realists, were so eager to export their American institutions that they sparked invasions and insurrections, the infamous filibusters, around the Caribbean in hopes of "exporting American institutions" by way of acquiring some new slave states.

Did the 1848 revolutions fail to resonate in America in any important sense? On the contrary, they became what historian Timothy Mason Roberts has called a veritable Rorschach test in domestic politics, especially during the presidential election of 1848. Whigs celebrated the ordered liberty enjoyed in the United States by contrast to the mob violence of Europeans (and implicitly the violence-prone Jacksonians in northern American cities). Northern Democrats celebrated the revolutions as popular challenges to power and privilege. Free Soilers and abolitionists celebrated the great international trend toward liberty. Southern elites, needless to say, saw proof of the dangers of revolutions from below. By 1849, when the tide of reaction triumphed everywhere (even in France when Louis Napoleon Bonaparte was elected president), all Americans gave nervous thanks for the order and liberty bestowed by what Lincoln called their political religion.

Catholic bishop John Hughes and idiosyncratic Catholic convert Orestes Brownson peered more deeply into the meanings of 1848 and found reason to fear for America's future. The very absence of feudal survivals like monarchy, aristocracy, and an established church in the United States, combined with free speech and free exercise of religion, meant Americans were uniquely free to take *vox populi vox Dei* seriously and create theologies to their own liking. How long would it be until they divided along sectional lines into two schismatic civil religions? The elderly James Fenimore Cooper sensed the danger, which is why he inscribed the 1851 edition of his novel *The Spy* (1821) as follows: "There is now no enemy to fear, but the one that resides within."

In the era of Classical ACR citizens liked to pretend that their enemy number one was monarchy. But as early as 1836 Abraham Lincoln bragged that "All the armies of Europe, Asia, and Africa combined, with all the treasure of the earth (our own excepted) in their military chest; with a Buonaparte for a commander, could not by force take a drink from the Ohio or make a track on the Blue Ridge, in a trial of a thousand years." Moreover, the United States maintained correct relations with all the European monarchies, including the Holy Alliance powers. Their prickliest relations were with the European power they most resembled because liberal Britain was the main geopolitical and ideological rival to the United States prior to the Civil War. In 1833 Parliament summarily voted to end slavery and compensate slave owners through the issue of government bonds. That pacific, humane resolution was simply not possible in the American federal republic. Parliament also expanded suffrage through the Reform Bill of 1832 and adopted free trade in 1846, thereby refuting the conceit that made the United States the vanguard of progress. Then, after the Revolutions of 1848 and Crimean War (1854), top-down reforms enacted by monarchies began to transform politics and economics all across Europe.

In other words, Americans wanted to believe the fate of the whole human race hinged on the outcome of their republic. But the all-too-familiar drumbeats of truth—the false Compromise of 1850; publication of *Uncle Tom's Cabin* (1852); Kansas-Nebraska Act (1854), which repealed the Missouri Compromise; Bleeding Kansas (1855–58); sudden rise of the Republican Party (1856); Dred Scott Decision (1857); financial panic and religious revival in the urban North (1857); Lincoln-Douglas debates (1858); John Brown raid (1859); and nomination of Lincoln for president (1860)—forced Americans to confess that an unbridgeable schism had indeed erupted in their civil religion to complete the lesser schisms that had occurred years before in some of their major Protestant denominations. Northerners were not abolitionists for the most part, but they could no longer in good conscience permit Southern planters to feel good about doing well and feared for their own livelihood so long as slavery persisted. Southerners were not outright secessionists for the most part, but they could no longer in good conscience permit Northern hustlers to feel good about doing well and feared for their own livelihood so long as the Union persisted.

Southerners had always rested their case on the Constitution, which implicitly blessed their peculiar institution. Now they took their stand on the Declaration of Independence, which justified rebellion against a tyrannical regime. Northerners had always rested their case on the Declaration, which said all men were endowed with the rights to life, liberty, and the pursuit of happiness. Now they took their stand on the Constitution, under which secession equated to anarchy and preservation of the Union was holy. South Carolina's attack on Fort Sumter made the contest a war, and war made foreign policy crucial because all four traditions of U.S. diplomacy—liberty, neutrality, the American system, and continental expansion—were thrown up for grabs. Should the Confederacy survive, then two sovereign and rival nations must arm against each other, make foreign alliances, contest for western lands (which might escape both), and compromise liberty through standing armies and the taxes and bureaucracies to support them. Since the surest way the Confederacy could survive was to win European recognition, trade, credits, and possibly co-belligerency, the purpose of Union diplomacy became mortally simple: uphold the Monroe Doctrine by keeping Britain and France out of the fray. The Lincoln administration had some bad moments, especially with regard to its naval blockade of Southern ports. But the Union's diplomatic acumen, skillful propaganda, economic clout (King Corn as opposed to King Cotton), and good fortune prevailed. Lord Palmerston's cabinet adopted a wait-and-see policy while Louis Napoleon (now Emperor Napoleon III) flouted the Monroe Doctrine only to pursue an imperial venture in Mexico. The Confederacy, left to its devices in a war of attrition, gradually suffocated.

Abraham Lincoln fell in love with the Classical ACR at least as early as his 1838 Lyceum Address, which exhorted youth to hold sacred their political faith. Throughout his career he employed logic and folksy wit to root out heresy and thereby establish orthodoxy, with the Lincoln-Douglas debates perhaps the crowning example. During the Civil War Lincoln experienced serial dark nights of the soul until at last surrendering to God's purposes. He bestowed on the United States a more coherent, somewhat more honest, political faith that became neo-Classical ACR. In the Gettysburg Address, for instance, Lincoln claimed humbly, "The world will little note, nor long remember what we say here" but in fact spoke for the ages. Lincoln claimed, "We cannot consecrate, cannot hallow this ground" but proceeded to do exactly that by proclaiming a new birth of freedom.

Historians have found several sources for that sublime sermon, one of which was the Hegelian Unitarianism of Theodore Parker. In "The Effect of Slavery on the American People" he called democracy "direct self-government, over all the people, for all the people, by all the people. . . . A government after the principles of eternal justice, the unchanging law of God; for shortness' sake, I will call it the idea of Freedom." Lincoln rejected the Declaration of Independence as a living letter insofar as his administration crushed the Confederacy's attempt to invoke it anew. But Lincoln also elevated the Declaration to iconic status and in so doing re-baptized the United States a teleocracy, a nation governed by its pursuit of an abstract idea, a nation with a purpose-driven life. Ralph Waldo Emerson, no stranger to coded rhetoric, observed of Lincoln, "Rarely was man so fitted to the event. The very dogs believe in him."

Did Lincoln do or say anything of similar theological significance with regard to U.S. foreign relations? In all Lincoln's voluminous writings there is not a single remark about what sort of foreign policy the United States should embrace except that it ought to cherish peace and reciprocity with all nations. Why, then, is it so often asserted that the Union victory in the Civil War somehow prepared the United States for its later career as a world power crusading for universal human rights? Certainly Lincoln was prophetic in the idiom of ACR. But far from being an advocate of democratic proselytism overseas, he fretted over whether self-government might survive at home. That was the meaning of his eloquent Second Annual Message to Congress of December 1862: "Fellow citizens, we cannot escape history. . . . We know how to save the Union. The world knows we do know how to save it. . . . In giving freedom to the slave, we assure freedom to the free—honorable alike in what we give, and what we preserve. We shall nobly save, or meanly lose, the last best hope of earth. Other means may succeed; this could not fail. The way is plain, peaceful, generous, just—a way which, if followed, the world will forever applaud, and God must forever bless." Lincoln was saying that the world was watching us, not we the world. And if we should fail, then what hope had the world? In short, Lincoln's concern was not the extension of liberty everywhere but the survival of liberty anywhere. Did the Union's survival and its destruction of a pseudo-aristocratic landed gentry in the name of democracy encourage liberals and nationalists over in Europe? Of course it did, but no one on either side of the ocean expected the United States to launch crusades beyond its own borders.

Lincoln's Second Inaugural Address was unambiguous, indeed saintly, in his forbearance. "With malice toward none, with charity for all, with firmness in the right as God gives us to see the right, let us strive on to finish the work we are in, to bind up the nation's wounds, to care for him who shall have borne the battle and for his widow and his orphan, to do all which may achieve and cherish a just and lasting peace among ourselves and with all nations." These are not the words of a crusading knight in search of monsters to destroy. These are the words of a penitent mystic bowing before an inscrutable God. By the end of the war Lincoln seemed to have completed his quest for the meaning of history as revealed in America's tribulation:

Both read the same Bible and pray to the same God, and each invokes His aid against the other. It may seem strange that any men should dare to ask a just God's assistance in wringing their bread from the sweat of other men's faces, but let us judge not, that we be not judged. The prayers of both could not be answered. That of neither has been answered fully. The Almighty has His own purposes. ... Fondly do we hope, fervently do we pray, that this mighty scourge of war may speedily pass away. Yet, if God wills that it continue until all the wealth piled by the bondsman's two hundred and fifty years of unrequited toil shall be sunk, and until every drop of blood drawn with the lash shall be paid by another drawn with the sword, as was said three thousand years ago, so still it must be said "the judgments of the Lord are true and righteous altogether."

The New Testament declares that all the kingdoms of this world are the devil's to dispose. St. Augustine's less jarring language assigns them all to the City of Man as opposed to the City of God. Lincoln never abandoned his civil religious faith in America, but he lived in the knowledge that his was merely "an almost chosen people," and he died acknowledging the people's obeisance. America, too, was under judgment.

Of course, Northerners were quick to deify Lincoln as the martyred messiah killed on Good Friday, the redeemer president who purged the nation of its original sin. Some got so carried away they harbored millenarian expectations. Prominent clergymen such as the abolitionist Methodist bishop Gilbert Haven imagined the Civil War ushering in a "world-Republic" based on perfect equality of all races of men. President Ulysses S. Grant invoked such a vision in his second inaugural address: "Rather do I believe that our Great Maker is preparing the world, in His own good time, to become one nation, speaking one language, and when armies and navies will be no longer required." Massachusetts senator Charles Sumner, the long-standing chairman of the Senate Foreign Relations Committee, awaited the Second Coming. Like John Adams before him, he collected prophetic signs and utterances regarding the providential role of America. But no American statesmen after the Civil War permitted such fantasies to affect foreign policy. Indeed, Sumner himself was a staunch defender of

John Quincy Adams's modest interpretation of the Monroe Doctrine, and it was Sumner who established the practice of having Washington's Farewell Address read aloud in the Senate. But perhaps the most telling testimony against those who attribute martial, universal ambitions to Abraham Lincoln was that of his son, Robert Lincoln. A successful lawyer who turned away all offers to run for office, he made a rare political gesture in 1912 when candidate Theodore Roosevelt invoked Lincoln's name. If his father were alive today, wrote Robert to the *Boston Herald*, he would abhor Roosevelt's imperialist platform.

The Civil War forged one nation out of the federal union and crafted a nationalism that maintained states' rights but abolished involuntary servitude and empowered the federal government to hasten the progress of agriculture, mining, transportation, science, and industry. Historians therefore speak of the Morrill Tariff and Land Grant Act, the Homestead Act and Department of Agriculture, the Pacific Railroad Act, and the National Banking Act as a second American revolution. But that was only the visible material expression of the neo-Classical ACR sealed by the Union's victory. To Northerners it was a good war, a holy war. But was it good because it was a war of aggression, an ideological conquest that, in Robert Kagan's imagination, taught a "new lesson, that war could serve what they regarded as just and moral ends"? David Hendrickson concludes, as Lincoln himself always insisted, that the war was good only if it was not a war of conquest, and the lesson it taught was that liberation of African Americans and reconstruction of the South were notoriously incomplete. Hence "America's first experiment in nation-building ended in disillusionment, recrimination, and renewed appreciation of limits of military power and its potential threat to republican principles."

Suffice to say the Republican leaders who dominated American politics for the rest of the century were almost all Civil War veterans. Almost all had a powerful aversion to war.

CHAPTER TEN

The Gilded Age

Last Years of Orthodoxy

U LYSSES S. GRANT HAD nursed a guilty conscience over the Mexican War for two decades. When the Civil War ended in 1865, he got the chance to atone for that national sin by hastening the end of Napoleon III's imperial gambit in Mexico. Grant deployed fifty thousand troops on the Rio Grande and instructed General Philip Sheridan to arm the opponents of self-proclaimed Emperor Maximilian. Those measured threats amply supported the stern protests of Seward's State Department. French troops withdrew in January 1867, and Maximilian was executed in June. Thus did the United States employ the Monroe Doctrine as John Quincy Adams intended, as a robust but ultimately peaceful defense of republicanism in the hemisphere.

Seward also gave President Andrew Johnson's otherwise ill-starred presidency a solid foreign policy triumph with the 1867 purchase of Alaska. Tsar Alexander II's offer to sell Russian America to the United States for a mere $7.2 million testified to the vulnerability of that remote colony in case of war. Indeed, only an Anglo-Russian side agreement to keep their respective North American colonies off-limits during the Crimean War had spared Alaska from easy conquest. Moreover, the tsar needed all the cash he could get in order to finance Russia's first railroads and factories. Finally, the deal testified to tsarist sympathy for the Union cause, a by-product of the fact that Russia faced its own secessionist movement in the Polish Revolt of 1863. But it is indicative of the mood of Congress, obsessed by the crushing national debt run up during the Civil War, that Seward had to beg Senator Sumner to persuade his colleagues to ratify the treaty and Russian minister Édouard de Stoeck had to bribe members of Congress to approve the appropriation.

The vigorous reassertion by Congress of its constitutional powers in foreign policy was one of the most striking features of postbellum politics. Another was the frugality of the legislative and executive branches alike. The federal budget shrank from $1.3 billion in 1865 to a lean $241 million in 1877 before inching back upward until the infamous 1889–91 "Billion-Dollar Congress" was condemned for spending that much over two years. Of course, the United States was blessed that its geopolitical neighborhood needed little active defense. Even the 1867 British North America Act, by which Parliament granted Canada federated home rule, was a defensive measure. But wise policy also ensured the United States made no enemies. No one imagined the United States meddling in the affairs of Europe, Africa, or Asia.

Latin America was another story. Indeed, the Monroe Doctrine was almost the sole subject of debate in U.S. foreign policy over the three post–Civil War decades. While all Americans could agree with *Harper's Weekly* that "the Monroe Doctrine is unquestionably a fixed principle of American political faith," they continued to quarrel, as they had in the 1840s and 1850s, over its meaning. Was it meant only to be a protective mantle thrown over the republics of the hemisphere, or did it invite the United States to expand or otherwise intervene in them? Southern filibusters obviously argued the latter, while northern Free Soilers argued the former. After the Civil War three tests of U.S. intentions and capabilities arose in the Caribbean. First, President Grant tried to annex the Dominican Republic in 1870. Its interest for him was strategic—a naval base to protect the eastern approaches of a future Central American canal—and racial— a potential new home for African American freedmen. All sorts of

profiteers and philanthropists, including Frederick Douglass, promoted the scheme. But the Dominican dictator, Buenaventura Baez,
stood to profit the most and rigged a Dominican plebiscite approving the sale. Nor did many Americans relish the notion of granting
statehood to poor, colored West Indians. Sumner opposed the treaty,
which fell short of a two-thirds majority.

The second test of the Monroe Doctrine came with a Cuban
rebellion against Spanish colonial rule from 1868 to 1878. Some
Republicans contemplated intervention for reasons financial, strategic, or humanitarian (slavery persisted in Cuba until 1886). But
neither Grant nor Secretary of State Hamilton Fish could stomach
the idea of a military adventure likely to drag the United States
into war. So far from claiming the Monroe Doctrine required U.S.
involvement, Fish hoped European powers could be persuaded to
mediate in Madrid.

The third test came with the elaborate project of French promoter Ferdinand de Lesseps to follow up his triumph at Suez with
an isthmian canal cutting through Nicaragua. Central American canal schemes dated back to the Forty-Niner gold rush in California,
which is why the Fillmore administration had negotiated the
Clayton-Bulwer Treaty of 1850. At that time the United States had
granted equal rights over an isthmian canal to Great Britain. Now
the Chester A. Arthur administration tried to check the French
project by negotiating a treaty with Nicaragua that awarded the
United States an exclusive right-of-way. Yet senators fearing the
treaty might lead to corrupting entanglements blocked ratification
until 1885, when the new Cleveland administration withdrew the
treaty.

Latin Americans were also on guard against any U.S. hegemonic ambitions. In 1889 Secretary of State James G. Blaine presided over the First Pan-American Conference in Washington,
D.C., in hopes that U.S. firms might displace their British competitors as the principal beneficiaries of South American commerce.
Preceding the conference Latin delegates were treated (or subjected) to a six-week railroad tour of northern industrial cities. As
historian Jay Sexton wryly observed, "The whole thing resembled
the train journeys Native American leaders such as Red Cloud took
to Washington before being bullied into signing away their tribal

lands. The parallel was not lost on observers at the time." Latin delegates, led by the Argentines, doggedly opposed the United States on every detail until Blaine had to promise to "meet together on terms of absolute equality." He never mouthed the words "Monroe Doctrine" and claimed the only U.S. objective was the annexation of trade. Even that objective was foiled when the Republican Congress passed a highly protectionist tariff in 1890.

Nation-building abroad tempted hardly any Americans in the Gilded Age. If anything, they mourned for the first time the fate of Indian tribes displaced or effaced by their own westward expansion. Helen Hunt Jackson, Hubert Howe Bancroft, Henry Adams, and constitutional historian Hermann Von Holst were just some of the best-selling authors who indicted the United States for its long history of broken treaties and massacres. Of course, the expropriation of Indian lands already under the American flag was something that could not be helped if civilization were to advance. But to suggest the same logic applied in densely populated lands not under the American flag was repulsive to moralists and racists alike in the 1870s and '80s. "Empire obtained by force," wrote Sumner, "is un-republican, and offensive to the first principle of our Union, according to which all just government stands only on the consent of the governed. Our country needs no such ally as war. Its destiny is mightier than war. Through peace it will have everything."

Grover Cleveland, the sole Democrat to serve as president between 1861 and 1913, was thoroughly orthodox in foreign affairs. At his 1885 inaugural he proclaimed the following:

> The genius of our institutions, the needs of our people in their home life, and the attention which is demanded for the settlement and development of the resources of our vast territory dictate the scrupulous avoidance of any departure from that foreign policy commended by the history, the traditions, and the prosperity of our Republic. It is the policy of independence, favored by our position and defended by our known love of justice and by our power. It is the policy of peace suitable to our interests. It is the policy of neutrality, rejecting any share in foreign broils and ambitions upon other continents and repelling their intrusion

here. It is the policy of Monroe and of Washington and Jefferson—"Peace, commerce, and honest friendship with all nations; entangling alliance with none."

He concluded with a civil religious benediction "humbly acknowledging the power and goodness of Almighty God, who presides over the destiny of nations, and who has at all times been revealed in our country's history" and asked for God's continued aid and blessings.

During his second (non-consecutive) term in the White House Cleveland even passed up a chance to annex Hawaii in 1893, when the *haole* (white) elite on Oahu overthrew Queen Liliuokalani. Yet, two years later it seemed the administration radically changed course when it intervened aggressively in a boundary dispute between British Guiana and Venezuela. Secretary of State Richard Olney drafted a haughty twelve-thousand-word brief that declared "the United States is practically sovereign on this continent and its fiat is law." The delighted president called it a twenty-inch gun. Many historians since have concluded that even Cleveland had now reinterpreted the Monroe Doctrine in order to prepare the way for imperialism. The truth is almost exactly the opposite. Cleveland's purposes were to steal the thunder from Republican jingoes so as not to compromise "limited and decentralized government and non-entanglement overseas" and to ward off European intervention. So he bade Olney not only to twist the British lion's tail, but also to reconfirm self-containment by renouncing the right to interfere in the internal affairs of other American states. When it was suggested to him that his note in fact inflated the Monroe Doctrine, Olney barked, "Nothing could be further from the truth. It, in reality, defined it and confined its application within narrower limits than had ever been fixed by previous administrations or public men."

Cleveland's vision of the United States as a modest republic seems quaint in retrospect only because we know what happened in 1898 and all the reasons why an American grasp for world power seems overdetermined. Since 1865 a new generation had grown up in a new America in the midst of a world made new by nationalism and imperialism. Industrialization accelerated after the Civil War to the point that manufacturing surpassed agriculture as the dominant economic sector, throwing enormous influence into the hands of capitalists such as Andrew Carnegie, John D. Rockefeller, and Edward H. Harriman. Urbanization advanced rapidly despite the opening of the Great Plains. A nation populated by farmers, tradesmen, proprietors, and professionals began to turn into a nation populated by dependent employees. Immigrants flooded American ports, triggering nativist fears. In 1882 Chinese were banned outright. Manufacturers concerned about overproduction looked for new markets abroad.

The world shrank. Jules Verne could pen *Around the World in Eighty Days* in 1873 thanks to the opening of the Suez Canal (1869), trans-India railroad (1870), and U.S. transcontinental railroad (1869). Europeans, having invented technologies that enabled them to acquire colonial empires on the cheap, partitioned nearly all of Africa, Asia, and the Pacific. Not only Britain, but also France, Russia, and Italy, then Germany and Japan, competed to build modern steel navies powered by coal and then oil. It appeared the United States must follow suit lest the Monroe Doctrine become a dead letter. Between the 1870s and 1890s bipartisan support steadily built in Congress for a new navy serving the interests of domestic industry and foreign trade. Even the Supreme Court seemed to clear the way for assertive foreign policy in a recondite 1890 decision *In re Neagle*. The court ruled the executive branch was endowed with power to do whatever was necessary to enforce the "rights, duties, and obligations growing out of the Constitution [and] our international relations." That stewardship theory might become an elastic clause in the hands of ambitious future presidents.

Ineffably important cultural turns also seemed to prepare late-nineteenth-century Americans for a sudden assertion of world power. Social Darwinism and its corollary, Anglo-Saxon supremacy, became an article of faith and reason to many white Americans thanks to the patronage they received from genteel northeastern elites, including the Harvard-trained historian John Fiske, Columbia political scientist John W. Burgess, General Secretary of the Evangelical Alliance Josiah Strong, U.S. civil service commissioner Theodore Roosevelt, and Naval War College professor A. T.

Mahan. Highbrow journals such as *Harper's, Scribner's*, the *Atlantic Monthly*, the *North American Review, The Century*, and *Putnam's Monthly* argued in favor of emulating the social and military policies of the European powers. Some historians even suspect the tedious, regimented lives of America's industrial workforce caused a crisis of masculinity. Roosevelt certainly deplored the enervation attending city life and exhorted, "Unless we keep the barbarian virtues, gaining the civilized ones will be of little avail."

A restless, half-conscious anticipation haunted Americans in the Gilded Age. History was speeding up, so if the United States were to fulfill its divine calling as the great nation of futurity, some great metamorphosis must be in gestation. That made the old utopian split-mindedness especially tempting. Perhaps the United States did have a mission beyond perfecting itself and setting an example for others. Private merchants and missionaries had long been at work in the global vineyard. Perhaps it was time for the U.S. government to take up the cause of exporting American material and spiritual blessings.

Consider George Kennan, the journalist and explorer whose 1891 best seller, *Siberia and the Exile System*, indicted tsarist Russia for its backwardness, superstition, oppression, and cruelty. Historian David Foglesong has described how Kennan's exposure to the "heroic self-sacrifice" of Russian prisoners had the curious side effect of wrecking his Calvinist faith. While "pondering the scripture on long arctic nights," Kennan came around to believing that Man, not God, was the source of pity, love, justice, and mercy, and America, not Jesus, was the messiah. He was hugely popular on the lecture circuit due to his tear-jerking tales of Siberian exiles paying secret homage to homemade Stars and Stripes. The Society of American Friends of Russian Freedom soon took up the cause of democratic revolution in Russia. The U.S. State Department formally protested on behalf of Jewish Americans caught up in the anti-Semitic pogroms encouraged by the tsarist regime.

Consider Julia Ward Howe, the abolitionist poet whose "Battle Hymn of the Republic" became an iconic anthem of neo-Classical ACR. The daughter of a Wall Street stockbroker, she moved to Boston upon marriage, became an enthusiastic Unitarian convert, and befriended prominent Transcendentalists. During the Jacksonian era, when many Americans got carried away by religious revivals, reform movements, and utopian cults, Howe traveled to Europe, where she was smitten by the romantic nationalist revolutions in Poland, Hungary, and Italy. She even scolded Pope Pius IX for turning against the Revolutions of 1848:

> Think ye, in these portentious times
> Of wrath, and hate, and wild distraction,
> Christ dwells within a church that rests
> A comfortable, cold abstraction?
> He cries: 'On brethren, draw the sword,
> Loose the bold tongue and pen, unfearing,
> The weakness of our human flesh
> Is ransomed by your persevering.

When the American Civil War broke out eleven years later, Howe naturally imagined it a mighty episode in all of humanity's self-liberation. Historian Richard Gamble has argued persuasively that Howe's Christ—the one who wields a terrible swift sword and died to make men holy—was a Unitarian-Universalist savior exhorting men to free themselves through a "radically reformed, creedless, activist Christianity dedicated to ending oppression at home and abroad."

Consider Walt Whitman, whose buoyant, mystical patriotism made him poet laureate of the civil religion. Before 1865 his verses chanted American democracy and nationalism and likened the Union's Civil War dead to martyred messiahs. After 1865 Whitman, like Howe, read a fiery gospel writ in burnished rows of steel, only the bayonets had become railroads and steamships. Whitman exulted in the human conquest of space and time through science and industry. His chants democratic became chants technocratic, and his paeans to America became paeans to humanity. The 1872 edition of *Leaves of Grass* celebrates "Years of the Modern! Years of the unperform'd! Your horizon rises—I see it parting away for more august dramas; I see not America only—I see not only Liberty's nation but other nations preparing." The transcontinental railroad was no sooner finished than imagined by Whitman (and others, including Seward) a portal to a global future and the very India Columbus had sought: "Ah Genoese, thy dream, thy dream! / Centuries after thou art laid in thy grave, / The shore thou foundest verifies thy dream."

What did it mean? Where was man's heroic technology taking him? Whitman's "Passage to India" suggested the answer:

> Lo, soul! seest thou not God's purpose from the first?
> The earth to be spann'd, connected by net-work,
> The people to become brothers and sisters,
> The race, neighbors to marry and be given in marriage,
> The oceans to be cross'd, the distant brought near,
> The lands to be welded together.

Not even Tennyson's "parliament of man" in the poem "Locksley Hall" expressed a more eloquent nineteenth-century vision of a global village.

In sum, it is easy to build an ex post facto argument that Americans were passing through some great transition in their national life that was inspiring some great new idea of their God-given place in history. But it would have surprised most Americans to learn that their hallowed foreign policy traditions were about to be jettisoned. That was certainly not their intention when they voted for Cleveland in 1884 or, for that matter, Benjamin Harrison in 1888 because he was just as orthodox in his adherence to neo-Classical ACR orthodoxy.

The son of a congressman and grandson of a president, Harrison attended Miami University of Ohio, where he married the daughter of its Presbyterian president. In 1854 he moved to Indianapolis to practice law, but when the Civil War broke out, he took an army commission. One of the first officers in Sherman's army to enter Atlanta, he retired a brigadier general. Harrison went into politics and quickly won a reputation for eloquence preaching civil and sectarian religion alike. In 1888 he captured the White House with 58 percent of the vote. Conventional wisdom teaches that the modern presidency was invented by William McKinley and especially Theodore Roosevelt. But the rhetorical presidency as bully pulpit was really pioneered by Harrison. He made almost three hundred speeches during his four years as president, roughly half the total of his twenty-two predecessors combined! One of the first was in April 1889 on the centennial of George Washington's inauguration. He said all the right things—Washington trusted in the "sustaining helpfulness and grace of that God who rules the world" and endeavored to "elevate the morals of the people; to hold up the law as that sacred thing which, like the ark of God of old, may not be touched by irreverent hands." He understood his high priestly functions and used them to further the cause of the Republican Party, which he deemed consonant with the cause of the American people under the cope of heaven.

Harrison took it for granted that God rewarded spiritual piety with material plenty. But he constantly reminded Americans that "it is not, after all, riches that exalt the Nation. It is a pure, clean, high, intellectual, moral, and God-fearing citizenship that is our glory and security as a Nation." Indeed, the centerpiece of Harrison's program was the moral economy based on the Republicans' protective tariff. Democrats said free trade meant cheaper goods, ignoring the fact that competition from "pauper labor" overseas meant lower wages for U.S. workers. "God forbid that the day should ever come when, in the American mind, the thought of man as a 'consumer' shall submerge the old American thought of man as a creature of God, endowed with 'unalienable rights.'" Finally, Harrison believed in a divinely appointed mission: "Our development will not find its climax until the purpose of God in establishing this Government shall have spread throughout the world." But note that he said "shall have spread," not "shall be spread," because he believed republicanism could spread only through sympathy and emulation.

Harrison preached what Lincoln had called the good old maxims of the Bible. He insisted America's real enemies were not great powers abroad but threats to integrity and purity at home. He warned the nation not to listen to those who hawked that "commercial carnival" called imperialism, and he never recanted his campaign slogan: "We Americans have no commission from God to police the world."

Wilson's World: The Civil Church Militant

Orestes Brownson (1803–76), the United States' most prolific political philosopher, sampled nearly every religious sect and political party on offer before doing the most politically incorrect thing imaginable. He converted to Roman Catholicism. But the son of Puritan New England never surrendered the civil faith he confessed in "Mission of America" (1856): "This manifest destiny of our country, showing that Providence has great designs in our regard, that he has given us the most glorious mission ever given to any people, should attach us to our country, kindle in our hearts the fire of a true and holy patriotism, and make us proud to be Americans." The Civil War tormented Brownson (besides costing him two sons), but unlike the warring schismatics of the North and South, he spied dangers even greater than disunion. So he went into cloisters to write a book that might reintroduce the United States to its citizens.

No nation in history was more in need of the ancient wisdom "Know thyself" because Americans were blinded by "the wild theories and fancies of its childhood." So began *The American Republic*, first published in 1865. All nations lived spiritual and moral lives in addition to physical and material ones, and God made use of them all. But Brownson believed the American republic unique since nothing resembling its institutions could be found among Aristotle's political types. Its mission was to realize both democracy without despotism and liberty without anarchy, thereby reconciling the rights of the whole with the rights of the individual. Many Americans thought government a necessary evil. On the contrary, government was the minister of wrath to wrongdoers, the protector of property and religious freedom, the promoter of science and art, the basis for civilization itself. "Next after religion, it is man's greatest good; and even religion without it can do only a small portion of her work." But citizens could pervert or destroy their government if they harbored false notions of its origin and purpose. Sovereignty, posited Brownson, cannot exist in theory. It emerges only as a historical fact whenever a self-conscious, organic community wrests control over a defined territory and wins recognition from existing sovereign states. We, the People, constituted the nation and defined it as the coeval *United* States and United *States*. That is, no Union absent the States, no States absent the Union, and no Union or States absent the sovereign, indissoluble People residing within indestructible borders.

Brownson believed Americans erred in tracing their origins to the Constitution and Declaration of Independence because those documents only constituted and declared a preexisting land and people. The real origin of the republic lay in the providential realization by colonial patriots that they had, in fact, become sovereign. (The revolution was first made in men's minds, said John Adams.) To be sure, the framers in Philadelphia did a miraculous job. But that was because the taproots of their constitution were not just the Reformation and Enlightenment (both prone to fanaticism, as illustrated by Cromwell and Robespierre) but the natural rights, ordered liberty, due process, and separation of church and state that dated from Medieval common law. Brownson went so far as to say that the American republic was truer to Catholic principles of dignity, law, and justice than any European regime. But it remained far from perfect because it contained only two of the three pillars required for a sturdy republic: people, state, and church. Its clever constitution sufficed to protect the people and state from each other, but sooner or later the two would collude in the destruction of dignity, law, and justice unless constrained by the conscience of an independent, orthodox church. That was the fatal flaw in the blueprint. Protestantism was no church, but a thousand churches that were creatures of the same public opinion driving politics.

Americans bent on pursuing their happiness had established a culture in which all were free to craft their own religions as if they were gods. Worse yet, Americans might claim the right to force their disparate moral agendas on others, again as if they were gods. Hence the twin dangers to the republic were egotism, license, and anarchy on the one hand, and bigotry, intimidation, and coercion on the other hand. Nor could anyone say Americans were too prudent to toy with those dangers in the aftermath of the Civil War.

Brownson distinguished among three sorts of democracy, only one of which was conducive to liberty, the one Benjamin Disraeli called "territorial democracy." By that he meant simply a sovereign people inhabiting a fixed territory subject to laws whose force was coterminous with the territory. That may sound anodyne until one contrasts it with the other sorts of democracy. The second sort, which Brownson labeled the Jeffersonian, interpreted government by consent of the governed to mean that states and citizens might freely scoff at unpopular laws or even secede from the union, whereupon all dissolved into anarchy. The third sort, which Brownson labeled the humanitarian, "scorns all geographical lines, effaces all individualities, and professes to plant itself on humanity." In short, he sensed a fanatical streak, a utopian urge, that might someday spill forth from American shores in crusades to reform the whole world.

In the Civil War the South fought to save Jeffersonian democracy while the North fought to save territorial democracy. But Yankee humanitarianism piggybacked on the Union's war effort, and its ambition was certain to grow along with American power. Brownson imagined supposedly philanthropic reformers targeting private property, private morals, private rights such as free speech, and even foreign countries in the name of perfecting mankind. Its logical conclusion was Rousseau's calamitous formula by which men are forced to be free. In a country where no religious authority was recognized save the court of public opinion, such philanthropists might easily imagine indelible sin to be erasable vice and make civil authority the eraser. That is why Americans needed Catholicity more than any other nation lest, in their liberty, power, and presumptive philanthropy, they run wild.

Brownson was under no illusion that Protestants and free thinkers would follow the logic of *The American Republic*. (Its author, quipped Van Wyck Brooks, was too Yankee for the Catholics and too Catholic for the Yankees.) But Brownson kept faith with the national destiny, believing "the American people need not trouble themselves about their exterior expansion. That will come of itself as fast as desirable. Let them devote their attention to their internal destiny, to the realization of their mission within, and they will gradually see the whole continent coming under their system, forming one grand nation, a really catholic nation, great, glorious, and free."

Within one generation of Brownson's death in the centennial year of 1876 his fears began to come true. But most Americans did not see any danger because they imagined reforms at home and interventions abroad to be leaps of progress, not falls from grace. History had entered an era defined by genius in science, industry, and management, and the United States was right where you would expect it to be, at the cutting edge.

The inauguration of William McKinley in 1897 was the first to be captured by Thomas A. Edison's motion picture camera and the first to be recorded by Edison's gramophone. In 1898 McKinley's administration was the first to set up a war room in the White House and a press room for newspapers, whose circulations would triple over the first decade of the twentieth century. In 1900 construction began on the New York City subway. In 1901 the first modern submarines were built for the U.S. Navy, and Guglielmo Marconi made the first transatlantic transmission via wireless radio. In 1902, Willis Carrier of Brooklyn invented the first air conditioner, and Ransom Olds's factory in Lansing, Michigan, began production-line manufacture of automobiles. In 1903 the Wright Brothers Flyer sputtered aloft on the dunes of the Outer Banks. In 1907 Leo Baekeland's New York laboratory produced the first synthetic polymer (plastic). By 1913, when Woodrow Wilson became president, motor cars, telephones, and appliances powered by alternating electric current were becoming routine in cities. So was premeditated research and development in the laboratories of General Electric, Bell Telephone, Du Pont, and Westinghouse, plus numerous German and British firms. Governments played an ever-increasing role because their navies were being transformed by steel armor, oil-fired engines, electric fire control, and radio. *H.M.S. Dreadnought* was launched in 1906.

The galloping progress exhilarated Americans but concerned them as well. Was the American Dream being fulfilled or killed? The 1890 census had measured inequality and revealed how wealthy (and powerful) the top 1 percent had become. That same year muckraking journalist Jacob Riis exposed *How the Other Half Lives* in northern slums whose denizens were worse off than slaves because their poverty was literally nobody's business. An ever-rising torrent of immigrants from Southern and Eastern Europe sustained corrupt big-city machines and challenged Anglo-Protestant culture. Ellis Island opened for business in 1892. Huge chunks of the national economy were controlled by trusts such as Standard Oil and U.S. Steel. Railroad monopolies gouged Midwestern farmers with variable shipping rates, and banks did the same with high interest rates. Populist and Greenback parties, the Grange movement, and at last the Democratic Party campaigned for monetary expansion through coinage of silver at a ratio of six-teen ounces to one ounce of gold. But the Republicans defeated that platform in 1896 and again in 1900, when L. Frank Baum spoofed the bimetallist debates in *The Wizard of Oz* (i.e., ounce). In 1889 the Sooner Land Rush in Oklahoma opened the last big Indian Territory to hustling land speculators and homesteaders, symbolically closing the American frontier. Some Sioux expressed their apocalyptic expectations in the Ghost Dance movement that ended in the 1890 Massacre at Wounded Knee. Back east, class warfare loomed between management and labor. The Haymarket Square riot and Southwestern Railroad Strike (1886), Homestead Strike (1892), Pullman Strike (1894), and Anthracite Coal Strike (1902) alarmed middle-class Americans and made villains or heroes of union leaders like Samuel Gompers and Eugene Debs.

By the first years of the twentieth century still newer trends dominated American politics, including the rise of salaried middle-class employees, suburbanization, mass immigration by Catholics and Jews, the advent of women in urban job markets, exposés by investigative journalists of waste and corruption in the public sector, and monopoly and pollution in the private sector. That is not to suggest that American society changed completely, or everywhere, or overnight. During the decades from 1890 to 1920 the United States just barely ceased to be a nation of farmers (65 percent rural in 1890 to 49 percent in 1920). Foreign trade, amounting to 6 or 7 percent of the economy, was still only of marginal concern. Foreign affairs only intruded upon the nearly perfect security still enjoyed by the United States. No single trend was enough to determine a lurch into activist foreign policies. But all the trends put together were more than sufficient to unleash American power into the Caribbean, then the Pacific, then the whole world, because all those century-old checks against foreign crusades—relative weakness, continental priorities, constitutional constraints, and theological humility—that had previously buttressed self-containment had eroded to the point where devolved Protestant fanaticism burst its chains, just as Brownson had feared.

Washington's World metamorphosed into Wilson's World.

CHAPTER ELEVEN

¡Cuba Libre!

W AY BACK IN 1978 James Field wrote a provoca-
tion entitled "American Imperialism: The Worst
Chapter in Almost Any Book." His point was that
all those historical forces welling up in the late
nineteenth century—Social Darwinism, the closing of the frontier,
the quest for foreign markets, labor and racial strife, the new navy
and new imperialism—were not a priori causes so much as ex post
facto justifications for the sudden assertion of world power that began with the Spanish-American War. They were too pat, linear,
and logical, untethered to actual human decisions. Field showed
that the leading exponents of those national moods such as naval
captain Mahan, the Reverend Josiah Strong, historian Brooks
Adams, and Professor John W. Burgess (Teddy Roosevelt's mentor)
were either absent from the fray or else opposed to the imperialism
of 1898. Racism was an outright deterrent against planting the flag
overseas. Colonialism still seemed un-American, even to the Social
Darwinist William Graham Sumner of Yale, as the title of his
ironic pamphlet suggests: "The Conquest of the United States by
Spain." Field concluded that U.S. acquisition of a protectorate over
Cuba and colonies in the Philippines, Guam, Puerto Rico, and the
Hawaiian Islands was not the aberration famously proclaimed by
historian Samuel Flagg Bemis but sheer accident.

Years later historian Richard Hamilton reached a similar conclusion. He researched the elites, including businessmen, party
bosses, elected officials, political mentors, press lords, and presidential appointees, and found that none of those groups had behaved
like a coherent belligerent lobby in 1898. Nor did his study of regional publications suggest that editors in places like St. Louis or
San Francisco had marched to the distant drums of the jingoist
William Randolph Hearst and Joseph Pulitzer flagships based in
New York. Nor did manufacturers, merchants, and shippers imagine
that the way to break into the China market was by going to war in
Cuba. Nor were presidential advisers Marcus Hanna, Myron
Herrick, Charles G. Dawes, and John Hay in favor of war. Nor did
Congress authorize $50 million for war preparations (the down pay-
ment on $250 million) in order to protect U.S. investments in Cuba
worth just $30 million. Nor did Americans suddenly look overseas
for new frontiers because University of Wisconsin history professor
Frederick Jackson Turner had declared the closing of the continental frontier in a lecture to the American Historical Association in
1893. The politics of the Cuban revolt also looked like a wash. In
1895–96 Republicans lambasted Grover Cleveland's indolence over
Cuba, while in 1897–98 Democrats scorned William McKinley's indolence, but the primary interest of both parties was the debate over
hard money. Indeed, the president's scrapbook of clippings reveals
little interest in Cuba until mid-January 1898, at which point 90
percent of his mail still favored peace. So what happened?

McKinley, like Cleveland, deplored the escalating mutual
atrocities during the Cuban revolt against Spanish rule dating from
1895. He, like Cleveland, deliberated among five options: (1) U.S.
non-involvement; (2) U.S.-mediated Cuban autonomy (which the
Cuban rebels emphatically rejected); (3) U.S-mediated Cuban independence (which the Spaniards emphatically rejected); (4) independence via U.S. armed intervention; (5) independence via U.S.
armed intervention but with a hidden agenda of U.S. domination.
Most businessmen favored options (1) or (2). Most interventionists
in the public and Congress favored options (3) or (4). Why then
did option (5) win out?

Intervention with ulterior motives prevailed thanks to a war
party (not an unfamiliar phenomenon in American history) led by

Assistant Secretary of the Navy Theodore Roosevelt, Senator Henry Cabot Lodge, and others promoting a "large policy" for naval expansion. But the war party might never have triumphed without support from an unlikely army of auxiliaries: Progressive Protestant clergy. ("You have no idea of the pressure on William from religious people," wrote McKinley's brother in January 1898.) The Republican war party was self-righteous and devious. The Protestant war party was self-righteous and naive. The advocates of the "large policy" wanted a network of strategic naval bases to command the approaches to Central America (where they hoped a canal would be dug); they wanted to enforce the Monroe Doctrine against European and Japanese interlopers and perhaps plant Old Glory somewhere in the western Pacific. By contrast, the advocates of *¡Cuba Libre!* wanted the United States to undertake a selfless humanitarian mission that involved little risk to itself, just ninety miles from its shores, against contemptible Spanish Catholic colonialists. Today it seems a no-brainer. Back then it conjured a sweet temptation to violate every American principle of peace, reciprocity, and non-interference. No wonder McKinley hesitated, delayed, agonized, even wept and prayed over what to do. It seemed even the religious lobby was calling on him to transgress.

The war party prevailed because five events over ten weeks played into its hands, while whipping Evangelicals into a frenzy. On January 12 Cubans rioted in Havana against a compromise based on autonomy but not independence. On February 9 Hearst's *New York Journal* printed a damning letter (intercepted and leaked by Cuban émigrés) in which the Spanish ambassador insulted the president and Republican jingoes. On February 15 the battleship *Maine* exploded and sank off Havana, killing 258 sailors. On March 17 Senator Redfield Proctor (R., Vt.), previously a skeptic on intervention, delivered a horrific eyewitness account of Spanish atrocities. On March 28 the navy's court of inquiry predictably blamed the *Maine* explosion on an external weapon. The war party exploited those events to pressure Congress and through it the White House. Though scorned as spineless by Roosevelt for not going to war, McKinley in fact showed his courage by standing athwart the stampede and stalling for time. The U.S. minister in Madrid, Stewart L. Woodford, assured the president by cable that the Spaniards were prepared to admit defeat and just wanted a face-saving way out. McKinley's personal aide later wrote: "The matter of which the President spoke with most feeling was his conviction that, if he had been left alone, he could have concluded an arrangement with the Spanish Government under which the Spanish troops would have withdrawn from Cuba without a war. Of this he spoke with great frankness, stating more explicitly his conviction that, but for the inflamed state of public opinion and the fact that Congress could no longer be held in check, a peaceful solution might have been had."

Americans today, having long since conceded all war powers to the president, reflexively ask what might have caused McKinley to change his mind. But in 1898 the Constitution was not yet a dead letter, war powers still rested with Congress, and the interesting question is how the president was able to resist the spasm of war fever as long as he did. The answer is that McKinley delayed as long as there was legitimate executive excuse for delay, but the train of events exhausted his options even as the war party turned up the pressure on the Congress. Representative Richard Bartholdt (R., Mo.) recalled that "messages by the score poured in on me peremptorily demanding that I either vote for war or resign." Some of the mail came from constituents but most was from "responsible party leaders and personal friends." Thirty years later Bartholdt confessed, "I regret that vote to this day."

Some historians, of whom Louis Pérez is most prominent, also suspect the war party really meant to ensure that Cuba did not become wholly free. Ever since Jefferson's time American statesmen had eyed Cuba as ripe fruit to be picked sooner or later, but their hand had been stayed for a century by sectional strife over slavery, or else Spain's refusal to sell its lucrative sugar island, or else the Classical ACR doctrine that the Constitution follows the flag. To annex Cuba meant to promise citizenship to its colored population; hence a scrupulous racism obligated the United States to abstain. But now the Cuban revolutionaries were on the verge of expelling the Spaniards and most likely confiscating private property in a frightening social revolution; hence an unscrupulous racism obligated the United States to invade. Once American soldiers and Marines were on the ground, the United States would be in position to impose a protectorate.

Impressive circumstantial evidence exists for this thesis, including the widespread belief among knowledgeable officials that the Cuban insurrection was nearly over and won. "Spain will lose Cuba," thought Secretary of State John Sherman. "That seems to me to be certain." Senator Lodge privately admitted that no armistice was possible because "the Cubans, on the eve of victory, of course, would not consent." Most telling was Woodford's report from Madrid in March 1898 to the effect that the Cubans were about to win independence but were unfit for self-government because the insurgents were almost all Negro. "I have at last come to believe that the only certainty of peace is under our flag. . . . I am, thus, reluctantly, slowly, but entirely a convert to the early American ownership and occupation of the island. If we recognize independence, we may turn the island over to a part of its inhabitants against the judgement of many of its most educated and wealthy residents." Suffice to say that the leader of the Cuban junta in exile, José Martí, asked, "Once the United States is in Cuba, who will drive them out?" His legal adviser called U.S. intervention "nothing less than a declaration of war by the United States against the Cuban revolutionaries." There is no denying the fact that the moment the United States intervened, the Cuban War of Independence disappeared from memory to be replaced by the Spanish-American War.

McKinley's message to Congress mentioned neither war nor independence. It simply requested authorization "to secure a full and final termination of hostilities between the government of Spain and the people of Cuba, and to secure in the island the establishment of a stable government, capable of maintaining order and observing its international obligations, insuring peace and tranquillity and the security of its citizens as well as our own, and to use the military and naval forces of the United States as may be necessary for these purposes." Spain's rather more honest reply was a declaration of war. Thanks to the new navy and in spite of the army's keystone-cop routines, American forces won a series of cheap victories, and peace talks began in August under French mediation. Cuba was to be free ostensibly, although U.S. war correspondents had already decided the Cubans were unfit for self-government: "We came to conquer for another people, vainly imagining that a new nation had been born. But there is no Cuba. There are no

Cuban people." One might have expected reporters to sympathize with the immensity of the political and economic reconstruction required and perhaps realize the U.S. Army itself was utterly unprepared to do nation-building on foreign soil. But the Cubans' incompetence offered a pretext for the formal U.S. protectorate declared by the 1901 Platt Amendment and 1904 Roosevelt Corollary to the Monroe Doctrine. Cuba was first in a long series of occupations characterized by Americans' ignorance of the realities of the mentalities of the localities.

What of the other cessions provided for in the Treaty of Paris? Puerto Rico and Guam, acquired for naval bases, were not controversial so long as they were not incorporated. The Supreme Court cleared the way with its so-called Insular Decisions of 1901–5, which ruled the Constitution need not follow the flag. The Philippines were another matter entirely. Once news leaked that McKinley was considering their retention, an anti-imperialist movement sprang up that attracted tens of thousands nationwide. Among its distinguished leaders was none other than Joseph Pulitzer, whose *New York World* now opposed the "unnatural and dangerous scheme for setting up satrapies for the sons of somebodies in the far Pacific and in Oceanica *[sic]* and converting a war for freeing Cuba into a war for conquest for the benefit of spoilsmen and adventurers." But in the end two-thirds of the Senate ratified the treaty with one vote to spare, and only because populist Democratic leader William Jennings Bryan urged Democrats to concede the battle in the interest of peace and focus on the next election (in 1900, when Bryan lost again). So what is one to make of this momentous year? When the purview shifts from big trends in geopolitics, economics, and demography to the human agents responsible for the lurch into war and empire, it seems all that is solid melts into air.

Historian H. W. Brands correctly observes that a "conflation of causes is a chronic hazard of American (and probably democratic) war-making." But whatever significance the events of 1898 had for U.S. grand strategy, one fact is sure: the year marked a huge theological shift in American Civil Religion born in a prairie fire of righteous Protestant indignation. Whereas just a few years before, the consensus held that foreign crusades were forbidden fruit, in

1898 the consensus felt sure that God Almighty was summoning his chosen nation to wage holy humanitarian war against atavistic Catholic tyranny. Even William Jennings Bryan was zealous for war, if not imperialism, while the clerical leaders of Progressive Protestantism exulted, none more so than theologian Walter Rauschenbusch. No year since the Civil War, said Rauschenbusch, had been "so momentous, so epoch-making. . . . To the historians of a hundred years hence, this year 1898 will be one of the great mountain ranges in the geography of times, a great watershed from which the rivers begin to flow toward new and distant oceans." Equating Americans to the Israelites in the desert, he professed: "The pillar of fire has lifted and moved. We must break camp and follow, though none of us have traveled the trackless future to tell whither we are going. As a nation we must learn to walk by faith and not by sight. And if we have needed the help and light of God in the past, how much more will we need him in the future." Rauschenbusch voiced a new gospel that was frankly heretical in the context of the Classical ACR. He claimed that God had not raised the United States to great power and wealth merely to be an example to other nations—that now seemed tantamount to hiding one's lamp under a bushel (Matthew 5:15)—but rather to act strenuously on behalf of righteousness in the world.

Did Protestant clergy realize they were making a radical alteration in the civil religion? To judge by an interventionist political cartoon in the February 20, 1898, *Los Angeles Times*, the answer is no. The cartoon, titled "Have We Degenerated?" depicted a desperate Cuban woman clutching to the skirts of an impassive Statue of Liberty, while above and behind her the ghosts of Revolutionary and Civil War heroes pass judgment on McKinley's refusal to ride to the rescue: "Her Appeal Would Not Have Been in Vain in Our Day." That is how heresy works. It stands doctrines on their heads and reinvents history to justify them but continues to call them by the same name.

Just eighteen months before going to war, McKinley promised the American people he would do no such thing. He was the last Civil War veteran to occupy the White House. He hated war and cherished the modest republic bequeathed by the Founders. He was devoted to his Masonic Lodge, to the Methodist Church, and to neo-Classical ACR. So McKinley began and ended his 1897 inaugural address with powerful references to the nation's divine patron and duty. "Our faith teaches that there is no safer reliance than upon the God of our fathers, who has so singularly favored the American people in every national trial, and who will not forsake us so long as we obey His commandments and walk humbly in his footsteps." Regarding foreign policy he hailed

> the policy of the United States since the foundation of the Government to cultivate relations of peace and amity with all the nations of the world, and this accords with my conception of our duty now. We have cherished the policy of non-interference with affairs of foreign governments wisely inaugurated by Washington, keeping ourselves free from entanglement, either as allies or foes. ... Our diplomacy should seek nothing more and accept nothing less than is due us. We want no wars of conquest; we must avoid the temptation of territorial aggression. War should never be entered upon until every agency of peace has failed; peace is preferable to war in almost every contingency. Arbitration is the true method of settlement of international as well as local or individual differences.

McKinley congratulated the country on overcoming its sectional divides and pledged to uphold the Constitution as "the obligation I have reverently taken before the Lord Most High."

McKinley's second inaugural address in March 1901, by contrast, contradicted his first in nearly every particular. He began by spinning the origins of the war so as to claim he had done "all that in honor could be done to avert the war, but without avail. It became inevitable. . . . It came." Lincoln, in his own second inaugural, had confessed human agency ("Both parties deprecated war, but one of them would make war rather than let the nation survive, and the other would accept war rather than let it perish") before famously saying, "And the war came." McKinley just said of his war: "It came. The result was signally favorable to American arms and in the highest degree honorable to the Government. It imposed upon us obligations from which we cannot escape and from which it is dishonorable to seek escape. We are now at peace with the world."

Only that was not true either. The U.S. Army was waging a counter-insurgency in the Philippines as brutal as the Spanish campaign in Cuba. But McKinley assured his countrymen: "The American people, intrenched in freedom at home, take their love for it wherever they go, and they reject as mistaken and unworthy the doctrine that we lose our own liberties by securing foundations of liberty to others. Our institutions will not deteriorate by extension, and our sense of justice will not abate under tropic suns in distant seas." Rather, we must "earnestly dedicate ourselves to the task upon which we have rightly entered. The path of progress is seldom smooth. New things are often found hard to do. Our fathers found them so. We find them so. They are inconvenient. They cost us something. But are we not made better for the effort and sacrifice, and are not those we serve lifted up and blessed?"

McKinley's civil religious tropes may seem cloying today, but in his day they were splendid. He flattered his audiences and identified with them by shifting to the first-person plural. He joined them in rejecting unpatriotic naysayers of little faith and assured his fellow Americans they were indeed following in their forefathers' footsteps. He praised them for their sacrifices (really very small, except for the army) and, by shifting to the interrogative, asked them to decide whether those sacrifices blessed and uplifted all parties. Of course they would answer yes so as to feel good about doing well. McKinley especially hailed the "reconstruction of Cuba as a free commonwealth on abiding foundations of right, justice, liberty, and assured order" (because Americans would assure it). Finally, the president solemnly addressed the Filipino issue. "We are not waging war against the inhabitants of the Philippine Islands. A portion of them are making war against the United States. By far the greater part of the inhabitants recognize American sovereignty and welcome it as a guaranty of order and of security, for life, property, liberty, freedom of conscience, and the pursuit of happiness. We will not leave the destiny of the loyal millions in the islands to the disloyal thousands who are in rebellion against the United States." Presidents ever since have claimed to make war on regimes or revolutions but never on people.

The imperialist cant drove German American statesman and Civil War general Carl Schurz out of the Republican Party. "No, do not deceive yourselves," he intoned. "If we turn that war which was so solemnly commended to the favor of mankind as a generous war of liberation and humanity into a victory for conquest and self-aggrandizement, we shall have thoroughly forfeited our moral credit with the world. Professions of unselfish virtue and benevolence, proclamations of noble humanitarian purposes coming from us will never, never be trusted again."

CHAPTER TWELVE

The Progressive Social Gospel

Historians do not agree on how to define or date the Progressive Era, but none deny that its spirit was all about reform. It burst forth at the tail end of the Great Depression (they called it that) of 1873–96, when it seemed obvious American institutions could not cope with industrialization and its attendant social pathologies. The Progressive response to all the problems posed by trusts, strikes, immigrants, corruption, education, public health, and more was scientific management through governance informed by credentialed experts. A modern society needed a modern state to fulfill the promise of rapid and permanent progress. Hence the following summation, written by historian William Leuchtenburg in 1952, remains valid today:

> The Progressives believed in a . . . national government directing the destinies of the nation at home and abroad. They had little but contempt for the strict construction of the Constitution by conservative judges, who would restrict the power of the national government to act against social evils and to extend the blessings of democracy to less favored lands. The real enemy was particularism, state rights, limited government which would mean the reign of plutocracy at home and a narrow, isolationist concept of national

117

destiny abroad, which would deny the democratic mission
of America and leave the brown peoples pawns of dynastic
wars and colonial exploitation.

Note the words "believed in," "contempt," "social evils," and
"real enemy." We think of Progressivism as a secular movement inspired in part by the scientific materialism of that era. Why then
does a language of faith versus evil come so easily to the historian
of Progressivism, and why does it go unnoticed by most readers?
The short answer is that secularism is a myth, or, to put it another
way, if you don't believe in a sectarian religion, you are likely to believe in a species of civil religion. For a hundred years after 1789
most Americans were not conscious of the potential conflict between their mostly Protestant faith and their civil faith because the
former was a support to republican virtue and the latter ensured
free exercise of religion. But under the stress of the Civil War and
the onslaught of modernism (Charles Darwin first published in
1859) mainline Protestant churches gradually surrendered their
prophetic role to the civil religion, surrendered their faith in an in-
errant Bible to science, and surrendered their cultural authority to
secular Progressives. That is why historian Bruce Kuklick has instructed: "We should associate Progressivism most with the rise of
a more relaxed Protestantism in higher education after the Civil
War." Ivy League universities, new universities such as Chicago
and Johns Hopkins, and land-grant state universities all devoted
themselves to secular research on the German model. The new
knowledge generated in science and engineering, modern languages, sociology, political science, and economics easily persuaded
politicians that the keys to the kingdom had passed from the clergy
to the intelligentsia, who—once empowered—could help them to
"manage God's universe for the benefit of mankind."

Progressives came into their own in the years surrounding the
Spanish-American War. They occupied a consciously middle position between stand-patters and socialists and in all aspects of society pressed the urgency of methodical reform through government
agencies. To be sure, various schools of thought contested over the
merits of national versus local solutions in issues of public health,
education, welfare, banking, and business regulation. At the state

level Robert La Follette in Wisconsin, Woodrow Wilson in New Jersey, Hiram Johnson in California, and Charles Evans Hughes and Theodore Roosevelt in New York pursued ambitious agendas. Labor lawyer Louis D. Brandeis coined the term "scientific management" and was known as the people's attorney prior to becoming the first Jewish Supreme Court justice in 1915. So-called Right Progressivism, represented by William Howard Taft and William Graham Sumner, clashed with the Left Progressivism of the young Walter Lippmann, Randolph Bourne, and John Dewey, and both camps distrusted the Centrist Progressives led by Roosevelt and Wilson. But all of them meant to break up capitalist concentrations of power and wealth; purge federal, state, and municipal governments of corruption; and protect and empower the people.

Progressive accomplishments (for better or worse) included enforcement of the Sherman Anti-Trust Act, the Pure Food and Drug Act, civil service reform, the income tax, the direct election of senators, and the federal reserve banking system. During that same era the Supreme Court's 1896 Plessy v. Ferguson decision enabled southern states and most northern cities to practice segregation through Jim Crow laws or extralegal customs. In that there was no contradiction at all because the Progressive science and social science taught at prestigious universities legitimized racial hierarchy. According to political scientist Rogers Smith, the moderate Progressives "agreed on the importance of cultural homogeneity, the dangers of immigration, the improvidence of black enfranchisement, the propriety of Anglo-Saxon racial domination, and the maintenance of some basic distinctions in the domestic and civic responsibility of men and women, even as they sincerely professed themselves to be committed to democracy and human rights." They also took for granted "the propriety of American imperialism."

What has all that to do with a more relaxed Protestantism? In fact, it has everything to do with a parallel movement in Protestant churches, sometimes called the Third Great Awakening or Social Gospel, which arose in the 1880s and 1890s. Its preachers, mostly Presbyterian and Methodist but including Episcopalians, Congregationalists, and others, meant to reconstruct the church, American society, and ultimately international affairs. They saw no difference between the laws of nature that applied to the physical and spiritual worlds. "The law of progress is the same in both," said the pastor of Brooklyn's famous Plymouth Church, Lyman Abbott. According to this developmental theology or applied Christianity, claimed Abbott, everything worked together for good in a democratic spirit of cooperation in "art, industry, invention, literature, learning, and government—all these are captives marching in Christ's triumphant procession up the hill of fame." The Social Gospel dismissed the Augustinian distinction between a fallen physical City of Man that exists in time and a perfect spiritual City of God beyond time. Its disciples accordingly stressed collective uplift rather than personal salvation. They made peace with evolution and science generally and looked to government for assistance in promoting charitable goals, missionary activity, and the perfection of American society. One of the most influential exponents was Johns Hopkins professor and Episcopal layman Richard T. Ely, who asserted in *The Social Aspects of Christianity* (1889) the (German historicist) idea that "if there is anything divine on this earth, it is the state, the product of the same God-given instincts which led to the establishment of the church and the family." The Progressive state, informed by university experts, could thus be viewed as the principal agency in the performance of what used to be the church's work. Walter Rauschenbusch exulted: "The social gospel registers the fact that for the first time in history the spirit of Christianity has had a chance to form a working partnership with real social and psychological science."

The Enlightenment's tyranny of reason had long ago challenged Biblical miracles. But the foundations of modern or liberal theology in the late nineteenth century included the literary and historical Higher Criticism of the Bible, Darwinian evolution, and discoveries in geology and paleontology, all of which appeared to debunk the book of Genesis and Biblical history generally. Sophisticated pastors responded predictably. They dispensed with strict Christian theology in favor of Christian ethics. That meant they began preaching salvation by works rather than salvation by faith—exactly the charge leveled at the Catholic Church by the original Protestants in the sixteenth century. Modernist clergy did not catch that irony. On the contrary, they considered Christ to be far more relevant as a prophet of social justice than as a redemptive messiah under a bar-

baric law of blood sacrifice. There was nothing especially new in that notion, which had long been held, for instance, by Unitarians. But only in the 1890s did a gospel of immanence rather than transcendence go mainstream. Many Social Gospel adherents were also post-millennialists who believed that America was called to build a literal heaven on earth in preparation for the Parousia, or Second Coming, rather than Jesus preparing a place in heaven for the church. The Rev. C. Arthur Lincoln of Buffalo even said Americans should become Christian, not to save their souls from hell, but to save the world from hell. No wonder old traditionalists and new fundamentalists accused modernists of preaching a new religion. In a manner of speaking, they did. Progressive Social Gospel really represented a metamorphosis in American Civil Religion that began on McKinley's otherwise Methodist watch.

Historians of religion have long understood that American Protestantism always displayed a decidedly Hebraic streak. The Social Gospel certainly did insofar as it socialized the Christian virtues of faith, hope, and charity into an ethic resembling the Jewish *tikkun olam*, the responsibility to repair the world from inside out. Hence the movement's primary concern became the communal consequences of sin, which were what thwarted the building of the kingdom of God in the here and now. That made the Social Gospel especially appealing to rich and powerful philanthropists who prided themselves on their own pragmatism and vision and assumed that the way to repair the world from within was to apply the same savvy, energy, and expertise they displayed in business or government. John D. Rockefeller donated millions to Harry Emerson Fosdick's Riverside Church in Morningside Heights and put Harry's brother, Raymond Fosdick, in charge of the Rockefeller Foundation. Theodore Roosevelt collaborated with Lyman Abbott and boasted of favoring the apostle James over Paul because the former taught that faith without works is dead. Men (and women like Jane Addams) built powerful public-private, political-religious partnerships for the promotion of grand projects ranging from Chicago's Hull House to the Panama Canal to Prohibition. Not least, they promoted globalization of the charitable impulse through foreign missions and humanitarian imperialism.

The truest of true believers was Senator Albert Beveridge (R., Ind.), a serious statesman whose works included a four-volume life of John Marshall and a shrewd book on the geopolitics of East Asia. In 1898 Beveridge exhorted Americans to realize that God had given to them a noble land with a glorious history but still more glorious future because the march of the American flag around the world was the fulfillment of God's purpose. He reasoned that if we were God's chosen people, then we could not fly from our duties, which included our benevolent rule over childlike colonial peoples. Indeed, the United States dared not retreat from "any soil where Providence has unfurled our banner . . . for liberty and civilization are God's promises fulfilled, the flag must henceforth be the symbol and the sign to all mankind." In fact, the American flag became a veritable fetish in the Progressive era and was often paired with the cross. William Guthrie, a University of Chicago professor and church rector, even preached a Religion of Old Glory with an "evolutional view of good and evil." He prophesied that the Stars and Stripes would become the flag of a federation of nations and ideal of the Kingdom of Heaven on earth.

Social Gospel was the marriage bed wherein mainline Protestantism mated with Progressivism to beget a heretical variant of the original ACR. The new theology devalorized virtue, prudence, humility, and small government in favor of power, glory, pride, and big government at home and, when possible, abroad. Take Josiah Strong, whose 1885 title made clear that the target of his jeremiads was *Our Country*. Just as Lyman Beecher's *Plea for the West* (1842) had imagined the frontier a threat to America's spiritual health, Strong feared a threat from the cities. Poverty, illiteracy, crime, drunkenness, prostitution, and pollution were presided over by political machines manipulating the immigrants; how long could democracy survive under such conditions? But the larger purpose behind Strong's urgent appeal for reform was democratic world evangelism. Anglo-Saxon Americans were called to export their values and institutions in league with government; why should the American missionary be the only man without a country? Anglo-Saxons were the most evolved race, the torchbearers of civil liberty and a pure spiritual Christianity. They must be their brother's keepers, sharing their money-making power, genius for colonization, explosive energy, and elastic institutions. His plea was not to "save America for America's sake, but, save America for the world's sake."

Everyone quotes Josiah Strong because he was so strident, popular, and prolific. But was he typical? The summer 1898 issue of *Homiletic Review*, a widely circulated digest of Protestant sermons, suggests he certainly was. Pastor L. B. Hartman preached: "Thus without the least consciousness of presumption or extravagance we recognize our republic as the politico-religious handmaid of Providence in the aggressive civilization of the world." William S. Rainsford, an Episcopal rector in New York City, assured his flock: "This war has not been cunningly devised by the strategists. America is being used to carry on the work of God in this war, which no politician could create, control, or gainsay." A Presbyterian in Philadelphia felt "the confidence of divine approval" in the war, and another in New York categorically stated, "I do not believe that there ever was a war more righteous than that which we have undertaken, nor one closer to the law of the self-sacrificing Christ that we bear one another's burdens."

What the war party discovered in 1898 was the broad political base that existed for expansive foreign policies so long as they could be draped in morality. Cuba was easy: Americans imagined themselves knights in shining armor freeing a damsel in distress. The Open Door policy in Asia was easy as well: Americans imagined themselves chivalrous guardians of Chinese sovereignty. Formal colonies were a harder sell but appealed to Protestants who imagined American intentions were pure by contrast to those of European imperialists. Progressive colonial governance seemed only to formalize the efforts of transnational moral movements that had already sprung up in the 1880s and 1890s, such as relief organizations for India, Russia, and Armenia; the World Women's Christian Temperance Union; the Student Volunteer Movement; and the YMCA, YWCA, and Young People's Society of Christian Endeavor. Just as almost all prominent Progressives were imperialist and vice versa, so were almost all the leaders of the Social Gospel, including Washington Gladden, Lyman Abbott, and Walter Rauschenbusch. To them and their flocks, annexation of the Spanish islands was a providential opportunity to convert their pagan (read: Catholic) inhabitants. In the event, the mostly Methodist missionaries who streamed into Cuba knew no Spanish and none of the history of a Hispanic culture 275 years older than that of the United States. Yet they expected to Americanize the island beginning with prohibition of rum, cock fighting, and Santería. They made few converts but saw no contradiction between empire and progress. Gladden swore, "If this is imperialism, I am an imperialist." Abbott baptized "the imperialism of liberty."

Senator Beveridge perfected the new conflation of politics and religion. During the 1900 presidential campaign he vigorously defended McKinley's colonial acquisitions:

> God has not been preparing the English-speaking and Teutonic peoples for a thousand years for nothing but vain and idle self-contemplation and self-admiration. No! He has made us master organizers of the world to establish system where chaos reigns. He has given us the spirit of progress to overwhelm the forces of reaction throughout the earth. He has made us adepts in government among savage and senile peoples. ... And of all our race He has marked the American people as His chosen nation to finally lead in the regeneration of the world. This is the divine mission of America, and it holds all the profit, all the glory, all the happiness possible to man. We are trustees of the world's progress, guardians of its righteous peace.

To be sure, the Progressive Era was loaded with contradictions. What era isn't? But there is something especially puzzling about it. If urban industrial society had become so squalid and U.S. institutions so dysfunctional as to require wholesale reform, why did Americans choose that moment to beatify their way of life and seek to export it? Perhaps it is because they become most anxious to prove their national greatness abroad when they grow least confident of it at home. In any event, the United States began to play God in 1898.

CHAPTER THIRTEEN

Benevolent Assimilation

P ROGRESSIVES WERE SO BRAZEN as to torture the text of Washington's Farewell Address to imply that it endorsed overseas empire. But their foreign adventures played out as calamities in exactly the ways John Quincy Adams had predicted. They also demonstrated how ill-suited American institutions, politics, and temperaments were to the task of nation-building overseas.

The conquest of the Philippine Islands was, of course, inadvertent. Assistant Secretary of the Navy Theodore Roosevelt had cabled orders to Commodore George Dewey of the U.S. Pacific Squadron (based at Hong Kong) to attack the Spanish ships at Manila Bay in the event of hostilities. Dewey achieved his mission in spectacular fashion on May 1, 1898, whereupon the Philippines had no further relevance to the fighting. But the War Department dispatched a U.S. Army expedition to occupy the island of Luzon, which in turn gave Congress a pretext to annex the Hawaiian Republic as a strategic way station. Meanwhile, Dewey encouraged Emilio Aguinaldo, leader of the islands' *ilustrado* elite, to think the United States would favor self-government. So the Filipino nationalist movement declared independence. But the Spanish commander in Manila made a secret deal to surrender only on condition that the Americans keep indigenous forces out of the capital. Aguinaldo turned suspicious, then hostile, during the months when McKinley fretted about how to dispose of the spoils of war. He believed the United States could not in good conscience restore the islands to Spain, or see them colonized by France or Germany (he did not mention Japan), or grant them self-government, for which Americans believed them unprepared, so there was nothing for it but to annex the whole archipelago and "by God's grace do the very best we could by them, as our fellow-men for whom Christ also died."

After the Treaty of Paris was signed on December 10, 1898, McKinley issued a proclamation assuring Filipinos that "the mission of the United States is one of benevolent assimilation substituting the mild sway of justice and right for arbitrary rule." Aguinaldo, styling himself president of a Philippine Republic, issued a counter-proclamation on January 1, 1899: "My government cannot remain indifferent in view of such a violent and aggressive seizure of a portion of its territory by a nation which arrogated to itself the title of champion of oppressed nations. ... I denounce these acts before the world, in order that the conscience of mankind may pronounce its infallible verdict as to who are true oppressors of nations and the tormentors of mankind." U.S. military authorities took that to be a declaration of war and commenced hostilities against the Filipino resistance.

That news was fresh off the wires when McKinley delivered a speech framed by portraits of Washington, Lincoln, and himself and a banner proclaiming them LIBERATORS. "I cannot bound my vision by the blood-stained trenches around Manila," he began, "where every red drop, whether from the veins of an American soldier or a misguided Filipino, is anguish to my heart—but by the broad range of future years, when ... [Filipinos] shall for ages hence bless the American republic because it emancipated and redeemed their fatherland, and set them in the pathway of the world's best civilization." He denied any imperial designs and promised "the largest measure of local self-government consistent with peace and good order." Aguinaldo read these words and wanted to test them. But the Filipino army commander seized control over his provisional government and launched a guerilla war.

General Elwell S. Otis presided over the initial phase, during which the U.S. Army deployed Gatling guns, Hotchkiss cannon, and steam-powered fire trucks that sprayed oil on burning villages. American soldiers condemned to fight this dirty war in torrid jungles twelve thousand miles from home quickly concluded that every dead "gugu" had been a rebel. The army used torture such as the water cure, summary executions, scorched earth tactics, and concentration camps, one of the Spanish outrages that had inflamed Yankee sensibilities in Cuba. But Filipinos, armed mostly with spears and bolo knives, fought on in hopes that William Jennings Bryan might win the presidency and withdraw U.S. forces. Republican secretary of war Elihu Root therefore accused Democrats of abetting the enemy. Meanwhile, McKinley replaced the toxic Otis with General Arthur MacArthur, who pledged to end the war in swift and sanitized fashion. He did, soon after the election of 1900, when Aguinaldo was fooled into captivity and called on his people to quit. Vicious localized fighting dragged on for another year.

McKinley himself was assassinated in September 1901, but his Second Philippine Commission under William Howard Taft executed benevolent assimilation. The Philippine Organic Act authorized the election of an assembly with limited powers, bestowed a Bill of Rights, and pardoned the *insurrectos*. President Theodore Roosevelt then took the occasion of the May 4, 1902, opening of Arlington National Cemetery to justify the Philippine War to the crowd of 30,000 and by extension the nation. Americans fought not only for the honor of the flag, but also for the very "triumph of civilization over forces which stand for the black chaos of savagery and barbarism." He did not mention the 20,000 Filipinos who died in battle or the 200,000–1,000,000 who perished from disease, starvation, and maltreatment. The war cost the United States $600 million, versus $250 million for the war against Spain, and 4,165 dead versus 2,910 in the war against Spain.

Americans on the left and Mugwump right recoiled. The *Philadelphia Ledger* charged, "Our men have been relentless; have killed to exterminate men, women, children, prisoners and captives, active insurgents and suspected people, from lads of ten and up, an idea prevailing that the Filipino, as such, was little better than a dog." E. L. Godkin of *The Nation* damned the pretense of claiming to civilize other peoples in the "absence from our system of any machinery for governing dependencies" and considered it all "a gross fraud for the first time by a Christian nation." Senator William E. Mason (R., Ill.) mocked the idea of spreading "civilization and Christian liberty hypodermically with thirteen inch guns." But nobody stuck in the craws of the war hawks more than George Frisbee Hoar (R., Mass.): "I believe that the highest service the American people can render to mankind is to preserve unstained and unchanged the Republic as it came to us from the Fathers. It is by example and not by guns or by bayonets that the great work of America for humanity is to be accomplished." Imperialists, bidding to establish a new orthodoxy, cried Judas!

In due time, Taft's managers, scientists, and engineers built infrastructure and lured private investment. But the Filipinos had not asked for their help, and the people who benefitted the most were Americans and their local collaborators. Missionaries quickened by the spirit of Social Gospel also arrived in force to fulfill McKinley's promise to evangelize Filipinos. The *Presbyterian Interior* boasted, "The churches will stand solidly against abandoning the islands." The *Foreign Missionary Journal* claimed it was "the invention of the devil to oppose foreign missions." A missionary in the Philippines even predicted, "By the time they are really ready for independence, they will not want it. . . . They will then realize what an honor it is to be a part of the greatest nation in the world." James Francis Smith, a veteran of Roosevelt's Rough Riders who served as governor-general of the Philippines from 1906 to 1909, enthused about U.S. engineering in the tropics: "Then for the first time since the world began did a nation, flushed with victory and mistress of the fate of conquered millions, turn her face from earth to heaven, and, catching some of that divine charity which inspired the Good Samaritan, set herself to lift a subject people to a higher plain of progress." Americans reading that could feel good about doing well. The reality, described by an Irish American soldier, was otherwise:

> Our flag floats o'er trenches, damp, ill-smelling,
> And reeking with the odors of the dead,
> While far and near yellow men loud yelling
> With sword and torch make all the vista red;
> Fighting with fever, and, O God! with Death,

In hospitals beneath a tropic sun,
No woman's hand to soothe the latest breath,
When, far from home, the soldier's work is done;
This is Empire.
Facing death in rice-fields which are shambles,
For yellow men who're fighting to be free;
Here, amid the cactus and the brambles,
Old Glory seems ashamed across the sea.

How to measure the war for benevolent assimilation? Its various motives were doubtless part pretense and part self-delusion. But effects count far more than motives in foreign relations, and the effects of the Philippine annexation were awful. Roosevelt soon called the islands an Achilles' heel. In retrospect, the Philippines need not have been annexed, occupied, or even attacked in 1898. Or the United States might have left it to the Spaniards to deal with their restless subjects, as Harvard president Charles W. Eliot advised at the time. Or the United States could have made a protectorate of a Filipino republic as it did in Cuba. If the navy wanted a base there to project maritime power or capitalists wanted an entrepôt there to exploit the China trade, the United States need only have asked. Filipino authorities would not have been in a position to refuse a lease on Subic Bay any more than authorities in Havana could resist the lease on Guantánamo Bay. What caused the McKinley administration to crash the Cuban and Filipino independence parties in the name of Progressive Imperialism was spiritual pride, formerly a sin in the civil religion but now a moral imperative. Few Americans had ears to hear Philippine nationalist Manuel Quezón: "I would prefer a government run like hell by Filipinos to one run like heaven by Americans."

CHAPTER FOURTEEN

Twentieth-Century Trends

INTELLECTUAL JOURNALS HAD ALWAYS paid close attention to European developments and measured the progress of the United States against them. In the late nineteenth century they paid special interest to the spread of political democracy in Britain and France and the modern social insurance programs of Bismarck's Germany. Perhaps Americans still had much to learn from the Old World, its monarchies, aristocracies, and established churches notwithstanding. Smug bias against the Old World seemed especially anachronistic when the Third French Republic bestowed Frédéric Auguste Bartholdi's Statue of Liberty on New York harbor in 1886. The Third Republic was both a democracy and the second greatest colonial power. Did that render it *hors de catégorie* or a harbinger of the future, and what might it portend for the United States?

Of course, the greatest colonial power was Britain, and no people thought more about America's future than the British because no nation threatened their global hegemony more than their North American offspring. In 1876 Thomas Henry Huxley, called "Darwin's Bulldog" for his stubborn defense of evolution at the bar of public opinion, sailed to the United States at the invitation of a committee of scientists. His first view from the deck of the steamer *Germanic* was of two towers soaring above the Manhattan skyline.

When told those were the headquarters of Western Union and the *New York Tribune*, he expressed keen interest. "In the Old World the first things you see as you approach a city are steeples; here you see, first, centers of intelligence." He was also struck by the hustle and bustle of the port, especially the purposeful tugboats. "If I were not a man, I think I should like to be a tug." But most telling were his thoughts upon departure. "Size is not grandeur, and your territory does not make a nation. . . . Truly America has a great future before her; great in toil, in care, and in responsibility; great in true glory if she be guided by wisdom and righteousness; great in shame if she fail." Huxley, professor of the survival of the fittest, sailed away uncertain how fit the Yanks really were.

In May 1898 the greatest statesman of the late Victorian era, the Third Marquess of Salisbury, was steering the British Empire through its last years of Splendid Isolation. As prime minister and foreign secretary, he observed the imperial wars and war scares of the day with patient detachment and condensed his thoughts in a speech to the Primrose League. "You may roughly divide the nations of the world as the living and the dying," Salisbury intoned; "the weak states are becoming weaker and the strong states are becoming stronger. . . . For one reason or another—from the necessities of politics or under the pretense of philanthropy—the living nations will gradually encroach on the territory of the dying, and the seeds and causes of conflict among civilised nations will speedily appear." The living nations included Germany, Japan, and the United States, "great countries of enormous power, growing in power every year, growing in wealth, growing in dominion, growing in the perfection of their organization." The dying nations included the Spanish, Portuguese, Ottoman, and Chinese empires, stagnant, backward, and corrupt. Salisbury was a Christian realist who damned the "race arrogance" whereby "seizing a colored man's land and giving it to the white man is an operation now generally known as the progress of colonization." But the world was in flux, and one suspects Salisbury's stiff upper lip concealed a concern that for Britain all change must be for the worse.

Six months later, in November 1898, Salisbury removed his Delphic mask and talked plainly. "It is the first year in which the mighty force of the American Republic has been introduced among the nations whose dominion is spent. . . . I am not refusing sympathy to the American Republic in the difficulties through which they have passed, but no one can deny that their appearance among the factors, at all event of Asiatic, and possibly of European, diplomacy, is not a grave and serious event which may not conduce to the interests of peace, though I think in any event they are likely to conduce to the interests of Great Britain." He went on to speculate about the prospects for a potentially fatal general war. "We have no land frontier, but if we ever allow our defense at sea to fall to such a point of inefficiency that it is as easy, or nearly as easy, to cross the sea as it is to cross a land frontier, our great empire . . . will come clattering to the ground once a blow at the metropolis of England is struck." At stake was Britain's "whole existence, not only our whole prosperity, but the whole fabric by which our millions are nourished and sustained" for a reason he did not need to supply. The British Isles had long become mortally dependent on imported food, mostly from North America. Sir John "Jacky" Fisher, the first sea lord, put it bluntly in 1906: "It's not invasion we have to fear if our navy is beaten. It's starvation."

William Thomas Stead had a solution for that. A flamboyant self-promoting muckraker, he was the virtual founder of investigative journalism and the tabloid press. He knew the power of a manipulated public opinion and even spoke of government by journalism. He was notorious for twisting facts and even making things up to spice a story but thought it wholly justified in the service of his three passions: Progressive reform, world peace, and theosophy. (Stead imagined himself a medium through which the dead spoke to the living.) He was also enthusiastic about Esperanto, the universal language, and expected that nations and civilizations would converge until the human race was united. It was in that spirit that he published *The Americanization of the World: The Trend of the Twentieth Century*, in 1901.

Stead addressed his fellow Brits, telling them not to treat Americanization as an affront but to feel pride of parentage and even imagine "that the American may stand to the Briton as Christianity stands to Judaism." Americans busily remaking the world in their image "have now arrived at such a pitch of power and prosperity as to have a right to claim the leading place among the English-speaking nations." Six chapters followed in which Stead described the growing influence of American politics, economics, and culture on the British Empire, especially Canada, Australia, and New Zealand. Four more chapters assessed the pace of Americanization in continental Europe, the Ottoman Empire, and Central and South America. He explained how Americans constantly renewed their religious spirit in revivals and spread it around the world through missions, temperance movements, and women's and youth organizations. The United States even absorbed Roman Catholics, which is why the papacy had recently condemned Americanism as a heresy.

Most of all, Americanization progressed by spontaneous, undirected export of literature, journalism, art, science, music, marital habits, social norms, sport, engineering, railway systems, shipping, business models, and all manner of consumer goods. Americans advertised themselves ceaselessly, and evidently other peoples wanted what they were selling. What was the secret of Americans' success? Stead granted their country's size and natural endowments, but mostly he credited their education, free enterprise, and democracy. The conclusion, he wrote, might be stated in a sentence. There lies before the people of Great Britain a choice of two alternatives. If they decide to merge the existence of the British Empire in the United States of the English-speaking World, they may continue for all time to be an integral part of the greatest of all world powers, supreme on sea and unassailable on land, permanently delivered from all fear of hostile attack, and capable of wielding irresistible influence in all parts of this planet." The alternative was "ultimate reduction to the status of an English-speaking Belgium."

Stead granted that a mighty Anglo-American union would give rise to the danger of pride. "It should be no ambition of ours to dominate the world save by the influence of ideas and the force of our example. The temptation to believe that we are the Viceregent of the Almighty, charged with the thunderbolt of heaven, for the punishment of evil-doers, is one of the subtle temptations by which the Evil One lures well-meaning people to embark upon a course of policy which soon becomes indistinguishable from buccaneering pure and simple." Yet Stead scored his rhapsody's coda for a choir of angels: "If you add to the propagation of civil liberty the propagation of the liberty of conscience, this empire, this patronage of the world, is the Kingdom of Christ."

All that was rubbish—in fact heresy—to G. K. Chesterton, the English Catholic who famously defined America as a nation with the soul of a church. He did not employ the term "civil religion," but his analysis implied as much since the United States was the only nation in the world founded on a creed. It postulated God as the author of human rights but left it up the people to fill it with content, and "in the matter of God and Government it is naturally God whose claim is taken more lightly." Chesterton noticed the rapid progress of Americanization, and it made him acutely uncomfortable. "We say that the Americans are doing something heroic or doing something insane, or doing it in an unworkable or unworthy fashion, instead of simply wondering what the devil they are doing."

Chesterton first commented on the United States in 1905 in "The Fallacy of the Young Nation." He denied that nations were destined to greatness or rise and decline. "All the absurd physical metaphors, such as youth and age, living and dying, are, when applied to nations, but pseudo-scientific attempts to conceal from men the awful liberty of their lonely souls." One might just as well ask whether America was dying. Regarding the three main symbols of greatness—heroism in government, arms, and art—America did not appear at all fresh or untouched. In fact, he heard coming out of America "a sweet and startling cry, as unmistakable as the cry of a dying man." The symptoms of decadence were already known to the grandsons of John Quincy Adams. Henry Adams believed ineluctable entropy must drain the United States of its vitality. The signs would include "falling birth rates, decline of rural population, growth in alcoholism and drug addiction, and increase in nervous exhaustion, suicides, and insanity." Brooks Adams imagined the United States degenerating into soulless, spineless materialism governed by and for financiers. He also foresaw horrible wars in the twentieth century touched off by the rise of Germany, Russia, and Japan. He predicted the United States and Britain would align and prevail in the first only to confront the continental victor—either Germany or Russia—in a sequel that would exhaust all parties. At that point his crystal ball grew cloudy, but he speculated that new empires might then arise on the shores of Asia.

What is the point of reviewing such prognostications? They illustrate the profound clarifications occurring in the most important bilateral relationship in the world: Britain and the United States. Around 1900 the British Empire was still at the pinnacle of its power. Imperial pink covered the map of the world. The Royal Navy still held to a two-power standard, meaning it surpassed the next two largest navies combined. British finance and commerce presided over global markets disciplined by the gold standard. But Britain's industrial production was already surpassed by the United States and Germany, signs of a strategic climacteric born of the inevitable spread of modern science, technology, and mass organization around the northern hemisphere. Many great and middle-range powers now competed for blue-water navies and colonies, and two of the most dangerous, France and Russia, were allied. When Edward VII was crowned after the death of Queen Victoria in 1901, a whole era seemed to pass away. Salisbury stepped down as foreign secretary in favor of Lord Lansdowne, who promptly jettisoned Splendid Isolation. In November of that year, almost simultaneous to the publication of Stead's book, the British ambassador and American secretary of state initialed the Hay-Pauncefoth Treaty. Tactically, it nullified the 1850 Clayton-Bulwer Treaty and surrendered to the United States full rights to dig and defend a Central American canal. Operationally, it symbolized British acceptance of U.S. naval hegemony in the Caribbean and central Pacific. Strategically, it expressed an assumption shared by all Brits and most (certainly most important) Americans that another Anglo-American war was out of the question. In 1902 the Foreign Office proceeded to make the Anglo-Japanese Alliance, in 1904 the Entente Cordiale with France, and in 1907 the Anglo-Russian Entente. In retrospect, it seemed obvious that these alignments were reactions to the growing threat posed by Germany. But they began with the United States and were all made with countries whose rising power threatened British naval security. Thanks to the Kaiser's willful stupidity, Germany, too, was becoming a naval threat, but Britain's realignments were about shedding enemies at least as much as wooing allies.

    Theodore Roosevelt noticed. During his presidency (1901–9) he exploited America's *carte blanche* from the British to practice an aggressive Progressive Imperialism in regions where the United

States was strong and a defensive one in regions where the United States was comparatively weak. He stage-managed the Panamanian revolution that freed that province from Colombia and bestowed the Canal Zone on the United States. He established the U.S. naval base at Guantánamo and reoccupied Cuba in 1906 to repress political strife and protect U.S. economic interests. His 1904 Roosevelt Corollary deterred European intervention in places like the Dominican Republic or Venezuela by asserting an exclusive American police power to engage in what we would call humanitarian interventions to rescue failed states. In the Far East, on the other hand, where the United States had its hands full in the Philippines, Roosevelt supported the British in their attempts to ward off the collapse and partition of imperial China and persuade the other imperialist powers to respect an Open Door policy with respect to trade and investment. When instead Britain's ally Japan went to war against Russia in 1904 over control of Korea and Manchuria, Roosevelt brokered peace in the 1905 Treaty of Portsmouth. He even sent Taft, now secretary of war, on a secret mission to bless Japanese expansion so long as Tokyo looked after American interests.

Roosevelt was no chicken hawk, having resigned from the Navy Department in 1898 to lead his Rough Riders through withering fire in the Battle of San Juan Heights. But neither can he be dismissed as a warmonger or racist. Rather, he was paradoxical—split-minded, if you will—in the manner his biographers' characterizations suggest. TR the Warrior was also a Nobel Peace Prize recipient. TR the Consummate Realist was also the Last Romantic. TR the Industrial Imperialist was also the Patron Saint of Conservation. In all things Roosevelt was a High Progressive born to govern, a privileged, unabashed scion of the American ruling class in an age when that class had become as cosmopolitan as it had been in the early years of the republic. He had many European friends. By contrast, the Progressive Democrat Woodrow Wilson was a provincial Southerner as anxious for acceptance as a Scotsman in Britain. Wilson rose on the strength of his academic credentials and had never traveled abroad. Roosevelt steered the ship of state with a geopolitical compass and moral rudder that rarely disagreed because both were calibrated by the national interest. He could pursue America's

God-given destiny without apology, doubt, or excess. When he sometimes overreached—for instance, in the Philippines—he learned never again to "swallow a porcupine wrong end-to." Wilson believed in the civil religion just as much, but it filled him with doubt and self-righteous stubbornness. He never learned from mistakes. Roosevelt believed national interests could often be advanced through international law because both expressed the ethical principles of Western civilization. Wilson elevated international law above all national interests with catastrophic results.

Most of all, Roosevelt was realistic in the sense of balancing ends and means, insisting Americans undertake no policies for which they were not prepared to pay. He understood the importance of national honor, prestige, and credibility, especially to deter aggression. The best and safest course was to promise little, keep one's promises, and otherwise speak softly and carry a big stick. Both his geopolitics and his moral vision were rooted in a sense of proportion and limits. He realized the world had shrunk and that the United States must fall into it; that it had a vital interest in stable balances of power in both Europe and East Asia; that it was fast becoming a first-rate naval power but otherwise relied on economic and moral strength, what we now call soft power. TR and Lodge once discussed the qualities most valuable in a diplomat. They listed experience in public life, courage to deal with other statesmen, deep understanding of European and Asian politics, instinctive feel for the balance of power, university training in great literature, and conscious membership in "the society whose rules are common to Western civilization." They were thinking, of course, of themselves, but the qualities chosen did not describe Wilson in any way except book learning. Wilson imagined the way to serve God was by sacrificing U.S. national interest on the altar of humanity. So calling TR a realistic nationalist and Wilson an idealistic internationalist is not incorrect. It just doesn't begin to capture the enormity of the gulf.

The United States was presented with three options in the years between 1867 and 1920: continue territorial expansion under constitutional equality, pursue overseas expansion under colonial inequality, or champion an entirely new world order based on arbitration and equal status for all. "As it turned out," historian Elizabeth Cobbs Hoffman pithily wrote, "Americans made all three choices, in an overlapping, but sequential fashion." The choices—including international law, perpetual peace through free trade or ideological affinity, arbitration, disarmament, expansion, and colonialism—had been around for decades or centuries, but they all burst on to the world's agenda during the Progressive Era. At the Hague Conventions of 1899 and 1907 the world's great powers went through the motions of agreeing to submit international disputes to arbitration even though the wars that were raging before, during, and after the conferences made a farce of the peace movement. But that did not stop Progressive clergy from interpreting the conventions as signs of humanity's progress toward world peace. Andrew Carnegie spoke of a coming United Nations of the World. An annual Lake Mohonk Conference on International Arbitration attracted hundreds of dignitaries who expected the United States to persuade the nations to beat their swords into ploughshares. Roosevelt was one of their heroes because he was the first world leader to submit a dispute for arbitration at the International Court at the Hague. Carnegie and W. T. Stead even hoped he might assume leadership of the World Federation League after his presidency. But TR kept a safe distance from the utopians. Instead, he spent his first post-presidential year on African safaris, during which time he read a book that Judge Learned Hand had sent him. Its thesis coincided almost exactly with his own view of the future and tempted him to jump back into politics. Herbert Croly's *The Promise of American Life* quickly became the Bible of Centrist Progressives.

Croly believed American history had been poisoned by a false conflict between Hamilton and Jefferson. He thought both embodied a form of self-interested liberalism that must be expunged if the United States were ever to realize the promise of democracy. Croly's ideal was Lincoln, the humble national citizen who found fulfillment in service. "If the promising career of any individual is not determined by a specific and worthy purpose, it rapidly drifts into a mere pursuit of success; and even if such a pursuit is successful, whatever promise it may have had, is buried in the grave of its triumph. So it is with a nation." In previous times America's destiny was just a matter of more people and more land. But in the twentieth century the national mission must be planned and conquered:

"Like all sacred causes, it must be propagated by the Word and by that right arm of the Word, which is the Sword." Old notions of freedom had to be jettisoned and the national destiny converted into a national purpose. Croly called for a new nationalism, the slogan TR would adopt for his 1912 presidential campaign. Croly had in mind a government staffed by specialists in business and politics who were empowered to mobilize industry, labor, and agriculture; generate and regulate new technologies; and harmonize individual interests with the public interest.

Croly looked abroad for models and found many in the nationalist, even militarist, institutions of Britain, France, and Germany. He spurned disarmament as a vain attempt "to exorcize the power of physical force in human affairs by the use of pious incantations and heavenly words. The Christian warrior must accompany the evangelist; and Christians are not by any means angels." It went without saying that U.S. diplomacy must serve democracy, but world competition was threatening "to convert the American democratic idea into a dangerously aggressive principle" and impart a "dangerously militant tendency to the foreign policy of the United States." Croly believed neutrality was still the best policy and "nobody serious proposes to depart from it." But defense of U.S. neutrality required firm measures: (1) a stable Pan-American system forged by U.S. cooperation with Argentina, Brazil, Chile, and Mexico; (2) a North American free trade zone stretching to Canada, Mexico, and beyond; (3) a security treaty in which the United States would ensure the sea lanes that carried North American food to Britain in case of a big war in Europe; (4) the imperial possessions needed to defend the Panama Canal; and (5) the Philippines, which had proven expensive but reminded Americans of their important relations with China and Japan. Croly granted that "intervention in a European conflict, carrying with it either the chance or the necessity of war, would at present be received with pious horror by the great majority of Americans." But note the prescient third point above. It was almost as if Croly, echoing Salisbury, Stead, and Brooks Adams, divined the exact circumstances under which the United States would intervene in a European war and recant once and for all its "absolute law—derived from sacred writings."

In 1913 American diplomat Lewis Einstein published an article arguing that U.S. security was contingent on the European balance of power. In fact, he warned it would be rueful blindness if America did not intervene to save England in a total war against Germany. The American East Coast elites already knew that, however improbable they might think the contingency. The American people had no idea about that at all. So in the event of a total war their president must choose very persuasive words to replace those of Washington and Monroe. The president in question made a terrible choice.

CHAPTER FIFTEEN

Wilson's War

PERHAPS THE UNITED STATES would have entered the Great War anyway because of security threats, economic interests, or cultural ties, "but one incontrovertible fact remains: the United States entered World War I because Woodrow Wilson decided to take the country in." John Milton Cooper, Wilson's latest biographer, makes a good case for that declarative statement, but perhaps even he does not realize how damning it is. Yes, the great crusade of 1917–18 was a war of choice. What is more, it was a choice made under the worst possible circumstances. By the time Wilson went before Congress to request a declaration of war against Germany in April 1917, he should have known that Senators Lodge, La Follette, William Borah, and their respective camps were hostile to his league of nations idea. He should have known that the Allied powers, led by Britain and France, were hostile to most of the principles he would espouse in his Fourteen Points. He should have known that most of those principles, not least national self-determination, could not be applied to most of the human race. He should have known that the vast majority of Germans, however war-weary and desperate, remained loyal to their emperor. He should have known that to earn a decisive voice at the peace conference the United States must wage a total ground war, not a limited naval war. He should have known that war would oblige him to sacrifice his

domestic agenda, violate civil liberties, and invite Americans to indulge violent and bigoted instincts (indeed, his own propaganda
campaign all but ensured it). Finally, he learned soon enough that
the United States must engage in revolutionary and counter-
revolutionary crusades at the same time. Despite knowing all (or any)
of that Wilson chose to flip the last civil religious "thou shalt nots"
into commandments.

The people should have seen it coming. At times Wilson could
sound as zany as Jefferson in split-minded moments—for instance,
when he told a Denver audience in May 1911 that "there are times
in the history of nations when they must take up the crude instruments of bloodshed in order to vindicate spiritual conceptions. For
liberty is a spiritual conception, and when men take up arms to set
other men free, there is something sacred and holy in the warfare. I
will not cry 'Peace' so long as there is sin and wrong in the world."
Such messianic delusions indicated this was a dangerous man liable
to make the United States a dangerous nation. Yet within two years
he was president. What were the voters thinking?

The election of 1912 is often described as a four-sided referendum on the role of government in the industrial age. The incumbent Republican, Taft, is said to have represented a stand-pat
conservatism that trusted big business. The renegade Roosevelt is
said to have represented a bold Progressivism that trusted big government to regulate big business and big labor. The Democrat
Wilson is said to have represented a rival Progressivism called the
"New Freedom," which was supposed to restore competition in the
interests of the common man. The Socialist Eugene Debs is said to
have represented the un-American project of state ownership of
the means of production in the interest of organized labor. But that
description is a bit of a caricature because American candidates
rarely say just what they intend to do (assuming they even know)
and rarely keep the vague promises made. American institutions
sharply constrain what a president can achieve. American voters
make up their minds for all sorts of reasons, including personality
and spin. But Wilson's campaign was bogus even by American
standards. Nominated on the forty-sixth ballot by a divided
Democratic Party and facing three opponents in the general election, Wilson desperately needed to shore up his base. Luckily the

Republican vote was divided, so that might be all that he needed to do. Consequently, he pretended to be some kind of small-government Populist, courted white voters in the solid South, and counted on William Jennings Bryan to corral the Great Plains. In the event, Wilson won in a landslide but only because he was able to win northern states like Massachusetts and Illinois with just 35 percent of their popular vote.

In his inaugural address Wilson claimed that the Nation (capitalized as if it were sacred) was using the Democratic Party to bring about moral change:

> The Nation has been deeply stirred, stirred by a solemn passion, stirred by the knowledge of wrong, of ideals lost, of government too often debauched and made an instrument of evil. The feelings with which we face this new age of right and opportunity sweep across our heartstrings like some air out of God's own presence, where justice and mercy are reconciled and the judge and the brother are one. We know our task to be no mere task of politics but a task which shall search us through and through, whether we be able to understand our time and the need of our people, whether we be indeed their spokesmen and interpreters, whether we have the pure heart to comprehend and the rectified will to choose our high course of action. This is not a day of triumph; it is a day of dedication. Here muster, not the forces of party, but the forces of humanity. Men's hearts wait upon us; men's lives hang in the balance; men's hopes call upon us to say what we will do. Who shall live up to the great trust? Who dares fail to try? I summon all honest men, all patriotic, all forward-looking men, to my side. God helping me, I will not fail them, if they will but counsel and sustain me!

That was the language of humanitarian democracy, the universal evangelism that Orestes Brownson feared would respect no boundaries at all.

In theory, Wilson ran on a platform that condemned imperialism "as an inexcusable blunder which has involved us in enormous expense, brought us weakness rather than strength, and laid our nation open to the charge of abandonment of the fundamental doctrine of self-government." In practice, Wilson ordered military occupations of Nicaragua, Haiti, and the Dominican Republic; invaded Mexico twice (ostensibly to teach Latin Americans to elect good men); and tried in vain to revive the Pan-American Movement. He made startling speeches such as the Annapolis address, when he told Naval Academy graduates the idea of America was to serve humanity, and the Mobile, Alabama, address, in which he told Southern businessmen of the coming millennium: "It is a very perilous thing to determine the foreign policy of a nation in terms of material interest. It is not only unfair to those with whom you are dealing, but it is degrading as regards your own actions. . . . We have breasted a considerable part of that climb and shall presently—it may be a generation or two—come out upon those great heights where there shines unobstructed the light of the justice of God." Wilson clearly held some pretty strange views on foreign affairs even before the Great War broke out. Only they weren't such strange views any more given the cresting tide of Progressive Social Gospel.

Historians routinely attribute Wilson's religious rhetoric to his upbringing as the son and grandson of Presbyterian preachers. That is not wrong, but it misses the power of civil religion to conflate the sacred and secular. Wilson insisted that faith was the basis for all his actions, especially in international relations, but it was not the orthodox faith of our fathers. It was the new Progressive faith, the heresy of a heresy, that Wilson wanted to make the new orthodoxy. In 1912 he boldly equated Calvinist Covenant theology with politics and promised heaven on earth:

> If I did not believe in Providence I would feel like a man going blindfolded through a haphazard world. I do believe in Providence. I believe that God presided over the inception of this nation; I believe that God planted in us the visions of liberty; I believe that men are emancipated in proportion as they lift themselves to the conception of Providence and of divine destiny, and therefore I cannot be deprived of the hope that is in me—in the hope not only

that concerns myself, but the confident hope that concerns the nation—that we are chosen and prominently chosen to show the way to the nations of the world how they shall walk in their paths of liberty.

He believed in a power that would "purify the whole air of American politics, chasten every selfish man, drive out every corrupt purpose," and cause men to say, "Behold the heavens are clear again! God's sun is in the heavens and all shall be right." So far from accepting the United States as a blessed, but inevitably flawed, nation struggling to discern and conform to God's will, Wilson imagined American policy (under his guidance) to be the measure of God's will.

Historians also routinely identify Wilson as an ivory tower professor who imagined the real world could be made to conform to theories. That, too, is accurate so far as it goes. But historian Thomas Fleming got Wilson right when he called him a real-life personification of *Philip Dru, Administrator*, the novel written by Wilson's political alter ego, Colonel Edward M. House. The book described a United States rent by sectional and economic divisions and beset by an evil plutocracy until Dru's benevolent dictatorship, based on scientific administration, put all to rights. Wilson, like House's character, did not really believe in self-determination because common people could not be trusted. Serious political questions, not least those of war and peace, must be left to "the selected leaders of public opinion and rulers of state policy." Throughout his career as a political scientist—an academic discipline invented by and for Progressives—Wilson constantly revisited the question "What is a nation?" and concluded (with German philosopher G. F. W. Hegel) that many, perhaps most, nations were not sufficiently evolved to form states. His civil religious agenda was implicit in his quest for the true canons of Americanism, and his Anglo-Saxon bias was explicit in *A History of the American People* (1902). Wilson's views on the presidency also evolved from the well-known *Congressional Government* (1885) to *Constitutional Government in the United States* (1908), in which he extolled the presidency as the only democratic expression of the whole nation. Its most important assets were leadership and rhetoric, and its most exclusive arena was foreign policy.

In foreign policy, of course, Wilson rejected balance of power in favor of what historian Lloyd Ambrosius terms a "community of power; not organized rivalries, but an organized common peace." But he also despised checks and balances in domestic politics, hated compromise, and (like Roosevelt) resented how hard it was to amend the Constitution. In fact, three amendments occurred on Wilson's watch: the income tax, Prohibition, and women's suffrage. Whereas the Founders had distrusted charismatic leaders as potential demagogues, Wilson idolized leaders and imagined his own charisma embodied the Hegelian Spirit of the Age. Wilson was the Cause, the Change, whose time had come. Finally, he believed in his rhetoric so completely that he was always shocked to discover that people might not always agree with him. When the election of 1918 perversely returned Republican majorities, Wilson insisted: "You may be sure the stubborn Scotch-Irish in me will be rendered no less stubborn and aggressive by the results!" When the Democrats lost the presidential election in 1920, dooming the League of Nations, he said of the voters: "They have disgraced us in the eyes of the world." Who is the "us" in that sentence except some idealized nation incarnated in Wilson himself? He drained whatever Christian humility was left in American Civil Religion in the belief he was a world historical figure.

An event of world historical importance occurred on August 15, 1914: the opening of the Panama Canal. But nobody in the Old World noticed because the Great War had broken out two weeks before. Despite horrific casualties, the initial battles were all indecisive. Instead of negotiating a truce, the belligerent governments mobilized their populations and economies for a total industrial war of attrition in the trenches. Ordinary Americans observed all this in stunned disbelief and certainly felt no impulse to intervene. So the public gave overwhelming support to President Wilson when he declared the United States too proud to fight, clung to neutrality for two and a half years, and tried several times to mediate truce talks. Meanwhile, Progressive clergy rent their garments over Europe's descent into atavistic barbarism. That was not supposed to happen in a Christendom progressing toward world federation. Nobody understood that the war was really a clash among nationalistic civil religions. All the Christian great powers and the sole Muslim one (the Ottoman Empire) mobilized their national clergy in support of their war efforts. All draped their public war aims in Manichean propaganda about the defense of civilization or culture. American churchmen wanted to know where God was in the midst of this bloodletting and what His own anointed country was expected to do?

Progressive Protestant clergy eventually sorted themselves into three schools of thought about how the United States might lead the world to perpetual peace. The first, a militarist camp led by Lyman Abbott, agreed with Theodore Roosevelt that peace must rest on righteousness, an aim that required the defeat of the pagan Germans. This school opposed Wilson's efforts to mediate and was ready to go global in the spirit of humanitarian crusade. The second, a pacifist camp led by Washington Gladden, believed going to war was a pact with the devil that would leave millions of Americans dead, a generation in debt, and all moral suasion cast away. It agreed with Wilson that only a negotiated peace without victory might last. The third, a moderate camp led by Sidney L. Gulick of the Federal Council of Churches and supported by Carnegie and Rockefeller, believed the United States should defend international law, by diplomatic means if possible and military means if necessary. Gulick insisted Americans stand for Golden Rule diplomacy but be prepared to suffer with Christ for the world's redemption. Wilson himself told a religious convention in December 1915 that the object of the church was "to save society in this world, not the next."

Political Progressives also splintered among pacifists; moderates, who founded the League to Enforce Peace under former president Taft; and belligerent Atlanticists, whose business-dominated National Security League supported Roosevelt's call for war on Germany after the 1915 sinking of the *Lusitania*. Clearly the situation cried out for strong presidential leadership of the sort Wilson had advocated. Instead, he gave Americans a counsel of perfection—be impartial in thought as well as in action—then derived a tortured policy from the minutiae of neutrality law that had zero chance of getting respect from Europeans locked in a death struggle. Above all, Wilson's policy was anything but impartial because he was a rabid Anglophile, and the only genuine neutralist in his Cabinet, Secretary of State Bryan, resigned in protest because Wilson refused to protest the British surface blockade as well as the German submarine blockade. His replacement, Robert Lansing; Secretary of the Treasury William McAdoo (Wilson's son-in-law); the secretaries of war and navy; and Colonel House were all Anglophile. So Wilson refused to embargo U.S. trade with all belligerents, refused to defend trade with all belligerents by ordering the navy across the ocean and daring either side to shoot first, and refused to instruct American citizens that they sailed on belligerent ships at their own risk. Instead, the president, who pretended it was perilous and degrading for a nation to pursue material interests, consistently served the interests of American cotton and grain exporters, manufacturers, and financiers, who made windfall profits from trade with the Allies. By 1916 Britain and France were getting 40 percent of their war materiel from U.S. suppliers. American banks liquidated European assets at fire-sale prices and purchased millions in Allied war bonds, reversing the transatlantic investment balance and making the United States the world's biggest creditor. The neutral rights Wilson invoked amounted to freedom for war profiteers to collude in the blockade of Germany.

British propagandists also manipulated U.S. opinion with ease. Since the Royal Navy had cut the German transatlantic cable, almost all war news came from the Allies, including lurid reports of German atrocities. British intelligence broke the German and American diplomatic codes and eavesdropped on all their traffic. The U.S. Embassy in London could be counted on to parrot the narrative originally promoted by Britain to the effect that this had become a war to end war and make the world safe for democracy. So even though millions of German Americans sympathized with the old country and Irish and Jewish Americans had good cause to hate England or Russia, their stories got drowned out. Nor was German propaganda about the defense of *Kultur* against Britain's nation of shopkeepers likely to resonate with Americans even more commercial than the British. Germany was authoritarian, militaristic, and the apparent aggressor. German submarines sank ships and drowned innocent people.

Still, Wilson earnestly abhorred the prospect of U.S. belligerence because he remained a Progressive of the 1898 generation. That meant he was on board with Progressive humanitarian interventions throughout the Americas and the Pacific but remained wedded to Washington's great rule when it came to involvement in European wars. He simply could not imagine, or else repressed the thought, that the United States might have to go to war in order to save Great Britain. Either the Allies would win or else his mediation efforts would succeed. In either case he expected to inaugurate a new epoch in history. Wilson's keynote address on the first anniversary of the League to Enforce Peace in May 1916 endorsed a universal association of the nations to uphold freedom of the seas, prevent unlawful war, and guarantee territorial integrity and political independence. In November, following his razor-thin reelection, Wilson relaunched his peace effort and refloated the notion of a league of nations. (It is significant that the Senate passed a resolution expressing its skepticism by a vote of 48 to 17.) In January 1917 Wilson stated categorically, "There will be no war. This country does not intend to become involved in war. We are the only one of the great White nations that is free from war today, and it would be a crime against civilization for us to go into it." That same month he called for Peace without Victory lest Europeans prolong the cycle of vengeance. Finally, Wilson floated the idea of extending the Monroe Doctrine to the world, a proposition that caused Senator William Borah to accuse him of treason and Senator Lodge to scoff, "If we have a Monroe Doctrine everywhere we may be perfectly certain that it will not exist anywhere." It turned out that mini-debate was a dress rehearsal for the fight two years later over the Treaty of Versailles.

The British had grown desperate. In December 1916, when David Lloyd George became prime minister, food supplies were perilously low and credit exhausted. A secret interdepartmental conference had already admitted the British war effort was completely dependent on the United States for munitions, steel, foodstuffs, oil, wheat, cotton, and lubricants. John Maynard Keynes calculated that 40 percent of the money required just to keep the war effort going into 1917 must come from Americans' savings. Chancellor of Exchequer Reginald McKenna even told an American journalist around Christmastime that Wilson could "force the Allies to their knees any time in a moment." Nothing was further from Wilson's mind, but he must also have been profoundly disappointed that the British had reached the end of their tether without either winning or negotiating a satisfactory end to the war.

The German high command had already made its decision to resume unrestricted submarine warfare on February 1. But to Americans that seemed a cynical response to the Peace without Victory speech and to the British, a godsend. Hence their own disappointment when Wilson armed merchant ships and broke off diplomatic relations but did not ask for a declaration of war against Germany. In fact, he gave vent to a flood of doubts. He asked his Cabinet whether the yellow races might gain a decisive advantage if Americans waded into the slaughter on the western front. He lamented to Navy Secretary Josephus Daniels that war would reverse the momentum of Progressive reform and put big business back in control. He told an editor that war would undermine tolerance and unleash a spirit of ruthless brutality in America. His second inaugural address, on March 5, sounded a strikingly uncertain trumpet:

> We are provincials no longer. The tragic events of the thirty months of vital turmoil through which we have just passed have made us citizens of the world. There can be no turning back. Our own fortunes as a nation are involved whether we would have it so or not. And yet we are not the less Americans on that account. We shall be the more American if we but remain true to the principles in which we have been bred. They are not the principles of a province or of a single continent. We have known and boasted all along that they were the principles of a liberated mankind. These, therefore, are the things we shall stand for, whether in war or in peace. . . . I need not argue these principles to you, my fellow countrymen; they are your own part and parcel of your own thinking and your own motives in affairs. They spring up native amongst us.

Wilson had not made up his mind. He did, however, universalize American principles and by a rhetorical trick ("I need not argue")

insinuate that all true Americans surely agreed with him. He ended
the speech with no fewer than eight appeals for national unity.

Many textbooks report that the infamous Zimmermann
Telegram was the last straw that finally made up the minds of the
president and the American people. But historian Thomas Boghardt's
recent book definitely proves it was not. The British secret service
and British Embassy in Washington had of course worked every an-
gle trying to curry American favor. It was time now for the chief of
British naval intelligence, William Reginald Hall, to play his last
card. He leaked a decoded telegram in which the German foreign
minister proposed a war alliance with Mexico. Surely that would outrage Americans and force the president to ask for war. But no, that
did not do the trick either because the German proposal was so obviously absurd that within two weeks of its publication (on March 1)
the Zimmermann Telegram had become an object of ridicule in the
newspapers. Even after the declaration of war few editors mentioned
it as a *casus belli*.

Nobody knows what tipped the president's thinking, but we
can well understand his anxiety. Wilson had no way of knowing
whether his free, diverse, and complacent nation would unite in a
war to defend some abstraction, be it international law, commercial
interests, or balance of power. Nor could it be pitched as an explicitly Christian duty because to many Americans that duty was still
pacific. No, the war must be pitched as a civil religious calling,
something for which his rhetorical skills were uniquely suited.
Biographer Cooper sensed just what was afoot in Wilson's mind by
noting how his war message echoed the language of Martin
Luther. Wilson, like Luther, resolved to sin boldly by plunging into
the European war. But there was even more to it than that. Wilson
was not trying to persuade Americans to engage in a necessary
evil. He was defining the bold sin out of existence by launching a
veritable reformation in the American Civil Religion.

In mid-March four U.S. merchant ships succumbed to U-boats.
Wilson polled his Cabinet and learned its opinion unanimously
conformed to those on Wall Street: all-out economic assistance to
Britain had not sufficed. The next day he scheduled a special session of Congress and went to work on a speech that doubled down
on American pretense but that most Progressive clergy could not

but support. He would preach a holy crusade. On the evening of April 2 Wilson performed that "distressing and oppressive duty" before a joint session of Congress. Declaring Germany's submarine campaign a war against all mankind, he revealed a new doctrine for the new Israel, a full-throated Progressive ACR:

> Neutrality is no longer feasible or desirable where the peace of the world is involved and the freedom of its peoples, and the menace to that peace and freedom lies in the existence of autocratic governments backed by organized force which is controlled wholly by their will, not by the will of their people. We have seen the last of neutrality in such circumstances. We are at the beginning of an age in which it will be insisted that the same standards of conduct and of responsibility for wrong done shall be observed among nations and their governments that are observed among the individual citizens of civilized states. We have no quarrel with the German people.

Wilson's war message soared: "The right is more precious than peace. . . . Make the world safe for democracy. . . . A universal dominion of right by a concert of free peoples. . . . America is privileged to spend her blood. . . . God helping her, she can do no other." But the extracted passage above was really the one that proclaimed a putative new world order. The Truman Doctrine is modest by comparison.

William J. Stone (D., Mo.), chairman of the Senate Foreign Relations Committee, warned that entering this war of choice would be "the greatest national blunder in history." George W. Norris (R., Neb.) believed, "We are putting the dollar sign on the American flag." La Follette (R., Wis.) burst into tears while rebutting Wilson's arguments point by point. If Germany was waging a war against all nations, he asked, why was the United States the only neutral to object? If the world was being made safe for democracy, why didn't the British practice democracy in Ireland, India, or Egypt? If Wilson was distinguishing between the common people and their oppressive rulers, how come more Germans supported the Kaiser than American voters supported Wilson? But

Congress bowed to the wishes of the executive. On April 6 the
Senate voted 82–6 in favor of war and the House, 373–50 the next
day. More than one representative privately confessed that many
members were opposed to war but dared not admit it. Ambassador
Cecil Spring-Rice reported to London that Americans went to war
"with the greatest reluctance."

Wilson claimed to have bowed to the inevitable when Prussian
militarism made it obvious that only by fighting could the United
States fulfill its destiny and earn a just and lasting peace. But as
high priest of the civil religion, it was his duty to market the war,
and he did so by taking the Progressive Social Gospel to its logical,
heretical conclusion. He recast the ACR as a fighting faith and
hurled the nation into a war among European civil religions in order to prove, like a pagan priest-king, that his tribal gods were
mightier than theirs.

CHAPTER SIXTEEN

Wilson's Peace

L YMAN ABBOTT CONSIDERED IT "something more than a coincidence" that the Senate went to war on Good Friday. He preached a theology that scores of Progressive preachers were quick to adopt: Germany was heathen, America righteous, and the war a climactic chapter in God's plan for redemption. Unseen forces of heaven were guiding the human race toward brotherhood and democracy with America leading the way like Moses. Dean of the Yale Divinity School Charles Reynolds Brown asked, "May we not believe that this country, strong and brave, generous and hopeful is called of God to be in its own way a Messianic nation?" Congregational pastor (and diplomatic historian) Tyler Dennett exulted, "Democracy is not merely a catchword of the War; it has become the watchword of the world." Evangelist Billy Sunday cried, "Christianity and Patriotism are synonymous terms, and hell and traitors are synonymous." The cross all but disappeared behind the American flag. Post-millennialists expected the war to usher in the kingdom of God on earth; pre-millennialists expected the Armageddon would trigger the Second Coming. Many became Zionists when the Balfour Declaration promised a homeland for Jews and British general Edmund Allenby captured Jerusalem in 1917. The Catholic Church proved its good citizenship by supporting Wilson's belligerency as fervently as it had previously supported his neutrality. Carnegie, Rockefeller, and their foundations scrambled aboard the war wagon hoping it might lead to world federation. "For the first time in history," boasted Herbert Croly's *New Republic*, "a wholly independent nation has entered a great and costly war under the influence of ideas rather than immediate interests."

Wilson encouraged the idea of holy war because it helped to unite and mobilize the nation. He meant to ship a million-man conscripted army over there to turn the tide of battle and win for him maximum leverage in peacemaking. So he praised as singular insight the Social Gospel book that declared Wilson's goal to be the kingdom of God. On Flag Day 1917 he declared a "People's War for freedom and self-government amongst all the nations of the world . . . [and] woe be to that man or that group of men that seeks to stand in our way in this day of high resolution." That solemn oath included the Allied powers because (Wilson confided to House) "England and France have not the same views with regard to peace that we have by any means." Accordingly, Wilson declared the United States an associated rather than allied power. Such language alerted the British and French, Italians and Japanese, that the United States was fighting against Germany but not necessarily alongside them.

In 1912 Presbyterian theologian William Adams Brown of Union Theological Seminary had published *The Christian Hope: A Study in the Doctrine of Immortality*. A champion of ecumenical Progressivism, Brown placed before his readers the vision of an American heaven that differed markedly from the angelic harps and clouds many Christians imagined. The American heaven was perfect precisely because it was not a place of untroubled bliss but rather a place where the church was reborn to a strenuous life. He imagined new challenges and worlds to conquer for heroes of faith lest a boring eternity of praise and worship "make heaven less desirable than earth." Five years later the Wilson administration pulled that heavenly vision down to earth. Not only would the American Expeditionary Forces wage war for righteousness, but also its very soldiers were urged to refrain from prostitutes and alcohol to purify themselves as crusading saints. The army newspaper *Stars and Stripes* unabashedly promoted a non-sectarian Protestantism that amounted to civil religion and framed the war against Germany as a redemptive reprise of the Civil War. Julia Ward Howe's "The Battle Hymn of the Republic" thus became the universal humanitarian hymn she had always intended. By contrast, the American Creed, composed by William Tyler Page and adopted by Congress on April 3, 1918, had no mystical content. But the American Legion insisted that all Protestant, Catholic, and Jewish denominations append the creed to their sectarian creeds as a form of loyalty oath.

Civil religious zealotry justified unprecedented censorship and repression. Wilson's Justice Department prosecuted over two thousand Americans for disloyalty under new Espionage and Sedition Acts. Eugene Debs was jailed. Suspect journals, including *The Nation*, were banned from the mails. Wilson's Committee on Public Information (CPI) commandeered three whole buildings for a global campaign of propaganda on behalf of what its director, Progressive journalist George Creel, called the gospel of Americanism. Creel reminded Wilson that the Vatican had coined the term "propaganda" to mean propagation of the faith, and it was in this positive sense that America would propagate its civil religion. The CPI did so via every possible medium, including feature-length films such as *Pershing's Crusaders* and *Hearts of the World*, directed by D. W. Griffith (whose *Birth of a Nation* had so impressed Woodrow Wilson). Mostly the CPI used standard commercial techniques in its advertisements—for instance, promising parents of soldiers "He Will Come Back a Better Man from His Adventure as a Victorious Crusader." Its daily agenda included censorship of the news, intimidation of dissidents, and depictions of the Germans as Huns and gorillas. Republican Progressives approved. Elihu Root spoke of "this great struggle between the principles of Christian civilization and the principles of pagan cruelty and brutal force." J. P. Morgan insisted, "The whole German Nation had started out on the war with the cry of 'world domination or annihilation,' and we recognized that world domination by Germany would bring complete destruction of the liberties of the rest of the world."

No one demonized the enemy more than keepers of the nation's conscience. Mainline Protestant clergy easily called Germany pagan and the Kaiser the devil. The Federal Council of Churches met in the nation's capital in May 1917 to offer its services to the state. Preachers recruited young men from their pulpits with lurid tales of German atrocities. Newell Dwight Hillis of Brooklyn's Plymouth Congregational Church served a Liberty Loan drive by delivering more than four hundred lectures in 162 cities. He claimed to share inside information—for instance, that German soldiers were issued medallions inscribed "I, the Kaiser of Germany, declare herewith on the authority committed to me by God Almighty, that the bearer of this token is permitted to commit any crime he may desire, and I, the Kaiser of Germany, will take upon myself the responsibility for such crime and to answer to God for the same." Hillis accused Germans of drinking blood from skulls, castrating prisoners, and raping women. The Rev. W. W. Bustard of Rockefeller's Euclid Avenue Baptist Church damned Wilhelm II to hell. Methodist bishop William Alfred Quayle said the real enemy was the German race. Billy Sunday cried, "I tell you it is Bill against Woodrow, Germany against America, Hell against Heaven. . . . All this talk about not fighting the German people is a lot of bunk." Lyman Abbott boasted of not being able to pray "Father, forgive them, for they know not what they do" because the Kaiser and his generals knew very well what they were doing. By summer 1918 only Quakers and a smattering of pacifists and socialists braved persecution by protesting "a nation drunk with hate."

Bear in mind this was the Kaiser's regime, not Hitler's. Imperial Germany was certainly militarist but also a constitutional pastiche of federal, parliamentary, and monarchical elements designed by Otto von Bismarck to accommodate and contain the onrush of industrialism, nationalism, and democracy. Far from being a dictator, Wilhelm II enjoyed no more prerogative than an American commander-in-chief in time of war. Wilson yielded nothing to him in terms of executive power, unbending will, or even civil religious pretensions. The Kaiser expressed the Germans' national creed at the onset of war—"So now I commend you to God. Go into your churches, kneel before God, and implore his help for our brave army"—and Lutheran pastor Johann Kessler spelled it out in his 1914 book, *Our Faith Is Victory:*

> We believe in the world calling of our nation. A nation that
> God has equipped with such gifts of the spirit and such

depths of mind that He called it to bear the gospel in the
days of the Reformation, that he chose it in the War of
Liberation [against Napoleon] to be the harbinger of a new
era, a nation to which God has given a Luther and Lessing,
a Goethe and Schiller, a Kant and Bismarck—this nation
cannot be cast aside. God has great things in store for such
a nation that could defy a world of enemies and still prevail.

Wasn't that German civil religion autocratic and oppressive toward
alien peoples? So was the American one vis-à-vis Mexicans, Indians,
and Africans. Wouldn't a German victory have made the world
unsafe for democracy? Even that is debatable. Given the extreme
sacrifices Germans made during the war, their powerful Social
Democratic, Catholic Center, and Progressive People's Parties
would probably have demanded democratic reforms in victory as
well as defeat. The Reichstag's peace resolution and the widespread
strikes that broke out in 1917 gave evidence of that. But Wilson,
despite his claim to have no quarrel with the German people, authorized vile propaganda and at the end acquiesced in the British
demand that the food blockade on Germany continue even after
the Armistice.

In his war message the president also asked, "Does not every
American feel that assurance has been added to our hope for the
future peace of the world by the wonderful and heartening things
that have been happening within the last few weeks in Russia?
Russia was known by those who knew it best to have been always
in fact democratic at heart." Wilson referred, of course, to the
March revolution (February on Russia's Julian calendar) that had
ousted the tsar in favor of a Provisional Government that promised
elections and a reinvigorated war effort. But in November
(October) 1917 Lenin's Bolshevik Party seized power in an armed
coup d'état and founded the world's first Communist state. All of a
sudden the United States was outflanked on the left, its identity as
the progressive nation cast into doubt. Lenin called on workers
and soldiers of all nations to overthrow their capitalist-imperialist
rulers and make a peace based on no annexations, no indemnities.
Wilson had to respond, but how? Americans were themselves capitalists (and imperialists) and had recently learned how ambivalent

they were toward social revolutions in Cuba, China, Russia in 1905, and Mexico. So Wilson's riposte, the famous Fourteen Points address of January 8, 1918, might have been a timely answer to the Bolshevik challenge. But with regard to the world war it was woefully premature. At that time only one U.S. infantry division had served at the front and only four were in France. It was far too soon for the president to name terms to his enemy or his associates, much less to define a vision of heaven on earth.

Wilson faked it eloquently, as La Follette perceived: "I sometimes think the man has no sense of things that penetrate below the surface. With him the rhetoric of a thing is the thing itself. . . . Words—phrases, felicity of expression and a blind egotism—have been his stock in trade." There is no need to repeat the well-worn text of the speech except to observe that the principles were vague and sure to be hotly contested: open covenants openly arrived at? absolute freedom of navigation in peace and in war? the removal of all economic barriers (even tariffs)? reduction of armaments to the minimum consistent with domestic (not international) security? adjustment of colonial claims with equal weight given to the interests of the inhabitants? a general association of nations affording mutual guarantees of political independence and territorial integrity? Most Progressives hailed the president's "unflinching insistence upon principles. . . . For the first time since the beginning of the war, its issues are clear and unmistakable." In fact, Wilson had no clue how his principles might play out in practice, and they were worse than a blank slate as a blueprint for peace. The British and French immediately plotted how to evade them. The Germans ultimately plotted how to exploit them. East Europeans, colonial peoples from Egypt and India to Korea and Vietnam, not to mention African Americans, dreamed futile dreams of self-determination during what historian Erez Manela has called "the Wilsonian Moment." Theodore Roosevelt, who actually had a kind word to say to the president after war was declared, reverted to angry opposition as a result of the vacuous Fourteen Points. He feared Wilson meant to impose himself as an umpire between Germany and the Allies, admit the defeated powers to his league's inner council, "abolish all armaments by sea and land, and then float to Heaven on one wide slushy sea of universal mush."

Whatever else it did, the Fourteen Points speech completed the transformation of the Great War from a two-sided affair into a four-way fight for the world's soul among three civil religions and an ideological atheism whose manifestations were German imperialism, Allied nationalism, Progressive Wilsonianism, and Marxism-Leninism. It is impossible to imagine the United States managing to force its will on all three competitors at once, but that is what Wilson led Americans to believe in order to justify the fantastic proposition of conscripting an army and hurtling it into the killing fields across the Atlantic. When in the summer of 1918 the bulk of the American Expeditionary Force finally set foot in France, General John J. Pershing insisted his soldiers fight as a separate army rather than be used as piecemeal reinforcements for Allied units. That was a patriotic decision, but among its consequences were appalling casualties because the raw and zealous doughboys launched costly frontal attacks. In just twenty-four weeks of serious fighting 50,000 Americans were killed in combat (plus 200,000 wounded), and the total death toll (counting disease, accidents, and suicides) was 120,139. But Pershing's independence and even his tactics maximized Wilson's political purpose, which was to make U.S. combat operations appear even more decisive than they were. After October 5, when the German government sent peace feelers to Wilson, he once again acted alone. The president traded three notes with the enemy before informing the incredulous, furious Allies. The French and British refused to consider an armistice unless and until Germany laid down its arms, evacuated all occupied territory, surrendered its fleet, submitted to Allied occupation of the Rhineland, and suffered the blockade to continue. The Allies paid no more than lip service to the Fourteen Points, which augured ill for the peace conference to come. But the first and hardest condition was Wilson's: the Kaiser must abdicate. That meant the fledgling German republic would be saddled with a stab-in-the-back theory as well as a draconian treaty.

Six days before the Armistice of November 11 Americans went to the polls. Wilson campaigned strenuously but to no avail. Republicans captured both houses of Congress. Lodge thought it a revolt against dictatorship. Roosevelt thought it a nationalist repudiation of the Fourteen Points. The *New Republic* attributed it to a reaction against censorship, persecution, and hysteria. Perhaps it was no more than the usual setback suffered by presidents in the midst of second terms. But if the United States had been a parliamentary system of government of the sort Professor Wilson had called for, then President Wilson would have been forced to resign. Instead, the lame duck pressed on for two more years, determined not to reach across the aisle.

German imperialism was slain. The Bolshevik regime was mired in a vast civil war that Western leaders—Wilson included—tried in vain to influence. So by default the Paris Peace Conference became a contest of wills between Allied nationalism, represented by British prime minister David Lloyd George and French premier Georges Clémenceau, and Wilson's reformed civil religion. The drama has been scripted as a morality play, a tragedy, a tragicomedy like *Don Quixote*, and a bitter farce because of Wilson's numerous unforced errors. He raised the hopes of common people everywhere to impossible heights, insisted on negotiating himself (the first U.S. president to do so) and thereby squandered his prestige in horse trading, and arrived in Paris with no economic plan and the vaguest of political plans. Most of all Wilson overestimated American military, political, and financial power, which dissipated the moment the Armistice was signed. If he had followed the advice of Roosevelt and Pershing and fought until unconditional surrender, the spring 1919 campaign would not only have driven defeat home to Germany but might also have greatly enhanced U.S. military and financial leverage over Britain and France. Instead, he put his faith in regime change.

Most of the political capital Wilson possessed in Paris he invested in the League of Nations Covenant, which he insisted the peace conference draft first. He spent most of the rest of his time in Paris either surrendering his principles or learning how inapplicable they were to real-world geography, politics, and economics. The treaty with Germany was sure to be very harsh given the carnage and devastation wrought by the war and French fears for their future security. Yet it was harsh in a strikingly Progressive way insofar as the document reeked of expertise and burst with stipulations. Wilson was accompanied in Paris by an elite, 21-member committee of scholars drawn from The Inquiry, which he had established in September 1917 to advise him on peacemaking. The peace conference as a whole combined 27 national delegations that staffed 58 committees that staged 1,646 (mostly tedious) meetings. The result was a punitive, nitpicking treaty designed to regulate nearly every aspect of German national life after the war. The famous Peace of Westphalia (1648), which ended the Thirty Years' War and transformed the whole international system of Europe, contained 128 articles and covers 42 pages in the *Major Peace Treaties of Modern History*. The Congress of Vienna (1815), which ended the Napoleonic wars and likewise transformed Europe, contained 121 articles over 56 pages. The Treaty of Versailles (1919) contained 440 articles over 268 pages, while the treaties with Germany's minor allies covered an additional 680 pages.

Contrary to Wilson's promise of open covenants, the preliminaries of peace published on May 7 were not preliminary but final, save for small cosmetic changes. They were then presented to Germany's democratic leaders on a sign-them-or-starve basis. That ensured that all Germans, not just diehard nationalists, deplored the *Diktat*. Wilson already knew that Senate Republicans had grave misgivings about the League. But the unkindest cut was dispatched by his own bitter supporters. *The Nation*'s editorial of May 17 railed against "The Madness of Versailles," because of which the "one-time idol of democracy stands today discredited and condemned." It just proved anew that "wherever liberalism strikes hands with war it inevitably goes down." The *New Republic* reluctantly echoed its radical competitor on May 24. "The Treaty of Versailles subjects all liberalism and particularly that kind of liberalism which breathes the Christian spirit to a decisive test. If a war which was supposed to put an end to war culminates without strenuous protest by humane men and women in a treaty of peace which renders peace impossible, the liberalism which preached this meaning for the war will have committed suicide." Those secular Progressive journals got it right, if belatedly. Wilsonianism was self-defeating because liberal internationalist reform of the world could not proceed unless important aggrieved nations, Germany most of all, were genuinely appeased. But insofar as the Allied powers resisted appeasement, they themselves became major barriers to Wilsonian reforms, which in turn invited Americans to abandon them. In retrospect, any serious U.S. commitment to Europe after the Great War would have to be highly conditional and dependent on the Germans and Allies alike agreeing to whatever terms the Americans declared necessary. Wilsonianism required a U.S. hegemony that simply did not exist in 1919.

For all practical purposes the familiar fight over ratification of the Treaty of Versailles, which contained the League Covenant, was a heresy trial with Wilson in the dock. Progressive Republicans might be internationalist, support arbitration agreements, and even be willing to extend a security commitment to France as Wilson had been persuaded to do. But they rejected his Progressive ACR on the grounds that it was not really American any more. Senator Lodge, who was a far more cosmopolitan statesman and scholar than Wilson, agreed that American power should be a global force for good—but it must be American power and not that of some assembly of nations. Most of all, Lodge and his colleagues were fiercely jealous of the constitutional powers of Congress. "I do not wish to plunge blindly forward, misled by phrases and generalities, into undertakings which threaten worse results than the imperfect conditions now existing." Nor was he under any illusion that human nature was about to be purged of folly or that American experience could be universalized. "The United States is the world's best hope," said Lodge in August 1919, "but if you fetter her in the interests and quarrels of other nations, if you tangle her in the intrigues of Europe, you will destroy her power for good, and endanger her very existence. Leave her to march freely through the centuries to come, as in the years that have gone. Strong, generous, confident, she has nobly served mankind. Beware how you trifle with your marvelous inheritance; this great land of ordered liberty. For if we stumble and fall, freedom and civilization everywhere will go down in ruin." Lodge and Elihu Root crafted Fourteen Reservations sheltering the Constitution, sovereignty, and freedom of action and then appended them to the Treaty of Versailles. Most controversial was their watering down of Article 10, the League Covenant's collective security provision.

The treaty failed for the reason that Wilson stubbornly insisted his loyal Democrats oppose any and all reservations. He just could not compromise what had become in his mind the ark of a new covenant, a holy thing that belonged not to him or the Senate but to God. The League of Nations justified the war's death and destruction, exonerated Wilson himself, and was meant to redeem all the nefarious power political compromises in the treaties of peace. Accordingly Wilson embarked on an exhausting whistle-stop tour certain that his conviction and eloquence would arouse public opinion. Instead, he collapsed and then suffered a stroke. Lodge brought the treaty up for a vote in November 1919, whereupon it failed to get a two-thirds majority with or without reservations.

The fight was not over yet because at that juncture Wilson's civil religious base in the liberal churches rallied to the stricken commander-in-chief. The *Christian Century* even claimed the League of Nations was the fulfillment of the Lord's Prayer (thy kingdom come). By January 1920 the National Council of Churches' Committee on the Moral Aims of the War deposed on the Senate a pro-League petition signed by seventeen thousand pastors. (Perhaps Lodge then realized what a monster his "war party" had helped to unleash back in 1898.) But once the war fever chilled and censorship was lifted, it also became evident that not all Protestant churches backed Wilson. A Christian anti-internationalist movement rose up to deny the propriety and even the possibility of cooperating with non-Christian states. Conservative theologians, led by the formidable Princeton Presbyterian John Gresham Machen, damned Wilson's treaty as a "terrible crime against the truth." Premillennialists, who believed only the Messiah could initiate the kingdom of God, inveighed against the man-made mockery called the League of Nations. Few senators paid attention to the quarreling pastors. When Lodge staged a final vote in March 1920, the treaty, with and without reservations, fell short again. Lodge's post mortem was simple. "We have succeeded twice in creating a situation where Wilson either had to take the treaty [with reservations] or else be obliged to defeat it. He has twice taken the second alternative. His personal selfishness goes beyond what I have ever seen in any human being. It is so extreme that it is entirely unenlightened and stupid."

Wilson, of course, said the same about Lodge. But in the end there is no reason to elevate their personality clash beyond the level of epiphenomenon. Nor is there reason to think that a healthy Wilson would have been any more willing to bargain than the invalid. Nor is there reason to think that history would have played out much differently if the United States had joined the League of Nations. What did play out very differently was the course of American Civil Religion. Defeat of the League meant Wilson's Progressive ACR failed to become a new orthodoxy, even though imperialism and world war had rendered the old orthodoxy as bygone as Washington's World. A long cusp ensued during which Americans fretted, fought over, or just forgot what God Almighty expected of them in the twentieth century.

Roosevelt's World: The Civil Church Agonistes

No American had better Progressive credentials than Fighting Bob La Follette, but like most Republicans, he opposed the League of Nations. "I do not covet for this country a position in the world which history has shown would make us the objcct of endless jealousies and hatreds, involve us in perpetual war, and lead to the extinction of our domestic liberty. I, for one, harbor no ambition to see this country start upon the path which has lured other nations to their ruin. ... We cannot, without sacrificing this Republic, maintain world dominion for ourselves."

World dominion or the old republic? Neither of those extremes seemed remotely possible given the fact and the failure of Wilson's crusade. Yet that question was the subtext of all the debates over U.S. identity during the long cusp that defined Franklin D. Roosevelt's World. The great man, like his country, was profoundly split-minded. He rose to prominence as a Wilsonian Democrat, endorsed his mentor's internationalist agenda, and ran for vice president in 1920. Yet like his distant Republican cousin Theodore, he had served as assistant secretary of the navy and was a lifelong promoter of national power. Likewise, serving as president during the Great Depression, he had to govern from the left and was called a traitor to his class. Yet the conservative purpose of his New Deal was to save corporate America during a decade when capitalism elsewhere was in headlong retreat. Likewise, he presided during the most materialistic era of American and world politics;

hence the New Deal was the first great reform movement in U.S. history that was wholly secular. Yet as high priest of the civil religion, he needed to persuade Americans that "the sufferings of this present time are not worthy to be compared with the glory that is to be revealed" (Romans 8:18). Could Roosevelt discover some synthesis that might resolve even one, much less all, of those tensions? The answer seemed decidedly negative, and that is why FDR employed rhetorical indirection, deception, pretense, and sleight-of-hand . . . until "The World of Tomorrow" dawned sunny and hot on April 30, 1939. That day, the 150th anniversary of George Washington's inauguration, marked the opening of the New York World's Fair, and it gave the president a clue.

The depression was far from over. In fact, the economy suffered a 4.5 percent relapse in 1938 that pushed unemployment back up to 19 percent. But the financial and political elites of New York, backed by virtually all the nation's great manufacturing firms, decided to throw an advance party for what Henry Luce would baptize "the American Century." Chicago's Century of Progress exhibition in 1933–34 had turned a profit in the midst of depression, and San Francisco was preparing its own Golden Gate International Exposition of 1939. So New York planned the biggest world's fair of all on a 1,262-acre site in Flushing Meadows. Its theme was the culture of abundance that American business was soon to bestow on the whole world through the magical power of applied science.

Control over science was hotly contested in the 1930s, not only in totalitarian countries, but also in democracies, where Progressive natural and social scientists such as Harold Urey and John Dewey despised its commercialization. They extolled the national benefits to be achieved through planned progress by government experts and even imagined the international scientific community as a model for world peace. Accordingly, physicist Gerald Wendt formed an advisory committee, chaired by Albert Einstein, to use the world's fair to educate the public about the potential of pure science. But the corporations and industrial designers who financed and built the exhibits politely ignored the academics. The resulting spectacle, beginning with the 610-foot-tall Trylon spire and 180-foot wide Perisphere, astounded the fair's 44 million visitors. Urey blasted them as meaningless symbols having nothing to do with science. But they had everything to do with marketing the Democracity displayed inside the sphere: a panoramic vision of the ideal future that corporate technology and mass production would soon make routine. Those symbols prepared the public for the specific wonders on display in the pavilions. Westinghouse boasted Electro the Moto-Man, a seven-foot robot that talked, discerned, and even smoked cigarettes. AT&T offered folks a free long-distance telephone call and tracked the progress of the signals on a huge electric map of the United States. Borden displayed an automatic milking machine. RCA and General Electric debuted the amazing new invention called television. Chrysler's exhibit on the future of transportation featured rocket travel in outer space. Du Pont revealed wonders of chemistry, including nylon and lucite; Kodak, the latest in color photography; and GE's House of Magic, all manner of gee-whiz electrical tricks. The fair, as historian of science Peter Kuznick put it, was a veritable "exercise in mechanolatry; it represented the greatest affirmation of technological faith in a decade ambivalent about the fruits of technological promise."

Nothing topped General Motors' Futurama, which transported visitors to a future America, the year 1960 to be exact. By clever projection and optical illusion the exhibit displayed an apparently life-sized world of fulsome farmlands and pristine cities (powered by "atomic energy"), linked by super-highways streaming with luxury automobiles every American was destined to own. The fair seems wishful thinking in retrospect given the world of 1939 was poised on the edge of a cliff. But 1960 was really just two decades away, and the displays were really just straightforward projections. In 1926, the year that planning for the U.S. highway system was finished, the price of a Model T Ford had been reduced to $260, and U.S. motor sales surpassed $3 billion. In 1929 the industry churned out 5.3 million units. By 1933 the federal Research Committee on Social Trends diagnosed the automobile psychology that had captured Americans. The Roosevelt administration spent over $4 billion on roads for an automobile fleet that continued to grow rapidly despite the depression. General Motors even organized a consortium of oil, tire, and construction firms to buy up trolley lines or else bribed officials to shut them down. Thus, Americans not easily seduced by advertising would be given no choice. The 1939 World's Fair's motto printed in the official guidebook even made the point explicit: "Science Finds—Industry Applies—Man Conforms."

Mainstream media mostly raved. Henry Luce's *Life* and *Fortune* magazines called the fair "a magnificent monument by and to American business" and a "great free-for-all of industrial public relations." To be sure, Walter Lippmann spied pretense behind the Futurama: "General Motors has spent a small fortune to convince the American public that if it wishes to enjoy the full benefit of private enterprise in motor manufacturing, it will have to rebuild its cities and its highways by public enterprise." What Lippmann did not anticipate was the gestating alliance between business and government that would make promotion of the auto and oil industries a major priority for Roosevelt's administration and those to come after the war.

The following year the German blitzkrieg overran the Low Countries and France and chased the British off the continent. On May 30, 1940, Roosevelt summoned to the White House the very leaders of American business he had denounced as money changers in the temple eight years before. He especially welcomed William Knudsen, the legendary production genius from General Motors, because Bernard Baruch, chairman of Woodrow Wilson's War Industries Board, had recommended him highly. Could he tell the president how to start and sustain a crash rearmament program throughout industry and across the nation? Knudsen not only could and did, but he also coined a term Roosevelt soon made famous: arsenal of democracy. Dr. New Deal in fact became Dr. Win-the-War on that day, although Roosevelt dared not tell the public that until Pearl Harbor, eighteen months in the future. The United States would become an empire of production through the power and ingenuity of its manufacturers and labor unions under stringent federal oversight, justified in turn by world war and validated by nationalism.

The name for that kind of system in Europe was corporatism, fascism, or national socialism. But the World of Tomorrow Roosevelt would design, Walt Disney would promote, and Superman would personify was to be a friendly fascism securing truth, justice, and the American way, freedom in abundance and abundance in freedom, ultimately for the whole human race. That was the magical synthesis FDR sought in order to reconcile Wilsonian internationalism with American nationalism, the New Deal with Big Business, and materialism with mission in an updated version of Progressive civil religion. If faith in Providence was losing its power to hold in thrall the American mind, faith in Progress must take its place. The name of the Lord who would trample out the vintage and loose the fateful lightning was Production.

Three months after Roosevelt launched his quiet rearmament campaign, an exile from Europe arrived in America. Salvador Dalí, the Spanish painter, was already known in New York for his art and hilarious self-promotion, including a bizarre pavilion at the World's Fair. The French Surrealist movement, which was heavily Communist, even excommunicated Dalí for selling out to American commercialism. Who else would write a wartime novel about a fashion salon for automobiles? But the métier of great artists is to feel the future and give it expression, whether or not they themselves understand what inspires them. In 1943 Dalí did exactly that when he painted the "Geopoliticus Child Watching the Birth of the New Man." His notes for it contain a list of words—parachute, paranaissance, protection, cupola, placenta, Catholicism, egg, earthly distortion, biological ellipse—that makes little sense until one views the painting, whereupon it makes perfect sense.

Dalí depicts the globe as a great egg, above and beneath which are drapes that represent a broken placenta. Out of the egg hatches a fully grown man, writhing with the effort of cracking the shell. A fluid runs down from the crack, but it is blood rather than yolk. ("For we know that the whole creation groans and suffers the pains of childbirth together until now" [Romans 8:22].) Since the man has burst through in North America, he obviously represents the United States. His head is not yet visible, but already the left hand has twisted around to clutch the British Isles in a gesture of possession as much as protection. Africa and Latin America seem enlarged and Europe diminished, as if Dalí sensed the tide turning, not only in this war, but also in the flow of world history. From the right foreground two naked figures observe this fantastic birth. One is an androgynous adult who points as if to say, "Behold!" But the adult casts a very short shadow, indicating perhaps that his/her era is reflecting the sun at high noon. The other, Geopoliticus Child, cowers behind the adult's legs but dares to peek at the egg. This toddler casts a very long shadow, indicating his/her geopolitical era is reflecting the sun at daybreak.

Nobody knows for sure what Dalí meant to convey or whether he had anything premeditated in mind. Like so much of his work, "Geopoliticus Child" seems like one of those dreams, neither sweet dream nor nightmare, all of us now call surreal. But the United States whose emergence he witnessed was surely the mightiest of all military-industrial complexes and determined to plough under foot anything that impeded construction of the World of Tomorrow. Europeans like Dalí would soon have to choose between the hard materialism of the Soviet Union and the soft materialism of the United States. It goes without saying that almost all of them favored the American version. Even Dalí's spiritual leader, Pope Pius XII, threw in his lot with the West. But they could not pretend to be happy about it.

CHAPTER SEVENTEEN

Modern Explosions

IT SHOULD NOT BE surprising that Americans pretended to crave a return to normalcy after the Great War and that Republican politicians pretended to give it to them. For the 1920s brought explosive change. It was, wrote the sagacious historian John Lukacs, "the modern decade—perhaps the last, perhaps the only modern decade." In Europe all traditional forms of political and cultural authority had been shattered by the war; hence the modern art, literature, music, architecture, theater, film, and totalitarian ideologies all expressed a Freudian mix of hedonism and despair—"anomie," the French called it. But in the United States the explosion of modernism was only the latest and most buoyant expression of the cult of progress. In the 1920s Henry Ford's model of lower prices for consumers and higher wages for workers through rationalized mass production became standard throughout American industry. Middle-class people (and some 80 percent of Americans defined themselves as middle-class) bought automobiles, household appliances, radios, and farm machinery; flocked to watch Hollywood movies in palatial theaters; marveled at skyscrapers in Chicago and New York; and made idols of sports figures and aviators. Education was valued as never before because it equated to progress and, in John Dewey's philosophy, democracy. Feminism, sex education, and even Prohibition were triumphs of Progressivism. Did not Ford himself say that booze had to go out when modern industry and the motor car came in?

Nevertheless, Progressive Americans felt real anxiety about their place in the world once Wilson's ideological bridle was removed. His civil religion had prophesied that a crusading America could transform the world, but that turned out to be heresy. Instead, it seemed the world was transforming America in frightening ways, most immediately through immigration.

By 1883, when Emma Lazarus wrote "Give me your tired, your poor, Your huddled masses yearning to breathe free," Congress had already passed a Chinese Exclusion Act. By 1903, when her poem was etched on the Statue of Liberty, Theodore Roosevelt was seeking an executive agreement to restrict Japanese immigration. By the end of the war the nation's Protestant majority grew sufficiently alarmed about millions of South and East European immigrants (the hyphenated Americans) to ban "white" immigration for the first time in history. The Emergency Quota Act of 1921 established an annual ceiling of 3 percent, based on each nationality's share of the U.S. population in 1890. The Immigration Act of 1924 reduced the quota to 2 percent and made it permanent. To dismiss those acts as racist misses the point. They reflected a lack of confidence in *The Melting Pot*, a civil religious romance popularized by the Russian Jewish playwright Israel Zangwill in 1908. The disturbing reality appeared to suggest that a portion, at least, of immigrants meant not to assimilate but to subvert America.

The Wilson administration bore no responsibility for the Bolshevik coup d'état (except insofar as it had urged Alexander Kerensky's Provisional Government to stay in the war against Germany). But the United States did perversely contribute to the survival of the Communist regime by (a) defeating Germany, the only outside power in a position to crush it, while (b) feeding Bolshevik propaganda by making an anodyne intervention in the Arctic, and (c) occupying eastern Siberia to keep it out of Japanese hands until, as it perversely turned out, the Soviets arrived to reclaim it. Meanwhile, in March 1919 Lenin founded the Third International, which committed all Communist parties to "the overthrow of the international bourgeoisie and for the creation of an international Soviet republic as a transition stage to the complete abolition of the State." Two American Communist parties numbering more than ten thousand members formed by late summer 1919. Only one in twenty was a native English speaker. "More than half of the agitators in the so-called Bolshevik movement were Yiddish" and based on Manhattan's Lower East Side. Or so a Methodist missionary just back from Russia told a Senate committee investigating (in a bizarre conflation of causes) "German and Jewish propaganda through brewing and liquor interests." In September 1919, just before his collapse, Wilson echoed the views of Secretary of State Robert Lansing, calling Bolshevism "the poison of disorder, the poison of revolt, the poison of chaos," and "the negation of everything that is American." The Senate responded by setting up a subcommittee to study the alien phenomenon, the first in a forty-year sequence of Congressional bodies defining and investigating un-American affairs.

The immediate upshot was the Justice Department's 1919–20 preemptive raids on the offices and safe houses of Bolsheviks, anarchists, and other radical leftists, led by Attorney General A. Mitchell Palmer. His agents arrested more than five hundred aliens and turned them over to the Labor Department for deportation. Palmer was assisted by an aggressive young lawyer named J. Edgar Hoover, whom he made head of the new Intelligence Division of the Bureau of Investigation. Meanwhile, a second threat emerged in the form of the shadowy Galleanists. In 1919 these Italian anarchists planted bombs in eight cities, one of which targeted Palmer and his New York neighbors, Franklin and Eleanor Roosevelt. Most likely the anarchists were also responsible for the bomb that exploded on Wall Street in 1920 and killed or seriously wounded 173 people.

Plenty of home-grown violence accompanied the collapse of Wilson's crusade. Labor unions reacted against wartime regimentation and postwar recession in a wave of strikes. The radical Industrial Workers of the World (IWW) helped to spark a general strike in Seattle in 1919, during which dockworkers refused to load ships bound for the American troops in Siberia. A 1921 United Mine Workers' strike in West Virginia turned into the Battle of Blair Mountain as management and labor both fielded armies stiffened by veterans of the trenches. Deadly race riots provoked by white fear and resentment killed and wounded hundreds in Chicago, Elaine (Ark.), East St. Louis, and Tulsa from 1917 to 1921. Jim Crow strengthened its grip north and south of the Ohio River as the Ku Klux Klan reached its flood tide and added Catholics, Jews, and alcohol to its list of enemies.

It seemed apparent in the 1920s that rural and small-town American Protestants were losing their grip on the culture and politics. That probably explains why patriotism was never more on public display. The American Legion became the new Grand Army of the Republic, rapidly expanding to nearly a million. Upon its founding, the Legion called on religious denominations to add the American Creed, composed during the war, to their sectarian creeds. Its own 1919 preamble declared: "For God and Country we associate ourselves together for the following purposes: To uphold and defend the Constitution of the United States of America; to maintain law and order; to foster and perpetuate a 100 Percent Americanism," which required, among other things, that its members "combat the autocracy of both the classes and the masses." Alas, one lodge in Washington state celebrated the Legion's creation by provoking a pitched battle with the local IWW post. But far from condemning such behavior, the Legion commander proudly likened his organization to the Italian Fascists combating leftists in the streets. As late as 1930 Mussolini was invited to address the American Legion convention.

During the 1920s reciting the pledge of allegiance became a daily ritual for American schoolchildren. The movement begun by Wilson to make "The Star-Spangled Banner" the national anthem triumphed in 1931. Towns and small cities turned out for a growing "church calendar" of civic holidays (the latest of which were Flag Day and Armistice Day) to hear local politicians posture and high school bands imitate John Philip Sousa. In the 1920s state legislatures passed laws to enforce politically correct conformity, especially for recent immigrants or their children. Progressive Wisconsin's law was especially revealing since it forbade "the teaching of any historical facts [sic] considered unpatriotic by politicians and the people." New Jersey banned textbooks deemed to "misrepresent, distort, doubt or deny the events leading up to the Declaration of Independence or to any war in which this country has been engaged." Back in the nineteenth century Americans wore their patriotism more lightly because the ethnic and religious composition of their nation was never in serious doubt. In fact, prior to the Civil War the only civic holidays observed were the Fourth of July and Washington's birthday. People honored the Stars and Stripes but made no fetish of the flag and consecrated no national anthem. Their public schools, following New England models, taught morals and discipline through patriotic textbooks that took it for granted the way to please God was to be a good citizen. All that began to change in the Progressive era because of the influx of foreign people, ideologies, and religions. By the 1920s American patriotism resembled a strident nationalism, hardened, defined, and, if necessary, imposed.

Most alarming, the modern explosions blew up the Protestant consensus. Fundamentalists and Progressives waged a cultural war, the national symbol of which was, of course, the 1925 Scopes Monkey Trial. It began as a publicity stunt in a small Tennessee town and became a *cause célèbre* because Progressive Chicago lawyer Clarence Darrow argued the case for Darwin and Nebraska Populist William Jennings Bryan argued the case for the Bible. But the outcome of the larger culture war was never in doubt. America's elites worshiped at the altars of science and material culture, which meant Jesus was relevant only insofar as he could be reinvented as a proto-American Progressive. Liberal theologians readily imagined Jesus the preacher of the Social Gospel. But after the war the rapid spread of professional business schools, the prestige of innovative industrialists, and the political ascendancy of Progressive Republicans combined to inspire a complementary view of Jesus as entrepreneurial capitalist! The 1925 mega–best seller *The Man Nobody Knows* portrayed Christ as a "virile go-getting he-man of business, the first great advertiser, a premier group organizer, master executive, a champion publicity-grabber." Business leaders praised the Lamb of God as the greatest salesman in history. The dean of the University of Chicago's Divinity School solemnly pronounced business the maker of morals. Hence Calvin Coolidge, the last (devolved) New England Puritan to occupy the White House, spoke conventional wisdom when he granted that the chief business of the American people was business but went on to emphasize that pursuit of wealth did not lead to moral decay. "Wealth is the product of industry, ambition, character and untiring effort. In all experience, the accumulation of wealth means the multiplication of schools, the increase of knowledge, the dissemination of intelligence, the encouragement of science, the broadening of outlook, the expansion of liberties, the widening of culture. . . . So long as wealth is made the means and not the end, we need not greatly fear it."

The Great War had made the United States the world's preeminent economic, financial, commercial, and naval power. But Wilson, like the cult leader William Miller in the 1830s, had promised Americans the millennium. When it did not occur, the clergy who had signed on to his civil religion were left to explain what, if anything, the blood sacrifice of 117,000 Americans had achieved. Indeed, the only denominations that emerged from the war with strange new respect were the Quakers and Mennonites, so recently damned for their pacifism. Otherwise, Protestants were all over the place in the 1920s. Clergy whose churches derived from Anglicanism, such as Episcopalians and Methodists, tended to support Britain's efforts to make the League of Nations work and hoped the United States might someday join. Those whose churches derived from Calvinism and Lutheranism split down the middle on the question of internationalism, while Baptists and other fundamentalists pronounced anathema on the belief that man could presume to create heaven on earth. In their view the Old World was incorrigible and the United States would only foul itself by joining its struggles for power.

Progressive clergy, however, never lost faith in America. To be sure, they repented of having trusted in war but otherwise insisted as fervently as before that America was destined to lead mankind to perpetual peace. In 1922 Sidney Gulick wrote *The Christian Crusade for a Warless World* and Samuel Zane Batten published *If America Fail: Our National Mission and Our Possible Future.* Throughout the Bible, wrote Batten, God used governments to fulfill his prophecies, and today "America is indeed a called and chosen nation." He assumed the key to American history could be found in the evolution of Israel. That is, just as it was God's will that Judaism spread to the Gentiles through Christianity, so it was God's will that

America perform a Messianic service. In short: "America is a gospel." Harry Emerson Fosdick and his brother Raymond of the Rockefeller Foundation believed the United States was destined to usher in world peace. So did Henry Ford, who had opposed U.S. belligerence in 1917 but became an avid supporter of the League of Nations.

No journal reflected Progressive Protestant opinion better than the *Christian Century*, which began publication out of Chicago in January 1900 and was closely connected with the University of Chicago, recently founded by John D. Rockefeller. Its first president, William Rainey Harper, raided the best universities in the United States and Europe (especially Germany) to staff the faculty with the most modern academics. In historian Elesha Coffman's words, Chicago's Divinity School became the "most conspicuous American exponent of the new methods of Biblical study" with an emphasis on pragmatism, entrepreneurship, and developmental theology. Harry Fosdick, Rockefeller's pastor, explained: "If the theology of a time is various and changing, it is because the life of the time is various, growing, and transitional." No place and time were more various than America in the twentieth century. From 1908 to 1947 its editor-bishop, Charles Clayton Morrison, made the *Christian Century* the flagship of Progressive Protestant thought by promoting liberal theology, the Social Gospel, and the ecumenism of the National and World Councils of Churches. On political and social issues it was virtually indistinguishable from *The Nation*, the *New Republic*, and the Progressive Catholic *Commonweal: A Review of Religion, Politics, and Culture*, founded in 1924. Thus did the currents in liberal Christianity (and Reform Judaism) meet and mix with the currents in secular opinion, but devoid of a cause around which to build a new civil religious orthodoxy.

What about anti-communism? Wasn't hostility to the evil, atheistic Soviet Union sufficient to unite all Americans except those few, mostly foreign, elements already fingered as traitors? Evidently not because Wilson's diplomacy toward the Russian Civil War had proven even less effective than his treatment of Germany. The Big Three had tried out four strategies at the Paris Peace Conference: a peace conference on the island of Prinkipo, American journalist William Bullitt's mission to Moscow, Winston

Churchill's appeal for a military crusade, and the Herbert Hoover–Fridtjof Nansen plan to provide food relief to the Russians. None of the four strategies (which would be tried again and again during the Cold War) got off the ground. So the Wilson administration just refused to recognize the Soviet regime unless it stopped promoting world revolution and compensated Americans for the nationalization of assets and repudiation of tsarist debts.

Non-recognition did not mean mutual isolation, however, because some American humanitarians and businessmen—so often the pioneers of U.S. foreign relations—readily engaged the Soviets. After the civil war ended and the USSR was declared, Hoover got his chance to deliver food to starving Russians, doubtless saving many lives but also (as he later admitted) helping the Communists consolidate their power. Capitalists spied opportunities in Russia after Lenin adopted the relaxed New Economic Policy and Armand Hammer opened the Amtorg commercial office. Recent Jewish immigrants to the United States cheered the Bolsheviks for purging Russia of anti-Semitism. Zara Witkin, a wealthy California construction engineer, was not the only one electrified by the Communist vision of the future. After all, Lenin's motto was "Communism equals Soviet power plus electrification of the whole country," a slogan that made him sound like a Progressive in a hurry. Better still was the longer version: "Communism = Soviet power + Prussian railway order + American technology and organization of trusts + American public education." To more radical Social Gospel adherents, like Chicago's Raymond Robins, the Bolsheviks seemed to be practicing effective Christianity, their atheism notwithstanding.

There were even rumors to the effect that Soviet atheism was retreating. In 1927 Chicago evangelist Paul Peterson returned from Russia full of excitement about a mighty revival that afforded "the greatest missionary opportunity of our time." That same year Julius F. Hecker argued in *Religion under the Soviets* that the classless society fulfilled a Christian ideal and thus prepared the ground for a spiritual culture. Then the Stalin era began, and renewed persecution of sectarians (Protestant converts) landed their pastors in prison. The *Literary Digest* wrote: "Red Russia's reported crucifixion of all faiths and mockery of God has at last set the whole world ablaze with indignation." Indeed, Protestants, Catholics, and Jews jointly supported the resolution of Congressman Hamilton Fish, Jr. (R., N.Y.) that declared repugnant the denial of religious freedom. But American fellow travelers never stopped hoping. In 1933, the year Franklin D. Roosevelt recognized the Soviet Union, prominent Methodist pastor Harry F. Ward published *In Place of Profit: Social Incentives in the Soviet Union.* Its cover displayed beams of heavenly light illuminating the Russian people.

Quarreling Protestant factions had one thing in common, at least. They all turned pacifist in their revulsion against Wilson's war and demanded disarmament, as if the demonic weapons and not human beings themselves had been the agents of evil.

CHAPTER EIGHTEEN

The Progressive Republican Denouement

THE PRESIDENTS WHO SERVED as the nation's high priests between 1921 and 1933 shunned messianic ambitions and reaffirmed most of the principles of neo-Classical ACR. But they continued to voice religious tropes, while their non-entanglement talk was pretense. All represented the Progressive wing of the Republican Party. In his 1921 inaugural address Warren G. Harding spoke candidly of his civil faith:

> I must utter my belief in the divine inspiration of the founding fathers. Surely there must have been God's intent in the making of this new-world Republic. ... We have seen civil, human, and religious liberty verified and glorified. In the beginning the Old World scoffed at our experiment; today our foundations of political and social belief stand unshaken, a precious inheritance to ourselves, an inspiring example of freedom and civilization to all mankind. Let us express renewed and strengthened devotion, in grateful reverence for the immortal beginning, and utter our confidence in the supreme fulfillment. ... We are ready to associate with the nations of the world [to promote dis-

armament and arbitration, but] a world supergovernment is
contrary to everything we cherish. . . . This is not selfishness, it is sanctity. It is not aloofness, it is security.

Having thus sanctified the American people's decision not to
compromise their sovereignty in the League of Nations, Harding
quickly assured the world that America would continue to "promote
that brotherhood of mankind which must be God's highest conception of human relationship." He closed by expressing his "reassur-
ance in the belief of the God-given destiny of our Republic,"
implored "the favor and guidance of God in His Heaven," and
asked "What doth the Lord require of thee but to do justly, and to
love mercy, and to walk humbly with thy God (Micah 6:8). This I
plight to God and country."

Harding's distinguished Cabinet, led by Secretary of State
Charles Evans Hughes, Secretary of the Treasury Andrew Mellon,
and Secretary of Commerce Herbert Hoover, did its best to translate the president's sermon into operational policies. They were
anything but isolationist. On the contrary, their energetic diplomacy and that of their successors appeared to resolve the crises in
Europe and Asia bequeathed by Wilson's war. Moreover, they were
abetted in their responsibilities by a newly self-conscious eastern
establishment. In 1921 former secretary of state Elihu Root
founded the Council on Foreign Relations to organize diplomats,
academics, and lawyers representing investment bankers and big
manufacturers into a Progressive steering committee. The council's
high-minded goal was to engineer foreign policy from the commanding heights on Wall Street in order to promote international
law and to create favorable conditions for American business
abroad. Its authoritative journal, *Foreign Affairs*, inspired by a former dean of the Harvard Business School, dated from 1922. Its
budget was supported by targeted donations from "the thousand
richest Americans" and later by generous grants from the Ford,
Rockefeller, and Carnegie Foundations. The council entertained a
variety of opinions but could be seen in retrospect to have anticipated U.S. foreign policy initiatives far more often than not.

That is not to suggest that a unitary big business cabal took
over the country. The U.S. economy was too large, complex, and

diverse for that. Rather, the agricultural, manufacturing, and banking sectors continued to clash over fiscal policy, regulation, and tariffs. Several powerful firms had mixed interests (e.g., J. P. Morgan's
acquisition of U.S. Steel), while whole geographical regions viewed
the world from strikingly different perspectives. What can be said
of the U.S. economy in the 1920s is that small farmers no longer
counted except as occasional objects of federal charity. Their bi-
metallism and Populist parties had been crushed, and rural America
was in full retreat, demographically and politically. The banking
sector, by contrast, was rapidly rising thanks to the friendly Federal
Reserve System created in 1913 (essentially a committee or club of
banks charged with policing itself) and thanks to the world war,
which made the U.S. dollar trumps. But New York bankers could
not write their own ticket because American industry, huge as it
was, had only begun to realize its potential. The steel, automotive,
tire, oil, chemical, electrical, medical, aeronautical, communications, processed food, mass marketing, construction, and dozens of
other industries wielded tremendous clout.

Manufacturers, through their lobbyists, were primarily responsible for persuading Congress to pass the Fordney-McCumber Tariff,
the highest in American history, in 1922. Its effects were baleful for
American farmers, whose wartime foreign markets had collapsed;
dubious for industrial firms that prioritized exports; and awkward
for international banks since Britain and France were blocked from
earning through exports the dollars needed to fund their war debts
to U.S. bond holders. Deadlock on war debts only gave Allies like
France more incentive to squeeze Germany for the war reparations
imposed in the Treaty of Versailles. That economic war after the
war culminated in the 1923 French occupation of the industrial
Ruhr valley. Germans retaliated through a general strike funded by
the Berlin government to the point that the deutsche mark was ru-
ined and Communists and Nazis agitated in the streets. That meant
Germany, too, needed American loans in order to back a new currency, save democracy, and establish a genuine peace in Europe.

Meanwhile, the tariff added injury to the insult Wilson had
delivered to Japan when he opposed a racial equality plank in the
Covenant of the League of Nations. White Americans feared a tide
of Japanese immigrants might wash up on their shores (as did

Canadians, Australians, and New Zealanders). Now the Congress was closing American ports to Japanese exports as well. That made it all the more imperative that crowded, industrial Japan expand, if necessary by force, into China. Given that Japan was one of the victorious powers in the Great War, had picked up Germany's Pacific colonies, maintained its 1902 alliance with Britain, and boasted a world-class navy, it behooved the U.S. State Department to reach some kind of modus vivendi to pacify the Pacific.

At his inaugural Harding had promised to foster the brotherhood of man desired by God. Charles Evans Hughes made good on that promise, at least for a while. In the Asian theater he invited Japan and all the European powers with concessions in China to the Washington Conference of 1921–22—but not before he "persuaded" the British to terminate their alliance with Tokyo by issuing veiled threats over naval armaments, war debts, and Irish home rule. Then he shocked the assembled delegates by insisting they freeze or roll back their navies. The Five-Power Treaty locked the U.S., British, and Japanese navies into a 10:10:6 ratio, thereby serving as a kind of halfway house on America's climb to supremacy. The Four-Power Treaty obliged the parties to recognize each other's Pacific possessions and cease to fortify bases. The Nine-Power Treaty required all parties to respect both the sovereignty of the new Chinese republic and the Open Door policy for international trade and investment. It all made William Jennings Bryan weep for joy in the gallery. Hundreds of American missionaries in China were elated as well. It seemed that the U.S. government was fulfilling the words of the prophet Isaiah to "make straight the way of the Lord" in the land with the largest harvest of souls on earth.

Hughes then turned his attention in Europe, where he waited until the French and Germans had worn themselves out before throwing them a lifeline in the 1924 Dawes Plan. Its terms included French evacuation of the Ruhr, German fulfillment of a reparations schedule, Allied oversight of the Reichsbank, and 800 million gold marks in loans from American banks. That allowed Germany, France, and Britain to return their currencies to the gold standard and their economies to 1913 levels of production. The 1925 Locarno security pacts, 1926 Franco-German commercial accords, and 1927 German entry into the League of Nations proceeded apace. Since all that was achieved without any commitment of U.S. soldiers or Treasury dollars, the public heartily approved. In fact, Treasury secretary Mellon's policy of lower tax rates worked so well that significantly more revenue was raised from wealthier Americans while poorer people paid almost nothing. The national debt, which Wilson's war had magnified nearly *eight times*, from $3.6 billion to $27.4 billion, fell to $17.6 billion.

Harding died in 1923, but his successor, Coolidge, reelected the following year, gave what in form was a standard second inaugural address in that it listed (with suitable humility, of course) the administration's first-term achievements. He applauded the limitation of armaments while declaring prudently that the United States would seek to maintain "a balanced force, intensely modern, capable of defense by sea and land, beneath the surface and in the air. But it should be so conducted that all the world may see in it, not a menace, but an instrument of security and peace." Coolidge took great satisfaction in Americans' postwar prosperity and willingness to help other nations. "Realizing that we can not live unto ourselves alone, we have contributed of our resources and our counsel to the relief of the suffering and the settlement of the disputes among the European nations. Because of what America is and what America has done, a firmer courage, a higher hope, inspires the heart of all humanity." Coolidge promised continued success so long as citizens remembered that economics involved moral issues. "It is not property but the right to hold property, both great and small, which our Constitution guarantees. All owners of property are charged with a service. These rights and duties have been revealed, through the conscience of society, to have a divine sanction. The very stability of our society rests upon production and conservation. For individuals or for governments to waste and squander their resources is to deny these rights and disregard these obligations. The result of economic dissipation to a nation is always moral decay."

Finally, Coolidge made a stirring invocation of old-time civil religion, delivered in a litany of flattering pronouncements of the sort Aristotle had taught were irresistibly seductive:

Here stands our country, an example of tranquillity at home, a patron of tranquillity abroad. Here stands its

Government, aware of its might but obedient to its conscience. Here it will continue to stand, seeking peace and prosperity, solicitous for the welfare of the wage earner, promoting enterprise, developing waterways and natural resources, attentive to the intuitive counsel of womanhood, encouraging education, desiring the advancement of religion, supporting the cause of justice and honor among the nations. America seeks no earthly empire built on blood and force. No ambition, no temptation, lures her to thought of foreign dominions. The legions which she sends forth are armed, not with the sword, but with the cross. The higher state to which she seeks the allegiance of all mankind is not of human, but of divine origin. She cherishes no purpose save to merit the favor of Almighty God.

The truth was not quite so pristine. For instance, Harding and Coolidge invoked the Roosevelt Corollary's police power to justify U.S. military protectorates over Cuba, the Dominican Republic, and Haiti and to send the Marines into Honduras and Nicaragua in 1924. Indeed, Roosevelt would no doubt have applauded the Progressive mix of nationalism and internationalism in the postwar Republican foreign policies. It even seemed in the mid-1920s that all good things went together: peace, prosperity, democracy, and disarmament, not only in North America, but also in Europe and East Asia. As for the United States itself, it simply enjoyed the most favorable geopolitics imaginable, a fact Coolidge celebrated in his 1926 State of the Union address: "We have no traditional enemies. We are not embarrassed over any disputed territory. We have no possessions that are coveted by others; they have none that are coveted by us. Our borders are unfortified. We fear no one; no one fears us."

That was the happy interlude that gave rise to the 1928 Kellogg-Briand Pact that renounced war as an instrument of national policy. French foreign minister Aristide Briand, who had become the incarnation of the League of Nations' Spirit of Geneva, suggested the pact in hopes of distracting attention from France's reluctance to pay down its war debts nor reduce its army. He might even dupe

the United States into making a moral commitment, at least, to uphold the Versailles boundaries in Europe. Secretary of State Frank
Kellogg turned the tables by suggesting a treaty all nations could
sign. But that invited numerous countries, France included, to append so many reservations that it was worse than no treaty at all.
Senator Lodge ruefully noted that "hundreds of newspapers are
hailing the treaty as a great step towards permanent peace, and
thousands of persons are being made to believe that something really has been done. . . . A sense of false security is thus created and
official sanction is thereby given to a most portentous misconcep-
tion. The conception of renouncing war by governmental fiat
seems inherently absurd." The Senate nevertheless ratified the
Kellogg-Briand Pact 85–1.

The treaty meant a great deal to Progressive Protestants, not
least Herbert Hoover, the Quaker who deemed the pact "auspicious
for the future happiness of mankind." Hoover predicted the renun-
ciation of war "will be felt in a large proportion of all future international acts. The magnificent opportunity and the compelling
duty now open to us should spur us on to the fulfillment of every
opportunity that is calculated to implement this Treaty and to extend the policy which it so nobly sets forth." In 1928, having served
as secretary of commerce for nearly eight years, Hoover stepped
down to run for president. He was a real-life "Philip Dru," whom
everyone recognized as a great engineer, humanitarian, and omni-
competent manager. Among Hoover's accomplishments were the
informal ententes he helped to establish among governments and
corporations for the organization of global markets in shipping, te-
legraphy, oil, and aviation. Though a dour campaigner, he won in a
landslide.

Hoover declared his 1929 inauguration another "consecration
under God to the highest office in service of our people. I assume
this trust in the humility of knowledge that only through the guidance of Almighty Providence can I hope to discharge its ever-
increasing burdens." He knew the American people understood
"the profound truth that our own progress, prosperity, and peace
are interlocked with the progress, prosperity, and peace of all humanity." He congratulated Americans "that we have no desire for
territorial expansion, for economic or other domination of other

peoples. Such purposes are repugnant to our ideals of human freedom. . . . We not only desire peace with the world, but to see peace maintained throughout the world. We wish to advance the reign of justice and reason toward the extinction of force." Accordingly, Hoover praised the Kellogg-Briand Pact as a big step forward toward the arbitration of international disputes but preached that peace "will become a reality only through self-restraint and active effort in friendliness and helpfulness. I covet for this administration a record of having further contributed to advance the cause of peace."

History happens, especially when leaders and nations think they have everything under control. Just seven months after Hoover's paean to peace the Wall Street Crash threw the United States into a Great Depression unlike all previous panics. This one could not be dismissed as divine punishment for slavery, greed, drink, or apostasy. This one punished even the most hard-working, abstemious families. This one defied the business cycle and the strenuous efforts of the great humanitarian in the White House. Congress made matters worse by pushing through an even higher Smoot-Hawley Tariff, exacerbating a beggar-thy-neighbor trade war that pushed other nations down the road to default, devaluation, unemployment, and autarky.

Hoover tried desperately to get nations to cooperate lest they all descend into the maelstrom, but nothing worked. The British and their dominions jettisoned the gold standard and free trade in favor of a system of imperial preference. Germans deserted their centrist parties for Nazis, Communists, and splinter groups, thereby voting democracy out of existence. Hoover hoped the nations might at least cut wasteful military spending in light of the depression, and the United States, Britain, and Japan did conclude a follow-up treaty in 1930. But the World Disarmament Conference in Geneva deadlocked because France refused to disarm, prompting Germany to insist on a right to rearm. Only in Latin America did Hoover make headway by retracting Roosevelt's Corollary to the Monroe Doctrine in 1930, withdrawing U.S. occupations in the Caribbean, and mediating a dangerous boundary dispute among Bolivia, Peru, and Chile. He thus anticipated the Good Neighbor Policy identified with his successor.

Japan posed the most immediate challenge. Buffeted by the depression, the American tariff and immigration restrictions, and Chinese hostility toward the Open Door policy, Japanese civil authorities surrendered initiative to their military. In September 1931 the Kwantung Army burst out of its concession in southern Manchuria, seized the entire mineral-rich province, and set up a puppet state. The League of Nations commission confined its response to a mild rebuke, which was sufficient to cause Japan to quit the League. The pacifist U.S. president had neither the will nor the means nor the national support to do more than refuse to recognize the Japanese conquest in what became known as the Stimson Doctrine.

Such was the denouement of the Progressive Republican era that followed the Wilsonian era that had failed to replace the Washingtonian civil religion with a new consensus Americans were prepared to accept. War had solved nothing, and now, it turned out, neither had peace. Progressive Republicans had been suckered by foreigners just as much as Wilsonians. They had acquiesced in a Japanese naval hegemony in their own waters, which only enabled the Japanese to declare a Monroe Doctrine of their own throughout East Asia. They had arranged hundreds of millions of dollars in loans to Germany, which now would not be repaid. Indeed, threadbare Americans were angrier with the British and French for reneging on their war debts than with anything the Japanese might be up to.

That is why, in the 1932 presidential election, Americans voted overwhelmingly against the internationalist candidate and for the isolationist one. Franklin D. Roosevelt took the oath of office in March 1933, six weeks after Adolf Hitler was invited to power in Germany.

CHAPTER NINETEEN

Roosevelt the Isolationist

ENGLISH-SPEAKING NATIONS SHOWED extraordinary patience during the Great Depression. In none of them did a serious threat arise to representative government or private property despite unprecedented distress. Yes, there was that Bonus Army that descended on Washington, D.C., in 1932, but the (disillusioned) world war veterans and their families were hoping to prick the conscience of their government, not overthrow it. In the United States unemployment (which in those days meant male heads of households) had soared to 23 percent by November 1932, yet the vote in that month's election included a measly 2.23 percent for Socialist candidate Norman Thomas and 0.26 percent for the Communist. In Germany President Paul von Hindenburg's emergency response was to hand the government over to Nazis. But American press magnate William Randolph Hearst's emergency response was just to bankroll a movie. *Gabriel in the White House*, a sort of updated *Philip Dru, Administrator*, told the tale of a corrupt, lackadaisical president who is thrown into a coma and emerges miraculously transformed into that Platonic ideal, the benevolent dictator. He defies big business, ends unemployment, breaks organized crime, repeals Prohibition, dissolves the recalcitrant Congress, suspends civil rights for enemies of the people, and enforces world peace through invincible air power.

Franklin Roosevelt got a kick out of screening *Gabriel* during his years in the White House. In fact, he consulted behind the scenes in its production.

During the campaign Hoover had called Roosevelt a chameleon in plaid, a description that was true. Unlike Hoover, FDR was a brilliant American politician; hence his public persona was a whorl of pretenses. For instance, he accused the Hoover administration of being the most spendthrift in peacetime history, only to double federal spending as a percentage of the economy. Moreover, many of the New Deal programs were derived from ones begun or planned by his predecessor. In one important respect, however, Roosevelt introduced a genuine novelty in American history: isolationism. He signaled the change in his inaugural address by making just one brief reference to foreign policy: "Our international trade relations, though vastly important, are in point of time and necessity secondary to the establishment of a sound national economy. I favor as a practical policy the putting of first things first. . . . In the field of world policy I would dedicate this Nation to the policy of the good neighbor—the neighbor who resolutely respects himself and, because he does so, respects the rights of others."

Roosevelt pretended that his recovery plans were "not narrowly nationalistic" but committed the nation to autarky. He pulled the dollar off the gold standard, completing the wreck of international finance; called the U.S. delegation home from the London Economic Conference, completing the wreck of international commerce; and cut defense spending sharply over his first three fiscal years. Meanwhile, the Democratic Congress passed—and the president signed—the Neutrality Acts of 1935, 1936, and 1937, meant to ensure that the United States did not acquire an economic stake in foreign wars. In other words, Americans in the 1930s willfully and preemptively sacrificed the neutral rights for which Woodrow Wilson had finally waged total war. When Mussolini's Italy invaded Abyssinia in 1935, Italian and African Americans demanded the United States favor one side or the other. But FDR contented himself with a moral embargo on Italy just as impotent as the limited economic sanctions Britain and France imposed through the League of Nations. When the Spanish Army, led by Catholic caudillo Francisco Franco, rebelled against the leftist republic in

1936—and Fascist Italy, Nazi Germany, and Stalinist Russia all intervened—Roosevelt faced a deeper dilemma. American liberals, radicals, and Communists agitated to help the anti-clerical republic, but Catholics just as avidly opposed the republic. Again FDR took refuge in the Neutrality Acts and again got political cover when Britain and France remained aloof from the Spanish Civil War.

Roman Catholics were much on President Roosevelt's mind, given their critical place in the New Deal coalition and the influence of Pope Pius XI (1922–39). Indeed, Vatican intellectuals were the first to lump communism and fascism together under the rubric of totalitarianism. But whereas the papacy condemned the Soviet Union unequivocally, it tried to shelter the rights of Catholics in Mussolini's Italy through the Lateran Pact of 1929; in Hitler's Germany through the Concordat of 1933; and in Spain, Austria, and Poland by supporting authoritarian regimes. Meanwhile, Protestant Americans began the process of granting Catholics a grudging citizenship following Al Smith's groundbreaking campaign for president in 1928. Hollywood started to celebrate Catholics as social reformers in 1930s films such as James Cagney's *Angels with Dirty Faces* and Spencer Tracy's *Boys Town*. Most important, Catholic clergy joined with the Protestant Federal Council of Churches in renouncing war and supporting isolationism.

In 1937 the Japanese invaded China proper, and American hearts were rent by missionary reports of atrocities such as the Rape of Nanking. Since the war was undeclared (like all other aggressions during the Kellogg-Briand era), Roosevelt decided not to invoke the Neutrality Acts. That allowed American aid and trade to flow to China but at a trivial level compared to U.S. commerce with Japan. Instead, he delivered a highly ambiguous speech in Chicago calling for a quarantine against gangster nations (none of whom he called by name) and warning that isolation and neutrality were no escape from the contagion of war. But his conclusion was all about peace:

> If civilization is to survive the principles of the Prince of
> Peace must be restored. Trust between nations must be revived. Most important of all, the will for peace on the part

of peace-loving nations must express itself to the end that
nations that may be tempted to violate their agreements
and the rights of others will desist from such a course.
There must be positive endeavors to preserve peace.
America hates war. America hopes for peace. Therefore,
America actively engages in the search for peace.

It is most telling that Roosevelt maintained correct diplomatic relations with Germany during the years when Hitler rearmed in violation of the Versailles Treaty, reoccupied the Rhineland in
violation of the Locarno Treaty, annexed Austria, and in September
1938 tried his best to provoke war over the Czech Sudetenland.
Americans either did not notice, believe, or care that Hitler's regime differed in any important respect from the Kaiser's.

Since FDR's successful Good Neighbor Policy was a carryover
from Hoover, his only real diplomatic initiative was the 1933 recognition of the Soviet Union. His timing could not have been
worse. As part of the First Five-Year Plan, a crash campaign for industrialization, Josef Stalin had ordered the forcible collectiviza-
tion of agriculture, which condemned Ukrainians to a massive
famine and virtual genocide. Stalin had also begun his series of
purges, first against alleged Trotskyists and saboteurs, later against
the Communist Party and Red Army. But, obsessed as he was with
building socialism in backward Russia, Stalin pursued a foreign
policy that was even more risk-averse than Roosevelt's. So FDR,
who evidently hoped the Soviets would contain Japan in the Far
East and/or open their market to American trade, was disappointed
on both scores. The principal effect of U.S. recognition was to
make it much easier for Soviet intelligence agencies to penetrate
the United States and coordinate with the American Communist
Party. The Congressional un-American activities committees and
the Federal Bureau of Investigation, formally established in 1935,
took notice.

Tendentious historians who assume isolationists were either mo-
rons or bigots have difficulty accounting for the fact that the beati-
fied Roosevelt deferred to them for so long. More objective
historians recognize that FDR himself was the chief isolationist

out of conviction, political convenience, or both. And why not? The arguments in favor of an isolationist (really a hemispheric) stance were many and mighty in the mid-1930s, whereas the arguments in favor of rearmament, intervention, and probable war were few and flaccid in the absence of a clear and present danger or deeply held civil religious consensus.

"Isolationism" was one of those curious political terms, like "Puritanism," that began life as a pejorative but was soon claimed by disparate persons and groups as a badge of honor. Left isolationists such as Eugene Debs, Randolph Bourne, Hull House's Jane Addams, peace activist Emily Greene Balch, Methodist bishop G. Bromley Oxnam, and Oswald Garrison Villard of *The Nation* combined their non-interventionism with anti-imperialism, anti-militarism, or anti-capitalism. Bourne, who coined the phrase "war is the health of the state" as a protest against Wilson's war, believed war had become the modern font of profit and privilege for government officials, businessmen, and not least "the intellectuals whose cooperation was essential to its success." But even the so-called right-wing isolationists were more complex than their caricature. For instance, most Midwestern and western Republicans were in fact Peace Progressives who were hostile toward eastern corporations, sympathetic toward labor unions, and tolerant or supportive of the New Deal. Roosevelt courted them assiduously.

Isolationists had very plausible arguments in their favor. First was the depression itself, which monopolized the nation's attention. Second was the fear that technology, especially aerial bombing, was sure to make the next war even more deadly than the last one and target every man, woman, and child in belligerent countries. Third was the historical revisionism that suggested the war of 1914 had not been Germany's exclusive fault but the accidental product of reciprocal threats or else the product of such long-range causes as militarism, imperialism, nationalism, yellow journalism, and alliance systems. To learn the lessons of 1914 meant to spurn such evils in the future. Fourth was the widespread belief that Wilson had been duped into going to war in 1917 by bankers and arms manufacturers greedy for profit. The 1934 best seller *Merchants of Death* caused such an outcry that a Special Committee on Investigation of the Munitions Industry, chaired by Senator

Gerald P. Nye (R., N.D.), held two years of hearings. Given that Republicans had shrunk to a mere 28 percent in the Senate, it was clear that the president approved. Only when Nye blasphemed by suggesting Wilson himself had lied did the Democrats pull the plug. Just as sensational was the public confession of Smedley Butler, the highest-ranking and most decorated U.S. Marine. In 1935 he rued his participation in a long list of bloody banana wars that served nobody's interests save Wall Street's. Fifth were the peace movements founded not only by Christian pacifists, but also by myriad secular movements defined by race, class, gender, and education. At Princeton, students formed a club called the Veterans of Future Wars, whose members wryly demanded their $1,000 veteran's bonus in advance since few would survive the next war. Suffice to say that a political movement uniting, among many others, heroes like pilot Charles Lindbergh, scientific geniuses like Albert Einstein, demagogues like radio priest Charles Coughlin, Catholic social workers like Dorothy Day, left-wing historians like Charles Beard and Carl Becker, right-wing newspaper moguls like Colonel Robert R. McCormick, and college presidents like Robert Maynard Hutchins constituted a sort of national negation. They formed no consensus whatsoever on what they believed in but were certain of what they all were against. Sixth and last was the widespread conviction among intellectuals of all stripes that another world war would push the United States down the road to fascism, socialism, or both. That meant any serious foreign policy initiative was certain to aggravate domestic divisions. Such were the deep and viscous political waters through which the crippled Roosevelt waded.

Then, at some point after the Munich Conference of September 1938, the president made up his mind that the gangster regimes could only be stopped by force. Perhaps Kristallnacht, the first clear evidence of Nazi violence against Jews, changed his thinking. Perhaps it was the occupation of Prague, the first clear evidence that Hitler could not be appeased. Perhaps it was the Nazi-Soviet Non-Aggression Pact of August 1939, which seemed to lift the veil of ideological confusion cloaking the totalitarians. Nobody knows for sure to this day because Roosevelt was so secretive, manipulative, and mercurial. Plausible portraits have been drawn of Roosevelt the Isolationist, Roosevelt the Statesman-Educator, Roosevelt the Reluctant Belligerent, Roosevelt the Militant Conspirator, and even Roosevelt the Frivolous Improviser who just made it up as he went along. Whichever image or composite of images historians choose, they encounter some embarrassing contradictions.

But whenever Roosevelt decided a war was coming, he had to strip down in order to don a new superhero disguise to be worn hidden beneath his existing disguise. That is, he had to pretend to remain Dr. New Deal while already devoting himself to Dr. Win-the-War's initial three tasks: mobilize a massive military-industrial complex, maneuver the bad guys into shooting first, and proselytize the American people—all the people—with a civil religious orthodoxy that might reconcile Wilson's internationalism and Lodge's nationalism by planning universal institutions to be run by small steering committees chaired by the United States.

As early as 1939–40 Roosevelt put people quietly to work on that agenda. Where did it come from? What spiritual or mental temperament inspired him? Those are risky questions to ask about anyone, not least a great political figure, but FDR's background was, in this one aspect, transparent. He was a socially prominent low-church Episcopalian inoculated with Social Gospel by every male role model in his life. His father, James Roosevelt, had been Dutch Reformed and his mother, Sara Delano, Unitarian, so like many upper-class American couples they compromised by joining an Episcopal parish that took status far more seriously than theology. What mattered was doing one's duty to one's fellow man, and the more blessed a man was with talent, money, and power, the higher his calling. Franklin's legendary headmaster at the Groton School, Endicott Peabody, reinforced what he had learned at home, including the sublime phrasing of the Book of Common Prayer, a Golden Rule morality, condescension toward the downtrodden that went beyond handouts, and the convictions that America had a special role to play in God's plan and that Peabody's boys had a special role to play in America.

Groton's motto, *cui servire est regnare*, is usually construed "whose service is perfect freedom," but the literal translation, "to whom to serve is to rule," best expresses the reality of the duality in the Progressive mentality. Given his family background, Roosevelt took power for granted as an entitlement, privilege, and responsibility. What is more, FDR knew how to exercise power in relaxed, jovial, indirect ways that were unthreatening and even disarming, at least to the general public. He was notorious for dividing responsibilities among people and bureaucracies so as to encourage a competition of ways and means and to retain for himself all final decisions. Many of his appointees were fellow Groton men (e.g., Dean Acheson, Francis Biddle, Averell Harriman, Sumner Welles) or other members of the eastern establishment. He also seasoned his administration with many more Jews and Catholics than any president before him.

Last but not least, FDR invoked religion constantly but never in a jarring, judgmental, or sectarian way. He just affirmed the simple faith of Americans that religion should be a source of comfort and morals, an aid to getting by and getting along with each other in this life, whatever might happen after we die. In sum, Roosevelt had no interest in sectarian theology and hated the fact that it drove people apart, but he had every interest in political theology that had the potential to unite all people in America and maybe even the world. In 1933 FDR was so bold as to tell Soviet ambassador Maxim Litvinov that his atheism was a pose and that he would think on the Jewish religion his parents had taught him before he died. (When Churchill heard of that, he promised to nominate Roosevelt for Archbishop of Canterbury.)

Finally, what can be said about Roosevelt's polio, which he contracted in 1921 at the age of thirty-nine and overcame with such grit, grace, and humor? It must have contributed mightily to his faith and self-confidence but also to his powers of pretense. From the moment he reentered the public arena in 1924 until the end of his life FDR hid his paralysis from the cameras and voters, making his daily life an elaborate charade. Where fantasy ended and reality began is a pertinent question because Roosevelt now laid on himself the high priestly mantle, not only in politics and economics, but also in war and diplomacy. He meant to create, through his optimistic, non-sectarian, Bible-drenched rhetoric, as communicated in person and print but especially by radio, a truly national civil church. Historian Gary Scott Smith drew a skeptical conclusion:

"Roosevelt exhibited a tendency to doctor the historical record and a deep concern about his reputation. Thus, how can we know what Roosevelt truly believed? Like other presidents, he clearly employed religious rhetoric to suit his purposes and promote his aims, whether it was winning elections, passing reform legislation, or defeating the Nazis. He skillfully raised the use of civil religion to new heights." Historian Andrew Preston speculated that Roosevelt's "practice of the American civil religion was successful because it seemed genuine." Both sensed that FDR weaponized faith for the coming war he dared not yet reveal.

In his February 1936 radio address for the National Conference of Christians and Jews' Brotherhood Day, Roosevelt alluded to the larger conflict beginning to brew in the world:

> The very state of the world is a summons to us to stand together. For as I see it, the chief religious issue is not between our various beliefs. It is between belief and unbelief. It is not your specific faith or mine that is being called into question—but all faith. Religion in wide areas of the earth is being confronted with irreligion; our faiths are being challenged. It is because of that threat that you and I must reach across the lines between our creeds, clasp hands, and make common cause.

At the Democratic convention that year, when FDR proclaimed, "This generation has a rendezvous with destiny," he explicitly secularized and implicitly internationalized the heavenly graces. "We do not see faith, hope, and charity as unattainable ideals, but we use them as stout supports of a nation fighting the fight for freedom in a modern civilization." Roosevelt declared America was already waging war, "a great and successful war. It is not alone a war against want and destitution and economic demoralization. It is more than that; it is a war for the survival of democracy . . . for ourselves and for the world."

CHAPTER TWENTY

Roosevelt the Interventionist

ROOSEVELT THE RECIDIVIST, THE reborn interventionist, recalled the blunders he had watched Woodrow Wilson commit and resolved to do otherwise. Wilson had tried to lead a deeply divided nation into a world war, hindered mobilization through excessive bureaucracy, made a premature armistice, worked against rather than with the Bolsheviks, snubbed rather than courted Republicans, and overplayed America's hand at the peace conference. The leadership of Roosevelt the Commander-in-Chief ensured the United States became that earth-cracking titan that Salvador Dalí would imagine in 1943. The leadership displayed by Roosevelt the High Priest would prove a more dubious proposition. The American people resisted his godly exhortations until given no choice and then went to war in a very uncivil, unreligious mood, hating their enemies and distrusting their allies.

After the Munich Conference the United States remained technically at peace for thirty-eight months, during which FDR tried to prepare his nation for war along three tracks. Politically he persuaded Congress to roll back the Neutrality Acts so the United States could help Britain defy Nazi Germany and defend the Atlantic. Militarily he worked with both parties, big corporations, and labor to launch a crash rearmament program. Spiritually he interpreted the world crisis to the American people in language increasingly apocalyptic, even as he pretended to cling to peace. His task was complicated by the usual second-term blues. In 1937 he had tried unsuccessfully to pack the Supreme Court, and in 1938 he had tried unsuccessfully to purge conservative Democrats from his coalition. Instead, Republicans made big gains in Congress and the Second New Deal petered out. That made it all the more imperative that Roosevelt's initiatives in foreign and defense policy seem bipartisan.

The 1939 State of the Union address sounded the keynote:

Storms from abroad directly challenge three institutions indispensable to Americans, now as always. The first is religion. It is the source of the other two—democracy and international good faith. Religion, by teaching man his relationship to God, gives the individual a sense of his own dignity and teaches him to respect himself by respecting his neighbors. Democracy, the practice of self-government, is a covenant among free men to respect the rights and liberties of their fellows. International good faith, a sister of democracy, springs from the will of civilized nations of men to respect the rights and liberties of other nations of men. . . . There comes a time in the affairs of men when they must prepare to defend, not their homes alone, but the tenets of faith and humanity on which their churches, their governments and their very civilization are founded. The defense of religion, of democracy and of good faith among nations is all the same fight. To save one we must now make up our minds to save all.

Roosevelt requested an additional $500 million for defense lest the United States be caught unprepared as in 1917.

Shocks were not long in coming. Two months later Hitler betrayed the Munich Pact by occupying the rest of Czechoslovakia, then demanded retrocession of the Polish Corridor stripped from Germany in the Versailles Treaty. Stalin alone seemed in a position to resist, but that prospect evaporated in August with news of the Nazi-Soviet Non-Aggression Pact. Germany invaded Poland on

September 1, 1939, and Britain and France declared forlorn war two days later. Roosevelt (unlike Wilson) did not ask Americans to be neutral in thought or in deed but instead introduced a bill to lift the arms embargo required under the Neutrality Acts. He called it a peace bill, which sounded innocent but in fact conjured a myth that he could never dispel: the myth that the way for America to stay out of the war was by giving "all aid short of war" to the British. The *Christian Century* wanted to know what the Nye hearings had been all about then! Would not selling arms to Britain and France on any terms inevitably drag America into the war? But the public overwhelmingly favored the Allies and by a margin of 64 to 7 percent expected them to win the war. In November Congress approved U.S. exports so long as they were on a "cash-and-carry" basis.

Meanwhile, the Nazi-Soviet Pact had caused both clarity and confusion. To be sure, the totalitarian parties were now exposed as naked, aggressive gangster regimes, but American non-interventionists distinguished between them and in fact regarded Stalin a greater long-run threat than Hitler. The *Chicago Tribune* declared "The Winner: Red Josef" in March 1940. Congressman Hamilton Fish predicted that "the Communist vulture will sweep down on the bloody remains of Europe" after the war. The *New York Daily News* feared America would end up "the only non-Communist nation left in the world." Even Walter Lippmann wondered, "What shall be the boundary of Europe against the expanding invasion of Russian imperial Bolshevism?" Roosevelt was reduced to a wistful assessment that made the Soviets sound like New Dealers gone bad. In their early days, he explained in February 1940, the Bolsheviks provided better education, health care, and opportunity to the "millions who had been kept in ignorance and serfdom" by the tsarist regime but sadly had banished religion. He clung to the hope that since "mankind has always believed in God, in spite of many abortive attempts to exile God," Russia might regain its faith and "become a peace-loving, popular government with a free ballot."

The next shock blew away any illusions about German power. In May 1940 blitzkrieg overran Western Europe. In June France surrendered, and its North African colonial empire seemed likely to fall into Nazi hands. Americans began to feel vulnerable if not yet exposed. Roosevelt exploited the crisis by pushing through a $10.5 billion rearmament package in July, thanks to reliable assistance from Senator Carl Vinson (D., Ga.) and Representative James W. Wadsworth (R., N.Y.). It included the Two-Ocean Navy Act, which authorized a 70 percent increase in combat ships, including eighteen aircraft carriers. That same month FDR replaced his secretaries of war and the navy with two eminent Republicans, Henry Stimson and Frank Knox, to manage the military expansion. But Roosevelt had good reason to fear opposition from a coalition of Republican non-interventionists and New Deal–hating businessmen augmented by pacifists and socialists. So he made a preemptive assault by organizing first. In 1940 FDR quietly gave the famous journalist William Allen White the task of founding a bipartisan grass-roots Committee to Defend America by Aiding the Allies. He also clandestinely discouraged opponents by adding prominent isolationists to the list of un-American activists under FBI investigation.

Non-interventionists fought back in force by founding the America First Committee (AFC), a richly financed national organization that grew to a membership of a quarter million. Its celebrity spokesmen included leaders of business, journalism, politics, labor, and culture, of which the most famous was aviator Charles A. Lindbergh. His vision of a technologically advanced, militarily tough Fortress America might almost be said to have represented a rival civil religious movement to the one Roosevelt wanted to forge.

In September 1940, against the background noise of the Battle of Britain, Congress passed the Selective Service and Training Act, which established the first peacetime conscription in American history. That same month Roosevelt made an executive agreement with Churchill to trade fifty old destroyers to the Royal Navy for bases ranging from Newfoundland to Bermuda to the Caribbean. The AFC's distrust hardened during the presidential campaign. Not only had Roosevelt chosen to break with precedent and seek a third term, but he had also forced the Democratic convention to swallow his new preference for vice president, the radical (and somewhat nutty) New Dealer Henry Wallace. Roosevelt then had the chutzpah to campaign as the peace candidate against Republican internationalist

Wendell Willkie. On October 30 he assured a jovial crowd in Boston, "I have said this before, but I shall say it again and again and again: Your boys are not going to be sent into any foreign wars. They are going into training to form a force so strong that, by its very existence, it will keep the threat of war far away from our shores. The purpose of our defense is defense." He won his third term in a landslide.

During the years Roosevelt pivoted toward intervention American pacifism beat a partial retreat before the Christian Realist movement led by Reinhold Niebuhr. He began his spiritual journey in the socialist wing of the peace movement, contributing regularly to the *Christian Century*. But his frustration as a community organizer among factory workers in Detroit and the influence of Karl Barth's neo-orthodox theology disabused Niebuhr of the conceit that society was perfectible. He reached the conclusion that human beings were indelibly flawed, especially when acting in national, racial, or economic groups. So even though people had a duty to struggle against evil, even (or especially) their most zealous efforts risked betraying their own cause. By the early 1930s Niebuhr had quit the *Christian Century* to form a neo-realist movement centered at Union Theological Seminary, where he won over influential colleagues including Paul Tillich, Henry Sloane Coffin, and Henry Van Dusen. Over the course of the decade he laid out a Protestant version of just war theory in articles for *The Nation*, the *New Republic*, and the *Atlantic Monthly*. He constantly warned against self-righteousness lest it breed jingoism and hatred. But his validation of resistance to radical evil gave theological cover for rearmament and intervention. In 1941 Niebuhr founded the Union for Democratic Action and a new journal, *Christianity and Crisis*.

Protestant opinion was thus beginning to come around when Roosevelt received the same bad news Wilson had gotten in December 1916. Britain was broke and would soon need American weapons and goods delivered free of charge. He began an elaborate campaign for a new formula in his December 29, 1940, Fireside Chat that introduced a new phrase—national security—and a new motto—Arsenal of Democracy. A week later Roosevelt's 1941 State of the Union address broadened the message by making a preemptive promise that all who supported strong and healthy democracy would be rewarded with equal opportunity, secure jobs, social security, civil liberties, the fruits of scientific progress, and rising standards of living. But that was only the lengthy preamble to the following:

> In the future days, which we seek to make secure, we look forward to a world founded upon four essential human freedoms. The first is freedom of speech and expression—everywhere in the world. The second is freedom of every person to worship God in his own way—everywhere in the world. The third is freedom from want—which, translated into world terms, means economic understandings which will secure to every nation a healthy peacetime life for its inhabitants—everywhere in the world. The fourth is freedom from fear—which, translated into world terms, means a world-wide reduction of armaments to such a point and in such a thorough fashion that no nation will be in a position to commit an act of physical aggression against any neighbor—anywhere in the world. That is no vision of a distant millennium. It is a definite basis for a kind of world attainable in our own time and generation. That kind of world is the very antithesis of the so-called new order of tyranny which the dictators seek to create with the crash of a bomb.

In February 1941 Roosevelt's campaign got a surprising boost from an unlikely source, press magnate Henry Luce. The penurious son of a missionary in China, Luce flourished at Yale by gumption and even got tapped for Skull and Bones. He went on to found three of the great magazines of the century—*Time, Fortune*, and *Life*—which celebrated the "modern progressive approach to business" and the consumers' utopia it might bestow on America and the world if only Roosevelt (whom Luce despised) would forget the New Deal and take the nation into the war. But Luce turned from advocacy to prophecy in a *Life* editorial, "The American Century," whose tone was brooding, even occult. Luce put his nation on the psychiatrist's couch and diagnosed deep depression. He dared tell his five million readers what the president still shied from saying: the United States was already at war. But Americans insisted on clinging to a false peace, thus shirking their duty and delaying their destiny. If they would but rise up, conquer the enemies of freedom, and play Good Samaritan to suffering humanity, they would rediscover their national calling and their own happiness as well. Swallowing his bile, Luce even called on Americans to make Franklin Roosevelt the greatest president ever.

In 1917 Progressive clergy had shouted Amen to such perfervid pleas, but in 1941 they recoiled. "This call for an American imperialism," replied the *Christian Century*, "makes an appeal to our national egotism, but it masks a deadly threat to our democracy. It is a counsel of madness . . . because no democracy can assume the master-slave relationship in world empire without imperiling its democratic soul." Luce's queer essay triggered no groundswell in favor of war, but it might have inspired Americans to support Roosevelt's plan for unconditional aid to Britain because polls now showed that over three-quarters of citizens approved. That made passage of the Bill to Promote the Defense of the United States— otherwise known as Lend-Lease—a foregone conclusion. The first witness was Willkie, who insisted it was Americans' best chance to defend liberty without going to war. Anti-interventionists knew that was a pretense since Britain could never hope to defeat the Third Reich alone. Senator Arthur Vandenberg (R., Mich.) cried, "We have tossed Washington's Farewell Address into the discard." But Americans colluded in their own deception. The bill passed in March 1941 by roughly two-to-one margins in both houses.

That was the spring when U.S. rearmament got going in earnest as the mostly Republican industrialists converted their factories to war production. The War Department guaranteed contracts, decentralized administration, and even encouraged a kind of crony capitalism to speed up coordination among firms. The New Deal was suspended in all but name. Roosevelt had learned from William Knudsen, the brilliant veteran of Ford and General Motors recommended to him by Bernard Baruch, that manufacturers must be *unleashed* rather than leashed. As historian Arthur Herman put it, "In Roosevelt's mind, it didn't matter how confused and disorganized Washington was, as long as mobilization became an irresistible, overwhelming force across the country." Secretary of War Henry Stimson put the point succinctly when he said if you wanted to prepare a democracy for war, you had to let business make money. Old New Dealers were not pleased. Neither were unions, many of whose leaders were isolationist. Perversely, they made 1941 a record year of labor unrest by mounting 3,500 strikes that cost 23 million man-days of labor.

Roosevelt resorted to scare tactics. His May 27 radio address from the Pan-American Union declared an "Unlimited National Emergency." It was now "unmistakably apparent" that Hitler's demonic goals were unlimited. "The Nazi world does not recognize any God except Hitler; for the Nazis are as ruthless as the Communists in the denial of God. What place has religion which preaches the dignity of the human being, the majesty of the human soul, in a world where moral standards are measured by treachery and bribery and fifth columnists? Will our children, too, wander off, goose-stepping in search of new gods?" Roosevelt told Americans what choice they must make. "We will accept only a world consecrated to freedom of speech and expression—freedom of every person to worship God in his own way—freedom from want—and freedom from terror. ... With a firm reliance on the protection of Divine Providence, we mutually pledge to each other our lives, our fortunes, and our sacred honor." Americans bought the premise of that rhetorical declaration of war because they swamped the White House with positive mail. But they refused the conclusion. Polls continued to show that most Americans still believed FDR's disingenuous claim that Lend-Lease was the best way to stay out of the war. Just 14 percent favored immediate entry.

When Nazi Germany invaded the Soviet Union on June 22 the world got even more confusing. Britain gained the great continental ally it needed to have hope of prevailing, but that only made the case for U.S. belligerence less compelling. Yet if the Soviets were defeated, as it certainly appeared they might be by the autumn of 1941, then even American entry might not make the difference. "People realize there is no choice for us," wrote the executive secretary of the AFC. "If Germany wins, Russia will go Fascist. If Russia wins, Germany will go Communist." The AFC officially declared that the "entry of Communist Russia into the war should settle once and for all the intervention issue here at home. The war party can hardly ask the people of America to take up arms behind the red flag of Stalin."

Roosevelt was eager to extend Lend-Lease aid to the USSR but was betrayed by his own rhetoric about the religious foundations of democracy and peace. Would not giving arms to "godless Communist murderers" (in the words of Igor Sikorsky) be "a betrayal of the very foundation of Christian idealism"? Only one-third of Americans favored aid to Russia. The Catholic Church was unalterably opposed, while many Protestants wanted to make U.S. aid contingent upon religious toleration. So Roosevelt compounded public delusion by voicing what would later be called "convergence theory." The USSR, he told his adviser Sumner Welles, had already progressed from communism toward a modified state socialism, while the New Deal had moved America toward the Communist model of political and social justice. He then made that fanciful notion operational by instructing his personal envoy to the Vatican, Myron C. Taylor, to sell Pope Pius XII on the idea, while his ambassador in Moscow, Averell Harriman, tried to nudge Stalin toward relaxing persecution. FDR even tried to persuade Americans that religious freedom was guaranteed under the 1936 Soviet constitution, but Catholic and Protestant leaders alike rejected that "clumsy portrayal." When Lend-Lease aid to the USSR came up for a vote in October, Congress approved it, but only on cold strategic grounds.

By then the United States itself had been waging undeclared war for over three months. On July 1 Roosevelt ordered the military to occupy Iceland and assist British patrols in the North Atlantic. In August he met with Winston Churchill off the coast of Newfoundland and assured him his strategy was to wage war even if he could not yet declare it. The president and prime minister reconfirmed a Europe First strategy in case of a simultaneous Pacific war and announced their war aims in the Atlantic Charter. Its liberal internationalist principles echoed Wilson's: self-determination, free trade, global economic cooperation and social welfare, freedom of the seas, and disarmament. It also anticipated "the final destruction of the Nazi tyranny," implicitly committing Americans to fight until unconditional surrender even before they had entered the war.

When Roosevelt and Churchill held hands on Sunday and sang Anglican hymns, it seemed that American civil religion had at last reunited with British civil religion. Only it hadn't—not by a long shot—because the State Department's officials made no secret of their intent to dismantle Britain's system of imperial preference as a first step toward decolonization. Americans might be persuaded to fight for British democracy but not for the British Empire.

On September 4 Roosevelt exploited a confused engagement between a destroyer and submarine to declare that U-boats were rattlesnakes to be shot at on sight. It was obvious he hoped to replicate 1917. But Hitler had given U-boat commanders strict orders not to do anything provocative, even in self-defense. Perhaps, then, some new Zimmermann Telegram might reveal Hitler's designs on the Americas. But all British intelligence could come up with was a fanciful map drawn by South American Nazi sympathizers. So its agents doctored the map to make it seem made in Berlin and leaked it to U.S. intelligence chief William Donovan. It is a measure of Roosevelt's desperation that he highlighted that lame fabrication in his October 27 Navy Day speech. "I have in my possession a secret map made in Germany by Hitler's Government—by the planners of the new world order." What is more, another document had come into his possession, "a detailed plan, which, for obvious reasons, the Nazis did not wish and do not wish to publicize." The plan was to replace all religions with an International Nazi Church, whose bible would be *Mein Kampf* and whose symbol would be the swastika. "The god of Blood and Iron will take the place of the God of Love and Mercy. Let us well ponder that statement which I have made tonight."

It didn't work. Then, on October 31, a U-boat sank the destroyer *Reuben James*, killing 115 American sailors. Even that didn't work. Such trusted advisers as Stimson, Harold Ickes, and speech writer Robert Sherwood urged Roosevelt to put the case squarely before Congress. But he evidently feared open debate might only expose the nation's divisions, not to mention his own devious tactics. A late October poll reported just 17 percent of Americans favored immediate entry into the war. That is what made the "back door" path to war—provoking an attack from Japan—an acceptable *pis aller*.

For nearly four years Roosevelt's response to Japanese aggression in China had been confined to anodyne protests and sanctions. He wanted a war in Europe, not in the Pacific. But the Nazi invasion of Russia raised the terrible prospect of a simultaneous Japanese attack on Siberia, which might help Germany defeat the Soviet Union and render the Axis invincible. However, the Japanese could not expand their continental commitments without petroleum imported from the United States. In August Roosevelt approved a trade embargo in the full knowledge that it might provoke Japan to attack Southeast Asia, including the Philippines, to secure the oil fields of the Dutch East Indies. At the same time he scuttled Tokyo's diplomatic quest for a "modus vivendi" by encouraging Secretary of State Cordell Hull's demands that the Japanese evacuate China and honor the terms of the Washington Conference treaties. In Tokyo the civilian prime minister, Prince Konoye, resigned in October and left the decision between war or surrender to General Tôjô Hideki. In Washington Roosevelt convened his war party, including Stimson, Knox, and Harry Hopkins, and asked how they could ensure "that Japan was put into the wrong and made the first bad move—overt move." Tôjô did that for them by approving the Imperial Navy's plans for a wider war in the event last-ditch negotiations failed. Thanks to the Pentagon's MAGIC decrypts, Roosevelt knew by late November that some overt move was imminent.

Then something fishy occurred. A top-secret copy of Rainbow 5, the Army-Navy Joint Planning Committee's blueprint for war, fell into the hands of Elinor "Cissy" Patterson, the isolationist publisher of the *Washington Times-Herald* and cousin of Robert McCormick, the isolationist owner of the *Chicago Tribune*. On December 4, 1941, both newspapers sensationally exposed FDR's war plan. Who leaked it and why? The mystery has never been solved. But General Albert Wedemeyer, a chief suspect later exonerated, confided in 1983: "I have no hard evidence but I have always been convinced, on some sort of intuitional level, that President Roosevelt authorized it." Did FDR leak the war plan in hopes of goading Hitler into declaring war in the wake of a Japanese attack on the United States? There were certainly grounds from the German perspective. Rainbow 5's Europe First strategy would obviously be derailed in the event of a Pacific war. By declaring war, Germany would be free to wage unlimited submarine warfare in the Atlantic. The plan itself stated the U.S. military would not be ready to intervene decisively in the European theater until 1943, by which time Hitler expected the war to be over and won. But all that is known is what Hitler told the Reichstag four days after Pearl Harbor. Germany had been provoked into war by American newspapers that revealed "a plan prepared by President Roosevelt . . . according to which his intention was to attack Germany in 1943 with all the resources of the United States. Thus our patience has come to a breaking point."

Meanwhile, Congress voted for a declaration of war on Japan by 388 to 1. The American people were far more united than in 1917 and indeed more united than FDR ever dared hope. But they were coerced into war because FDR never persuaded them to volunteer in defense of the Four Freedoms everywhere in the world. The long cusp in the civil religion still had not come to an end.

CHAPTER TWENTY-ONE

World War II

The Great Masquerade

ORLD WAR II WAS not the two-sided conflict between Allies and Axis as depicted by Roosevelt. It was a free-for-all born of the overlapping wars started by Italy in 1935, Japan in 1937, and Germany in 1939, and it escalated by the sneak attacks on the USSR and United States in 1941. The Grand Alliance was not a coalition of democracies fighting for the Four Freedoms as depicted by Roosevelt. It was an awkward popular front comprising an imperial monarchy (Britain), a liberal democracy (United States), and a Communist dictatorship (Soviet Union). The United Nations Organization was not the principal war aim of a neo-Wilsonian administration as depicted by Roosevelt. It was the institutional drapery masking the American pursuit of benevolent hegemony over the world. Not for nothing did the president quip, "You know I am a juggler, and I never let my right hand know what my left hand does. . . . I may be entirely inconsistent, and furthermore I am perfectly willing to mislead and tell untruths if it will help win this war." In other words, the most brutally real dance of death in modern times was also Roosevelt's grandest masquerade ball.

He was able to make it so because geography permitted the United States to postpone belligerence until its enemies were already trapped in exhausting wars of attrition. Geography also allowed the United States to mobilize its incomparable agricultural, industrial, and scientific resources in conditions of near-perfect security. That mobilization, in the crucible of high-industrial total war, laid the foundations for the New York World's Fair's Futurama and Henry Luce's American Century. God was not on the side of the big battalions—such a choice would have favored the USSR and China. God was not on the side of the most advanced technology—such a choice would have favored Germany and Britain as much as the United States. Rather, as historian Paul Kennedy later chronicled, God was on the side of sheer productivity. The U.S. war economy quickly proved its overwhelming superiority to National Socialism, communism, and the New Deal alike, the very models James Burnham argued were the trends of the time in his 1941 classic, *The Managerial Revolution*.

Donald Nelson understood that when he half-joked, "This is a hell of a congregation I'm pastor of." Nelson was the Sears and Roebuck executive Roosevelt made chairman of the War Production Board (WPB) following Pearl Harbor. He was granted even more power than Bill Knudsen, who now joined the War Department, had wielded. The WPB could force manufacturers to accept contracts and unions to suspend strikes, which they mostly did because Nelson was a New Deal Democrat and Congress had passed an excess profits tax. Still, acting as czar of the whole U.S. economy exposed Nelson to complaints from all sides (not least, the War Department). But the WPB, assisted by dozens of dollar-a-year men from corporate America, allocated capital, raw materials, labor, and transport to defense-related industries and then got out of the way. "Industry—in fact, the entire economy—shivered under the impact of conversion throughout the first six months of 1942," Nelson recalled. When Roosevelt assured Churchill that U.S. aircraft production would triple and then triple again, the prime minister privately scoffed. The prediction proved modest. By autumn 1942 America was already outproducing all the Axis powers combined.

The U.S. gross national product grew by 52.4 percent from 1939 to 1944 as war production rose from 2 to 40 percent of the economy. Aircraft production increased by a factor of 28, explosives by 20, and shipbuilding by 17, supporting a total wartime output of 300,000 airplanes, 86,700 tanks, and ships displacing 60 million tons. The United States not only equipped its own armed forces, but it also heaped Lend-Lease supplies on its comrades-in-arms (they were not exactly allies) to the tune of $32.5 billion (almost $500 billion today). To be sure, the national debt ballooned from $40 billion (43 percent of GNP) in 1939 to $251 billion (112 percent) in 1945, but the United States would emerge from the war with 35 percent of the world's economy and 67 percent of the world's gold. The Roosevelt administration anticipated as much. In April 1941 Harry Hopkins had already called the New Deal "the Designate and Invincible Adversary of the New Order of Hitler" and predicted a new world order based on universal democracy. But to prevail the United States must wage "total war against totalitarian war. It must exceed the Nazi in fury, ruthlessness and efficiency."

The so-called Grand Alliance was really the Strange Alliance. The British and Americans, who Churchill fancied had a special relationship, created a combined chiefs of staff to coordinate military strategy. But in fact their military commanders quarreled incessantly over where and when to deploy their resources. Otherwise the United States and Britain were just allies of a kind because their war aims sharply diverged. The Americans were determined to create an Open Door world and expected the British to reciprocate for Lend-Lease with a commitment to end their imperial preference. The Roosevelts (Eleanor even more emphatically than Franklin) enraged Churchill by insisting that Britain shed its empire after the war, beginning with India. The other bilateral relationships during World War II were even more acrimonious. The Americans, British, and Soviets viewed each other with profound distrust, and none of them cooperated effectively with Nationalist China.

Yet Roosevelt declared that a transcendent alliance had come into being on January 1, 1942, when twenty-six countries pledged to fight until complete victory over the Axis. Their principles included those of the Atlantic Charter plus religious freedom (cynically conceded by the Soviets). Roosevelt christened the twenty-six the "United Nations" because, well, that sounded more united than the League of Nations had ever been and because it made a comforting echo of "United States." Needless to say, that was the alliance, not the perverse coalition of his daily experience, that Roosevelt chose to trumpet in his 1942 State of the Union address:

> But we of the United Nations are not making all this sacrifice of human effort and human lives to return to the kind of world we had after the last world war.
>
> We are fighting today for security, for progress, and for peace, not only for ourselves but for all men, not only for one generation but for all generations. We are fighting to cleanse the world of ancient evils, ancient ills.
>
> Our enemies are guided by brutal cynicism, by unholy contempt for the human race. We are inspired by a faith that goes back through all the years to the first chapter of the Book of Genesis: God created man in His own image.
>
> We on our side are striving to be true to that divine heritage. We are fighting, as our fathers have fought, to uphold the doctrine that all men are equal in the sight of God. Those on the other side are striving to destroy this deep belief and to create a world in their own image—a world of tyranny and cruelty and serfdom. That is the conflict that day and night now pervades our lives. No compromise can end that conflict. There never has been—there never can be—successful compromise between good and evil. Only total victory can reward the champions of tolerance, and decency, and freedom, and faith.

In light of what Nazi and Japanese imperialism represented one cannot fault the president for placing the United States on the side of the angels. But no regimes were more determined to create a world in their own image than Roosevelt's America. On Memorial Day 1942 his confidante Sumner Welles bluntly declared, "Our victory must bring in its train the liberation of all peoples. Discrimination between peoples because of their race, creed or color must be abolished. The age of imperialism is ended." When Harry Hopkins reported in London the American ideas about international trusteeships for former colonies, Churchill threw an obscene tirade that lasted two hours. That was what prompted his famous oath before Parliament: "I have not become the King's First Minister to preside over the liquidation of the British Empire." But American pressure was relentless. Wendell Willkie toured the allied nations, met with the British, and returned to write his 1943 book, *One World*, which called for "the orderly but scheduled abolition of the colonial system."

The Roosevelt administration's ambitions scarcely knew any limits. The State Department, the War and Navy Departments, and private interests ranging from corporations to foundations to missionaries took for granted that this time the war must end in the Americanization of the world. Europe was taken for granted from the start. In 1942 Pearl Buck declared, "If the American way of life is to prevail in the world it must prevail in Asia." Japan would be forcibly demilitarized and democratized, its *zaibatsu* trusts broken up. China would become an economically open, politically democratic partner of the United States and one of the "four policemen" Roosevelt expected to enforce the new world order. The allure of the vast China market dazzled Americans across the political spectrum. Business economist Eliot Janeway cautioned the United States would "have to find customers for an unprecedented volume of export business" after the war; hence it must ensure "reliable friends and potential allies," above all in China. Leftist Owen Lattimore of *Amerasia* magazine described Asian markets as a new economic frontier that could ensure the United States did not slide back into depression. Vice President Henry Wallace returned from China excited about the vast commercial opportunities. Nelson of the WPB believed a market of enormous size would open for U.S. exports. Harvard Sinologist John King Fairbank called China "a battleground where American values are in conflict with other values, and where we should seek to make our values prevail." But China was only the start. Southeast Asia's rich resources, India's gigantic market, the Persian Gulf's oil reserves—all the opportunities of the world's largest, most populous continent could be brought on stream once pried loose from Europe's colonial overlords.

How was that to be achieved? Roosevelt had secretly begun postwar planning more than two years before Pearl Harbor. His goal was what political scientists call extra-regional hegemony in the expectation the United States would eventually have the means, motive, and opportunity to achieve it. In September 1939 he asked Secretary of State Hull to appoint a committee, chaired by Sumner Welles, "to survey the basic principles which should underlie a desirable world order to be evolved after the termination of the present hostilities and with primary reference to the best interests of the United States." On New Year's Day 1940 Hull added that the United States would in its own interest use its "moral and material influence in the direction of creating a stable and enduring world order" so as to prevent another "breeding ground of economic conflict, social insecurity, and, again, war." They kept their work under wraps because the America First Committee would have cried bloody murder if it had learned the president was already plotting a peace only total war could produce! The initial deliberations focused on making collective security effective, perhaps through a great power council and international army. Over the course of 1941 Roosevelt's thinking gradually settled on the practical goals of converting Congress to internationalism, maximizing American military and financial power, cloaking the exercise of that power through multilateral institutions, and selling the whole package as the will of God.

That last task fell in part to Vice President Henry Wallace, a teetotaling Social Gospel Presbyterian and tribune for the masses. On May 8, 1942, he made a grand public address that called the war a culmination of the people's revolution that began on Lexington Green in 1775. "Some have spoken of the American Century. I say the century on which we are now entering, the century that will come out of this war, can and must be the century of the common man. The people's revolution is on the march and the devil and all his angels cannot prevail against it. They cannot prevail, for on the side of the people is the Lord." British Embassy official Isaiah Berlin called it "the most unbridled expression to date of the New Deal as the New Islam, divinely inspired to save the world."

The new revelation gathered tremendous momentum from the parallel rise of the Christian Realist movement that displaced the pacifist Protestant establishment following Pearl Harbor. The Union Theological Seminary faculty and other proponents of "crisis theology" all but took over the Federal Council of Churches with the help of Wall Street attorney and devout Presbyterian John Foster Dulles. He had attended the 1937 Oxford ecumenical conference that had planned for a World Council of Churches and had come home convinced that churches had a transnational duty to promote world order. He now persuaded the FCC to create a Commission on a Just and Durable Peace, to be led by Henry Van Dusen, Reinhold Niebuhr, and Samuel Cavert. Its first conference, at Ohio Wesleyan University in March 1942, attracted 377 clergy who declared it "the purpose of God to create a world-wide community in Jesus Christ, transcending nation, race and class."

Of course Dulles knew that government, not the church, would be the ultimate authority in any worldwide community. So the following year he distilled the commission's principles down to Six Pillars supporting a secular global edifice: Allied collaboration in perpetuity, universal free trade, adaptable treaty structures, decolonization, suppression of militarism, and protection of human rights. He then arranged for the FCC to promote the pillars in a national campaign. Dulles and Senator Joseph H. Ball (R., Minn.) sounded the keynote at New York's Cathedral of St. John the Divine, and Luce's magazines provided publicity throughout the autumn of 1943. Among other things, people were told they could do their part for world peace with a three-cent stamp. So Capitol Hill was buried with letters denouncing any postwar return to isolationism as un-Christian. Methodist bishop G. Bromley Oxnam declared it a "Crusade for a New World Order."

In any case, there seemed no alternative. In his prewar Fireside Chats Roosevelt had already said the Atlantic Ocean had become again what it had been when the republic was young: a potential avenue of attack. He now turned his February 23, 1942, broadcast into a global geography lesson: "I'm going to ask the American people to take out their maps." Indeed, many citizens owned them because stores had sold out of maps, atlases, and globes the week after Pearl Harbor. FDR spoke of a "battlefield for civilization," thereby infusing geography with political and spiritual content. But radio offered no visual content and movie newsreels just a fleeting glimpse, which made the artwork of Richard Edes Harrison richly serendipitous. Working for *Fortune* magazine, Harrison designed maps with strikingly new projections and proper curvature so that whole theaters of war loomed up from the horizon. North America no longer appeared as an invulnerable island but as an integral part of a global continuum made even more intimate by aviation. Roosevelt loved that. Throughout the war he constantly sounded the "Air Age" theme and linked it to the One World theme sounded by Willkie, whose own radio speech recounting his world tour was heard by some 36 million people. Finally, Hollywood dutifully churned out propaganda films such as Disney's *Victory through Air Power* (1943), Frank Capra's *Why We Fight* series (1943–45), and Twentieth-Century Fox's hagiographic *Mr. Wilson* (1944).

Congress satisfied public opinion and the White House alike by committing itself in advance to "some sort of organization of nations after the war." J. William Fulbright (D., Ark.), chairman of the House Committee on Foreign Affairs, introduced a resolution in favor of "a specific plan or system" for international peace and security, and Congress approved it 360–29 on September 17, 1943. The following month Tom Connally (D., Tex.) introduced a similar resolution, thereby kicking off what the *New York Times* called the most momentous Senate debate since the Treaty of Versailles. Only there was no debate. Instead, Senator Vandenberg invited Republicans to caucus on Mackinac Island, where they decided to favor "responsible participation by the United States in a post-war cooperative organization among sovereign nations to prevent aggression." The resolution passed in November by a vote of 85–5, and 85 percent of the public approved.

Americans had no idea what the words "responsible," "cooperative," or "sovereign" might turn out in practice to mean. They knew even less after the four conferences staged in 1943. At Casablanca Roosevelt and Churchill tried to reassure Stalin through their Unconditional Surrender pledge. At Moscow Cordell Hull appeared to win British, Chinese, and Soviet adherence to a declaration renouncing the balance of power in favor of collective security through a united nations organization. At Cairo Roosevelt pretended to elevate Nationalist China to a rank of equality with the United States, Britain, and the Soviet Union as one of the Four Policemen expected to enforce international law after the war. At Teheran Roosevelt remuddled the issue of whether he imagined the peace to come would derive from hard-headed spheres of influence or from an organization of truly united nations.

Meanwhile, the first agency bearing the name of the United Nations came into existence for what appeared to be purely humanitarian purposes. Reversing yet another of Woodrow Wilson's mistakes, the Roosevelt administration conceived of the U.N. Relief and Rehabilitation Agency (UNRRA) to succor the war-stricken peoples of Europe and Asia. But almost two years of behind-the-scenes bickering ensued because British, Soviet, and even Canadian officials resisted U.S. efforts to dominate the agency. Since the United States would contribute most of the money, medicine, and food, Americans expected to call the shots. Founded in November 1943 by delegates from forty-four nations meeting in Atlantic City, the UNRRA would eventually be credited with repatriating nearly a million refugees and delivering vital necessities to 100 million people in a score of countries. But it also served as a powerful American lever in the broader negotiations for a new world order, exactly the result that Assistant Secretary of State Dean Acheson intended.

Those same forty-four nations answered the summons in July 1944 to the Bretton Woods Conference in New Hampshire, where they would learn the larger plans the Americans had for them. There was no question the European war would be won thanks mostly to the Red Army. It had been fighting between 60 and 80 percent of the Wehrmacht for three years at horrendous cost and was now advancing at will into Eastern Europe. But the Americans, at a fraction of the cost, were busy taking over the rest of the world. Their forces had now conquered Rome and invaded Normandy; launched devastating bombing campaigns over German cities; broken the back of the Japanese navy; and island-hopped to the Marianas, whose capture put U.S. air power within range of Japan. It was still too soon to tell how far American power would reach by the end of the war, but it is safe to say Roosevelt and the military chiefs expected to dominate the Atlantic and Pacific Oceans and the littoral regions of Europe and East Asia, in addition to the Western Hemisphere. Those conquests would meet all the conditions for world hegemony laid down by Yale professor Nicholas Spykman in his geopolitical classics, *America's Strategy in World*

Politics (1942) and *The Geography of the Peace* (1944). Contrary to the German and British geographers Andreas Haushofer and Halford Mackinder, who thought a land empire might dominate the world by controlling Eurasia's heartland, Spykman believed a maritime empire might dominate by securing Eurasia's rimlands. The United States, with Britain in tow, was manifesting that destiny by mid-1944.

The economic counterpart to that military realm was the Open Door economic regime designed by the Federal Reserve Board's economist Charles Kindleberger for the Council on Foreign Relations in 1942. It was liberal insofar as it promoted free trade and access to materials and markets; private insofar as it promoted free enterprise; cooperative insofar as it was non-discriminatory and international; and governed insofar as it was subject to multi-national institutions. But since the institutions would be designed, paid for, and led by American officials, it was obvious who expected to be top dog. One could hardly expect anything else given the widespread fear that peace might hurl the industrial world back into depression or at least another postwar recession exacerbated by hyperinflation, international indebtedness, and high tariffs. So the U.S. Treasury drew the obvious conclusions and took prophylactic measures. An International Monetary Fund (IMF) would function as lender of last resort, an International Bank for Reconstruction and Development would finance the rebuilding of war-torn Europe, and a Bretton Woods monetary system would peg all currencies against the U.S. dollar, pegged in turn at $35 per ounce of gold. For its part, the State Department would seek universal adherence to an international trade organization dedicated to lowering tariff barriers and opening up more opportunities for U.S. investment banks and exporters. The world would thus get easy access to American capital and goods, while U.S. firms would do well by doing good. In author Stewart Patrick's words, it amounted to a "consensual and pluralistic style of hegemonic leadership."

Treasury Secretary Henry Morgenthau boasted that Roosevelt's "deliberate policy of organized plenty" amounted to "a kind of New Deal for a new world." Its roots lay in part in the domestic New Deal, especially the Tennessee Valley Authority (TVA). If the federal government could transform backward parts of the United States through planned application of capital and technology, why not other parts of the world? As David E. Lilienthal, the TVA chairman, boasted: "No English interpreter is needed when a Chinese or a Peruvian sees this series of working dams, or electricity flowing into a single farmhouse, or acres that phosphate had brought back to life." Philanthropic foundations, missionary societies, and private corporations pioneered overseas development projects, but government bureaucracy, foreign policy, and the natural and social sciences added to the momentum. It was said Eleanor Roosevelt imagined the whole world her personal welfare project, while her husband made global welfare the nation's project. But the roots of the project were nourished at least as much in wartime mobilization of the private sector. Roosevelt obliquely admitted that fact when he changed costumes from Dr. New Deal to Dr. Win-the-War and made postwar recovery almost wholly dependent on Progressive businessmen. So Henry Luce had won and Henry Wallace had lost, as prominent historians have all recently suggested. The United States would achieve *Dominance by Design* (Michael Adas), bestow *A New Deal for the World* (Elizabeth Borgwardt), export its principles by *Inventing the "American Way"* (Wendy Wall), modernize the world through *The Great American Mission* (David Ekbladh), and spread its *Irresistible Empire* of consumption (Victoria de Grazia).

Of course, all other empires must die, and not only the evil ones. It was Lord Halifax, the British ambassador, who reported that men like Wendell Willkie, Bernard Baruch, and Thomas Lamont, the chairman at J. P. Morgan, were "energetic technicians and businessmen filled with a romantic . . . self-confident economic imperialism, eager to convert the world to the American pattern." Such men could not abide reciprocity but must always "rule the roost."

Oxford professor J. R. R. Tolkien, bemoaning the virtual occupation of Britain by Americans soldiers, sailors, and airmen, made the same point rather more colorfully in a December 1943 letter to his son:

> Humph, well! I wonder (if we survive this war) if there will be any niche, even of sufferance, left for reactionary back numbers like me (and you). The bigger things get the smaller and duller or flatter the globe gets. It is getting to

be all one blasted little provincial suburb. When they have introduced American sanitation, morale-pep, feminism, and mass production throughout the Near East, Middle East, Far East, U.S.S.R., the Pampas, el Gran Chaco, the Danubian Basin, Equatorial Africa, Hither Further and Inner Mumbo-land, Godhwanaland, Lhasa, the villages of darkest Berkshire, how happy we shall be. At any rate it ought to cut down travel. There will be nowhere to go.

CHAPTER TWENTY-TWO

Roosevelt the Failed High Priest

"THE WAR AS A necessary evil has been soberly accepted and squarely faced. But it is not a crusade such as we saw in 1917." Isaiah Berlin thus realized early on what author Studs Terkel later documented at length: World War II was not a good war at all in the minds of Americans. On the contrary, their mood was bitter, stoic, grim, impatient, and vengeful. Nor was it fought by a "greatest generation," if that phrase meant anything more than unlucky. The home front did not display a uniformly patriotic team spirit. Widespread cheating on rations, absenteeism, profiteering, draft dodging, and malingering distressed the War Production Board and even the president. Overseas the GIs were often sullen and risk-averse, a mood amply documented by *Studies in Social Psychology in World War II: The American Soldier*, made under the direction of sociologist Samuel Stouffer for U.S. Army chief of staff George C. Marshall.

Enlisted men understood that Pearl Harbor meant war and that once in the war, the United States had to win. But two-thirds of them suspected the country had been dragged into it by big businessmen and imperialists. Just 15 percent interpreted the conflict in terms of moral goals like destroying fascism or securing the Four Freedoms (which the vast majority could not name). Soldiers were skeptical of all propaganda, including their own, which meant

Roosevelt could not effectively recycle Wilsonian calls to make the world safe for democracy. Moreover, the servicemen were well aware that a U.S. victory also meant victory for the British Empire and Soviet Union, both of which they deeply distrusted. Nor did most believe in a war to end war because two-thirds expected another world war to break out within twenty-five years, with Russia by far the most likely opponent. The War Department tried to motivate soldiers through orientation sessions and stirring documentaries, but knowing their enemies were evil did not seem to improve morale. The military also greatly expanded the chaplaincy corps, adding especially rabbis and Catholic priests, and blessed the USO, created by ecumenical religious bodies. But that, too, had no discernible effect except perhaps to encourage private prayer among men in combat. The Army Research Branch concluded the following: "The general picture in this volume of men preoccupied with [their own comfort and safety and getting out of the army as soon as possible] does not suggest a particularly inspired work performance in the American Army."

When forced to fight, of course, U.S. soldiers usually displayed courage, tenacity, and ingenuity. But the rates of desertion, self-inflicted wounds, venereal disease, alcohol abuse, and malingering alarmed General Dwight D. Eisenhower. He fumed privately about the absence of an aggressive spirit or even of anger on the part of his soldiers by comparison to the Germans. (When the U.S. Army liberated its first Nazi concentration camp in 1945, Ike snapped at a soldier, "Still having trouble hating them?") The surveys also belied the baptism-of-fire myth, a discovery that helped to explain a shocking rate of combat exhaustion. GIs confessed by a three-to-one margin that the more combat they experienced, the more frightened they became. Self-preservation, self-respect, unit loyalty, and the chance to go home were their principal motivations. Just one soldier in twenty spoke of "making a better world, defeating aggression, patriotism, or freedom," and over three-quarters confessed to frequent or occasional doubts about whether the war was even worth fighting. To be sure, internationalism appeared to win over servicemen because two-thirds favored U.S. membership in some new league of nations. But few expected it to prevent future wars. Hence the Army Research Branch team's conclusion that the

soldiers had no pronounced expectations of anything positive coming out of the war. This time there would be no disillusionment
because most Americans had no illusions to start with.

Woodrow Wilson had been passive for three years before
preaching a sudden crusade that stampeded Americans into war
and succeeded in filling their heads with illusions. Franklin
Roosevelt had the opposite problem. He had been active for three
years, trying to get the nation ready for a crusade, but never succeeded. Somehow Roosevelt needed to harness provincialism in
pursuit of internationalist ends so that the enormous military and
financial power the United States was accumulating could reshape
the world. It seemed in the wake of the Bretton Woods Conference
that a hegemonic United States would emerge from the war with
power to cajole or coerce all other powers but only if the American
people willed it. That explains why internationalists in both political parties were at pains to re-illusion themselves and the public.

Wartime wishful thinking almost begs credulity. For instance,
no sooner had Hitler betrayed Stalin on June 22, 1941, than the
tide of propaganda reversed its flow. The *New York Times'* Moscow
bureau chief and U.S. ambassador rushed out best-selling books
that made excuses for Stalin's famines, purges, show trials, and pact
with the Nazis. Hollywood produced two dozen movies on pro-
Russian themes during the war. The chiefs of the Office of War
Information, Archibald MacLeish and Robert Sherwood, told
newspaper editors that the decisive battlefield of this war would be
American public opinion and that the principal barrier to lasting
peace was colonialism. The Soviet Union, if anything, was an ally.
The world's future was at stake, said Henry Wallace: "Unless
Russia and the United States come to a satisfactory understanding
before the war ends, I very much fear that World War Number
Three will be inevitable." Wendell Willkie reported that Stalin was
earthy, charming, tough-minded, and admiring of the United
States: "Russia is neither going to eat us or seduce us." Still, he
deemed it imperative that the United Nations agree fundamentally
on the shape of the peace lest the Atlantic Charter go the way of
the Fourteen Points. Left-wing journalist Max Lerner assured
Americans that Russia would become a "responsible partner in a
common peace." Right-wing publisher Henry Luce made Stalin

Time's Man of the Year in January 1943 and depicted the Russians in a special issue of *Life* as "one hell of a people [who] look like Americans, dress like Americans, and think like Americans." It even described the NKVD secret police as just "a national police similar to the FBI." Roosevelt repeated his conviction that the American and Soviet regimes were somehow converging.

Manufactured good will for "our brave Russian allies" bordered on hyperbole beginning in September 1942, when some two hundred Republican bankers and businessmen toasted the Red Army at a gala luncheon, and in November, when New York mayor Fiorello La Guardia declared a Stalingrad Day. The mass rally that jammed Madison Square Garden heard a Notre Dame professor praise Stalinist Russia and declare any unnecessary delay in the opening of a second front "a crime against religion." Vice President Wallace spoke to the conference of Christian Realists at Ohio Wesleyan University, warning the worst peacetime scenario would probably be "in case we double-cross Russia." A National Council of American-Soviet Friendship promoted the cause among conservative groups such as American Legion posts, Masonic lodges, and chambers of commerce. Protestant, Catholic, and Jewish leaders welcomed reports that the Communists were easing up on religious persecution. All Americans were told that democracy and even consumerism were spreading in the wartime USSR so that there was cause to be hopeful about postwar cooperation. Predictably, 93 percent of Americans in 1943 expressed confidence that Russia would be a friendly partner of the United States. What does that tell us? Since 93 percent is not a real number in the democratic political world—even Roosevelt got only 55 percent of the vote—it tells us that the basis of American support for the Stalinist regime was a mile wide and an inch deep.

Roosevelt waded ever more deeply into fantasyland because his top priority was to keep the Grand Alliance intact both during and after the war. When incontrovertible evidence of the Soviets' Katyn Forest massacre of thousands of Polish officers surfaced in 1943, the president said privately he would pretend not to believe it. During the run-up to the Teheran Conference that November he told Churchill that he could handle Stalin "better than your Foreign Office or my State Department." At Teheran he blithely assumed the Soviet dictator was get-able, and the way to get him was to parrot the Communist line about the evils of imperialism. After Teheran he reported in a Fireside Chat that "I got along fine with Marshal Stalin," who spoke with "complete frankness." It seemed as if Roosevelt imagined the cold bureaucratic executioner was just a big union boss who only needed to be cut in on the deal.

Stalin had abolished the Comintern in 1943 because the USSR could hardly pretend to be a loyal ally while sponsoring subversion against all capitalist nations. One might even ask what took him so long to make that goodwill gesture. But Soviet intelligence agencies, unbeknownst to the Roosevelt administration, waged an unrestrained espionage campaign against the United States from 1942 to 1945. The Venona code decrypts made after the war provided evidence that Soviet agents had recruited at least 349 American citizens as active spies, and reasonable extrapolations suggest the real number might have been several thousand. The foundations were laid by operatives working out of the Soviet Embassy following Roosevelt's recognition of the USSR in 1933. Young idealists who flocked to Washington, D.C., to serve in the early New Deal were one group susceptible to Communist blandishments. Others were gleaned from American leftists who had volunteered for the Abraham Lincoln Brigade in the Spanish Civil War. Jewish communities were both infiltrated and targeted by Stalinists ordered to root out the Polecats (code name for Trotskyists) and Rats (Zionists). Several hundred more agents were lodged in the secret apparatus for internal security of the American Communist Party.

The wartime alliance flung the doors wide open. Under Lend-Lease agreements several thousand Soviet soldiers, technicians, officials, and spies roamed North America; snooped around military bases, factories, and laboratories; and harvested bumper crops of military-industrial-scientific intelligence. The Office of Strategic Services, Roosevelt's own foreign intelligence agency, was peppered with at least fifteen double agents, most prominently chief of research Maurice Halperin. The State Department contained at least six informants, led by Alger Hiss; the Treasury had another six, led by Harry Dexter White. Top-secret aeronautical and scientific projects, not least the atomic program, were compromised.

But since nobody's cover was blown during the war, the only people fooled were Americans.

Eisenhower later titled his wartime memoirs *Crusade in Europe*, but the Roosevelt administration fooled itself again by pretending its own war effort was a civil religious crusade for human rights and fundamental freedoms. It set up concentration camps for U.S. citizens of Japanese ancestry, ignored evidence of the Nazi Holocaust, and persisted in racial segregation of the armed forces despite Willkie's caution that such imperialism at home sullied the American cause. Meanwhile, the British and U.S. commands abandoned even the pretense of humanitarianism by perfecting the Fascist way of war: the carpet bombing of cities, which killed a million German and Japanese civilians by war's end. As for Roosevelt's claim that "we are fighting to cleanse the world of ancient evils, ancient ills," that was mocked by Stalin's annexationist goals, which he made explicit as early as December 1941 and inflated after July 1943, when the Battle of Kursk turned the tide on the eastern front. In August 1944, with the Red Army on the outskirts of Warsaw, the Polish underground rose in revolt against its German occupiers. Stalin cynically ordered his army to sit for two months while the Nazi SS exterminated thousands more Polish patriots. He obviously meant to install the Communist Lublin Committee as the government of a liberated Poland, citing as precedent the 1943 Anglo-American occupation of Italy, which notably excluded Communists. Stalin believed that each side would impose its system as far as its armies reached and that it could not be otherwise. The dictator told the truth. The democrat could not.

Finally, the idealistic gloss of a New Deal for the World faded even before its first application was finished. The Soviets displayed no intention of joining the Bretton Woods system, while their demand for a Security Council veto at the Dumbarton Oaks Conference augured poorly for a consensus on the U.N. Charter. Cordell Hull threatened to declare the talks a failure even if that put FDR's reelection at risk. The Soviets called the bluff, and Hull folded: his communiqué called Dumbarton Oaks a signal success. By October 1944 Churchill was sufficiently worried about Stalin's ambitions that he flew to Moscow and made a bilateral deal on

Balkan spheres of influences. The Roosevelt administration's illusions of control over its allies were already crumbling.

It did not have to end that way. By 1944 other voices and visions from the Progressive movement's own camp were on offer. The brilliant, unpredictable Walter Lippmann published a book calling for a tough, commonsense foreign policy based on national interests. The Red Army was going to occupy Eastern Europe, and the Soviets were not going to tolerate unfriendly regimes on their borders. If Americans refused to accept that reality, the alliance would shatter and the U.S. Army would have to stand guard in Western Europe. A naive reliance on international law and parliaments would only lure Americans into complacency or overextension. The leftist historian Carl Becker thought along similar lines. People who imagined this war must carry the human race beyond nationalism and sovereignty could not be more mistaken. The war was strengthening the nation-state's role as the principal agent of modernization and underscoring the fact that international politics were all about power. He advised the Roosevelt administration to stop attributing imaginary virtues to Russia and imaginary vices to Britain and seek genuine compromise with both. Reinhold Niebuhr's fears were darker and subtler. He sensed power-hungry elites lurking behind the utopian plans for postwar collective security: "Thus our policy moves toward a cynical expression of American power, while our avowed war aims are as pure as gold. It would be fatal to assume that the wiser and more sensitive forces of America have already lost the battle against an irresponsible expression of American power in the postwar world. But if the battle is to be won, we will have to draw upon profounder insights of our Christian faith than is our wont."

Finally, George F. Kennan—no Progressive, but a bonafide Russian expert—wrote from the U.S. Embassy in Moscow, urging a change of course before it was too late. Stalin no longer had any incentive to make a separate peace, hence did not need to be coddled. His armies were about to spill over a dozen international boundaries. But American leverage was also cresting, and the Soviets still needed Lend-Lease. Kennan advised the Roosevelt administration to engage the Soviets at once, drive a hard bargain, and divide up the spoils of war while their countries were still nominal allies. The State Department, let alone the White House, ignored him. Years later, in 1970, Kennan reflected on the damage done by Roosevelt's pretense: "I think it never pays not to tell the people the truth." The truth was the democracies had desperately needed Soviet help to defeat Nazi Germany and would have to pay a bitter price for it. But FDR insisted the Grand Alliance was on a moral crusade. According to Kennan, "This was the great deceit that was practiced on the American public: to try to make them believe that really, at bottom, the Russians and we were after the same things. This was not right."

Roosevelt, ill and rapidly aging, displayed enormous courage in February 1945 by traveling all the way to the Crimea for strenuous negotiations with Churchill and Stalin at Yalta. But in so doing, he made the same mistake Wilson had made by sailing over to Paris in 1919. Whatever came out of Yalta would be his personal program, diluted by whatever concessions he was obliged to make to his Soviet host to keep up appearances of Allied unity. As historian Walter LaFeber noted, Roosevelt had no Plan B, which meant his Wilsonian language was not a policy but "a disease that not even FDR—searching for a consensus for policies in 1945 he knew could not work—was immune to." At Yalta the Big Three made accords on U.N. procedures, the partition of Germany into occupation zones, German reparations, and the composition of the Polish regime. They also issued a Declaration on Liberated Europe, in which they promised to realize the principles of the Atlantic Charter in liberated countries. All those accords were tentative, ambiguous, and left up to the parties to interpret as they pleased.

Equally significant was a subject that the Soviets had previously broached but that did not come up at Yalta: postwar American loans to the USSR. The reason was that Cordell Hull and Ambassador Averell Harriman insisted the Soviets embrace the Bretton Woods system and Open Door in return, whereupon the Soviets fell silent. So much for the New Deal for the World. Finally, Roosevelt made a portentous deal to ensure the USSR entered the war against Japan within three months of a German surrender. In return he promised to pressure Chiang Kai-Shek into granting the Soviets all the imperial concessions in the Far East possessed by the tsars. Such a treaty would presumably give Stalin a strong incentive to support the Nationalist Chinese rather than the Communist Chinese after the war. Conspicuous by its absence at Yalta was the Anglo-American special relationship. No wonder Churchill (who had secured his eastern Mediterranean lifeline of empire through that Balkans spheres-of-influence deal) fretted more about Roosevelt's intentions than Stalin's. The long-term American plan was obviously to break up the British Empire and supplant it.

The Yalta Conference was not a sellout but rather the last dance of the masquerade ball. Its ambiguous terms shrouded, one last time, the incompatible aims of the improbable popular front that Axis aggression had brought into being. Moreover, FDR still needed that shroud because he believed a final sales pitch was needed at home to ensure that the Congress and American public were on board with internationalism. Luckily for Roosevelt, it was not needed because his sales pitch to a joint session of Congress on March 1, 1945, was pathetic. The charismatic president's powers had deserted him. For the first time he appeared in his wheelchair and spoke openly of his handicap. He was gaunt, hollowed out, and at times incoherent. He had lost the use of one hand and possibly one eye. But Roosevelt performed what he imagined his duty when he told the nation some bright shining lies. The first was that his health was fine; indeed he had never felt better: "Roosevelts are not, as you may suspect, averse to travel. We seem to thrive on it!" The second was that Americans were uniquely responsible for making the United Nations a success. "Speaking in all frankness, the question of whether [my journey] is entirely fruitful lies to a great extent in your hands. For unless you here in the halls of the American Congress—with the support of the American people—concur in the general conclusions reached at Yalta, and give them your active support, the meeting will not have produced lasting results."

The third was that Yalta ensured perpetual peace. No less than twenty-five times did FDR promise the Congress peace in various forms: "international peace ... a world of peace ... lasting peace ... the peace of the world ... peace and security ... peace and the civilization ... peace-loving nations ... ideal of lasting peace ... secur[ing of] the peace ... world peace. ... Republicans want peace

... structure of world peace ... not just an American peace, or a British peace, or a Russian peace. ... [It] cannot be a peace of large Nations or of small Nations [but] a peace which rests on the cooperative effort of the whole world. ... It can be a peace—and it will be a peace—which rests on the sound and just principles of the Atlantic Charter. ... The solution of problems that may arise to endanger the peace. ... tremendous influence in the cause of peace ... responsibility for keeping the peace ... common ground of peace ... a universal organization in which all peace-loving Nations will finally have a chance to join ... a permanent structure of peace." In retrospect, he was only right about one thing and that only ironically. He said that "under the agreements reached at Yalta, there will be a more stable political Europe than ever before."

Roosevelt, like Lincoln, was spared the heartbreaking wreck of his cause. The president succumbed to a killer stroke on April 12 at his polio retreat in Warm Springs, Georgia. He was spared having to agonize over dropping the atomic bomb on Japan, spared having to break relations with Stalin, spared having to face a Congress he had so badly misled. But as beloved as FDR was to the millions of Americans who looked to his inspiring leadership during depression and war, he had also earned the enmity of a large minority, did not die a martyr, and did not get instant admission to the civil religious pantheon. On the contrary, one of the first acts of Republicans upon regaining a Congressional majority in the landslide midterms of 1946 was to pass the Twenty-Second Amendment, limiting presidents to two elected terms. Franklin D. Roosevelt was posthumously impeached.

The San Francisco Conference on International Organization opened on April 25, 1945, five days before Hitler committed suicide. The delegates revised the tentative texts drafted at Dumbarton Oaks but invited submission of ideas from the outside. So it was that the Christian Realists' Commission on a Just and Durable Peace got some input after all. Four of their nine suggestions contributed to the U.N. Charter: a statement of moral purpose in the preamble; the development of customary international law; the colonial trusteeship; and a proclamation of human rights. The charter was opened for signature by representatives of fifty nations on June 26 and heralded by President Harry Truman, who, not surprisingly, was determined to realize the agenda of his great predecessor: "The Charter of the United Nations which you have just signed is a solid structure upon which we can build a better world. History will honor you for it. Between the victory in Europe and the final victory, in this most destructive of all wars, you have won a victory against war itself. . . . This new structure of peace is rising upon strong foundations. Let us not fail to grasp this supreme chance to establish a world-wide rule of reason—to create an enduring peace under the guidance of God."

The final victory to which Truman referred was agonizingly elusive because the Pacific War's coda seemed an interminable cadence of unspeakably violent crescendos. It was almost as if the Americans themselves had been driven mad by their enemy's madness. The armada of B-29s that firebombed Tokyo made March 9, 1945, the deadliest day in the history of warfare. Almost all of the over ninety thousand victims were civilians. The Army Air Forces then systematically incinerated defenseless cities until General Curtis LeMay complained he was running out of targets. But over those same months Japanese soldiers and kamikaze pilots defended Iwo Jima and Okinawa ferociously. U.S. commanders could only imagine the carnage an invasion of the home islands would cause, not least because the enemy was certain to fortify the few likely invasion beaches on Kyushu. The U.S. naval blockade might eventually starve the islands into submission, but how long would that take? In July 1945 a third option appeared.

President Truman was attending the Potsdam Conference outside the ruins of Berlin when he learned of the atomic test at Alamogordo, New Mexico. Cooperation with the Soviet Union was already breaking down but had not yet turned into hostility. The president and the new secretary of state, James F. Byrnes, were simply resigned to the fact that the occupying powers in Germany were going to do as they wished in their own zones—in other words, de facto dismemberment—and the Soviets were likely to define democracy however they wished throughout Eastern Europe. Historian Marc Trachtenberg has called this an amicable divorce because the United States really had no clear policy regarding Eastern Europe in the last half of 1945. To be sure, Byrnes rued the fact that the USSR had managed to emerge from the war with so much power, and Truman confided to his diary that the atomic bomb might prompt a Japanese surrender before the Soviets got into the Pacific War. But neither was thinking in Cold War terms at Potsdam, nor did they try to intimidate Stalin or suggest that a decision to use the atomic bombs was controversial. The orders regarding use of the warheads simply proceeded through military channels from the deputy chief of staff on July 25, nine days after the initial test. Only a presidential intervention countermanding the orders would have been controversial.

The atomic bombs effaced Hiroshima on August 6 and Nagasaki on August 9, with a hasty Soviet declaration of war on Japan in between. The emperor at last intervened on behalf of a cease-fire in return for a vague American promise to let him remain on the throne. General Douglas MacArthur received the instrument of surrender on September 2. The war ended. Americans cheered and sobbed. But the New Deal for the World and harmonious United Nations evaporated within a year because FDR, no less than Wilson, had failed to establish Progressive ACR as the new orthodoxy in foreign affairs.

Kennedy's World: The Civil Church Triumphant

Baby boomers took American power, prosperity, and technological progress for granted. They learned from their parents, teachers, coaches, and clergy that the United States was one nation under an ecumenical God who blessed a republic with liberty and justice for all. Nominal Protestants, Catholics, and Jews might not observe sectarian holy days, but everyone celebrated civil holidays, including the Fourth of July, Thanksgiving, Lincoln's and Washington's birthdays (now Presidents' Day), Decoration Day (now Memorial Day), Armistice Day (now Veterans' Day), and Flag Day. In schools children recited the Pledge of Allegiance and a vaguely Unitarian prayer and learned the United States won all its wars and led the Free World. Later they learned how the free enterprise system, suitably regulated by Keynesian economics, ensured full employment and perpetual growth through planned research and development. Many boomers would eventually rebel against racial discrimination, poverty, nuclear weapons, and imperial wars. But with few exceptions they rebelled in the name of the ideals they had been told America stood for. Their very protestations validated a newly orthodox ACR.

In that "mid-century moment," as journalist Michael Barone aptly called it, a unique conflation of demographic, political, and technological trends rendered Americans more connected with each other than ever before or since. From the late 1940s to the late 1960s big government, big business, and big labor were seemingly on the same team, as they had been in World War II, cooperating for great national goals. White-collar organization men conformed to corporate cultures and got lifetime careers and pensions in return. Blue-collar workers joined powerful unions and got lifetime employment and pensions in return. Everyone qualified for Social Security. Everyone got telephone, electricity, gas, water, and sewer services from the same regulated monopolies. Everyone bought cars from the Big Three manufacturers (Ford, General Motors, and Chrysler), consumed entertainment and news from the three television networks (NBC, ABC, CBS), and chose among three news magazines *(Time, Newsweek, and U.S. News and World Report)*. White, middle-class Americans bought similar homes in similar suburbs, heard similar sermons in similar churches and synagogues, and held remarkably similar political views.

Almost everybody got richer. The U.S. gross domestic product doubled in real terms between 1950 and 1965, and per capita income increased 50 percent. Home ownership climbed from 50 to 63 percent. The Dow Jones index more than tripled between 1949 and 1965. The numbers, size, and muscle of automobiles reached crazy proportions, while the price of gasoline held stable at about thirty-five cents per gallon. The Interstate Highway System, modeled on the German autobahns Eisenhower admired, already linked most major cities by 1965. Jet aviation fulfilled the One World and Air Age prophecies of Willkie and Roosevelt. Air conditioning was turning the torrid South into a sunbelt far more attractive than cold northern cities. But so, too, were the charms of myriad American localities being swiftly occulted by restaurant chains, motel chains, and shopping malls.

The Free World in which baby boomers grew up was no less Americans' oyster. To be sure, Stalin had frustrated Roosevelt's ambitious design for a truly unified planet. But the Communists behaved so egregiously that within four years they conjured into existence the Truman administration's far more manageable design for a sub-world led by the United States. As McGeorge Bundy explained in *Foreign Affairs* in 1949, the Soviets faced three choices after the war: fulfill the Yalta accords, quietly cheat without causing alarm, or brazenly break their promises. Luckily they had chosen the third. "For what saved Western Europe from Communism was American public opinion, and it was the Russians, not Wall Street, that armed this mighty force." Once Americans were convinced their own security and prosperity required global commitments, the civil religious implications were clear. God must be calling Americans to shelter and succor all peoples threatened by atheistic communism. As Secretary of the Navy James Forrestal reasoned in 1947, "You cannot talk about American security without talking Europe, the Middle East, the freedom and security of the sea lanes, and the hundreds of millions of underfed, frustrated human beings throughout the world."

President Truman made the new orthodoxy explicit in his 1949 inaugural address, a paean to faith. History had reached a major turning point that obliged Americans

> to proclaim to the world the essential principles of the faith by which we live, and to declare our aims to all peoples. The American people stand firm in the faith which has inspired this Nation from the beginning. We believe that all men have a right to equal justice under law and equal opportunity to share in the common good. We believe that all men have the right to freedom of thought and expression. We believe that all men are created equal because they are created in the image of God. From this faith we will not be moved.

Democracy was threatened by the false philosophy of communism, but the United States and its partners were seizing the initiative in this struggle by supporting the United Nations, promoting economic recovery, strengthening collective security, and embarking "on a bold new program for making the benefits of our scientific advances and industrial progress available for the improvement and growth of underdeveloped areas. More than half the people of the world are living in conditions approaching misery. . . . For the first time in history, humanity possesses the knowledge and the skill to relieve the suffering of these people." Since the United States uniquely possessed the capital, productivity, and "inexhaustible" technical knowledge, it would achieve peace, plenty, and freedom for all "who hunger and thirst after righteousness" (Matthew 5:6). Truman closed with a vow: "Steadfast in our faith in the Almighty, we will advance toward a world where man's freedom is secure. To that end we will devote our strength, our resources, and our firmness of resolve."

Baby boomers did not remember that speech, but many of them were old enough to hear President John F. Kennedy's even more zealous inaugural in 1961. He reminded Americans (and the world) that "the rights of man come not from the generosity of the state, but from the hand of God." He pledged to Americans (and the world) that "we shall pay any price, bear any burden, meet any hardship, support any friend, oppose any foe, in order to assure the survival and the success of liberty." He called on citizens of America (and the world) to wage "a long twilight struggle, year in and year out, 'rejoicing in hope, patient in tribulation' [Romans 12:12]—a struggle against the common enemies of man: tyranny, poverty, disease, and war itself." Having renewed Truman's vow, Kennedy closed with an "altar call" challenging younger generations to join the crusade:

> The energy, the faith, the devotion which we bring to this endeavor will light our country and all who serve it—and the glow from that fire can truly light the world. And so, my fellow Americans: ask not what your country can do for you—ask what you can do for your country. ... With a good conscience our only sure reward, with history the final judge of our deeds, let us go forth to lead the land we love, asking His blessing and His help, but knowing that here on earth God's work must truly be our own.

Robert Frost had composed a poem for Kennedy's inaugural but could not read it because, he claimed, his eyes were old and the light was poor. He recited a poem from memory instead. But Arthur M. Schlesinger, Jr., reported that Frost's intention had been to prophesy a glorious new Augustan age in which Kennedy's America—proud, powerful, poetic, and ambitious—might confidently enter the lists "in any game the nations want to play."

How ironic that social theorist Lewis Mumford chose the same analogy in his philosophical critique, *The Myth of the Machine.* He damned the technocratic hubris that prevailed on both sides of the Iron Curtain. But whereas the Soviet sort was candidly atheist, the Western sort seemed to him a new religion akin to that of the

Augustan age, when "the Roman power system, supported and extended by its massive engineering and military machines, had reached the height of its authority and influence. Who then guessed that the law and order of the Pax Romana were not so solidly established as to be virtually impregnable? Despite the earlier warnings of the historian Polybius, the Henry Adams of his day, the Romans expected that their way of life would last indefinitely." To baby boomers, that way of life was their birthright.

For a few years Americans' confidence was shaken by the inexplicable lead the Soviets grabbed in the grandest game the nations had ever played: space exploration. In 1957 they launched Sputnik, the first artificial earth satellite, atop a test ICBM, and made cosmonaut Yuri Gagarin the first man in space in 1961. But President Kennedy asked Congress to fund a crash program to send Americans to the moon, and he reassured the world about U.S. superiority at the opening of Seattle's Century 21 Exposition in April 1962. Its original theme, the progress of the Pacific Northwest, had fallen flat, but Sputnik inspired the promoters to stage a world's fair of science advertising American technology. The Federal Science Pavilion, a cathedral fronted by towering vaults of steel, housed a Spacearium where spectators toured the solar system and galaxy. In its World of Tomorrow gallery patrons in transparent plastic balls called Bubbleators gasped at the techno-utopia that human beings would build if they could only avoid nuclear war. Most memorable were the Seattle fair's symbols: the 605-foot Space Needle and 1.3 mile Monorail connecting the fair to downtown. After six profitable months the city fathers looked forward to Kennedy presiding again at the closing ceremonies, but he had more pressing business in October 1962: avoiding nuclear war in the Cuban Missile Crisis.

Just eighteen months later the New York World's Fair of 1964–65 opened to enormous hype at the same locale in Flushing Meadows where the 1939 fair was staged. Kennedy was dead by then, but Kennedy's World was on spectacular display. In the vast Hall of Science Frank Capra's film *Rendezvous in Space* took visitors into orbit with NASA's Gemini astronauts. In the Space Park outside NASA showed off its Jupiter, Atlas, and Titan space boosters (all of military provenance), and the F-1 engines designed for the

Apollo Program's Saturn 5 moon rocket. Americans never thought twice (or even once) about the pagan names attached to their hardware. Indeed, the Christian Life Convention sponsored a Sermons from Science exhibit reassuring the public that faith and science were never in conflict. The Oak Ridge Nuclear Laboratory even presented Atomsville, a please-touch children's display that made nuclear fission your friend, while General Electric promised "There's a Great Big Beautiful Tomorrow" thanks to safe, limitless energy from nuclear fusion. Ford introduced its Mustang model, General Motors reprised its 1939 Futurama, and IBM gave millions of visitors their first interaction with a computer. U.S. corporations spent up to $50 million dollars ($380 million today) on their pavilions, but the undisputed champion was Walt Disney, the P. T. Barnum of the twentieth century. Disney debuted audio-animatronic technology that breathed life into wax figures and made the GE, Ford, Pepsi, and Illinois (a robotic Abe Lincoln) pavilions the fair's biggest hits. *Time* summed up: "The 1964 fair both celebrates and illustrates the fact that in the last 25 years science has so far expanded the human imagination that anything seems possible."

Even more was possible, even inevitable. For the fair's regal promoters, including Mayor Robert F. Wagner, Jr., master builder Robert Moses, and Nelson and David Rockefeller, meant to showcase not only the promise of technology, but also the promise of globalization through American enterprise and culture. The official themes were "Peace through Understanding" and "Man's Achievement on a Shrinking Globe in an Expanding Universe." The opening words by President Lyndon Johnson declared a global manifest destiny: "I prophesy peace is not only possible in our generation. I predict that it is coming much earlier." By the time of the next world's fair, he said, the United States would be free of poverty and racial discrimination and lead "a world in which all men are equal." The symbol of the fair, the Unisphere, was a twelve-story-high stainless steel globe ringed (or lassoed) by satellite orbits. The globe displayed Earth's major physical features but no political boundaries.

The fair marketed globalization with subtle, feel-good techniques. Johnson Wax made a hit with its film *To Be Alive!* celebrating the joys common to all cultures in one brotherhood of man. Coca-Cola offered a "Global Holiday" and "World of Refreshment" that celebrated the marketing of Coke in 125 countries. But the most evocative pavilion by far was sponsored by Pepsi-Cola and produced by Disney. Visitors rode around the world in cute little cars, listening to happy children sing "It's a Small World after All." The countries (notably minus the Communist bloc) were distinguished by their traditional costumes, but the children's faces were identical, as if they were cloned. Thus did Pepsi and Disney anticipate by a few years Coke's famous "Hilltop Ad." This time the global chorus was comprised of real teenagers and therefore diverse, except for the fact that they all sang in unison, as if they were programmed, about teaching the whole world harmony and buying the world a Coke.

The 1964–65 fair put religiosity on display despite the fact that the Supreme Court had just struck down school prayer as a violation of the separation of church and state. But that should come as no surprise. Every Cold War administration, together with most corporations and foundations, encouraged an ecumenical, material faith that really amounted to civil religion. So it was, after the Soviets declined to participate in the New York World's Fair, that Robert Moses chuckled, "Into the gap left by the departing Communists the saints have come marching in." The Church of Latter-Day Saints (Mormons), whose pavilion replicated the eastern facade of the temple in Salt Lake City, was already an American civil religion of sorts. The uncontroversial Vatican City pavilion featured Michaelangelo's *Pietà*. The Greek and Russian Orthodox, Evangelical, and Christian Science communities all participated, but the American Synagogue Council, after long debate, did not. So Judaism was represented instead by the Zionist movement in the American-Israeli Pavilion. Mainline Protestant churches were likewise at a loss over how to present their message or whether they even had one. In the end they chose a suitably civil religious relic—the charred cross from Coventry Cathedral, bombed by the Germans in 1940—and a twenty-two-minute film that displayed Jesus as a "donkey-riding circus clown." The fair's council worried it might give offense but in the end let the public decide. The public, for the most part, approved.

In his 1962 book *The Image, or Whatever Happened to the American Dream*, Daniel Boorstin wrote that when the gods wish to punish us, they make us believe our own advertising. It seemed to him that "the God of American destiny has answered our prayers beyond Jules Verne's imaginings. ... But no power is without price." He sensed America was under imminent threat, but not from the Soviet Union or the tyranny, poverty, disease, and ignorance plaguing so much of the world. Rather, it was "the menace of unreality. ... We are the most illusioned people on earth. Yet we dare not become disillusioned, because our illusions are the very house in which we live; they are our news, our heroes, our adventure, our forms of art, our very experience. ... We have come to believe in our own images, till we have projected ourselves out of this world." Boorstin discerned that Kennedy's World was a hall of mirrors. Whichever way Americans looked, they saw distorted reflections of themselves. They believed the future must inevitably be shaped by the three things they assumed all people wanted—freedom, science, and stuff—and they believed that God had bestowed upon them the resources, knowledge, power, and right to deliver those blessings. The United States, in the words of historian Michael Adas, had become "the law-giver and arbiter of mankind."

In their classrooms baby boomers were prompted by *My Weekly Reader* (with a grade school circulation of 13 million) to cheer U.S. leadership of the Free World and United Nations, especially its newly decolonized members. In their own rooms at home the boomers were prompted by Marvel and DC Comics to cheer the patriotic thaumaturgy of Superman, Captain America, the Justice League of America, and other superheroes. But nothing expressed the technical and political magic of Kennedy's World so much as Gene Roddenberry's *Star Trek*, the television series that premiered in 1966 and became a cult franchise, especially a decade later, when the *Star Wars* films began to appear. *Star Trek* was set in the twenty-third century, by which time all intelligent species had transcended their historic religions in favor of an ethical civil code. The cultures of earth, long since united, had joined with more than 150 extraterrestrial cultures in a United Federation of Planets, which dispatched scientific-military expeditions throughout the galaxy. The crew of the Starship *Enterprise*, diverse by 1960s standards, included a Russian, a Scot, an East African, a generic Asian, and an alien from the planet Vulcan. But the captain, of course, was American, and the captain's name was "church" (Kirk).

In Kennedy's World it could not have been otherwise.

CHAPTER TWENTY-THREE

The Cradles of Cold War Theology

OR MANY PEOPLE THE first reaction was fear, the second shame, and the third awe upon catching a glimpse of a world without God in which man was the master of destiny. A singularity had occurred. The atom was split and the future seemed grim, for wherever "the power of mass murder is in the hands of a few, democracy labors for breath."

Thus did the Anglo-Catholic monseigneur Ronald Knox record his initial thoughts on Hiroshima in *God and the Atom*. "The churches, we say, have made themselves look ridiculous and worse by lending themselves to the service of chauvinist propaganda. Organized religion is the scape-goat we drive into the wilderness, loaded with the burden of our own unspoken remorse. But, deep in our hearts, the scruple still rankles. There is blood on our hands, and not all the perfumes of Arabia will wash them clean." The atom had become the symbol of mankind's release from all self-control, such that world domination would belong "not to the cause which has right on its side, but to the cause which has the best-equipped laboratories on its side. We, too, will be fiery particles, bombinating in a world of unrest." Knox thought it unrealistic to believe the democracies might have refrained from using the ultimate weapon, and he already guessed at conflicts to come with the Soviets. But at least the atomic bombs had ended a war, which gave humanity time to reflect before the next war began. Indeed, "the Allied Powers have done the next best thing to not dropping the bomb on Hiroshima. They have dropped it."

Churchill imagined the atomic bomb the Second Coming in wrath. Truman called it the greatest thing since Creation. Anne O'Hare McCormick, the Pulitzer Prize–winning foreign correspondent, believed the bomb caused "an explosion in men's minds as shattering as the obliteration of Hiroshima." *Life* magazine introduced the mushroom cloud to the American people in its August 20, 1945, issue and correctly judged that the escalation of strategic bombing had led ineluctably to Hiroshima, which "was, and was intended to be, almost pure *Schrecklichkeit*" (terror). Numerous editorials leapt to the conclusion that humanity had invented the means of its own destruction. The public did not agree. Four out of five people polled in the weeks after the Japanese surrender considered the bomb a good thing because it ended the war, spared countless lives, and was safely in American hands. Moral considerations were a luxury for the clergy, who were in any case hopelessly split. At one end of the spectrum the National Association of Evangelicals declared, "Our concern is not so much about the atomic bomb as about the people who control it. If the people are saved Christians, it will do the world no harm." On the other end Progressive pastors, led by Harry Emerson Fosdick, sent an open letter to the president expressing horror over the bomb's use and implications. In the middle of the spectrum John Foster Dulles and Bishop G. Bromley Oxnam, president of the FCC, wrote the White House expressing pride over the scientific achievement but concern for the future. They hoped for national self-restraint and atomic controls through the United Nations.

Protestant leaders attempted to forge a common stance on an issue whose existential nature they could hardly ignore, but their abject failure all but invited government to fill the consequent vacuum. In December 1945 the FCC's blue-ribbon Calhoun Commission on the conduct of war denounced the atomic bombings as a wanton outrage. Its March 1946 report, "Atomic Warfare and the Christian Faith," said Americans ought to be "deeply penitent [for the] morally indefensible" pyre of Japanese non-combatants and work to abolish nuclear weapons and war. But few Americans donned sackcloth and ashes. To be sure, polls in 1946 revealed a growing concern over atomic weapons but only because Americans were beginning to fear they might someday be used against them. The Iron Curtain was descending. Communist atomic spy rings were in the news.

Then cloture came. On August 31, 1946, *New Yorker* magazine devoted its entire issue to John Hersey's essay, "Hiroshima," a humane but coolly journalistic account of the bomb as experienced by six innocent Japanese. Critics compared it to *Common Sense* and *Uncle Tom's Cabin*, but unlike those manifestos it contained no call to arms. On the contrary, it allowed Americans to say to themselves, "We have confronted what happened. We have been told what we did and experienced its horror. But we must get on with our lives. We can put all of that behind us." Nor was that unusual. It just meant that Hersey did for victims of the atomic bomb (and by extension all the civilians killed by strategic bombing) what James Fenimore Cooper, Henry Wadsworth Longfellow, Willa Cather, Helen Hunt Jackson, and other great authors had done for prior peoples trod underfoot by the march of American civilization. He memorialized them, which permitted readers to shed a few tears and move on.

Meanwhile, the charade of atomic controls played out in the United Nations, where the General Assembly's first resolution called for elimination of atomic weapons in January 1946. Truman appointed a high-powered committee under Acheson and Lilienthal whose report, in March, concluded that only by taking atomic energy out of military hands, and indeed national hands, could a frightful arms race be forestalled. But Secretary of State James Byrnes, concerned lest the United States surrender its nuclear secrets under less than airtight controls, persuaded Truman to appoint one of FDR's toughest enforcers, financier Bernard Baruch, to serve as chief negotiator. In July Baruch presented his plan with mock melodrama as a choice between the quick and the dead, punctuated by the first postwar U.S. atomic tests at Bikini atoll. His rigid conditions included unrestricted on-site inspection of the USSR, elaborate control systems, abolition of the Soviet veto in atomic affairs, a sanctions protocol threatening preemptive attacks against suspected cheaters, and no surrender of the U.S. arsenal until all the above was in place. He also insisted on a vote before the membership on the U.N. committee rotated. In the end even Britain, Canada, and France begged for revisions but could not afford to be left out of what Baruch bluntly called "our world." In December 1946 ten of the twelve member nations voted in favor, thereby giving a propaganda victory to the United States, but the USSR and Poland abstained, which was tantamount to a veto. Byrnes later lamented that the choice of Baruch was the worst mistake he ever made.

It was really pretense on almost everyone's part. A top secret report on American relations with the Soviet Union, drafted by White House counsel Clark Clifford in September, described surprising agreement among administration officials "that proposals outlawing atomic warfare and long-range offensive weapons would greatly limit United States strength, while only modestly affecting the Soviet Union." It was extremely unlikely that the White House, Pentagon, Congress, and most ordinary Americans would give up their nuclear monopoly on any terms, let alone terms acceptable to Stalin. Indeed, the more fear that politicians, educators, physicists, and clergy generated among the public, the more reluctant Americans became to entrust their nuclear secrets to some international body or even their own military, which is why Congress passed the 1946 McMahon Act creating a civilian Atomic Energy Commission (AEC). Even the earnest physicists, whose *Bulletin of the Atomic Scientists* warned it was seven minutes to midnight, defeated their own purpose because scare talk, in historian Paul Boyer's words, "created fertile psychological soil for the ideology of American nuclear superiority and an all-out crusade against Communism." Nuclear fear was like a Chinese finger trap: the more people tried to pull out, the tighter it gripped.

In 1947 the Catholic Association for International Peace broke that church's official silence with a decidedly ambivalent statement. It found atomic bombs ethically impermissible because they amounted to disproportionate use of force, but it shrank from categorical condemnation since their very existence might prevent war. Pope Pius XII waited until 1948 to pronounce on the issue, by which time it was clear the Soviet Union was racing to acquire the bomb. The Vatican feared communism even more than it had fascism and sided almost unconditionally with the United States in the emerging Cold War. So the pope refrained from anathematizing nuclear deterrence, warning instead that all scientific discoveries were susceptible to perversion. He even expressed admiration for an American Jesuit's book, *Total War*, which argued the case for a preemptive strike against the Soviet atomic program.

By then the Truman administration was deep in debate over whether to develop the thousand-times more powerful hydrogen bomb. A majority of the AEC's General Advisory Committee considered nuclear fusion bombs to be innately genocidal, while a "revolt of the admirals" objected strongly to air-atomic war plans. But the Joint Chiefs of Staff said it was "folly to argue whether one weapon is more immoral than another," while the newly independent U.S. Air Force insisted that Soviet superiority in conventional arms made it all the more imperative for the United States to maintain its lead in nuclear arms. Then, on September 24, 1949, the Soviets conducted their first atomic test. George Kennan wrote a compelling eighty-page brief opposing the H-bomb, but Acheson, ever a bellwether, kept it from the president. Truman later said he made no decision on the hydrogen bomb because there was no choice to be made. To him, disarmament by example was just appeasement by a different name.

With the Cold War and nuclear arms race faits accomplis, mainline Protestant churches tacked and fell into line behind the flagship of state. In 1950 another FCC commission, chaired by Episcopal bishop Angus Dun, issued *The Christian Conscience and Weapons of Mass Destruction*. Reinhold Niebuhr's fingerprints were all over it. His reputation had soared in 1947–48, when he had helped to found the Cold War liberal Americans for Democratic Action and the World Council of Churches. He even appeared on the cover of *Time* magazine's twenty-fifth anniversary issue. So the Dun Commission now endorsed deterrence and retaliation: "For the United States to abandon its atomic weapons, or to give the impression that they would not be used, would leave the non-Communist world with totally inadequate defense." Catholics, Evangelicals, and mainline Protestants thus deferred to the national security state on the most morally charged issue of the day. Historian Robert Jewett has called this the "high point in the acculturation of religion under the impact of civil religion."

Back in 1941 Niebuhr had written the following in *Christianity and Crisis:* "Only those who have no sense of the profundities of history would deny that various nations and classes, various social groups and races are at various times placed in such a position that a special measure of the divine mission in history falls to them. In that sense, God has chosen us in this fateful period of world history." Seven years later Truman preached the same homily to an audience of newspaper editors: "We are now faced with what Almighty God intended us to be faced with in 1920. We are faced with the leadership of the free peoples of the world. . . . Get these things in your mind, and use your influence to do what God Almighty intended us to do: to get the right sort of peace in the world."

Preliminary blueprints for the right sort of peace already existed. They were the Roosevelt administration's heady plans for a United Nations that was to be the United States writ large, a Bretton Woods monetary system that was to be the dollar zone writ large, and an International Trade Organization (ITO) that was to be the American market writ large. Ironically, the ITO would fail in the Congress, but the General Agreement on Tariffs and Trade (GATT) emerged in its stead to promote the global Open Door policy. So Roosevelt's model for a new world order survived, but—luckily for Truman—the world itself split apart when the Cold War broke out. That relieved his administration of the responsibility to police and reconstruct all of Eurasia, a burden beyond the powers of the United States even assuming American voters had been willing to shoulder it. By contrast, the Cold War restricted U.S. responsibility to what became known as the Free World, while giving Americans ample cause to shoulder it through policies serving national defense, humanitarianism, and economic self-interest. Moreover, Americans got ample justification for all that because the long cusp in their ACR came at last to an end. Most citizens rallied to a new orthodoxy, a militant, Cold War neo-Progressive civil religion.

The Truman administration did not begin with the intention of forging a new civil religious consensus. Rather, it began with tasks left over from World War II, including the occupations of Germany and Japan; UNRRA assistance for displaced and starving peoples; consolidation of the Pacific basin into a U.S. security sphere; the inception of U.S. oil diplomacy in the Middle East; the Nuremberg war crimes trials; and decolonization of the Philippines, British India, and Palestine, climaxing in Truman's recognition of the state of Israel in 1948. Not least, the energetic advocacy of Eleanor Roosevelt, reinforced by the Carnegie, Ford, and Rockefeller Foundations and Catholic, Jewish, Quaker, and African American lobbies, inspired the U.N.'s Universal Declaration of Human Rights, also in 1948. That remarkable document would have been inconceivable without World War II and the Holocaust. But its thirty articles, endowing all human beings with myriad rights and freedoms "without distinction of any kind, such as race, colour, sex, language, religion, political or other opinion, national or social origin, property, birth or other status," would weigh most heavily on the democracies since dictatorial and authoritarian regimes might ignore them with impunity. Suffice to say the Communist regimes abstained from the nearly unanimous U.N. vote for the declaration.

It cannot be known what else the United States might have been willing or able to do in the event that Roosevelt's Four Policemen had stumbled into the future as allies of a kind. Perhaps Walter Lippmann's realistic critique, *The Cold War: A Study in U.S. Foreign Policy* (1947), might have persuaded U.S. elites that indiscriminate resistance to communism would expose the nation to geopolitical and psychological overextension on behalf of a bewildering array of clients, dependencies, and puppets. Perhaps the noninterventionism of Robert Taft's *A Foreign Policy for America* (1951) might have won over the Republican Party and sooner or later the presidency. Perhaps Churchill, who had all but declared the Cold War in his Iron Curtain address, might have persuaded Americans in 1948 to finalize a spheres-of-influence deal with the Soviets while their leverage remained high. Perhaps Henry Wallace's leftist *Toward World Peace* (1948) might have gained support for a program that focused on domestic reform while granting "fair play" for Russia.

As it was, Truman just tried to carry out Roosevelt's agenda, which meant the initial and principal target of American diplomacy was the British Empire. In July 1946 Congress acceded to the administration's desire to make a postwar loan to Britain on apparently generous terms. But the $3.75 billion in credit was scarcely offered out of Anglophilia, much less to underwrite the Labour Party's socialist agenda. Rather, State Department officials such as Acheson and Under Secretary of State for Economic Affairs Will Clayton were determined to lever the British into making the pound sterling convertible and ending export controls in the pursuit of American interest as much as a vague international interest. Soviet economist Evgeny Varga noticed at once a phenomenon predicted by Marxist theory. "Historical development is unquestionably driving towards the disintegration of the British colonial empire." If the Americans succeeded in breaking down imperial preference and the sterling bloc, the "United States will then remain the only capitalist Great Power."

Toward the Soviet Union, by contrast, the Truman administration had no a priori agenda. For all the president's tough talk, the truth was the United States largely demobilized, took no offensive initiatives, and clung to the Yalta Accords long after they became a dead letter. But the question is moot because the perception of Soviet threats soon inspired the strategy of Containment, which in turn justified military and economic commitments so vast as to lie beyond anything Americans ever imagined might be in the national interest or even legal under the Constitution. They made those commitments out of faith and fear, and from them was born (like Dalí's *Geopoliticus Child*) a civil religious consensus that retained all of Roosevelt's One World promises but deferred them for the duration so far as the Communist bloc was concerned. The neo-Progressive ACR emerged as a fighting faith based on a new dispensation that positively required the United States to go abroad in search of monsters to destroy and crusade for its values and institutions out of fear of the threat from communism.

Which came first, the faith or the fear? Without a doubt it was fear of atomic holocaust, fear of a worldwide Communist conspiracy, fear of falling back into depression unless the world were pried open to American investments and exports. It should not be forgotten that the 1930s and 1940s were decades of wholesale retreat for capitalism and democracy, and their prospects of thriving in the ruins of war seemed remote. Acheson freely confessed to exploiting those fears in order to promote Cold War policies. But since those policies were alien to their previously hallowed traditions, Americans needed assurance that this time an authority even higher than George Washington and their sacred Constitution—a heavenly authority in fact—now summoned their blessed nation to leadership of the world.

Local crises and conflicts always erupt after great wars, like after-shocks from an earthquake. What distinguished the tremors after World War II was their alarming tendency to grow in frequency and magnitude. In 1945 the Red Army overran most of Eastern Europe, and the Soviets installed either Communist or compliant regimes. Early in 1946 Stalin announced his military-industrial pri-orities in a hostile speech on the postwar Five-Year Plan, while chief ideologue Andrei Zhdanov proclaimed a "Two Camps" theory that divided the world into peace-loving socialist and war-mongering imperialist camps. In February George Kennan wrote his famous Long Telegram from the U.S. Embassy in Moscow in order to explain Russia's insecurity, sense of inferiority, and para-noia, overlaid since 1917 by the fig leaf of Communist ideology. The deadlock over U.N. control of atomic energy was then fol-lowed by the frigid winter of 1946–47. Bereft of coal, oil, and dol-lars (even the U.S. loan to Britain was quickly expended), Western Europe made little progress toward economic recovery. Meanwhile, Stalin pressured Turkey to grant Russia's age-old ambition for a na-val base and transit rights through the Dardanelles and apparently funneled aid to Greek insurgents (in fact, it was the independent Yugoslav Communist, Josip Broz [Tito]).

For two centuries the British had sheltered the eastern Mediterranean from Russian or German external threats. But on February 21, 1947, the British ambassador informed the State Department that His Majesty's Government was broke and must cease assistance to Athens and Ankara by April 1. Ever since the turn of the century various prescient observers had foreseen this sort of changing of the guard. So the smart people in Washington, D.C., should not have been stunned. They should have anticipated the costs of assuming Britain's global burdens one port, one gulf, one sea, one ocean at a time. Instead, the process played out in a crisis atmosphere over the famous fifteen weeks in 1947.

First came the Truman Doctrine. A joint report by the Departments of State, War, and the Navy urged immediate succor for Greece and Turkey, a move that Acheson justified by the first iteration of a domino theory. The Russians were muscling Greece and Turkey while large Communist parties agitated in Italy, France, and Iran. Should any of those countries fall, the others were likely to topple until the Soviets controlled the entire Mediterranean and Middle East. Senator Arthur H. Vandenberg, the famed convert from isolationism and now chairman of the Foreign Relations Committee, promised to help but warned that Truman must scare the hell out of the American people. Speech writers huddled, wondering whether to restrict the request to Greece and Turkey or to hazard a principle that presidents might apply anywhere. Kennan was appalled by the implications of a universal commitment, but Acheson prevailed with a specious appeal to authority: "If FDR were alive I think I know what he'd do. He would make a statement of global policy but confine his request for money right now to Greece and Turkey." Abraham Lincoln had warned one hundred years before against yielding such blanket prerogatives to the president. Now it was done. The new doctrine Truman announced on March 12 justified the $400 million in aid on the grounds that peace and prosperity were indivisible; hence the United States must support all free peoples threatened from within or without. "If we falter in our leadership, we may endanger the peace of the world— and we shall surely endanger the welfare of our own nation."

Next came the Marshall Plan, which the president called the other half of the same walnut. One need not be a Marxist to assert that economic structures play a dominant, if not determinant, role in historical causation. That is, no public policy, political system, ideology, or civil religion that is unsupported by an economic base is likely to last long. The economic foundations of the United States were at first agricultural, sectional, and commercial, then industrial and national as well, and finally financial and international as well. The preferred policies of these sectors (each with their sub-sectors) varied over time, as did their political clout. But in the wake of World War II, for the first time, nearly all sectors coalesced in favor of free flows of capital, manufactures, and commodities across national boundaries: the global Open Door. William Appleman Williams, who imagined American history as a tale of relentless capitalist expansion, might have gotten earlier eras wrong but got his own substantially right. The 1940s, '50s, and '60s were the first era during which bankers, manufacturers, exporters, and commodities producers all feared the consequences of closed markets and saw tremendous advantage in open ones.

So the State Department went to work on a plan for economic assistance to all European countries willing to play by American rules. That was the obvious way to avoid the mistakes made after World War I, the obvious way to serve humanitarian ends, the obvious way to strengthen democratic capitalism, and the obvious way to meet the needs of all four sectors of the U.S. economy. It was a moment, said a key State Department official, "surely unique in statecraft. It was not whether the United States should aid Europe, or even how much aid should be proposed, but how to make the transfer of billions of dollars to countries that had not asked for them and would not ask for them." Acheson kicked off the publicity campaign for the Marshall Plan with a high-profile speech before Mississippi Delta cotton merchants that emphasized this was no giveaway program but rather an investment "to preserve our own freedoms and our own democratic institutions." Vandenberg, a major spokesman for northern industrial interests, sold the plan on Capitol Hill, a task made simpler by the fact that business-friendly Republicans had recaptured Congress in 1946. Finally, Secretary of State Marshall's speech on June 5, 1947, made it clear that recipient governments must coordinate their investment of the American aid—eventually $17 billion—and thereby kick-start the process of European integration. It all aimed, Acheson later recalled, at "the creation of half a world without destroying the whole."

Kennan's "X" article in *Foreign Affairs* appeared the following month to promote the new strategy of Containment. He later explained that he meant to advocate political, economic, and psychological measures like the Marshall Plan rather than military measures. He also limited his strategic focus to Western Europe and Japan, and since he believed the Soviet Union was already overextended, the subliminal purpose of Kennan's article was really to contain the

United States. But "Containment" inevitably became the catchword that justified the Truman Doctrine and the National Security Act of July 1947. That act created a unified Defense Department and Joint Chiefs of Staff, the U.S. Air Force with its atomic-armed Strategic Air Command, the Central Intelligence Agency (CIA), and the National Security Council. The Pentagon, which Roosevelt had imagined becoming a vacant warehouse after the war, became headquarters of the neo-Progressive ACR's global crusade.

It began in 1948, when Communists seized power in Czechoslovakia and the Red Army blockaded West Berlin. Congress responded with the Selective Service Act, which established a permanent peacetime draft, and the Vandenberg Amendment, which ratified in advance whatever security pacts the State Department deemed necessary. The North Atlantic Treaty Organization—the first U.S. peacetime alliance since 1800—emerged in April 1949. In August of that *annus horribilis* the Soviets got the bomb, and in October Mao Zedong proclaimed the People's Republic of China. The Nationalist Chinese, despite $2 billion in American aid, had lost the civil war in the world's most populous nation. Those earth-shaking events turned the so-called Lippmann Gap between military commitments and resources into a chasm. So Truman appointed a secret committee that produced NSC-68 in April 1950. The document described the Cold War as spiritual combat against "a new fanatic faith, antithetical to our own," which "seeks to impose its absolute authority over the rest of the world." The authors rejected the status quo, isolation, and preventive war as no solutions at all (the last being odious to a democracy). Instead, they recommended still more financial resources to relieve Europe's and Japan's dollar gaps, plus a huge buildup of U.S. military power to deter Soviet aggression. The eventual goal was to foster fundamental change in the Soviet system. Two months later Communist North Korea invaded the south, whereupon U.S. defense spending shot up from 5.0 to 14.2 percent of the gross domestic product.

The Korean War was not really a war, said Truman, but a "police action" under the auspices of the United Nations. The Korean War was a limited conflict because Truman dared not risk escalation after General Douglas MacArthur's reckless foray to the Yalu River drew in the Chinese. The Korean War panicked Americans over Communist infiltration and subversion, threatened civilian control of the military, and never officially ended since the 1953 Panmunjom truce remains in effect. The Korean War persuaded incoming president Dwight D. Eisenhower that the United States must solve what he called the "Great Equation" between economic health and military spending by avoiding such brush fire wars in the future. He meant to do so via two more departures in U.S. foreign relations. First, Eisenhower authorized the CIA secretly to support friendly regimes, like those in France and Italy, and topple unfriendly regimes, like Prime Minister Mohammed Mosaddegh's in Iran and President Jacobo Árbenz's in Guatemala. Second, Eisenhower sent the NSC back to the drawing board in Project Solarium. What emerged in NSC-162/2 was a strategy for the long haul based on blunt nuclear deterrence (more bang for the buck) and a ring of Eurasian alliances sheltered by the U.S. nuclear umbrella. If the Soviets or Chinese dared cross those trip wires, they risked massive retaliation by the United States at times and places of its own choosing. Just as Monseigneur Knox had foreseen in 1945, the power of mass murder came to rest in the hands of a few and democracy labored for breath. Eisenhower knew and later lamented that very fact.

Finally, World War II consummated a quiet, decades-long trend in which presidents substituted executive agreements with foreign governments for treaties subject to Senate ratification. From 1789 to 1839 they made 60 treaties and just 27 executive agreements. From 1839 to 1889 the numbers were about even: 215 versus 238. But from 1889 to 1939 treaties rose to 524, whereas agreements soared to 917. Then over just five years, from 1940 to 1945, Roosevelt signed 38 treaties as against 256 agreements, including that greatest of all executive agreements: the Yalta Accords. By 1953 Senator John W. Bricker (R., Ohio) was fed up. He proposed an amendment that might be considered the post–World War II echo of Lodge's Reservations to the League Covenant. It limited the president's power to make executive agreements and prohibited treaties that eroded the powers of Congress. Eisenhower hated the Bricker Amendment and secretly worked to defeat it with the help of Senate majority leader Lyndon B. Johnson.

The point of reviewing this familiar Cold War chronology is simply to highlight the constitutional amputations enabling what historians Daniel Yergin and Michael Hogan have indelibly labeled the "national security state." In just a few years Congress surrendered its war powers to the president, curtailed its power to advise and consent to treaties, abandoned its responsibility to raise and support armies for not more than two years, acquiesced in covert intelligence operations on foreign soil, made enormous commitments of taxpayers' dollars to foreign governments, and mandated peacetime conscription. Henceforth an American citizen's rights to life, liberty, property, and privacy were subject to sequester whenever the president deemed necessary. One could argue that all those de facto repeals of portions of the Constitution and Bill of Rights were necessary under Cold War conditions in the nuclear and missile age. One could also argue that provocative warnings about a garrison state proved alarmist. Finally, one could argue that members of Congress have welcomed executive usurpations that relieved them of responsibility yet left them free to criticize when a president's adventures turned sour (as in Korea). But the fact remained that this second postwar era brought nothing resembling a return to normalcy. Americans now lived in what Senator Hubert Humphrey (D., Minn.) called a "permanent struggle in which war and peace had become inseparable."

It seemed the United States had swept out the unclean spirit of fascism only to find the world beset by more unclean spirits it could not directly engage without risking nuclear holocaust. The frustrating, protracted Cold War demanded vigilance, mobilization, global engagement, steely nerves, strong stomachs, and patience, traits very unlike those that Americans habitually took into war. No wonder Truman and Eisenhower sensed the people's need for a powerful civil religious consensus and self-consciously called their people to prayer.

CHAPTER TWENTY-FOUR

High Priestly Prayers

ENRY LUCE'S 1941 prophecy of the American Century was cautious compared to the "Permanent Revolution" he revealed in a special February 1951 issue of *Fortune*. The United States was that revolution because it was destined to bring the American Way of Life to all nations, not least those emerging from colonial empires. Some cultural leaders might grumble about it, but he encouraged his readers to hearken instead to the captains of industry, war, and government, who grasped the mystical meaning of progress. Once exposed to U.S. management styles, production modes, technologies, and habits of consumption, every people would crave them; hence "the question of Americans thrusting themselves on anybody can never really arise." This was the real march of time, the divine will for mankind that nothing must be allowed to delay. International bankers and corporate executives, Pentagon managers, and Cold War politicians were eager to sing hallelujah for reasons both sincere and self-interested. Was that not the appeal of every version of American Civil Religion: the right to feel good about doing well? Standard Oil of New Jersey treasurer Leo D. Welch even boasted that being "the largest source of capital, and the biggest contributor to the global mechanism, we must set the pace and assume the responsibility of the majority stockholder in this corporation known as the world. . . . This is a permanent obligation."

Luce took it hard when Roosevelt's and Willkie's One World aborted. He took even harder the 1949 fall of Nationalist China, where he had been born into a family of missionaries. But the Korean War revived his spirits to the point that some confidantes suspected Luce secretly craved the Big War with Russia. Seeking a spiritual basis for his corporate gospel, he fell under the sway of Harvard philosopher William Ernest Hocking, whose 1912 book, *The Meaning of God in Human Experience,* denied revelation but affirmed a spirituality derived from history. His wife, Clare Boothe Luce, went to the other extreme by converting to Roman Catholicism. But that only made the power couple a living representation of the ecumenical civil religion that had triumphed in the early Cold War. Both believed world politics had something to do with morals and thus something to do with God. In 1952 the Luces urged Eisenhower to embrace religion only to be told, "I would have nothing but contempt for myself if I were to join a church in order to be nominated President of the United States." But Ike not only exhorted citizens to faith thirteen times in his inaugural address, he also got himself baptized and joined the National Presbyterian Church, then located near Dupont Circle, just north of the White House.

Truman and Eisenhower breathed soul into Containment, in historian William Inboden's evocative phrase, with their high priestly prayers and non-sectarian mobilization of opinion and organization. Their civil religious Cold War crusade began when Truman addressed the Federal Council of Churches on March 5, 1946, the day following Churchill's Iron Curtain speech. "Both religion and democracy are founded on one basic principle, the worth and dignity of the individual man and woman," declared the president. "If the civilized world as we know it today is to survive, the gigantic power which man has acquired through atomic energy must be matched by spiritual strength of greater magnitude. All mankind now stands in the doorway to destruction—or, upon the threshold of the greatest age in history." Anticipating both the Cold War and the nuclear arms race, he urged Protestants, Catholics, and Jews to make a spiritual revival lest terror and destruction ensue. Truman was no theologian. He was not even a very good Southern Baptist to judge from his fondness for bourbon, poker, and profanity. Nor did his celebrated aversion to ritual prevent him from serving as grand master of Missouri Freemasons. But his very laxity plus strong acquaintance with the Bible suited him perfectly for the civil priesthood. "I am by religion like everything else. I think there is more in acting than in talking," said Truman. As for nuclear weapons: "It is an awful responsibility which has come to us. We thank God that it has come to us, instead of to our enemies; and we pray that He may guide us to use it in His ways and for His purposes."

Since Truman was the first high priest under the new dispensation (not to mention a partisan politician), he made some faux pas and geopolitical blunders. But the American consensus survived because Truman was not given to pretense. He took ownership of the Cold War initiatives his advisers devised because he really believed the United States was called to minister to all God-fearing human beings by resisting the threats and exposing the lies of the Communists. But the unmistakable implication of Truman's hyperbole about the limitless power of technology to extinguish poverty, disease, ignorance, and oppression was that the United States would prevail in that spiritual war by material means, as if "Seek ye first the kingdom of all God . . . and all these things shall be added unto you" (Matthew 6:33) was an operational doctrine. Very few Americans understood at the time, but that put a decidedly postmillennial Progressive Protestant stamp on Cold War ACR that committed the Free World to building a veritable heaven on earth.

Truman began with an ecumenical campaign. He made FDR's emissary Myron C. Taylor his own liaison to the Vatican and was gratified when Pius XII proclaimed, "Into the hands of America God has placed the destinies of an afflicted mankind." The new CIA subsidized Christian Democrat political parties in Italy, France, and West Germany, and the Voice of America, Radio Free Europe, and Radio Liberation (later Radio Liberty) broadcast religious programming behind the Iron Curtain. Back home, bigoted Protestant protests frustrated Truman's effort to extend full diplomatic recognition to Vatican City. But Catholics now had full membership in the American civil church because of their service during World War II and especially their staunch anti-communism. Eloquent bishop Fulton Sheen, a star of the new medium, television; New York's cardinal archbishop Francis Spellman; patriotic Jesuit John Courtney Murray; Senator Joseph McCarthy (R., Wisc.); and his earnest supporter, Senator John F. Kennedy (D., Mass.), were among the prominent faces of Cold War Catholicism.

Jewish Americans naturally identified with an ecumenical civil religion that guaranteed freedom of religion in theory and delegitimized anti-Semitism in fact. Even leftist Jews supported the Cold War inasmuch as many had been anti-Stalinist Trotskyists. Truman then sealed the support of the Jewish community when he recognized the Zionist State of Israel in 1948. In so doing, he bucked the nearly unanimous advice of State Department and Pentagon officials who feared the consequences of alienating Arab states. Finally, Truman gave powerful evidence that his neo-Progressive ACR was a new and inclusive orthodoxy by integrating the U.S. armed forces. Imagine that happening under Woodrow Wilson! It so alienated Southern white voters that they bolted in 1948 to a Dixiecrat third party. But Truman won a surprise victory without them, whereupon he turned his inaugural address into a Cold War sermon. It began with a litany contrasting American faith with Communist falsity and listed the many ways the United States intended to combat oppression, hunger, misery, and despair. "To that end we will devote our strength, our resources, and our firmness of resolve. With God's help, the future of mankind will be assured in a world of justice, harmony, and peace." In November 1949 Truman told the National Conference of Christians and Jews, "We have achieved our unity in this country, not by eliminating our differences in religion . . . but by holding to a concept which rises above them all, the concept of the brotherhood of man." Truman even tried to bring Muslim and Buddhist leaders into the alliance, pledging to do "everything of which I am capable to organize the moral forces of the world to meet this situation."

By 1950 Truman had fashioned what historian Jonathan Herzog described as a "spiritual-industrial complex" in which civilian agencies, the military, industry, and the media cooperated to stir up religiosity and direct it against communism. It "was conceived in boardrooms rather than camp meetings, steered by

Madison Avenue and Hollywood suits rather than traveling preachers, and measured with a statistical precision that old-time revivalists ... would have envied." The Committee on Religion and Welfare in the Armed Forces, directed by Jewish activist Frank L. Weil, instructed chaplains to preach military service as a sacred calling. Attorney General Tom C. Clark toured the nation in a Freedom Train that displayed America's founding documents and interpreted them according to Biblical principles. FBI Director J. Edgar Hoover launched a publicity campaign touting spirituality as the essence of Americanism. Magazines, newspapers, textbooks, comic books, radio, television, and movies turned homes, workplaces, schools, and theaters into Cold War classrooms. In 1950 Truman put General George Elsey in charge of a global crusade in the belief that the "greatest obstacle to peace is a modern tyranny led by a small group who have abandoned their faith in God. These tyrants have forsaken ethical and moral beliefs. They believe that only force makes right."

The neo-Progressive ACR complex came together and almost came apart during the Korean War. In the short run the blunt aggression by Communist North Korea, presumably with the imprimatur of Moscow, justified a massive U.S. military buildup, continuing flood of dollars to Europe, peace treaty and alliance with Japan, and eventual rearmament of West Germany. As one of Acheson's aides cynically said, "Thank God, Korea came along." But the Chinese invaded Korea in force during the autumn of 1950, whereupon a victorious police action turned into a frozen nightmare. For reasons of domestic politics Truman had to defend Korea simply because he had appeared to lose China. For reasons of international politics Truman had to fight lest his Containment strategy lose all credibility. For reasons of cosmic politics Truman had given his country no choice inasmuch as his rhetoric identified the United States with the divine mission to liberate and to prosper the whole human race. In 1951 he even preached from a pulpit in Washington, D.C.: "We are under divine orders—not only to refrain from doing evil, but also to do good and to make this world a better place in which to live." However, limited war for a presumably unlimited cause was a very hard sell.

In fact, Korea was a botched discretionary expedition charac-terized, according to historian Robert Dallek, by "poor leadership and misjudgments by the heads of government in Pyongyang, Moscow, Peking, Seoul, and Washington, none of whose calcula-tions proved prescient." But Truman and Secretary of State Dean Acheson took full advantage of the conflict to erode or de facto re-peal the enumerated powers of the legislative branch in regard to defense and foreign affairs. In other words, the administration made the war an object of pretense from its very inception. The president's first act was to instruct newsmen to be low key, not alarmist. His next was to scold Edward R. Barrett, Acheson's public affairs officer, for saying North Korea was Donald Duck to the Soviet Union's Walt Disney because the United States did not want to provoke Soviet intervention. That compelled Truman to deny it was really a war and then deny it was really a proxy war, even though his Containment strategy assumed a unified global Communist conspiracy. But the spin worked because 81 percent of the public supported the initial decision to defend South Korea. However, when General Douglas MacArthur lodged a request for eight combat divisions, the White House needed to alter its spin. So Truman explained by radio to 130 million Americans that while Korea was "a small country, thousands of miles away," the sneak at-tack there was "a direct challenge to the efforts of the free nations to build the kind of world in which men can live in freedom and peace." Yet he promised to keep the conflict limited and even fired Secretary of Defense Louis Johnson for remarking that the real front was Europe and the real enemy the USSR. How quickly the world had turned upside down. No wonder the American people grew dizzy.

After MacArthur's Inchon landing routed the North Koreans, Acheson recommended a cease-fire in the spirit of the Containment strategy. But now the opposite civil religious logic kicked in. Congressional Republicans, backed by opinion polls, asked how the United States could justify a truce with the devil, especially when the side of the angels was winning. So Truman, assured by MacArthur that Red China would not intervene, gave him a green light to roll back communism. Instead, two hundred thousand Chinese soldiers crossed the Yalu River in November and drove U.N. forces all the way back to Seoul. That forced the White House to change spin again. Truman now declared the homeland was threatened—"Our homes, our nation, all the things we believe in, are in great danger"—and blamed the rulers in the Kremlin. On December 20, 1950, Herbert Hoover appeared like the Ghost of Christmas Past to deliver a national radio speech damning the folly of land wars in Asia and urging Americans to rely on air and sea power to deter communism. A great debate ensued in Congress between General MacArthur's position that there was no substitute for victory and Senator Taft's position, which attacked "the wide influence of the administration with editors, columnists, commentators, and others" who blindly followed the president's every zig and zag. But the administration dared not withdraw from Korea nor risk World War III, which is why most of those pundits supported Truman again when he sacked MacArthur in April 1951 and engaged in frustrating truce talks. U.S. soldiers now called it "to die for a tie." Two-thirds of U.S. civilians now called it a mistake. But to civil theologians limited war was the crown of thorns a chosen nation must bear.

Reinhold Niebuhr was never more enigmatic than in *The Irony of American History* (1952). He still espoused Christian Realism but exposed the pretense of a nation that promoted, not spirituality and individualism, but the same materialism and conformity of which it accused the Communists and harbored the same sort of messianic delusions. When World War II bestowed on America enormous power, the responsible use of which is a precondition of survival, the irony became complete: "A strong America is less completely master of its own destiny than was a comparatively weak America." Hence Niebuhr's ironic view of history "under the scrutiny of a divine judge who laughs at human pretensions without being hostile to human aspirations."

Was Niebuhr's a courageous dissenting voice denouncing both pacifist isolationists who were embarrassed by power and bellicose interventionists who made a virtue of power? That is how he is usually described because his voluminous, split-minded oeuvre includes proof texts for nearly all political camps. But Niebuhr must have known or expected that his books were misunderstood or else exploited as theological cover for power politics. As the reflective sociologist of religion Will Herberg imagined a few years later, "An irony of *Irony* was that it might produce a kind of stealth hubris; one could take on the Niebuhrian pose of being troubled by the implications of power—only without remorse or charity."

The Korean War wrecked Truman's presidency but not the Cold War ACR. That was because both candidates in 1952 endorsed the Truman Doctrine and national security state and criticized Truman's Korean decisions only on tactical grounds. Both parties assumed the enemy was very real and stronger than ever. But the most important reason the new ACR survived was Eisenhower himself. Perhaps it was inevitable that a World War II commander would serve two terms as president and thereby consolidate his battlefield victories in the manner of Washington, Jackson, Grant, and TR. In fact nearly everything about Ike's background, career, and personality prepared him for the role of ecumenical high priest. He might have consolidated the civil theology simply by not challenging it, the way he consolidated the New Deal. Instead, Eisenhower blessed and personified the national faith as if he were an American pope.

Almost every president's inaugural address paid lip service, by one epithet or another, to the Almighty. Only Eisenhower's began by asking "the privilege of uttering a little private prayer of my own." Of course he needed no one's permission and promptly exerted pastoral authority by adding, "And I ask that you bow your heads." After the Amen he addressed the nation in terms more apocalyptic than Truman's.

> We sense with all our faculties that forces of good and evil are massed and armed and opposed as rarely before in history. . . . How far have we come in man's long pilgrimage from darkness toward light? Are we nearing the light—a day of freedom and of peace for all mankind? Or are the shadows of another night closing in upon us. . . . This trial comes at a moment when man's power to achieve good or to inflict evil surpasses the brightest hopes and the sharpest fears of all ages. . . . At such a time in history, we who are free must proclaim anew our faith. This faith is the abiding creed of our fathers. It is our faith in the deathless dignity

of man, governed by eternal moral and natural laws. . . .
The enemies of this faith know no god but force, no devo-
tion but its use. They tutor men in treason. They feed upon
the hunger of others. Whatever defies them, they torture,
especially the truth. Here, then, is joined no argument between slightly differing philosophies. This conflict strikes
directly at the faith of our fathers and the lives of our sons.
No principle or treasure that we hold, from the spiritual
knowledge of our free schools and churches to the creative
magic of free labor and capital, nothing lies safely beyond
the reach of this struggle. Freedom is pitted against slavery;
lightness against the dark. The faith we hold belongs not to
us alone but to the free of all the world.

Eisenhower's use of the rhetorical "We" invited his audience to nod
in subconscious agreement with his description of a Manichean
struggle that drew Americans outward, into a tormented world, and
threatened the mystical union between their "spiritual knowledge"
and the "creative magic" of free enterprise. That was no accident
but rather an essential element of Eisenhower's dream for a corporate commonwealth. He was a great military commander who
acutely observed the behavior of individuals in large systems. It
should come as no surprise that Ike rejected both socialism and
laissez-faire capitalism as solvents of national unity and aspired instead to a democratic version of the corporatism pursued by
Mussolini's regime. Ike wanted bankers, manufacturers, small businessmen, tradesmen, factory workers, farmers, and people from all
regions of the country to behave as teammates the way they had
during the war. Historian Robert Griffith has called this a "deeply
conservative image of a good society in which conflict would yield
to cooperation, greed to discipline, coercion to self-government."
If civil religion could inspire Americans to such teamwork, they
would surely win the Cold War as decisively as they had won
World War II.

In 1953 Eisenhower wrote his secretary of state, John Foster
Dulles, that communism was a mortal danger because it threatened
to close off the United States from industrial Western Europe and
the raw materials of Asia and Africa. However, if nations, like

Americans internally, cooperated on issues of trade for everyone's long-range good, then "we could laugh at the so-called 'contradictions' in our system and ... be so secure against the Communist menace that it would gradually dry up and wither away." By then it was clear that nuclear war was unthinkable and limited conventional wars unsustainable, lest the United States spend itself to death. The logical conclusion was that the Cold War must eventually be decided through political, spiritual, and economic competition. Nikita Khrushchev made that logic official Soviet ideology in 1956, when he declared no alternative to peaceful coexistence. Eisenhower proclaimed it the moment he took office and spent two terms waging peace (the title of his post-presidential memoirs) by seeking to end the arms race, balance budgets, and manage prosperity at home and abroad. Khrushchev might boast of Soviet economic growth, promising "We will bury you!" But Vice President Richard Nixon won the 1959 Moscow "Kitchen Debate" amid an exhibit of American household appliances.

Eisenhower was determined to keep the world economy open even at the risk of extending the U.S. nuclear umbrella over two dozen countries. It was certainly not his intention to turn people into mindless consumers. Yet that is exactly what happened when big business and big labor took advantage of Ike's corporate commonwealth, plus world markets, cheap raw materials, and the almighty dollar to manufacture consumer demand for wants rather than needs. Madison Avenue not only practiced demand creation at home but ably seconded the government's campaigns to sell Europeans (including women) on American business management, production, marketing, retailing, and shopping. Over the 1950s a spate of books recorded (not necessarily celebrated) the non-ideological consensus underpinned by prosperity.

How could Eisenhower preside like Pharaoh over peace and prosperity without losing his people to hedonism? By imparting a religiosity he came by honestly via his pious mother. Obviously Ike shook off his pacifist Mennonite heritage by attending West Point and during his army career did not go to church. But on his second Sunday as president he joined, as noted above, the Presbyterian congregation of Dr. Edward L. R. Elson, a prominent former chaplain. Postwar families followed Ike's example to the point where over half of Americans claimed to attend weekly services, church and synagogue construction boomed, religious books topped best seller lists, and seminaries burst their seams. Eisenhower opened Cabinet meetings with prayer—Mormon secretary of agriculture Ezra Taft Benson offered the first—and instituted the Prayer Breakfast and National Day of Prayer. In 1954 he encouraged Elson to found a Foundation for Religious Action in the Social and Civil Order to promote democracy through ecumenical faith. On Flag Day that year he signed into law the bill inserting "under God" into the Pledge of Allegiance. In 1955 he keynoted the American Legion's Back to God convention, explaining, "Without God there could be no American form of government, nor an American way of life. Recognition of the Supreme Being is the first—the most basic—expression of Americanism." In 1955–56 he signed resolutions to put "In God We Trust" on currency and make it the national motto. In 1957, following the Suez Crisis in the Middle East, Eisenhower dedicated the Islamic Center of Washington, D.C., devoted to the "peaceful progress of all men under one God." Most notoriously he announced, "In other words, our form of Government has no sense unless it is founded in a deeply held religious faith, and I don't care what it is." Though often misquoted and deprived of context, the remark deserves the moniker "civil religious proof text."

During the 1950s people like Jackie Robinson, Elvis Presley, Marilyn Monroe, *Playboy* publisher Hugh Hefner, and *Mad* magazine creator Harvey Kurtzman roiled the surface of popular culture. But high above them a chorus of angels in politics and the media filled the air with so much comforting God talk that Americans soon took it for granted. Meanwhile, mainline Protestants, ever in flux, re-coalesced into an angst-ridden liberal faction led by the National Council of Churches, an angst-ridden conservative faction resigned to Christian Realism, and an angst-free Evangelical faction that eliminated tension between church and state simply by fusing them. Its most prominent and politically active preacher was Billy Graham. All Protestants claimed to want a Christian foreign policy, but without unity or authority they left it up to the White House to craft what Inboden has called a "diplomatic theology of containment."

Cold War civil religion had a ready-made demonology and martyrology, but it needed a creation myth. Until the late 1940s the dominant narrative taught in American colleges and high schools was the Western Civ curriculum developed at Columbia University during World War I. It depicted history as a pageant of progress rooted in ancient Jerusalem, Athens, and Rome, blossoming in modern Europe, and culminating in scientific enlightenment and liberal democracy, of which the United States was the paragon. The Russians had no part in the story, while the Germans had fallen from grace. But the values of the Atlantic nations were sure to prevail throughout what used to be called Christendom. That was useful history to a generation of Progressive educators. The Cold War required a new twist, a history that depicted America not as an offshoot of Europe but as a distinct civilization with a mission to transform other civilizations. Historian Perry Miller had already laid the groundwork in books that traced the roots of modern America to the seventeenth-century New England mind. The Puritans, he explained, were on an errand in the wilderness to raise a godly city upon a hill from which their descendants might redeem Old England and in time the world. Miller's interpretation has since been disputed, but his books (as Niebuhr remarked) succeeded as therapeutic history because they provided the mythical basis for another postwar catch phrase: American exceptionalism.

Contrary to popular belief, that loaded term was not an archetype but an artifact of the Cold War. In the 1830s Alexis de Tocqueville had described America's exceptional geography, but he never imagined an –ism. In 1899 Pope Leo III condemned Americanism as a heresy that diluted the faith and practice of Catholic immigrants, but he did not use the term exceptionalism. In 1906 the German sociologist Werner Sombart asked why socialism had gained no traction among industrial workers in Pittsburgh or Detroit. He concluded their unique opportunities and culture placed Americans at an extreme by comparison with other industrial societies, but they were not exceptional, not off the charts. The real authors of the phrase were none other than Communist Jay Lovestone, who suggested American exceptionalism might delay the proletarian revolution, and Josef Stalin, who condemned that suggestion in 1930. The concept was bandied about in left-wing

circles until the Cold War broke out, whereupon it was only a matter of time before someone turned a term of derision into a patriotic badge of honor and stamped it on American history. That
someone was Max Lerner, a former Trotskyist and editor of *The
Nation* who published *America as a Civilization* in 1957.

Exceptionalism made a neat shorthand for what Harvard political scientist Louis Hartz called the liberal tradition. Americans,
born free of aristocracy and established church, had no need for
European-style ideologies whether radical or conservative. They
alone were free to self-actualize and carry their freedom to the rest
of the world. Historians such as Daniel Boorstin, Richard
Hofstadter, and Clinton Rossiter made exceptionalism the principal
trope for a generation of textbooks. Sociologists such as Seymour
Martin Lipset used it as a heuristic device by which to test other
nations. Most obviously, the notion of an America set apart by
Providence against the day when it was called to export its values
and institutions suited Cold War civil religion to a T. Never mind
the grotesque contradiction of values and institutions being somehow exceptional yet universal at the same time.

Most historians, however they judge the Eisenhower administration's manifold foreign policies, agree they were prudent by contrast with those that preceded and followed. That was due in good
part to the fact that Ike never let civil religion interfere with his
strategy, operations, or tactics. Secure in his belief that America's
goals were righteous, Ike sought practical, tough-minded solutions
through a National Security Council that functioned like a General
Staff. He ended the war in Korea, solidified U.S. alliances in the
Pacific, buttressed NATO, enabled Western Europe's economic
miracle, and encouraged its integration. His other policies, however, proved no solution at all. For instance, the nuclear arms race
Ike passionately denounced as a "Cross of Iron" in 1953 escalated
throughout his two terms. The Soviets rejected his 1955 Open
Skies proposal for verifiable arms control treaties and exploded the
1960 summit after shooting down a CIA spy plane. The Soviets
won prestige for launching the Space Age in 1957, partly because
Eisenhower needed to cloak a secret U.S. program for spy satellites.
His clumsy handling of the Suez and Hungarian crises in 1956

soured U.S. relations with Britain, France, the Soviet Union, Israel, and the Arabs all at once, while exposing as pretense Dulles's pledge to assist captive nations in Eastern Europe. Indecisive U.S. support of the Fulgencio Batista regime in Cuba reaped a whirlwind in 1959, when Fidel Castro seized power. Most ominously, Ike's refusal to recognize the 1954 Geneva Accords on Indochina stuck the United States to the tar baby called South Vietnam. Meanwhile, at every juncture, Eisenhower authorized Allen Dulles's CIA to engage in espionage, subversion, coups d'état, and assassinations, including that of Congolese prime minister Patrice Lumumba.

In sum, Eisenhower not only accepted the neo-Progressive ACR, but he also deployed it as a moral umbrella that shielded Americans from the dangers outside while blinding them to the dangers American power posed to outsiders. Remember the presidential rhetoric of the 1920s, when Coolidge thanked God for the fact that America was never more secure, more at peace, more prosperous? What a contrast to Eisenhower, who when he spoke of security only reminded Americans how insecure they had become. Moreover, the balance of terror and Soviet intransigence meant victory would not come any time soon. That obliged Eisenhower to pretend Containment really was Eden or purgatory really a paradise. So long as Americans practiced what historian Ira Chernus has called "apocalypse management," the Free World could prosper even though "the demise of communism was postponed to an eschatological horizon."

Will Herberg, who was a former Communist turned Cold Warrior, saw danger in that. In 1955 he published *Protestant, Catholic, Jew*, a book that exposed Americans' dubious religiosity. In their postwar pursuit of affluence they busily blurred their sectarian distinctions in order to worship an American Way of Life that tolerated everyone except Communists. This civic religion was intensely pragmatic and materialistic but also empowered citizens to congratulate themselves on their humanitarian idealism. Every struggle America waged had to be a crusade anchored in the Puritan idea of a New Israel in a new Promised Land. Historic Jewish and Christian faiths had been so Americanized and secularized that they had become compatible with—or indistinguishable from—an official religion based on a mere faith in faith. Herberg concluded that

Americans were prone to sanctify their cause and turn their "undeniable moral superiority over Communist tyranny into pretensions to unqualified wisdom and virtue." The danger was that the identification of religion with national purpose engendered the messianic need "to bring the American Way of Life, compounded almost equally of democracy and free enterprise, to every corner of the globe."

Eisenhower had spent eight years trying to identify religion with national purpose. But by the end of his tenure Ike saw the danger that permanent prosperity combined with permanent mobilization were more apt to corrupt than to sanctify the nation. Meanwhile, the permanent high-tech arms race granted defense industries a permanent claim on the federal budget, while rendering elected officials incompetent to judge weapons programs only physicists and engineers understood. A democratic people, bought off with goodies, might be easily tempted to surrender control of their country. Accordingly, Eisenhower used his Farewell Address to warn against the military-industrial complex, whose "total influence—economic, political, even spiritual" was ubiquitous and unwarranted, and against the scientific-technological elite that threatened to take public policy captive. Ike offered no advice about how a free society might survive those threats because he had none. The speech was a eulogy. So he ended his presidency the way he had begun, with a prayer.

CHAPTER TWENTY-FIVE

Impossible Dreams

"IN THIS SUCCESS-BLINDED country ... [a] long-accepted national axiom has been that money equals wisdom. Never mind that some of the most narrow-minded idiots I have ever encountered are successful businessmen." So recorded lyricist Alan Jay Lerner to explain why he and his partners, composer Fritz Loewe and playwright Moss Hart, decided not to seek out a financial angel to back their new musical, *Camelot*, based on T. H. White's *The Once and Future King*. The European-born Loewe even thought it ridiculous to imagine that the legend of Arthur, Launcelot, and Guinevere could be styled as a tragedy: "Zat king vass a cuckold!" The others, already dreaming up ways to wring tears from audiences through the tale of chivalry wrecked by forbidden love, assured him otherwise. "Vell," sighed Loewe, "zat's only because you Americans and English are such children." Precisely so. "Stripped of its tales of derring-do, its magic, love potions, and medieval trimmings and trappings," wrote Lerner, the Anglo-Saxon myth of the Round Table evinced the very "aspirations of mankind" for brotherhood.

Camelot opened on Broadway in December 1960, six weeks before John F. Kennedy's inauguration, and closed in January 1963, ten months before his assassination. *Camelot* would have been linked to his administration even if he and Lerner had not been

classmates at Choate and Harvard and even if JFK had not repeatedly played the original cast recording before going to bed. But
Jacqueline Kennedy indelibly branded her husband's administration through a *Life* magazine interview with Theodore White a
week after his death. "Don't let it be forgot," she quoted Lerner's
lyrics, "that once there was a spot, for one brief shining moment
that was known as Camelot."

Utopian romance intoxicated the American 1960s. That may
seem counter-intuitive given the decade's thralldom to high technology, systems analysis, militarism, applied social science, and the
administrative state. But polytechnic hegemony over culture, civilization, and society—what philosopher Lewis Mumford called the
myth of the machine—positively required that ordinary people foster romantic faith in the progress on display at those Seattle and
New York world's fairs. The nation might perhaps be excused that
Promethean folly. After all, their neo-Progressive ACR made the
United States responsible for minding every other nation's business
as well as its own, and it is axiomatic that God does not assign missions to people and nations without equipping them with the
means to discharge them. Accordingly, economic, political, military,
and academic elites took for granted their competence to design
the future of a Free World and on some distant day a converted
Communist bloc. "Will the coming world order be the American
universal empire?" asked Austrian émigré Robert Strausz-Hupé in
the first issue of *Orbis: A Journal of World Affairs*. "The mission of
the American people is to bury the nation-states, lead their be-
reaved peoples into larger unions, and overawe with [America's]
might the would-be saboteurs of the new order. . . . The American
empire and mankind will not be opposites but merely two names
for the universal order under peace and happiness."

The goal of Cold War ACR, in other words, was to hold the
fort until the triumph of a Millennial ACR, which would double as
the first global civil religion. Imagine a world without walls, shorn
of ignorance, hatred, and poverty; united in democracy, peace, and
human rights; enjoying free movement of people, goods, capital,
and ideas. That was the Camelot dreamed of in the sixties.

Eisenhower's frugal husbandry bequeathed to his successor a
robust economy and a peacetime military of unprecedented power.

Perversely, that is what made possible the romantic binges to follow. Only in deep retrospect was it evident that American power had already begun to abate in relative terms. The Suez Crisis of 1956 accelerated British and French decolonization, which soon generated gigantic Third World responsibilities for which Ike had not budgeted. In 1956 U.S. commercial hegemony began to give way before the European and Japanese economic miracles nurtured by the export of U.S. production, distribution, and consumption models. In 1956 white-collar workers surpassed blue-collar ones, and cities began to lose population, early signs of de-industrialization. In 1956 the consumer price index began to inflate and the annual balance of payments turned negative, which meant the clock began to run out on the artificial Bretton Woods dollar system.

That deficit stemmed in large part from U.S. military deployments in Europe and Asia. But where Eisenhower had hoped to reduce them, Kennedy sharply increased them, even as his administration undertook social engineering on a global scale. Truman had founded the State Department Policy Planning Staff and National Security Council. Eisenhower had founded the President's Science Advisory Committee and the 1960 Commission on National Goals. But under Kennedy Progressive planning characterized nearly all federal programs, including weapons technology, space exploration, and Third World development, as if American central planning must be valid just because Communist central planning was bogus.

There is a name for that solecism, derived from Plato but developed by sociologist Karl Mannheim: the life-giving lie. Social classes aspiring to rule devise ideologies. Once in power, they discover their ideologies cannot deliver, so instead they promise utopias—lies—in the form of future perfection. All civil religions are variations of life-giving lies whose function is to unite, discipline, and motivate a nation under specific historical conditions. But sooner or later the lie is debunked by some new ideology, so the cycle repeats. In 1936, when Mannheim wrote, the ideologies-in-power all claimed to overcome irrationality. But whereas communism purged it through dialectical reason and fascism harnessed it through dynamism, liberalism tried "with undaunted optimism" to hyper-rationalize the world such that it spawned a new irrationality. Mannheim defined liberal utopia as the unhampered development of the personality and put it in the same category of wish fulfillment as chiliastic religions, myths, and fairy tales. Thus did Progressives reason themselves into Camelot.

On the Fourth of July 1946 the young candidate for Congress assured his Boston audience that Americans believed "they have always stood at the barricades by the side of God. Now, in the postwar world, this deep religious conviction that this is truly God's country and we are truly God's people will meet its greatest trial." Fourteen years later president-elect John F. Kennedy bade Boston good-bye with another speech invoking the recently minted trope "City upon a Hill." During the campaign Protestant leaders had urged Richard Nixon to raise the religious issue, but he was clever enough to know that would backfire in an era of neo-Progressive ACR. Kennedy's cradle religion ensured he would be more Catholic than the pope when it came to civil religion. Indeed, he was perfectly candid when he told the clergy of Houston that he considered the separation of church and state to be absolute. "I am not the Catholic candidate for president. I am the Democratic candidate who happens to be Catholic."

Kennedy's inaugural address struck such deafening civil religious chords that even Eisenhower was abashed. The sermon sounded a certain trumpet—"We shall pay any price, bear any burden"—and ended in that altar call—"Ask not what your country can do for you but what you can do for your country." But like so much civil religious rhetoric it cloaked a grand pretense because Kennedy's exhortation to sacrifice was really an enthymeme—an incomplete syllogism—that invited the audience to draw the unstated conclusion. That is, you won't really be asked to pay or bear beyond your tolerance because I (unlike my niggardly predecessor) will mobilize America's inexhaustible resources. Moreover, the last line—"knowing that here on earth God's work must truly be our own"—invited listeners to pretend that we could know, must do, and therefore must already be equipped to do God's perfect will.

But who were the "we" in Kennedy's speech? The audience might assume that "we" referred ritually to all Americans. More specifically, the "we" might refer to that idealistic new generation to which the president said "the torch has been passed." Most specifically, the "royal we" might refer to Kennedy himself, whose intelligence, erudition, vigor, ambition, and impatience (perhaps because of his severe health problems) supposedly qualified him to lead the wagon train to the new frontier. But where Eisenhower enjoyed Zane Gray's Western novels, Kennedy's favorite light reading was Ian Fleming's spy novels. Did he imagine himself a James Bond, Agent 007: glamorous, handsome, sophisticated, seductive, resourceful, lethal, armed with futuristic technology, and possessed of a license to kill for righteousness's sake, like a space-age Sir Launcelot? Certainly covert and special operations—the CIA and Green Berets—flourished during the sixties. But perhaps that rhetorical "we" referred to the extended self that was Kennedy's administration, all the undaunted optimists of Mannheim's model. Journalist David Halberstam ironically dubbed them "the Best and the Brightest." Historians Bruce Kuklick and Derek Leebaert call them "blind oracles" and "emergency men" given to magical thinking about their power to manage history.

A self-conscious body of foreign policy experts first assembled in Woodrow Wilson's Inquiry and was then institutionalized in the Council on Foreign Relations. But they captured a big, permanent niche in Washington, D.C., through the national security state. The experts' initial specialties were nuclear strategy, international finance, and systems analysis, but scholars were quick to colonize every specialty linked, however remotely, to national security. They invented game theory, modernization theory, the bureaucratic politics model, the rational actor model, conflict resolution, crisis management, assured destruction, graduated response, escalation dominance, and cost-benefit analysis. They founded the RAND Corporation and copycat think tanks, plus dozens of university centers for policy studies and international relations to which they comfortably retreated while out of office, regardless of how well or poorly they had served.

Cold War intellectuals also spawned progeny among the brigades of doctoral candidates who flocked to the social sciences and new area studies programs endowed by the Ford, Carnegie, and Rockefeller Foundations and federal agencies. Universities created centers for the study of various geographical regions the better to inform governmental efforts to steer foreign countries' development. The funding parties usually preferred that such centers be placed in the hands of political scientists or economists because their abstract theories (unlike historians' stubborn facts) were easily malleable. Hence, defense intellectuals tended to view the world from one perspective—Washington's—and employ one or another methodology to simplify complex human realities.

Emergency men (they were nearly all male) were supremely confident of their logic and objectivity, yet they frequently quarreled over how to handle the latest crisis. That led Kuklick to conclude that these unelected wizards of Armageddon did not make foreign policy so much as rationalize strategies chosen by their political patrons. But almost all American elites in the 1960s fell prey to six romantic traits. They believed urgent action was always superior to restraint. They trusted in business management techniques. They pandered to the public's craving for celebrity experts. They promised tremendous results despite embracing half-measures that only proved to foreign audiences that they weren't really serious. To American audiences they justified grand initiatives with flawed historical analogies and postulated the eagerness of foreign countries to be transformed with American help. But worst of all was the illusion that they had no illusions. According to Leebaert, the knights of Camelot made "the fatal mistake of believing their own propaganda" until the "whole government succumbed to an ideological hubris."

Kennedy's aggressive policies were wasteful and risky. The first reconnaissance satellites proved the Democrats' missile gap was a fiction, but they could not admit their demagogy nor go public with secret intelligence data. Accordingly, in his March 1961 "second State of the Union address" Kennedy called for sharp increases in the triad of nuclear delivery systems—Minuteman ICBMs, B-52 bombers, and Polaris submarines. But the president wanted more military options than those offered by massive retaliation because he meant to do more than deter Communist threats to core allies and vital interests. He wanted to be free to use limited force on behalf of limited national interests. He therefore adopted a strategy of flexible response, which required a sharp increase in conventional forces and special forces trained in counter-insurgency. It added up to a preemptive, across-the-board buildup that further entrenched the military-industrial complex Ike had warned against just a few months before and, not incidentally, created a gap on the Soviet side that drove Khrushchev to take dangerous risks.

In another special address to Congress on May 25, 1961, Kennedy declared the "great battleground for the defense and expansion of freedom today is the whole southern half of the globe—Asia, Latin America, Africa and the Middle East—the lands of the rising peoples." He granted that no simple policy could promote the independence and equality of all nations, that no one nation had the power or wisdom to solve all their problems, that not all commitments enhanced U.S. security, and that no initiative was without risk. Then he promptly forgot all those caveats to push for a long list of "urgent national needs." First was a strong full-employment economy at home. Second was a sharp increase in foreign aid through an Agency for International Development. Third was a big increase in public diplomacy (Voice of America), especially in Latin America and Southeast Asia. Fourth was an increase in military assistance to allies and friends on all continents. Fifth was reform of the army and Marines to prepare for non-nuclear contingencies. Sixth was civil defense focused on bomb shelters. Seventh was the founding of an Arms Control and Disarmament Agency to work toward a nuclear test ban. Eighth and last was the space program. The Soviets had stolen another spectacular first the month before when cosmonaut Yuri Gagarin orbited the earth, and Kennedy was anxious to leapfrog them. So he requested crash funding for the Apollo Program, aimed at landing a man on the moon and returning him safely to the earth by the end of the decade. That glorious but expensive initiative jettisoned Eisenhower's methodical building-blocks plan to develop infrastructure for space operations in favor of a race for prestige that predictably lost public support the moment the race had been won. Apollo might serve as the purest symbol of the decade's romantic, magical mood.

The speech ended with an announcement of a summit meeting to be held later that year. Kennedy assured the Soviets that Americans "seek no conquests, no satellites, no riches—that we seek only the day when 'nation shall not lift up sword against nation, neither shall they learn war any more'" (Isaiah 2:4). Those words played to the home crowd, but they must have made Khrushchev chortle. Just five weeks earlier Kennedy had authorized a sneak attack under false pretenses on a neighboring sovereign country. Moreover, he botched the Bay of Pigs invasion so badly that Castro's army quickly killed or captured the entire force of U.S.-armed Cuban émigrés. That brilliant disaster, as historian Jim Rasenberger describes it, proved how hyper-rational men in power could manufacture their own irrationality. Someone might have drawn the following conclusion: if the smartest among us can so misunderstand Cuba—a country with whom Americans have had intimate, unhappy relations since 1898—how can we presume to manipulate post-colonial peoples much further afield and far more alien? But nobody did. Instead, Cuba became a source of encouragement to the defense intellectuals because of the role it soon played in the stabilization of the Cold War in Europe.

Kennedy appeared weak and indecisive at the Vienna summit, which emboldened Khrushchev to permit the East German regime to seal off West Berlin in August 1961. The Kennedy administration acquiesced, viewing it no doubt as a welcome alternative to more Berlin crises (better a wall than a war). Nervous negotiations ensued among the NATO allies over strategies, command structures, and nuclear weapons—would West Germany get them or at least get a finger on the button? The Soviets were anxious to influence the debates, but their strategic vulnerability grew steadily worse as a result of Kennedy's nuclear buildup plus the deployment of Jupiter missiles in Turkey. So Khrushchev tried to even the score by smuggling intermediate-range missiles to Cuba. When U-2 spy planes discovered the bases under construction, the tensest of Cold War crises played out over a fortnight in October 1962. At length Kennedy agreed to withdraw U.S. missiles from Turkey and promised not to invade Cuba in exchange for the withdrawal of Soviet missiles. But the administration imagined its doctrines of conflict management and graduated escalation had forced the adversary to blink.

In the wake of the crisis the rivals took steps to prevent a recurrence, including a hotline linking the White House and Kremlin. They also put an end to radioactive fallout in the atmosphere through a partial nuclear test ban treaty. Most important, the NATO allies arrived at policies acceptable to Moscow so that confrontation gave way to a premature form of détente. After 1964 the Soviets under Leonid Brezhnev devoted the rest of the decade to achieving rough nuclear parity with the United States. The resulting balance of terror, called mutual assured destruction, stalemated the arms race even as Europe was stalemated. But the Cold War dragged on because mighty domestic interests in the United States and Soviet Union had acquired too big a stake in it and because new geopolitical imperatives came into play. Radical nationalist movements in the decolonized world plus the seemingly crazy Red Chinese (armed as of 1964 with nuclear weapons) posed existential threats to the apostles of communism and Progressivism alike. So instead of ending the Cold War, they globalized it.

Truman and Eisenhower had shelved much of FDR's anti-colonial agenda in the interest of Western solidarity. They were not thrilled about having to replace or else pay for the British and French imperial presence in so much of Asia and Africa. By contrast, Kennedy's advisers, including Robert McNamara, Dean Rusk, McGeorge Bundy and his brother William, and Eugene Rostow and his brother Walt were eager to prove that modernization theory could work alchemical wonders in any country regardless of history, culture, or climate. To be sure, the experts divided over chickens and eggs. One school of thought preached a global social gospel whereby sufficient investment could boost developing nations to the takeoff point for self-sustained growth, which in turn would nurture a liberal middle class. Another school of thought preached a global prosperity gospel whereby developing nations that began by securing property rights and the rule of law would attract the investment required for self-sustaining growth. But both approaches rested on a tacit assumption that the Third World was clay, that Americans were master potters, and that metrics could measure success.

Unfortunately, Communist wreckers could be expected to hijack the process of modernization by stoking the resentments and fears of displaced social groups. So modernization theory under Cold War conditions gave the U.S. government additional marching orders. It must assist nation-building by providing newly independent regimes with military defense, social reforms, and aid programs, the instruments for which were the Green Berets, Peace Corps, Alliance for Progress, CIA, and Agency for International Development. The purpose was to win the hearts and minds of Third World peoples through the export of U.S. money, power, and good will. The perverse results often included the multiplication of enemies, alienation of friends, toleration of friendly dictatorships, and the confusion of Americans naively seduced by Kennedy's rhetoric.

The United States was not an official party to the 1954 Geneva Accords, which liquidated French Indochina and gave birth to Laos, Cambodia, and the promise of a reunified Vietnam. Instead, the CIA transformed South Vietnam into a client state under President Ngo Dinh Diem, a Roman Catholic with strong American ties. That mattered because of the zealous Catholic adherence to neo-Progressive ACR. For instance, Cardinal Spellman published anti-Communist articles in the mass circulation *Reader's Digest*, and Dr. Thomas Dooley undertook highly publicized humanitarian missions on behalf of the six hundred thousand–odd North Vietnamese Catholics that U.S. agencies encouraged to flee to the south. Eisenhower patronized Diem's regime and warned that its fall might topple other dominoes throughout resource-rich Southeast Asia.

Kennedy's advisers not only agreed with that assessment, they made South Vietnam a test case for their own counter-insurgency and nation-building techniques, which must succeed lest the Communists be encouraged to launch more wars of national liberation. In fact, they got everything upside down. The USSR and China were now bitter competitors, especially in the Third World. The Vietnamese were wary of both, particularly their old enemy China. The Soviets did not press Hanoi for a guerilla war but in fact promoted peaceful coexistence after the Geneva Accords. Even Ho Chi Minh was content to build socialism in the north and wait on events in the south. But Le Duc Tho and Le Duan, who favored armed struggle in South Vietnam, managed to take control of the Politburo. By 1962 their cadres in the south, dubbed Viet Cong (traitors) by the Diem regime, launched a guerilla war that exposed the weakness of South Vietnam's army and government.

Kennedy, a leader of the American Friends of Vietnam, had told a conference in 1956 that "Vietnam represents the cornerstone of the Free World in Southeast Asia, the keystone in the arch, the finger in the dike" against "the red tide of Communism" and is an "inspiration to those seeking to obtain and maintain their liberty in all parts of Asia—and indeed the world." So he steadily increased U.S. support until, by 1963, more than sixteen thousand military advisers were in-country. Americans who noticed mostly approved. That was the year the best-selling novel *The Ugly American* became a hit movie starring Marlon Brando. The ugly American, by contrast to beautiful Americans ensconced in embassies and hotels, worked beside peasants to win hearts and minds. The hero warned that the stakes were enormous: "If the only price we are willing to pay is the dollar price, then we might as well pull out before we're thrown out. If we are not prepared to pay the human price, we had better retreat to our shores, build Fortress America, learn to live without international trade and communications, and accept the mediocrity, the low standard of living, and the loom of world Communism which would accompany such a move."

By 1963 Kennedy's team was perplexed by the surge in Viet Cong violence and its apparent popular support. It naturally decided that Diem's mandarin arrogance, ruthless secret police, and feckless army were wasting U.S. assistance. Diem was even rumored to be secretly negotiating with Hanoi. So after much deliberation and several unheeded warnings the White House acquiesced in a generals' coup, during which Diem was murdered. Did that event give the United States an excuse to pull out, or did it in fact make the commitment irrevocable? Since Kennedy's own assassination came three weeks later, historians can only guess. On one side is the hearsay evidence of an aide to whom the president said he could not withdraw from Vietnam until after his reelection. On the other side is the evidence that Kennedy doggedly looked for ways to win in Vietnam. He bet his presidency on it and forged bureaucracies around it. He put boots on the ground in the south and approved secret operations against the north. The coup itself was a war measure: what was the point of regime change if Kennedy planned to get out? But perhaps the most telling fact is that U.S. credibility was at stake—not political credibility (European allies in particular were apprehensive about this U.S. war of choice) but theological credibility because a pullout would have involved a repudiation of neo-Progressive ACR so great as to verge on apostasy. Suffice to say that the president planned, in the Dallas speech prepared for November 22, 1963, to boast of having sextupled the military advisers in South Vietnam and to tell Americans they "dare not weary of the task," no matter "how risky and costly" it proved to be.

Lyndon B. Johnson embodied the ecumenical faith in faith that lay at the heart of the civil religion. He was raised Evangelical but attended services at Episcopal, Catholic, Lutheran, Baptist, and Disciples of Christ churches. He kept Billy Graham close for reasons both political (it looked good) and personal (he feared the judgment to come), but mostly LBJ believed in the Franklin and Eleanor Roosevelt visions of Progressive utopia. That a poor teacher from the Texas hill country grew up to become a kingpin in Congress was no surprise. The Old South specialized in such types. But what on the surface seems truly surprising is Johnson's role in championing and maneuvering through Congress the legislative revolution of 1964–68: the Civil Rights Act, Voting Rights Act (despite knowing "we might have lost the South for a generation"), Great Society, War on Poverty, Head Start Program, Education Act, Economic Opportunity Act, Housing Act (Model Cities), Urban Mass Transportation Act, updated Social Security Act, Medicare, Medicaid, Food Stamps, Work Study, National Endowments for the Arts and Humanities, Public Broadcasting, Gun Control Act, and Immigration and Nationality Act of 1965, which eliminated discrimination on the basis of national origin.

In retrospect it seems as though some great backlog of public demand finally burst the dike on the wave of sentiment following Kennedy's martyrdom. For instance, the African American civil rights movement had been marching for decades to its own drummers, most recently that of Dr. Martin Luther King, Jr., and according to its own non-violent tactics. If anything, its legislative victories were probably overdue for the reason that Eisenhower was tone deaf on issues of race. But the timing of this third great wave of American Progressivism appears obvious. The Cold War forced the hands of recalcitrant Dixiecrats and Republicans because the civil religion now required the United States to pretend (at least) to practice what it preached about racial equality and social uplift lest it make a mockery of its own propaganda throughout the decolonized world.

The United States had anointed itself the world's savior and custodian of all those human rights proclaimed by the United Nations in 1948. But the USSR and People's Republic of China trumpeted their own support for national liberation movements in the Third World, and the burst of decolonization after 1960 gave them ample opportunity to make mischief. Ergo the United States had to embrace wholesale domestic reforms in support of its Cold War strategy. But the Johnson administration, with Congress in tow, dared not admit that reforming human nature was impossible and that even altering attitudes and behaviors could take a generation. So it contented itself with the romantic delusion that just passing some laws sufficed (as LBJ put it at the New York's World Fair) to eliminate poverty and racial discrimination and create "a world in which all men are equal." That was the message of the LBJ reelection campaign's notorious daisy ad. It wasn't about Barry Goldwater's brinkmanship and the threat of nuclear war. It was about Goldwater's opposition to the Civil Rights Act and the consequent threat of race war. Decolonization merged with the U.S. civil rights movement to form a transnational revolt that the Kennedy and Johnson administrations somehow had to appease.

Americans were told that Third World countries could not be expected to choose democratic capitalism so long as racism and poverty existed in the United States itself (as if Vietnamese or Congolese peasants had a clue about life on the South Side of Chicago). The neo-Progressive ACR made it incumbent upon the federal government to take immediate steps to relieve the plight of the helpless poor and to give maximum opportunity to the able poor. Had not every president since Roosevelt promised that America now had the technology, knowledge, and wealth to end hunger, disease, and ignorance worldwide? What would the world think if Americans neglected to use such power even at home? The federal government thus reasoned itself to the magical conclusion that showers of money could make misery disappear.

The leadership vacuum in Saigon invited Americanization of the Vietnam War, which is what McNamara, Rusk, and the others had wanted all along. The only thing holding them back was the campaign of 1964, in which LBJ, like FDR and Wilson before him, ran as the peace candidate. But Johnson had already drafted a Congressional resolution granting him authority to use unspecified force to protect U.S. interests in Southeast Asia. The bogus Tonkin Gulf incident in August 1964 served as the convenient pretext. Johnson's 1965 inaugural address contained no hint that the nation was on the brink of another land war in Asia. His self-congratulatory rhetoric simply assured his "nation of believers" that the enemy would be confounded by "the faith they could not see or that they could not even imagine. It brought us victory. And it will again. For this is what America is all about. It is the uncrossed desert and the unclimbed ridge. It is the star that is not reached and the harvest sleeping in the unplowed ground. Is our world gone? We say 'Farewell.' Is a new world coming? We welcome it—and we will bend it to the hopes of man."

In March 1965 the first U.S. combat units arrived in South Vietnam and aircraft carriers launched Operation Rolling Thunder, the calibrated bombing of North Vietnam. It soon became evident that CIA and military intelligence had vastly underestimated Viet Cong strength, not to mention the determination of North Vietnam to support the insurgency. General William Westmoreland chose a strategy of attrition based on search-and-destroy operations, confident that U.S. firepower and mobility must overwhelm the enemy. But those tactics might require several hundred thousand troops, based on the formula that counterinsurgency requires a 10:1 superiority. In June Johnson asked for his options and was told he could: (1) bomb North Vietnam back to the Stone Age but risk Chinese intervention; (2) cut his losses and swallow the consequences of defeat; (3) keep U.S. forces at the current level and take casualties to no purpose; (4) mobilize for war, with whatever domestic sacrifice and control that required; or (5) do what was needed to sustain the present situation, but do nothing that might provoke the Soviet Union and Red China. Needless to say, he and his advisers chose the equivocal fifth option for the sake of expediency but also because they did not really expect to win the war militarily. They expected to buy time for nation-building programs to manufacture a popular, prosperous South Vietnam capable of defending itself. Here is what LBJ told reporters the day after quasi-committing the nation to a Vietnam conflict (still not a war) with no definition of victory:

> It is now my opportunity to help every child get an educa-
> tion, to help every Negro and every American citizen have
> an equal opportunity, to help every family get a decent
> home, and to help bring healing to the sick and dignity to
> the old. ... But I also know, as a realistic public servant,
> that as long as there are men who hate and destroy, we
> must have the courage to resist, or we will see it all, all that
> we have built, all that we hope to build, all of our dreams
> for freedom—all, all will be swept away on the flood of
> conquest. So, too, this shall not happen. We will stand in
> Vietnam.

To Johnson that was not a non sequitur.

The architects of the conflict assumed Vietnam would not be another Korea, and it wasn't: it was worse. But the casualties, moral doubts, and impatience developed more gradually, which in the short run meant Johnson had less trouble than Truman in selling the war to the media, Congress, and public. Correspondents such as Peter Arnett, David Halberstam, Neil Sheehan, and Peter Brown initially believed in the cause and supported the troops. Official propaganda such as the Frank Capra–inspired film *Why Vietnam?* drew the Munich analogy by insisting that "aggression unchallenged is aggression unleashed" and warning that if "freedom is to survive in any American home it must be preserved in such places as South Vietnam." U.S. citizens, distracted by the Great Society, a soaring stock market, and NASA's moon race, mostly nodded their heads. They were watching what historian Marilyn Young rightly called "war as performance," designed to assure them the United States was doing its duty at acceptable cost.

Johnson meant to prevail not only in Vietnam, but also through Vietnam, by giving its people a revolution so superior to the one the Communists offered as to convert all developing nations. When David Lilienthal expressed reluctance about trying to modernize a country in the midst of a war, Clark Clifford explained: "It isn't about winning the war, it isn't the military operations that are closest to the

President's mind. It isn't even South Vietnam. It is a pattern for a kind of life that the people of all Southeast Asia can begin to enjoy that is at issue. . . . So what the President wants is to make a demonstration, a demonstration in South Vietnam." No one had greater faith in technocracy than Lilienthal, who yearned to realize LBJ's dream of a TVA on the Mekong River. But upon hearing in a secret White House briefing that the war might drag on interminably, he wrote in his diary: "I find myself sad, sad, sad. Unalterably sad."

The Tet Offensive in 1968 belied Johnson's talk of a light at the end of the tunnel. By the time it was over, U.S. personnel in South Vietnam surpassed 540,000 and U.S. deaths surpassed 25,000. Johnson withdrew from the presidential campaign. Peace talks began and quickly stalemated in Paris. A state of siege gripped American cities and campuses. The experts evidently had not foreseen those unintended consequences when they decided to draft American boys off the block, ship them halfway around the world to a country whose language and customs were alien, and tell them to slog through jungles and paddies in 110° heat, threatened by ambushes and booby traps, in the midst of strange small people who might be friends or foes, with no clear instructions except to find the Commies and kill them.

Man of la Mancha, Dale Wasserman's musical retelling of *Don Quixote*, opened in a Greenwich Village theater on November 22, 1965, two years to the day after the Kennedy assassination. He imagined that Cervantes, accused by the Spanish Inquisition, staged the play as a brief for his own defense and played the title role himself. Since the other characters alternately mock or humor the mad knight's behavior, truth and illusion get all mixed up. Quixote's chivalric errantry mostly wreaks havoc. For instance, the mercy he shows some rude muleteers enables their rape of the lady (really a whore) whom Quixote chastely adores. The climax comes when his archenemy, the Enchanter (really a doctor hoping to cure Cervantes), attacks Quixote with knights whose shields are dazzling mirrors. The romantic idealist at last sees himself as others see him and falls tearfully to the ground. But the prostitute now believes in his quest, prompting the whole cast to reprise "The Impossible Dream" and sing of marching to hell for a heavenly cause.

The hit show moved to Broadway for another three years and 2,329 total performances. Wasserman was amused that reviews of the show were either "brickbats or bouquets." After opening night, critics noted the "aggressive idealism" it expressed "on the second anniversary of the loss of American innocence." If anything, *Man of la Mancha* really proved how little innocence had been lost. "The Impossible Dream," wrote Wasserman years later, had been "used to promote everything under the sun and some in the shade. It's been used in sales pitches by General Mills, General Motors, and General Westmoreland. Also, by baseball teams and bidets and by sleazy politicians and by charlatans of all breeds and vocations. . . . When I see these references—and I see them every day—my impulse is to holler, 'Pay attention, damn it, the operative word is not 'dream,' the operative word is 'impossible'!"

CHAPTER TWENTY-SIX

Age of Aquarius

"WHAT I BELIEVED IN the 60s: Everything. You name it and I believed it. I believed love was all you need. . . . I believed drugs could make you a better person. I believed I could hitchhike to California with 35 cents and people would be glad to feed me. I believed Mao was cute. I believed private property was wrong. I believed my girl friend was a witch. I believed my parents were Nazi space monsters." But mostly satirist P. J. O'Rourke learned "the awful power of make-believe. There is a deep-seated and frighteningly strong human need to make believe things are different than they are."

Authors sensed the neuroses lurking beneath the surface of postwar American culture. Norman Mailer's *The Naked and the Dead* punctured the myths of World War II as early as 1948. J. D. Salinger's Holden Caulfield sensed how phony the grown-up world was in the 1951 novel *The Catcher in the Rye*. In 1953 science fiction genius Ray Bradbury published *Fahrenheit 451* about a future America in which books had been banned. By 1962 historian Daniel Boorstin had diagnosed the nation's penchant for self-deception in *The Image*. But the sentence that best encapsulated the clashing pathologies of the Greatest, Silent, and Baby Boomer Generations was the unheeded warning in Kurt Vonnegut's 1966 novel *Mother Night:* "We are what we pretend to be, so we must be careful about what we pretend to be."

In the 1960s pretty much all Americans who were upscale, vocal, and white strutted like supermen. If politicians representing the corporate establishment promised to end racism, poverty, and oppression through a top-down national effort and waged a hyperbolic war in Southeast Asia to prove it, so did self-styled leaders of the New Left promise to end racism, poverty, oppression, and war through a bottom-up global youth movement. Such fantasies of omnipotence were sustained by phenomenal wealth and the promise of still more to come. Over that decade the U.S. economy grew at a real average annual rate of 5.2 percent and imparted tremendous momentum toward globalization. Transoceanic jet aviation and telephone cables increased business traffic by a factor of twenty, inspiring Canadian philosopher Marshall McLuhan to coin the term "global village" in 1962. That was the year NASA launched AT&T's Telstar, the first experimental communications satellite. Three years later Hughes Aircraft's Early Bird geo-synchronous satellites (stationed above the equator one-tenth of the way to the moon) made the new COMSAT Corporation a routine utility. When representatives from many nations later approved a charter for the INTELSAT system science fiction writer Arthur C. Clarke, who first conceived of comsats in 1946, solemnly said they had signed "the first draft of the articles of the Federation of the United States of the Earth."

The United States was rapidly realizing the Open Door earth. The General Agreement on Tariffs and Trade's Kennedy Round of negotiations involved sixty-six nations accounting for 80 percent of world trade. When its sharp, across-the-board tariff reductions were approved in 1967, no one was more thrilled than Undersecretary of State for Economic Affairs George Ball. Historians usually note him for being the lone voice opposing escalation in Vietnam, but his most important role was that of Wall Street lawyer in the service of multinational corporations. Ball even promoted a cosmocorp theory advocating supranational councils to administer global rules without political interference. The multinational corporation was the model of the future, while the nation-state, "rooted in archaic concepts unsympathetic to the needs of our complex world," was the model of the past. Ball was instrumental in the Kennedy Round, which had world historical effects because of its Cold War asymmetry. The State and Commerce Departments self-consciously flung open the doors to the American market while acquiescing in Asian (especially Japanese) and European (especially French) restrictions on U.S. exports. Moreover, the technology to handle the ensuing tsunami of foreign automobiles, electronics, and durable goods was already in place because an American firm had introduced the container ship in 1956. A decade later compatible docks had increased the speed with which longshoremen could process cargo by a factor of fifty.

Corporations adjusted by going global with a vengeance. The foreign subsidiaries they founded quadrupled U.S. investments abroad from $25.4 billion in 1957 to $103.7 billion in 1973. Nor did the United States seem likely to lose its technological lead since its firms accounted for five out of every six patents and the federal government two-thirds of the world's research and development. No wonder observers ranging from Adlai Stevenson to Zbigniew Brzezinski theorized that Americans had discovered the philosopher's stone enabling progress to accelerate at an ever-increasing rate. No wonder the Gaullist journalist Jean-Jacques Servan-Schreiber warned Europeans in 1967 of an American challenge more formidable than the military threat from the Soviet Union. To be sure, the costs of empire and the dollar's role as the Free World's reserve currency meant the U.S. balance of payments continued to deteriorate. But the Treasury under Kennedy and Johnson kicked that can down the road.

Neo-Progressive ACR clearly worked, or so it seemed in the 1960s. Even as the Cold War dragged on, Americans got busy building the technological and institutional foundations for the Millennial ACR, the teleological era of global civil religion. On that great-come-and-get-it day—to quote a lyric from Broadway's *Finian's Rainbow*—all human needs would be met and all barriers to the free movement of people, goods, services, and capital would disappear. Diverse, divisive cultures would be homogenized into one civilization, one society, ultimately one marketplace as nations melted into each other. That was the Progressive romance peddled by corporate and political elites that most college-age Americans in

the 1960s had been taught to believe. Why, then, were racism, violence, injustice, and poverty so prevalent in the world, even in the
United States itself? When the grown-ups had no plausible answer,
the youngsters threw a tantrum.

Who could blame them? Baby boomers were like foreigners to the
traumatized Greatest and Silent Generations who had begotten
and raised them. Americans shaped by the Depression and World
War II had gotten used to dealing with scarcity, regimentation, and
conformity. When at last rewarded with postwar prosperity, they
were determined to enjoy the best years of their lives. They had
plenty of babies but also plenty of fun in their suburban living
rooms. They unabashedly drank, smoked, gorged, and partied
(their children noticed). But they remained obedient to their big
bureaucracies, corporations, and unions, and they reacted stoically
when told the nation must remain on a war footing for the duration of what Kennedy called a long, twilight struggle. But to the 38
million children born between 1946 and 1955 and the equal number of late boomers born before 1965, the Depression was ancient
history and World War II the subject of exciting movies, TV shows,
books, and board games. The only reality they knew was now.

Middle- and upper-middle-class boomers, famously indulged
by parents who wanted them to have all the things that they hadn't,
grew up either unregimented or rebellious. Boomers took it for
granted that America was a cornucopia, had never lost a war, and
stood for liberty and justice. Boomers got little or no theology in
their liberal churches and synagogues except that people should be
tolerant and nice to each other (especially minorities). Boomers
watched television shows and commercials scripted on Sunset
Boulevard and Madison Avenue that taught them to want much
and expect instant gratification. But television role models also
compelled boomers to realize (or repress) how dysfunctional their
own families were by comparison to those on *Ozzie and Harriet* or
Father Knows Best. Boomers were the first youngsters to have broad
access to automobiles, transistor radios, and mainstream pornography, hence to fantasy lives beyond the reach of their parents and
teachers. Boomers reached adolescence in a nation trapped by its
own utopian promises and not surprisingly questioned authority,

asking, "Who says?" and "Why not?" about every taboo. Not least, if upscale whites noticed the chasms between illusion and truth, then *a fortiori* working-class whites and Negroes (as they were politely called) noticed them even more.

It goes without saying that most baby boomers did not burn their draft cards, flee to Canada, join radical movements, trash urban ghettoes, drop acid, live in communes, or even protest the Vietnam War. Fewer still flirted with Leninist and Maoist ideology or revolutionary violence. But all baby boomers faced challenges for which freedom and opulence ill equipped them. The first was the funnel effect of too many people competing for places in institutions designed for far fewer. The educational system accommodated the demographic bubble of college-bound students but only through huge state universities that fostered alienation and mediocrity. The economic system eventually accommodated the swelling numbers of professional and white-collar boomers but not blue-collar workers—white and now black, male and now female—who faced unemployment or stagnant wages because U.S. manufacturers began to ship jobs overseas those very same years.

A second challenge was the civil rights movement, which confounded, shamed, or threatened older Americans but fascinated and intimidated the boomers. Jews naturally sympathized with the black exodus, while Protestants and Catholics as well observed how white authorities and institutions buckled in the face of courageous, non-violent protest. A third challenge was military conscription, annoying in peacetime (it took Elvis Presley away for two years) and downright scary in wartime. So the boomers rebelled through open defiance or sullen passive-aggression. But what was it they were rebelling against? American Civil Religion? Not really. In foreign policy the privileged youth of the sixties generation certainly rebelled against the military-industrial complex and nuclear weapons in particular (please don't blow up the world); against Cold War regimentation and Vietnam in particular (please don't get me killed or make me a killer); against the mores of liberal empire (make love, not war); and against the very persistence of rival nation-states (imagine there are no countries). But stripped of its radical fringes, the sixties phenomenon was a rebellion against the neo-Progressive ACR in the name of the Millennial ACR, a rejection of the embattled present on behalf of the transcendent future the United States claimed to be forging. That explains why the original New Left program was so moderate and its protests so romantic, at least until paranoia hardened all hearts. It also suggests that the boomer revolt, whatever else it entailed, was a spontaneous religious revival.

"Say what you will about the Sixties' failures, limits, disasters, America's political and cultural space would probably not have opened up as much as it did without the movement's divine delirium." So recalled Todd Gitlin, principal chronicler of the antiwar movement. In retrospect, he believed, it made breakthroughs to "a politics in which difference (race, gender, nation, sexuality) does not imply deference; the idea of a single globe and the limits that have to be set on human power." But did it hasten the end of the Vietnam War? Adam Garfinkle has argued the opposite, that in fact the protests so alienated a majority of Americans that they perversely prolonged the war. Nor does he think Vietnam the primary catalyst for the agitation of the sixties, which Garfinkle explains in terms of those generational shocks to the American system. But he, too, thinks the sixties spawned "a religious movement among youth," a chiliastic search for meaning, even a children's crusade.

The first, mystical expression of that religious revival, no less than of the Protestant Reformation itself, could be found in its music. The 1950s revival of authentic American folk music, especially Scots-Irish ballads from Appalachia, led the way. But they soon gave way to coffee house tear jerkers and cocaine-laced plaints that in turn got overwhelmed after 1960 by quickly crosspollinating rhythm and blues, gospel, country, rockabilly, rock and roll, folk rock, soul, and psychedelic. Each new commercial genre (masquerading as rebellion) liberated artists to experiment in so many ways that the years 1955–70 were the most creative, evocative era of popular music ever. Top-40 hits had traditionally expressed adolescent heartbreak or joy, but album-length folk and folk-rock recordings included anthems persuading sheltered white kids they could feel the pain of exploited workers and ghetto blacks, sharecroppers and Third World peasants, not to mention the anxieties of sheltered white kids. The best of them made people want to cry, then storm the barricades for no particular cause. Think Bob Dylan's "When the Ship Comes In" or Peter, Paul, and Mary's "If I Had a Hammer." Music blessed boomers with a secret, spontaneous language through which they communicated, as much by feelings and symbols as language, with each other and received revelations from their prophets. The young owned this music; their parents did not.

The second, activist expression of that religious revival, no less than of the American Revolution itself, could be found in its organization. In 1960 the defunct Student League for Industrial Democracy was reborn as Students for a Democratic Society (SDS) under a twenty-one-year-old president, Tom Hayden. He oversaw the SDS convention that issued the notorious Port Huron Statement in June 1962. Only the delegates were mostly well-scrubbed college kids in crew cuts, and their statement read less like a revolutionary manifesto than a wistful appeal from the American Friends Service Committee. (Satirist Tom Lehrer described the temperament as, "We all hate poverty, war, and injustice, unlike the rest of you squares.") The SDS authors certainly took ideology seriously, but their inspirations were American professors like C. Wright Mills and Arno J. Mayer, not Europeans like Marx and Lenin.

Accordingly, Port Huron's Agenda for a Generation protested a "democracy without publics" that made "cheerful robots" of Americans. It held up as a model the non-violent activism of Southern black churches. It defined human beings as "infinitely precious and possessed of unfulfilled capacities for reason, freedom, and love"; hence it opposed ideas, institutions, and technologies that reduced men to mere things. It especially warned against utopian ideologies whose vague appeals to posterity were used to "justify the mutilations of the present." But neither did SDS endorse an egotistic individualism destructive of social conscience. Hence the Cold War must be made to transcend people and nation-states alike and become "an international civil war throughout the unrespected and unprotected *civitas* which spans the world." Thus did Port Huron anticipate the "global 1968" protests against both Cold War blocs.

The way out, SDS imagined, was through "the simultaneous creation of international rule-making and enforcement machinery beginning under the United Nations, and the gradual transfer of sovereignties—such as national armies and national determination of 'international' law—to such machinery." Thus did Port Huron anticipate Bill Clinton's Assertive Multilateralism and humanitarian intervention. In the interim, SDS proposed that the principal goal of the United States should be the creation of "a world where hunger, poverty, disease, ignorance, violence, and exploitation are replaced as central features by abundance, reason, love, and international cooperation." Thus did Port Huron take Kennedy's global meliorist rhetoric literally. Moreover, industrialization of the Third World was "too huge an undertaking to be formulated or carried out by private interests. Foreign economic assistance is a national problem." Thus did Port Huron take Truman's Point Four seriously and anticipate LBJ's Johns Hopkins address. "We must reverse the trend of aiding corrupt anti-communist regimes. To support dictators like Diem while trying to destroy ones like Castro will only enforce international cynicism about American 'principles.'" Thus did Port Huron anticipate Jimmy Carter's emphasis on human rights. Finally, SDS imagined liberals might "expunge the Dixiecrats from the ranks of the Democratic Party" so that "massive Negro voting in the South could destroy the vice-like grip reactionary Southerners have on the Congressional legislative process." Thus did Port Huron anticipate Richard Nixon's Southern strategy, if in reverse.

The united, equal, humane world imagined at Port Huron was not at all un-American. It was nothing other than the Millennial ACR promised by the neo-Progressive ACR when and if the Cold War was won. But impatient boomers got the impression the Cold War had climaxed in the Berlin and Cuban crises and believed the ensuing détente must hasten the growing convergence between East and West. Kennedy had promised no less in his American University speech of June 1963: "I am talking about genuine peace—the kind of peace that makes life on earth worth living ... not merely peace for Americans but peace for all men and women—not merely peace in our time but peace in all time." History happened instead. Kennedy was shot, Johnson went to war, the arms race continued, the civil rights movement turned violent, and federal and state authorities treated protestors as if they were Bolsheviks. What were the coming-of-age boomers to make of it all? The Berkeley Free Speech Movement answered that question by making explicit the generational cleavage—"Don't trust anyone over 30"—and the international civil war—"Berkeley equals Mississippi equals Vietnam."

As early as 1965 the new SDS president, Carl Oglesby, raised the roof with a speech explaining that those who "push the buttons and tally the dead . . . are not moral monsters. They are all honorable men. They are all liberals. . . . We have become a nation of young, bright-eyed, hard-hearted, slim-wasted, bullet-headed make-out artists, a nation—may I say it?—of beardless liberals." The son of an Akron tire plant worker, Oglesby insisted it wasn't he who was un-American but "those who mouthed my liberal values and broke my American heart." The power elite, it now appeared, was not an aberration susceptible to reform but an entrenched machine to be raged against until overthrown. Suddenly the topsy-turvy interpretations of revisionist historians who blamed U.S. Open Door imperialism for the Cold War appeared plausible, even self-evident. Vietnam was just racist, capitalist America's latest Indian war.

Churches, having long since surrendered to the civil religion, were almost nowhere to be found. In October 1965 Pastor Richard John Neuhaus, Father Daniel Berrigan, and Rabbi Abraham Heschel founded the Clergy and Laymen Concerned about Vietnam, later joined by the National Council of Churches, Yale Divinity School, Jewish Theological Seminary, and Union Theological Seminary. But across the nation very few pulpits opposed the war on theological grounds. For many Americans a crisis of conscience came in April 1967, when Martin Luther King, Jr., damned the war, but many a conscience only found cause to damn King. The vast majority of Catholics and Evangelicals, with Cardinal Spellman and Billy Graham leading the way, remained hawkish well into the 1970s. Equally conspicuous by their absence were Old Left Progressives and card-carrying Communists. But the antiwar movement swelled as more and more boomers turned eighteen. To be sure, the first target of their rebellion against pretense was *in loco parentis*, those college rules constraining undergraduates' freedom in matters of speech, housing, alcohol, drugs, and sex. Privileged boomers ceased even to pay lip service to the Ten Commandments, and why should

they have when the mainline clergy preached relativism and situa-
tional ethics in place of the historic creeds? That was the question
Henry Luce probably meant to pose in April 1966, when *Time* magazine's shocking red cover asked "Is God Dead?" But the God who
commanded, "If it feels good it, do it," in the American Church of
What's Happenin' Now was very alive and indeed hotly contested.

By 1966 the sheer duration of the Vietnam War—never mind
its morality or futility—began to worry tens of thousands of boomers soon to graduate and confront the draft. With plenty of time on
their hands and cash in their jeans, boomers followed the lead of
the SDS and took to the streets in the belief that displays of collective outrage ("Hey, Hey, LBJ! How many kids did you kill today?")
could raise a nation's consciousness. Moreover, getting stoned and
getting laid made it easy to feel good about doing well. But these
mass demonstrations, however impressive they looked on the seven
o'clock news (six o'clock Central Time), could not have been less
like an ideological, European-style revolutionary movement.

In at least six fundamental traits the baby boomer radicalism
differed from that of previous Progressive eras. First, the Old Left
was intellectually rigorous, tested ideology against empirical evidence, and argued and revised party lines. The New Left gave converts instant wisdom and drew no distinctions, as the founder of
the Liberation News Service recalled: "From Vietnam I learned
to despise my countrymen, my government, and the entire English-
speaking world, with its history of genocide and international
conquest. I was a normal kid." Hence, while the Old Left bred disciples, the New Left spawned masters free to be you and me and to
do as they pleased (don't follow leaders, Dylan had warned).
Second, the Old Left was a family affair, especially among Jewish
immigrants and their red diaper babies. The New Left was a generational revolt against the values, beliefs, and traditions of parents
and grandparents. Third, the Old Left included authentic proletari-
ans. The post-scarcity New Left, as Gitlin described it, was composed overwhelmingly of would-be professionals. Fourth, the Old
Left emulated Bolshevik organization and tactics. The New Left
rejected Soviet-style communism and pretended instead to lionize
Third World rebels ("Ho, Ho, Ho Chi Minh! NLF is gonna win!"),
who bravely resisted "Amerika," as in "swastika." Fifth, the Old Left

was stoic and sacrificial. The New Left was Dionysian in its hedonistic escapism, ritual madness, and theatrical and religious ecstasy. Sixth, the Old Left spoke in the first-person plural. The New Left spoke in the first-person singular. The point of even taking a political position, observed Christopher Lasch, was "to get the self going." In Garfinkle's summation, the New Left was not a serious social movement at all but rather the collective spasm of an unprepared generation seeking a spiritual wormhole to a heavenly future.

The sixties mix of politics, music, pathos, religion, and sex was as thorough and sensual as the bells and smells of a Catholic High Mass. Hairy, naked children breathing sweet marijuana while grooving on psychedelic music amid black lights and lava lamps experienced mystical highs and communal bonds they had never imagined possible while growing up absurd in postwar suburbs. That sixties liturgy, moreover, was ostensibly devoted to the most sublime aspiration of all, which is love. The message preached every day in the temple—by Joan Baez and Paul Simon, Bob Dylan and Donovan, the Beatles and Byrds, in songs like "Love Train" ("Tell all the folks in Russia and China, too"); "Get Together" ("Come on people now, smile on your brother"); "Imagine" ("I hope someday you'll join us, and the world will live as one") and in Broadway revues like *Joseph and the Amazing Technicolor Dreamcoat*, *Jesus Christ Superstar*, and *Godspell*—was simply peace through understanding in a small world after all: precisely the mottos of the 1964 World's Fair.

That was the historical passage in the midst of which U.C. Berkeley sociologist Robert Bellah first noticed the "habit of the heart" he called American civil religion. His truly seminal article peered through the rood screen cloaking the national altar, and he risked accusations of blasphemy by revealing what he observed. Bellah exhumed the Founders' faith in a Providential United States, Lincoln's faith in an almost chosen people, and the ritualistic invocations of God in presidential inaugurals. But it was Kennedy who caught Bellah's attention precisely because he was Catholic. Clearly the ritual and rhetoric of American political culture were more than a sop to the Bible Belt. The rituals, the rhetoric, the panoply of civil church holidays, heroes, martyrs, and myths all expressed a "genuine apprehension of universal and transcendent religious reality as seen in or, one could almost say, as revealed through the experience of the American people." Bellah appreciated the power of civil religion to cement national unity and secure personal liberty. But he also saw dangers, especially with respect to "America's role in the world." The theme of the New Israel, problematical from the start, had devolved into Manifest Destiny, then imperialism, then Cold War universalism. Now the civil religion that had survived the eras of the American Revolution and Civil War was confronted by a third great crisis, the problem of what constituted responsible action in a revolutionary world. Bellah thought the United States could negotiate this crisis but only through the emergence of a genuine transnational sovereignty that "would result in American civil religion becoming simply one part of a new civil religion of the world." Of course, the Bible would have to be left behind, but that need not disrupt historical continuity. "A world civil religion could be accepted as a fulfillment and not a denial of American civil religion. . . . To deny such an outcome would be to deny the meaning of America itself."

Except the love train of Millennial ACR was still stuck on the tracks of Cold War, which tore at a nation already torn by its own demographics. The snap was sudden. As late as 1964 boys still had crew cuts, girls wore dresses and stockings, the Beatles sang "I Want to Hold Your Hand," and Hillary Rodham worked for the Goldwater campaign. Just three years later the Spring Mobilization Committee to End the War in Vietnam assembled four hundred thousand protestors for an April march through Manhattan, and one hundred thousand hippies hung out at San Francisco's Summer of Love. Across the Bay in Oakland the new Black Panther Party chanted, "The Revolution has come! Off the pigs!" which caused FBI chief J. Edgar Hoover to name them public enemy number one. In October another one hundred thousand demonstrators protested at the Lincoln Memorial, after which thirty thousand marched across the Potomac to watch beat poet Allen Ginsberg and yippies Abbie Hoffman and Jerry Rubin try to levitate the Pentagon.

Todd Gitlin recalled wistfully, "Think how far we had come. In 1960, when I was seventeen, we put together a demonstration of forty students. In 1962, we got eight thousand people in Washington to protest nuclear testing and the fallout shelter movement. In 1965, we got twenty-five thousand people. By 1968, there were antiwar activities all over the country. Everything in our experience contributed to a rather grandiose sense that we were the stars and spear-carriers of history." What happened instead was another *annus horribilis:* the Tet Offensive, the King assassination, the bloody Columbia University sit-in, the Bobby Kennedy assassination, the Soviet invasion of Czechoslovakia, the Chicago police riot during the Democratic convention, and the denouement of a three-way race featuring no antiwar candidates at all. Gitlin continues: "That was the psychological underpinning of various severe misjudgments as to where we were in relation to the rest of the country. We were seen, not inaccurately, as part of a radical ensemble that really wanted to turn a great deal upside down. Most of the country didn't want to have that much turned upside down." That's putting it mildly. Opinion polls in 1968 revealed the antiwar movement to be the most hated group in America, even among those who favored withdrawal from Vietnam.

In the wake of the 1968 election a New Mobilization Committee to End the War in Vietnam helped SDS organize more monster demonstrations in fall 1969 and again in spring 1970, following the Kent State fatalities. But that was the New Left's last hurrah. President Nixon shrewdly adopted a draft lottery in 1969 and began to phase out conscription in 1971. A critical mass of the baby boom bubble reached the age of ambition, if not discretion, and began to turn into yuppies. Females whose experience in the movement was often that of sexual auxiliaries raised their own consciousness and turned feminist. The SDS leaders themselves either burned out or wandered off into splinter groups (e.g., Young Socialists, Wobblies, Spartacists, Maoists), while a lunatic fringe turned terrorist (e.g., Weather Underground, Black Liberation Party, Symbionese Liberation Army). The final New Left campaign to build a worker-student alliance might have been the most demoralizing of all because the young agitators at the factory gates encountered firsthand the deep resentments, not to say fists, of blue-collar union men.

Those who remained committed to causes decided they must work within the system. So veterans of the radical sixties began their Long March through the institutions and would eventually

seize the commanding heights in politics, law, academics, and foundations. Along the way they asked themselves and each other why
the oppressed back in the sixties had failed to unite against their
common enemies in the power elites. As tenured radicals, they
found answers in the transnational history of race, class, and gender, which they imposed on their institutions as the new hegemonic discourse. The New Left apparently won out in the end.

On the evening of September 11, 2001, Gitlin picked up
George Orwell's 1945 essay "Notes on Nationalism" to meditate
on the distinction between healthy, defensive patriotism and sick,
aggressive nationalism. From the perspective of the sixties it
seemed a distinction without a difference because the radicals' assault on the latter looked to mainstream Americans like a denial of
the former. He concluded: "The tragedy of the left is that, having
achieved an unprecedented victory in helping stop an appalling
war, it then proceeded to commit suicide." But he also realized that
over the course of his lifetime patriotism had lost its grip on sophisticated Americans because it got in the way of their preferred
identities as individuals and cosmopolitans. Hence their imagined
community (in social scientist Benedict Anderson's phrase) was no
longer the nation-state but the global nexus.

If Gitlin is right—and all the evidence suggests that he is—
then the dawning of the Age of Aquarius meant the New Left had
won the cultural heights only to surrender the economic heights to
finance capitalism. Henry Luce had won, too.

CHAPTER TWENTY-SEVEN

A Purgatory in Time

"AS WE LOOK AT America, we see cities enveloped in
smoke and flame. We hear sirens in the night. We see
Americans dying on distant battlefields abroad. We see
Americans hating each other; killing each other at
home. And as we see and hear these things, millions of Americans
cry out in anguish: Did we come all this way for this?" In his 1968
campaign speech Richard Nixon heard an answer in "a quiet voice
in the tumult of the shouting. It is the voice of the great majority
of Americans, the forgotten Americans." It was time, they said, for
new leadership. "We extend the hand of friendship to all people. To
the Russian people. To the Chinese people. To all people in the
world. And we work toward the goal of an open world, open skies,
open cities, open hearts, open minds." Thus did Nixon promise a
radical change of means but a radical continuity of ends with the
prophecies of his high priestly predecessors.

Someday historians will record that no presidents other than
Lincoln and Franklin Roosevelt took office in more trying times
than did Nixon. Abroad, he inherited a war his predecessor could
neither win nor end, plus 540,000 demoralized soldiers. Beyond
Vietnam he confronted a world more dangerous than ever before
because the Soviet Union had achieved parity in ICBMs, China had
joined the atomic club, and many Third World countries flirted

with one or with both. Even NATO allies seemed pleased that Vietnam had taken the haughty United States down a peg. At home, Nixon inherited paranoid cities wracked by mob violence, a youth culture in rebellion against traditional authority, and an economy sapped by guns-and-butter programs that inflated the dollar and hemorrhaged gold. The new president also had a dubious mandate, having gotten just 43 percent of the vote because third-party segregationist George Wallace won angry white voters even in the North. ("Alabama has not joined the nation," he boasted. "The nation has joined Alabama!") Finally, Nixon's adversaries included Democratic majorities in the Congress and most of the media and eastern establishment. Under those awful conditions he was obliged to surmount old crises engendered by Cold War hubris and new crises engendered by a diffusion of power historians refer to as the "shock of the global." No wonder a character in Garry Trudeau's comic strip *Doonesbury* called it a kidney stone of a decade and the Rolling Stones rock group titled an album *Sucking in the Seventies.* Yes, those were the seventies, when everything sucked.

During that decade the United States passed through three cycles of painful purgation. First, the Nixon administration purged the nation of its sixties romanticism through a stunning combination of diplomatic détente and domestic liberalism that nonplused Republicans, disarmed Democrats, and marginalized the New Left. But Nixon's triumphs were too personal, his motives too suspect, and his means too devious for an establishment already nervous about the imperial presidency. So the elites purged the nation of Nixon through the convenient Watergate scandal. Finally, Jimmy Carter purged the nation of cynicism by re-moralizing foreign policy then reviving the Cold War. Hence, while Robert Bellah lamented in advance of the Bicentennial that "American civil religion is an empty and broken shell," the nation was already building up to an ecstatic neo-Progressive ACR revival.

Richard Nixon had no particular faith except in America, which enabled his radical pragmatism. He shed his cradle Quakerism as inconsistent with the civil religion; scoffed at the mainline Protestants' pathetic efforts to be politically relevant; and clung only to Billy Graham, who could be trusted to bless all his maneuvers. In a post-presidential book Nixon characterized his faith as "intensely personal and intensely private" and said what really mattered was that people recognize the nation's spiritual roots. "If the choice is godless capitalism, which rewards greed, or godless communism . . . we are in deep trouble." Quoting Fyodor Dostoevsky, he admonished, "The one essential condition of human existence is that men should always be able to bow down before something infinitely great. If men are deprived of the infinitely great, they will not go on living and will die of despair." As president, Nixon did not just attend church, he turned the White House into a church on Sunday mornings by hosting services for an ecumenical (albeit politically safe) assortment of clergy. Rabbi Louis Finkelstein even predicted future historians would conclude the finger of God had touched Nixon with the vision and wisdom to save civilization. On July 4, 1970, which the president designated Honor America Day, Billy Graham exhorted citizens to rededicate themselves to God and the American Dream. That was the year W. Clement Stone's Religious Heritage foundation named Nixon Churchman of the Year for having prepared a "return to the spiritual, moral, and ethical values of the Founding Fathers." But the editor of *Christianity Today* interviewed Nixon and found him to be "remarkably imprecise" about spiritual and ethical issues.

In short, Nixon's agenda bore a striking resemblance to Eisenhower's, which was to end his predecessor's land war in Asia and right the economy his predecessor had mismanaged while reinforcing his predecessor's civil religion. Accordingly, Nixon's inaugural address eerily echoed Kennedy's New Frontier. He issued Americans a "summons to greatness," building on the giant strides made in agriculture, science, and industry.

> We have shared our wealth more broadly than ever. We have learned at last to manage a modern economy to assure its continued growth. We have given freedom new reach, and we have begun to make its promise real for black as well as for white. We see the hope of tomorrow in the youth of today. I know America's youth. I believe in them. We can be proud that they are better educated, more committed, more passionately driven by conscience than any

generation in our history. No people has ever been so close to the achievement of a just and abundant society, or so possessed of the will to achieve it.

Nixon even echoed Johnson's Great Society when he celebrated the fact that "government has passed more laws, spent more money, initiated more programs, than in all our previous history. In pursuing our goals of full employment, better housing, excellence in education; in rebuilding our cities and improving our rural areas; in protecting our environment and enhancing the quality of life—in all these and more, we will and must press urgently forward." But Americans must also join hands with the whole human race.

> Let us take as our goal: where peace is unknown, make it welcome; where peace is fragile, make it strong; where peace is temporary, make it permanent. After a period of confrontation, we are entering an era of negotiation. Let all nations know that during this administration our lines of communication will be open. We seek an open world— open to ideas, open to the exchange of goods and people— a world in which no people, great or small, will live in angry isolation.

Just weeks before, on Christmas Eve 1968, the astronauts of Apollo 8 had captured an iconic photograph looking back from the moon to the fragile blue orb that nurtured the only known life in the universe. So Nixon inevitably closed by bidding all riders on the earth to drink from a chalice of opportunity: "Let us go forward, firm in our faith, steadfast in our purpose, cautious of the dangers; but sustained by our confidence in the will of God and the promise of man."

Nixon granted in passing that Americans had suffered a crisis caused by inflated rhetoric and false promises. But that did not mean the United States must renounce its utopian project. It meant only that tactics must change and burdens must shift, at home and around the world, as dictated by pragmatism. Attorney General John Mitchell put it bluntly: "Instead of listening to what we say ... watch what we do." What the Nixon administration *did* was to administer shock therapy through diplomatic and financial reversals that adjusted American institutions to new realities in the global markets of power and wealth. Those realities obliged the United States to compromise with Communist rivals and capitalist friends alike. For the seventies were not only the decade of Cold War détente. They were also the decade when the U.S. empire of production metamorphosed into an empire of consumption.

Nixon had no plan to win the Vietnam War. He did not believe it could ever be won since a Korea-like truce was the most that could be achieved under realistic constraints. But he also believed it his sacred duty not to lose the war, despite the fact that a growing number of Congressional Democrats now believed it very unhealthy if the United States were somehow to win. Hence Nixon's task as commander-in-chief was to extricate U.S. ground forces through Vietnamization while transforming the global chessboard through détente with Beijing and Moscow. But it would take years for that grand design to fall into place; hence Nixon's task as high priest was to buy time by appealing directly to Republicans, Southerners, and white ethnic voters over the heads of the media, protestors, and racial minorities.

Nixon manipulated his audience with masterful indirection. First, at the Air Force Academy in June 1969, he elevated U.S. global commitments to literally Olympian heights: "When a nation believes in itself—as Athenians did in their Golden Age, as Italians did in their Renaissance—that nation can perform miracles. ... That is why I believe a resurgence of American idealism can bring about a modern miracle in a world order of peace and justice." Next, his Nixon Doctrine, proclaimed on Guam in July, limited U.S. commitments in contingencies such as South Vietnam, even as it hinted the American nuclear umbrella would be draped over the People's Republic of China. Finally, in his November 1969 address from the Oval Office Nixon warned that a sudden pullout from Vietnam would cause a bloodbath, topple dominos all over Southeast Asia, and encourage more Communist aggression. So Nixon invoked the parable of the Good Samaritan—"Let historians not record that when America was the most powerful nation in the world we passed on the other side of the road"—and preached patience "to you, the great silent majority of my fellow Americans—I ask for your support. Let us be united for peace. Let us also be united against defeat. Because let us understand: North Vietnam cannot defeat or humiliate the United States. Only Americans can do that."

Nixon and his national security adviser, Henry Kissinger, both came to power convinced the time was ripe to exploit the Sino-Soviet split. In 1967 Nixon had written in *Foreign Affairs* that "we cannot afford to leave China forever outside the family of nations, there to nurture its fantasies, cherish its hates and threaten its neighbors." In 1968 Kissinger had advised Nelson Rockefeller that by nurturing a subtle triangle among Washington, Beijing, and Moscow "we improve the possibilities of accommodations with each as we increase our options toward both." When the Soviets provoked bloody clashes on the Siberian frontier with China in 1969, Nixon signaled Beijing that the United States considered China "a nation whose survival we consider vital to our security" and thus signaled Moscow not to contemplate a preemptive strike. All lesser questions, including the defense of Taiwan, paled by comparison to that geopolitical stake. So secret negotiations commenced through which Nixon, Kissinger, Mao Zedong, and Zhou Enlai groped for a formula to repeal their respective anathemas. Moreover, Nixon and Kissinger rightly suspected—contrary to conventional wisdom—that a Sino-American rapprochement would make the Soviets more eager to pursue détente themselves.

Tectonic shifts on a continental scale brought about these transformations. The Soviets had achieved superpower status, but their command economy had turned stagnant now that postwar rebuilding had ended. The Soviets needed access to Western technology, a cap on the arms race, and grain imports to feed their own people. The 1968 Prague Spring exposed the fragility of their grip over Eastern Europe. But most of all they worried about China's nuclear weapons and long-range missiles. China, traumatized by Mao's 1966–69 Cultural Revolution and threatened by the USSR, needed U.S. protection and assistance. Finally, the United States needed relief from military and economic overstretch and the shattering of the Cold War consensus at home and abroad. French president Charles de Gaulle had pursued détente for a decade, and now West German chancellor Willy Brandt reached out to the Soviet bloc through *Ostpolitik*. All that suggests détente was a way for all three world powers to collude in the tamping down of internal challenges to their status. But détente was also the international political piece in a grand design that extended to international economics, domestic politics, and domestic economics. In the context of the Cold War it amounted to a radical mid-course correction made necessary by the end of postwar U.S. hegemony. In the context of the civil religion it amounted to a great leap forward toward a globalized interdependent world. But every feature of the grand design was sure to be regarded as a betrayal by some important constituency. So if Nixon wanted to get anything done (and he wanted to get many things done), he had little choice but to centralize decision making, operate secretly, dissemble, and manipulate.

The New Nixon of 1968 had positioned himself as a bridge between the conservative, nationalist Goldwater wing of the Republican Party and the liberal, internationalist Rockefeller wing. Since neither trusted him, the White House threw up smoke and mirrors in every direction to cloak its intentions. So the president made conservative noises but in fact matched Johnson's avalanche of liberal legislation. Between 1969 and 1974 the Nixon administration more than doubled federal spending for food stamps, aid to dependent children, and other welfare programs to the point where the budget for the Department of Health, Education, and Welfare surpassed that of the Pentagon. It established wage and price controls, full-employment bills, and revenue sharing in hopes of stimulating the economy while slowing inflation. It launched the Environmental Protection Agency, Occupational Safety and Health Administration, National Oceanic and Atmospheric Administration, Amtrak, and the Space Shuttle program, plus major initiatives in urban renewal, transportation, consumer protection, and the arts and humanities. It promoted desegregation of schools and labor unions, began affirmative action, supported the Equal Rights Amendment, and appointed more women than any before. It ended conscription through the All-Volunteer Force; presided over the amendment to lower the voting age to eighteen; and declared well-financed wars on cancer, drugs, and crime. The ghettoes and campuses fell silent.

Nixon also made nationalist noises, but his Realpolitik invariably embedded the United States in networks of dependence and governance promoted by the investment banks, multinational corporations, international organizations, foundations, and nongovernmental organizations. The Nixon Doctrine even became the disguise for an extension of U.S. commitments to embrace the whole Indian Ocean, while détente implied accommodation of the interests of China and the USSR as well as Europe and Japan in a pentagonal new world order. The president lectured a NATO summit: "Those who think simply in terms of 'good' nations and 'bad' nations—of a world of staunch allies and sworn enemies—live in a world of their own. Imprisoned by stereotypes, they do not live in the real world." He told newspaper editors it "was not a bad thing" that the United States was losing its predominance because the era of negotiations he and Kissinger were inaugurating could bequeath a whole generation of peace. Finally, détente made perfect sense for a rapidly globalizing economy because it provided people like Chase Manhattan president David Rockefeller, IBM president Jacques Maisonrouge, Pepsi-Cola's Donald Kendall (a Nixon crony), and U.S. exporters generally (not least agribusiness) with the lever they needed to pry open enormous Communist markets. Those were the years when Walter Wriston of Citibank boasted, "Mankind now has a completely integrated international financial and information marketplace, capable of moving money and ideas to any place on this planet within minutes." Those were the years when American, Japanese, and European financiers founded the Trilateral Commission to influence governments and ensure the global economy would not be subject to fickle and messy democracy.

Sociologist Franz Schurmann grasped what was happening almost in real time. Nixon's goal, he wrote, was "to start moving the United States away from its position as the foremost nation-state, with friends, allies, and clients, to becoming the center of a new world system that encompassed much of the planet." Kissinger was not much interested in economics but concurred wholeheartedly in the grand design. Just ten years before he had drafted eloquent speeches for Nelson Rockefeller that portrayed polycentrism and globalization as the foundation of world federalism. Now, he played master tactician in Nixon's strategy to transcend ideology and free the United States from the burdens of Atlas.

For nearly two years the White House made little headway on détente or the Vietnam peace talks and appeared to lose control of the tumultuous Middle East, where the politics of oil, the Arab-Israeli conflict, and the Cold War intersected. The Palestine Liberation Organization had turned terrorist following the Zionist victories in the 1967 Six Day War. The secular Arab regimes of Egypt, Syria, and Iraq had become Soviet clients. Worst of all, the British announced their military withdrawal from east of Suez as of March 1, 1971. That obliged the U.S. Navy to construct a major new base on Diego Garcia and Nixon and Kissinger to cast about for some regional power to help police the Persian Gulf. Finally, Muammar Gaddafi led a colonels' revolt that overthrew the pliant Libyan monarchy in 1969 and threw open its rich oil fields to the highest bidder. Ever since World War II the buyers' cartel known as the Seven Sisters, in cooperation with the British and American governments, had negotiated *en bloc* with the Arab, Iranian, and Venezuelan regimes. That had made possible the strikingly stable oil prices that fueled the greatest economic growth in history. But Gaddafi queered the pitch by driving harder bargains and dealing with independent U.S. and European firms, which emboldened the Organization of Petroleum Exporting Countries (OPEC) to insist on separate deals with the major oil companies at its December 1970 meeting.

John J. McCloy, one of the Truman administration's towering "wise men," represented the Seven Sisters and expected the Nixon administration to provide the usual diplomatic support. He was flabbergasted when instead Undersecretary of State John M. Irwin returned from Teheran to recommend the oil companies gratify the Shah of Iran and other leaders of OPEC by negotiating separately and competitively. As a result, the 1971 Teheran and Tripoli Accords imposed higher prices for crude oil and higher taxes on company profits. Evidently Nixon judged the halcyon era of Anglo-American hegemony was coming to a close, so the United

States might better serve its geopolitical interests by enriching the shah in return for his purchase of an American arsenal and service as key regional ally in the spirit of the Nixon Doctrine. To be sure, other newly empowered OPEC states proceeded to nationalize their oil industries, demand majority ownership, and/or raise prices. But since the United States had just begun to import foreign oil, the costs of this new global oil market would presumably fall on the Europeans and Japanese, who, the Nixon administration decided, had been free riders long enough.

The truth was the United States could no longer afford the world it had built in the late 1940s. The annual balance of payments deficit climbed to an alarming $10 billion by 1971. Imported goods from Europe and Japan flooded American markets while the overvalued dollar depressed U.S. exports. So the balance of trade also turned negative in 1971. American multinationals were cashing in on the rapidly growing foreign economies, but they repatriated less and less of their profits. An estimated hundred billion Eurodollars sloshed around foreign banks without any sovereign controls, while the U.S. unemployment and inflation rates hovered around a then unacceptable 6 percent. Warning signs had been evident for a decade, but Kennedy and Johnson had found excuses to ignore them. Nixon and Treasury Secretary John Connally bit the bullet and did so in a fashion that turned otherwise nationalistic policies into mechanisms for international cooperation.

In a televised address on August 15, 1971, Nixon announced a "new economic policy" to address "the challenges of peace." He abruptly ended the Bretton Woods monetary system by closing the gold window and allowing the dollar to float. He backed off the GATT's free trade commitment by imposing a 10 percent surcharge on imports and called on American business to enforce a voluntary freeze on wages and prices at home. Of course, he draped those provocative acts in civil religious garb, asking "whether we as a people have faith in ourselves or lose that faith; whether we hold fast to the strength that makes peace and freedom possible in this world, or lose our grip. . . . I say, let Americans reply, 'Our best days lie ahead.'"

Europeans cried foul play and Japanese damned the Nixon *shokku*. But this was not 1933, and no major country was even tempted to practice beggar-thy-neighbor autarky. On the contrary, central banks intervened to support the dollar while the IMF's Group of Ten negotiated the Smithsonian Agreement of December 1971. It pegged the dollar at $38 per ounce with a 2.25 percent trading range, and other countries re-pegged their currencies to the dollar. Nixon, who had already called Apollo 11 the greatest week since Creation, said this new Bretton Woods accord was "the most significant monetary achievement in the history of the world." Only it didn't work. By 1973 new pressures obliged the Nixon administration to jettison fixed exchange rates and devalue the dollar by as much as 40 percent versus the deutsche mark. Economic historian Charles Kindleberger pronounced the epitaph: "The nation-state is just about through as an economic unit." Even the United States now had to play by the same rules as everyone else, which meant globalization trumped American exceptionalism.

Diplomatic breakthroughs also occurred in 1971, beginning with Kissinger's secret trip to Beijing in July. Mao, obviously fearing the USSR more than the United States, abruptly dropped all the preconditions China had insisted upon for twenty years. Zhou and Kissinger were pleased to find in the other a like-minded interlocutor. They quickly reached agreement on a conceptual framework for Sino-American rapprochement that in fact amounted to an informal strategic alliance against aspirants to hegemony. In February 1972 a planeload of gawking American journalists accompanied Nixon to China for what he called "the week that changed the world." Not that the leaders' Shanghai Communiqué contained much of substance. The two governments merely pledged to work toward normalization; reduce the danger of war; renounce hegemony in the Asia-Pacific; and agree to disagree over Taiwan, Vietnam, and the trends of history. But Sino-American détente in fact reversed the momentum in the Cold War and ensured the United States would emerge from Vietnam with more potential geopolitical leverage than at any time since 1950.

Nixon's and Kissinger's instincts about the likely Soviet reaction were also proven correct when Leonid Brezhnev dropped the Kremlin's long-standing preconditions for arms control talks and invited Nixon to Moscow. That worried the North Vietnamese. On March 30, 1972, they launched a blitzkrieg invasion across the DMZ that Nixon thwarted with an unprecedented exertion of U.S.

air and sea power. But Brezhnev did not cancel the summit. He welcomed the president to Moscow with bear hugs and signed a whole series of treaties and accords on strategic arms limitation, trade, and scientific, technological, and cultural exchange. Finally, the secret peace talks in Paris bore fruit when Le Duc Tho suddenly dropped North Vietnam's long-standing preconditions and agreed on terms for a truce. An elated Kissinger announced, "Peace is at hand" on October 26, twelve days after which Nixon won a landslide reelection. Only that didn't work because South Vietnamese president Nguyen Van Thieu rejected a truce that would leave North Vietnamese soldiers on his country's soil and oblige him to negotiate with the Viet Cong's National Liberation Front. So Nixon ordered the so-called Christmas Bombing, ostensibly to oblige Hanoi to accept modifications but really to reassure Thieu that U.S. air power would enforce the truce.

The American people did not want to think about that. So far as they were concerned, the Paris accords of January 27, 1973, meant the agony of Vietnam was over.

Nixon's second inaugural address celebrated his administration's alleged achievements, including peace with honor in Vietnam and a structure of peace to last generations:

> We shall answer to God, to history, and to our conscience for the way in which we use these years. ... Today, I ask your prayers that in the years ahead I may have God's help in making decisions that are right for America, and I pray for your help so that together we may be worthy of our challenge. ... Let us go forward from here confident in hope, strong in our faith in one another, sustained by our faith in God who created us, and striving always to serve His purpose.

Nixon's speech was uniquely ill-starred for four ironic reasons. The first was that his 1972 electoral victory was so thorough as to scare his lukewarm supporters in the eastern establishment. With the tiny exceptions of Massachusetts and the District of Columbia, the electoral map was solid blue (the Republican color back then). To be sure, Wall Street, the media, and mainstream Congressional

Democrats had to approve when Nixon cracked down on radical movements, wound down the war, came to terms with Cold War adversaries, freed the economy of its Bretton Woods burden, signed all sorts of Progressive legislation, and defeated George McGovern's "Come Home, America" non-interventionism. But the Nixon landslide was so vindicating as to encourage vindictiveness that manifested itself immediately.

"One day we will get them on the ground where we want them, and will stick our heels in, step on them hard and twist," Nixon had vowed, referring to his political enemies in Congress, the media, academe, Wall Street, and even his own administration. The election returns gave him the chance. He demanded letters of resignation from his entire Cabinet and personal staff, restocked the executive branch with loyalists, and created four "super-secretaries" to exercise the same control over domestic affairs that Kissinger had over foreign affairs. He challenged the legislative powers of Congress by impounding funds through the White House Office of Management and Budget. Finally, he ordered the Justice Department to exploit the grand jury system against political targets. It seemed Nixon meant to exploit his landslide to assault all three branches of government in what amounted to a presidential coup. No wonder a certain powerful editor remarked, "There's got to be a bloodletting. We've got to make sure nobody even thinks of doing anything like this again." Almost at once Nixon's clumsy efforts to cover up the Watergate burglary exposed the presidency to attack, and the more vulnerable he became, the more everybody piled on.

The second ironic reason the inaugural address was ill-starred was that Nixon's acrobatic diplomacy reduced Cold War tensions to the point where the presidency might again be subjected to peacetime standards of probity. In other words, Nixon took the fall for all the sins committed by imperial presidents beginning with Roosevelt. Long before, in the 1830s, Alexis de Tocqueville had deduced from the Constitution that long-term external threats might empower the president with royal prerogatives. Since Pearl Harbor that had become the norm. Every president usurped power, abused authority, and invoked executive privilege in the name of national security. Congress grew increasingly restive until 1973, when the

coincidence of a hated and feared Republican president, a large
Democratic majority in Congress, and détente invited a counterat-
tack. Congress voted in June 1973 to cut off funding for military
operations in Southeast Asia, slashed economic assistance to South
Vietnam, and never even considered the reconstruction aid promised North Vietnam. In November Congress passed (over Nixon's
veto) the War Powers Resolution, which theoretically obliged the
commander-in-chief to seek prompt Congressional approval of future combat deployments. Next, the Senate began hearings into covert intelligence operations that would culminate in the Church
Committee's exposé of CIA secrets—the agency's crown jewels—in
1975. All those acts—not to mention impeachment—became think-
able because of the momentary relaxation of Cold War tensions.

A third ironic circumstance confounding the piety of Nixon's
speech was that the Realpolitik necessary for détente did not com-
pute on any level of American Civil Religion. However much
Nixon insisted he was an ardent Wilsonian and Quaker for whom
peacemaking was the highest calling, however much Kissinger insisted the prudent pursuit of national interest was the only ethical
form of statecraft, the truth was their realism confused and disori-
ented Americans searching for psychological solace and self-
justification. Stoic hawks who clung to the neo-Progressive ACR
damned a diplomacy that legitimized and respected the interests of
Communist regimes, while Aquarian doves who dreamed of a
Millennial ACR damned a diplomacy that pursued balance of power
at the expense of human rights. Kissinger later wrote that Nixon
had to play power politics because Vietnam had rent American idealism asunder. Whether or not one agrees that Nixon's decisions
were "highly moral and intellectually correct," it is hard to argue
with Kissinger's judgment that in the American system "the burden
which Nixon took upon himself was not meant to be borne by just
one man."

The fourth ironic circumstance that mocked Nixon's inaugural
was the almost immediate demonstration of how little control the
United States had over the Third World in general and Middle
East in particular. In October 1973 Egyptian president Anwar
Sadat defied pleas from both superpowers and launched surprise
attacks against Israeli forces across the Suez Canal. During this

Yom Kippur/Ramadan War the Nixon administration ordered a nuclear alert to deter Soviet intervention and airlifted supplies to Israel. When the crisis subsided, Kissinger began the shuttle diplomacy that brokered a disengagement in the Sinai. But the Arab members of OPEC retaliated with an embargo, followed by a 400 percent increase in oil prices that plunged the capitalist world into severe recession. In the United States inflation climbed above 12 percent, and the Dow Jones stock index fell 45 percent.

Kissinger convened a Washington Energy Conference in February 1974, where he managed to hold the oil-consuming democracies together. Then he pulled off a coup by brokering secret deals in which the Saudi Arabian Monetary Authority mollified three of the most powerful sectors of the U.S. economy. First, the Saudis agreed to recycle their petrodollars through American and British banks, while purchasing billions in U.S. treasury bonds. Second, the Saudis agreed to permit the major oil companies to retain control of refineries and distribution so they could pass on their added costs to customers. Third, the Saudis agreed to purchase an arsenal of weapons from U.S. aerospace firms badly in need of business during the years of détente. But American consumers and Rust Belt industries got clobbered.

In the years surrounding Nixon's resignation in August 1974 the tidy Free World of the American Century just disassembled. North Vietnam, with impeccable timing, staged another full-scale invasion that buried the Saigon regime in April 1975. That same month the sociopath Khmer Rouge seized power in Cambodia. The Soviets, judging the correlation of forces had swung in their favor, patronized client states, insurgencies, and political parties on four continents. Cuban troops intervened in Angola. At the United Nations the Group of 77 developing countries denounced multinational corporations and demanded a new world economic order. The Catholic Church, especially in Latin America, entertained *dependencia* theory and liberation theology. In Western Europe home-grown terrorism erupted and Communist parties made a comeback. Democracy degenerated to the point that in 1975 the U.N. General Assembly denounced Zionism as a form of racism by a vote of 72 to 35, while cheering wildly for Uganda's tyrant, Idi Amin. Meanwhile, détente ran its course just long enough to carry

Americans, Europeans, and Soviets to the Helsinki Final Act of August 1975. Its declaration of principles included reciprocal recognition of national sovereignty, frontiers, and a pledge of non-interference in the internal affairs of other countries. So NATO at last bestowed legitimacy on Stalin's Communist bloc. American hawks called it the worst sellout since Yalta. Doves called it betrayal since no one expected the Soviets to respect Helsinki's commitment to "human rights and fundamental freedoms, including the freedom of thought, conscience, religion or belief."

The Bicentennial year arrived with the civil religion in tatters. Americans who had boasted of limitless growth just a decade before now took for granted the limits to growth. Stagflation eroded the jobs and savings of middle-class families eroded in turn by the breakdown of social convention and cultural authority. Sixties hedonism went mainstream in the seventies as open marriage, no-fault divorce, abortion, pornography, illegal drugs, and New Age spirituality migrated inland from Boston and Berkeley. Thanks to President Gerald Ford's calm, self-effacing leadership and distinguished Cabinet, the ship of state stayed afloat. But his electoral chances in 1976 were not robust given his pardon of Nixon, the backlash against Republicans, and the wretched economy. The closest Ford ever came to playing high priest was during his plaintive State of the Union addresses. In 1975 he confessed the following:

> I must say to you that the state of the Union is not good. Millions of Americans are out of work. Recession and inflation are eroding the money of millions more. Prices are too high, and sales are too slow. This year's Federal deficit will be about $30 billion; next year's probably $45 billion. The national debt will rise to over $500 billion. Our plant capacity and productivity are not increasing fast enough. We depend on others for essential energy.

In 1976 Ford confessed, "We have not remade paradise on Earth. We know perfection will not be found here." Still, he bade citizens chant in unison, "I am proud of America, and I am proud to be an American. Life will be a little better here for my children than for me."

CHAPTER TWENTY-EIGHT

The Power of Words

WHILE MEDITATING ON THE Bicentennial, Lutheran pastor and antiwar activist Richard John Neuhaus sorted through the pretenses of "thoughtless patriotism and vacuous radicalism" and came to the conclusion that "the best game in town is the interplay between explicit Christianity and America's civil religion." When Jimmy Carter won the 1976 presidential election, Neuhaus thought he might be the Lincolnesque figure the times called for. Neuhaus was wrong. It turned out Carter was ill suited to serve as the ACR's high priest because he was too earnestly Christian. Not that he wore his sectarian faith on his sleeve. As a good Baptist, Carter believed strongly in the separation of church and state, considered respect for diversity a Christian duty, and strove to reassure voters he was not a religious weirdo. James Wall, the editor of the *Christian Century* who ran Carter's Illinois campaign, said it would be "unconstitutional, impolitic, and just plain bad theology" to suggest the Bible gave specific answers to political questions. The ironic result was that Carter, save for one scripture verse at the start, omitted God from his inaugural address and made fewer religious allusions than any Cold War president. To be sure, he prayed daily, promoted a global Social Gospel, and might have been the most introspective president since Lincoln. But his inability to confess a comfortable faith in an

American God magnified the impact of his unpopular policies and very bad luck.

Carter's ACR deficit was lost on the Wall Street elites who set out in 1973 to recapture the Democratic Party from the McGovernites. Few of the movers and shakers in finance or the media even knew what "being born again" meant until *Newsweek* retrospectively dubbed 1976 the Year of the Evangelical. What David Rockefeller and the Trilateral Commission sought was simply a candidate able to reunite prairie populists, big labor, and liberals and win back Wallace voters without alienating black voters. Everything pointed to a progressive, clean-cut Southern governor who could pose as an anti-Nixon. Carter was eligible and—just as important— educable. He not only joined the Trilateral Commission, he staffed his administration with twenty additional members, led by Secretary of State Cyrus Vance, National Security Adviser Zbigniew Brzezinski, and Henry D. Owen, who served as ambassador to the G-6 economic summit meetings begun in 1975. Carter offered the Treasury and Federal Reserve posts to David Rockefeller himself, who declined (preferring, like Cosimo dé Medici, private influence to public office). To voters the Georgia peanut farmer seemed a refreshing outsider but in fact was a creature of the establishment.

Carter played an indispensable role in Cold War history by remoralizing U.S. foreign policy and thereby performing the third and final purgation that defined the 1970s. Its effects might have been nugatory for the most part, but its rhetoric permitted Americans to pretend again that their motives were pure. Carter promised never to lie to the people (impossible for a politician), pledged a government as good as the people (a dubious proposition), and closed the book on the sixties by pardoning draft dodgers. Most of all, Carter made a virtual fetish of human rights.

FDR's wartime civil religion had begotten the human rights revolution, which the United Nations then baptized in 1948. But the Cold War dashed hopes that the Universal Declaration of Human Rights might be enforced, while providing the superpowers with a pretext for abusing the rights of millions caught in their crossfire. Then, in the 1970s, the moral world started to shift. In Western Europe the impacts of decolonization, economic integration, the protests of 1968, and *Ostpolitik* and in Eastern Europe the testimony of dissidents such as Bronisław Geremek, Václav Havel, Andrei Sakharov, and Alexander Solzhenitsyn—all promoted the vision of a common humanity. Ironically, the Commission on Security and Cooperation in Europe (CSCE), which sponsored the Helsinki Conference, initially got more support in Moscow than in suspicious Washington. But by 1974 human rights had moved to the top of the agenda, not only of the European Community, but also of big American foundations, the Trilateral Commission, and even Kissinger's State Department insofar as the CSCE was a child of détente. To his credit Gerald Ford stood firmly behind the 1975 Helsinki Accords despite loud opposition from conservatives co-alescing around California's Republican governor Ronald Reagan and neo-conservatives coalescing around Washington's Democratic senator Henry Jackson. But Ford famously fumbled his interpreta-tion of the accords in a televised presidential debate, which contributed to his narrow defeat.

President Carter made former Supreme Court justice Arthur Goldberg his ambassador to the CSCE, where the tough negotia-tor put Communist regimes on notice that their compliance with Helsinki's "Basket Three" human rights provisions would be closely monitored. Congresswoman Millicent Fenwick (R., N.J.) promptly founded the Helsinki Watch, which joined Amnesty International and Freedom House in a burgeoning transnational network. In April 1977 Carter sounded the keynote in his speech at the University of Notre Dame. He declared Americans "free of that inordinate fear of communism which once led us to embrace any dictator who joined us in that fear. . . . This approach failed, with Vietnam the best example of its intellectual and moral pov-erty. But through failure we have now found our way back to our own principles and values, and we have regained our lost confi-dence." Ending the fixation on East-West issues would permit the United States to address North-South issues like the promotion of democracy and economic development in the Third World.

Carter's timing was good from the standpoints of psychology and domestic politics. But from the standpoints of economics and foreign politics his timing could not have been worse. Vietnam should have taught American doves as well as hawks that even the most powerful and progressive country cannot design and build nations, especially among people of an alien culture. Moreover, if that were so in the 1960s, how much more so it was in the 1970s, when global stagflation limited the resources of First World governments and drove many Third World governments into default. Moreover, Carter's moralism inevitably collided with geopolitical realities. His agenda assumed détente would continue, and he eagerly wanted a SALT-II treaty, but that required him not to pressure the Soviets on human rights. He eagerly wanted full diplomatic relations with China, but that required him not to pressure the People's Republic (and its murderous client state in Cambodia) on human rights. He was determined to stop coddling friendly dictators but deepened U.S. dependence on the authoritarian Shah of Iran. To be sure, his appointment of African American Andrew Young as U.N. ambassador was highly symbolic, as was his stance against apartheid in Rhodesia and South Africa. His administration also completed two transformative projects begun by Nixon and Kissinger: the 1978 treaty that established full diplomatic and commercial relations with China without abandoning Taiwan and the Camp David Accords, which laid the basis for the 1979 Egyptian-Israeli peace treaty. But Carter could not escape any more than his predecessors the Niebuhrian dilemmas of power.

Nixon had said America was losing its centrality and must find its place in a multipolar world. Brzezinski went further in 1974 when he said, "Nation-states are losing their centrality amidst a shift from traditional international politics to a new global process." Candidate Carter announced, "Balance of power politics must be supplemented by world order politics." President Carter proclaimed, "The United States has no choice but to be engaged in a protracted architectural process to reform and reshape the international system." Brave words, but that architectural process required the digging of a foundation hole so deep as to bury any one president. The years 1978–79 were calamitous and 1980 was wasted. What happened?

One thing that happened was the sudden end of the Keynesian era. Labor bosses like the United Auto Workers' Dewey Burton had endorsed Carter in 1976 expecting he would adopt an industrial policy to halt the decline of American manufacturing. It never happened. The double whammy of high inflation and high unemployment in a post–Bretton Woods global economy imposed constraints that hobbled even a Democratic president and made the 1978 Humphrey-Hawkins Full Employment Act an exercise in nostalgia. The choice between policies to fight inflation or to relieve unemployment was not even Carter's to make. The choice would be made by the Federal Reserve Board, which represented U.S. banks, which in turn were part of a transnational financial community hell bent on choking inflation. So the gnomes of Zurich got their way. The Federal Reserve raised interest rates sharply in 1978 and again in 1979, when Carter appointed Paul Volcker (the Trilateral Commission's choice) to be chairman. Liberals and unions, led by Vice President Walter Mondale and the AFL-CIO's Lane Kirkland, felt betrayed because Volcker's reputation suggested he would court international opinion. That was precisely the point. He won the support of European central banks by promising U.S. rates would remain high but stable, while the White House and Congress restrained spending and even raised taxes in the midst of recession. One economist called it "burning down the house to roast a pig." The austerity eventually worked, but it obliged the president to fall on his sword.

Second, the world spun scarily out of control. Carter spent New Year's 1978 in Iran, where he praised the shah's great leadership, which had made his country "an island of stability." It was only a matter of weeks before the protests began that turned into the revolution led by Shi'ite Muslims loyal to the exiled ayatollah Ruhollah Khomeini. Nobody saw it coming, least of all the CIA, but within a year the shah had gone and Iran had become a theocratic Islamic republic for which the United States was the Great Satan. OPEC took advantage by jacking up oil prices four more times during 1979. For the second time in six years Americans queued up for scarce gasoline. The recession deepened.

Carter decided he needed to address the nation's sullen mood. In July he cleared his calendar for over a week and repaired to Camp David, where he invited a parade of officials, politicians, businessmen, academics, and clergy to offer their insights. One of the most influential was pollster Patrick Caddell, whose seventy-five-page memorandum, "Of Crisis and Opportunity," described the nation's problems as more psychological than material. That might have suited the president's temperament but not a public accustomed to thinking that spiritual and material blessings were all of a piece. Mondale thought Carter's draft speech sounded too grouchy. Staffers called it "Apocalypse Now." But on July 15, in a televised address from the Oval Office, the president told the truth as he saw it. He began by reciting twenty quotations from ordinary Americans lamenting the decline in civil virtue and hope and diagnosed as a crisis of confidence:

> We've always believed in something called progress. We've always had a faith that the days of our children would be better than our own. . . . Our progress has been part of the living history of America, even the world. We always believed that we were part of a great movement of humanity itself called democracy, involved in the search for freedom, and that belief has always strengthened us in our purpose. But just as we are losing our confidence in the future, we are also beginning to close the door on our past.
>
> In a nation that was proud of hard work, strong families, close-knit communities, and our faith in God, too many of us now tend to worship self-indulgence and consumption. Human identity is no longer defined by what one does, but by what one owns. But we've discovered that owning things and consuming things does not satisfy our longing for meaning. We've learned that piling up material goods cannot fill the emptiness of lives which have no confidence or purpose.

Carter granted the shocks and tragedy—the Kennedy and King assassinations, Vietnam, Watergate—that left people disillusioned but felt the root cause was loss of faith in America. What could be done to rekindle that faith? "First of all, we must face the truth, and then we can change our course. We simply must have faith in each other, faith in our ability to govern ourselves, and faith in the future of this Nation. Restoring that faith and that confidence to America is now the most important task we face." Carter then outlined six initiatives to address the energy crisis (on which the president predictably declared war) before closing with an appeal for unity. "With God's help and for the sake of our Nation, it is time for us to join hands in America. Let us commit ourselves together to a rebirth of the American spirit."

Owning and consuming too many things were not exactly uppermost in the minds of ordinary citizens punch drunk from bad economic news. Still, reactions to the speech were not disparaging until subsequent events caused it to be remembered with scorn. In October Carter answered a plea from David Rockefeller (among others) by granting the shah a medical visa to the United States. Students in Teheran used that as a pretext to invade the U.S. Embassy and take sixty-six hostages. Just two months later the Red Army invaded Afghanistan. Brezhnev's motives were in fact defensive—a pro-Soviet regime had been overthrown in Kabul—but the campaign looked like an aggressive thrust toward the Persian Gulf. Carter, who had imagined Americans escaping the fear of communism and dependence on foreign oil, now revived Cold War angst and doubled-down on defense of the oil fields. His 1980 State of the Union address proclaimed the Carter Doctrine, by which he pledged to repel, if necessary by force, any attempt by an outside force to control the Persian Gulf. Carter also withdrew the SALT-II Treaty that month and authorized secret military cooperation with China.

Operation Eagle Claw, the botched effort in April 1980 to rescue the U.S. hostages, after which Cyrus Vance resigned in protest, completed the reversal of Carter's foreign policy. During his final year in office he either authorized or accelerated the neutron bomb, MX missile, deployment of theater-range missiles in Europe, and a buildup of conventional forces. Most ominously, Presidential Directive 59 in July 1980 tilted U.S. nuclear strategy away from a counter-value, war-deterring strategy and toward a counter-force, war-fighting strategy. Finally, Carter boycotted the 1980 Moscow Olympics, terminated grain sales to the Soviet Union, and extended covert assistance to the Afghan *mujaheddin*.

Americans got very confused by 1980. White male workers were angry but unsure whom to blame. All they knew was that plant closures, union de-certifications, women in the workforce, inflation, racial integration, and busing attacked them right where they lived. Those were the years when even steelworkers and roughnecks grew ponytails and smoked pot, when country-and-western music and clothes were the rage, and when truckers with CB radios occupied Washington's mall in protest against gasoline prices. Musical outlaws like Willie Nelson gave eloquent voice to redneck anger, Bruce Springsteen to blue-collar rage, Bob Dylan to born-again gospel, and the Bee Gees to the urban escapism of disco. It seemed to the radical theorist Michael Harrington that the nation was "moving vigorously left, right, and center at the same time." In the midst of it all Carter staved off a primary challenge from Edward M. Kennedy but trailed the Republican front-runner Ronald Reagan in polls. If the election became a referendum on Carter, said Caddell, he was dead. So the campaign labored vainly to paint Reagan as a Goldwater extremist. The former Hollywood actor parried the punches by insisting that government was not the solution but the cause of the nation's problems and claiming it was still morning in America. Reagan just said no to the 1970s in the manner of humorist Garrison Keillor, who said sometimes you needed to be willing to look reality in the eye and deny it.

Reagan's campaign had little to say about foreign policy except that America would stand tall again. That suited the establishment, which had worried about Reagan in 1976 but now found him acceptable, especially with George H. W. Bush as his running mate and Alexander Haig, Caspar Weinberger, and George Shultz likely to lead his Cabinet. And to confused voters Reagan's pastoral style contrasted with Carter's "Sinners, repent" in perfect chiaroscuro. In 1980 television preachers such as Rex Hubbard, Jerry Falwell, Pat Robertson, Jim Bakker, and Jimmy Swaggart positively encouraged Evangelicals to conflate the cross and the flag, whereupon the religious right gravitated naturally to Reagan. So did many Catholics, who imagined the Irishman a kindred spirit. On election day he won every demographic except blacks, carried forty-four states, and coat-tailed Republicans to their first Senate majority in twenty-six years.

Ronald Reagan, untethered by history, was an expert at erasing the past. For instance, Lyndon Johnson had addressed a joint session of Congress five days after the Kennedy assassination and called

America a sick society that needed to heal itself. Reagan addressed a joint session of Congress in April 1981, following an assassination attempt on himself, and said the avalanche of support he had received in the hospital proved America was anything but a sick society. The following month Reagan erased Carter's 1977 Notre Dame speech with a 1981 Notre Dame speech of his own: "The years ahead are great ones for this country, for the cause of freedom and the spread of civilization. The West won't contain communism, it will transcend communism. It won't bother to . . . denounce it, it will dismiss it as some bizarre chapter in human history whose last pages are even now being written." Reagan even redid the dour 1976 Bicentennial by declaring the Fourth of July 1986 to be Liberty Weekend. On board the aircraft carrier *John F. Kennedy*, he blessed the lofty-masted ships assembled in New York harbor: "Perhaps, indeed, these vessels embody our conception of liberty itself: to have before one no impediments, only open spaces; to chart one's own course and take the adventure of life as it comes; to be free as the wind—as free as the tall ships themselves." Most famously, Reagan erased the resignation expressed in Kennedy's "Ich bin ein Berliner" speech with his own 1987 Berlin speech calling on Mikhail Gorbachev to "tear down this wall." In the words of historian Sean Wilentz, "There never was a politician less interested in the past."

Reagan has captivated historians of all stripes because his temperament and policies seem as liberal and dovish as they do conservative and hawkish, while his record belies the efforts of all the factions presuming to claim him. As Kissinger put it, "Reagan's was an astonishing performance—and, to academic observers nearly incomprehensible." The man was thoroughly secure in himself and in his beliefs. The trouble is in deciding what were his beliefs. Although plenty of evidence suggests Reagan professed Christianity, his Presbyterian pastor, Donn Moomaw, admitted it was "a deep private faith that has not been instructed too much by Bible classes, prayer meetings, or worship services." The nearest Reagan came to a conversion experience was a touching Social Gospel story his mother gave him at age eleven. Otherwise he grew up a small-town Midwesterner who was tolerant and benevolent and believed God was too. He never relinquished his simple faith that God had a plan for everyone, even when his religious observance became, as it were, indifferent during his long career in Hollywood and California politics.

Like Walt Whitman, Reagan contained multitudes. What historian Andrew Roberts calls his "enigmatic syncretism" made room for everything from astrology to apocalyptic mysticism. Kissinger said that he appeared to treat the Book of Revelation and Armageddon as "operational predictions." Patrick Buchanan thought him a primitive focused on a "personal relationship with God." Garry Wills imagined that Reagan carried God around "in his pocket with his other amulets and rabbit's feet." But most observers agree that Reagan's religion was quintessentially civil. He told patriotic Alabamans that democracy was just a political reading of the Bible and a Dallas prayer breakfast that "If we ever forget that we're one nation under God, then we will be a nation gone under." He told the Irish Parliament, "The struggle between freedom and totalitarianism today is not ultimately a test of arms or missiles, but a test of faith and spirit. And in this spiritual struggle, the Western mind and will is the crucial battleground." No president invoked religious themes and images more often than Reagan; no president had a heavier hand in writing his own speeches. So whereas Carter agonized over church and state, it never occurred to Reagan to draw such distinctions because his creed was American Civil Religion *tout court*. Who but a fervent adherent of neo-Progressive ACR could describe his Cold War strategy this way: "We win; they lose."

Carter mourned that Americans had lost touch with their values and become self-indulgent materialists. Reagan's inaugural address called Americans heroes and promised, "Your dreams, your hopes, your goals are going to be the dreams, the hopes, and the goals of this administration, so help me God." It laid out no plan for the Cold War and barely mentioned foreign relations except to say that America "will again be the exemplar of freedom and a beacon of hope for those who do not now have freedom." He pledged to pursue peace through strength, but otherwise "we must realize that no arsenal, or no weapon in the arsenals of the world, is so formidable as the will and moral courage of free men and women. It is a weapon our adversaries in the world do not have." To Reagan such rhetoric was not boilerplate because he really believed in his script. He believed it when he waved communism good-bye at Notre Dame, when he consigned Marxism-Leninism to the ash heap of history before the British Parliament in 1982, and when he called the USSR an evil empire in his 1983 sermon to the National Association of Evangelicals.

Reagan's convictions matured over decades, beginning with his exposure to Bolshevik tactics in the Screen Actors Guild. His influences included the witness of ex-Communist Whittaker Chambers, the conservative philosophy of James Burnham, the libertarian economics of Ludwig von Mises and Friedrich von Hayek, and the highbrow geniality of journalist William F. Buckley, Jr. But Reagan chiseled his own style in the commentaries he wrote out in longhand, painstakingly revised and read over the radio during the 1970s. More than half of them dealt with foreign policy and comparative economics, which persuaded Reagan that the pundits, defense intellectuals, and Sovietologists had to be wrong when they described the USSR as robust. A command economy in which a corrupt, dictatorial bureaucracy made every decision in defiance of the price mechanism, profit motive, and promotion by merit was so contrary to human nature that it could not possibly work. Reagan came to office sure the Soviet Union was a Potemkin Village and the United States was healthier than it appeared. Once unleashed, its economy would deliver into its hands "a powerful weapon in our battle against Communism—money." Reagan's national security strategy of May 1982 was specifically designed to "weaken the Soviet alliance system by forcing the USSR to bear the brunt of its economic shortcomings, and to encourage long-term liberalizing and nationalist tendencies within the Soviet Union and allied countries."

How much of Reagan's new era was new? The defense buildup, second Cold War, and high interest rates to wring out inflation were all inherited from Carter's last years. So was Reagan's stress on human rights, but with the decisive twist that he swiveled his moral artillery away from Third World dictators and trained it with devastating effect on the Soviet bloc. The rest of his fiscal policy, known as Reaganomics or supply-side economics, was new. Its four prongs were a 30 percent tax cut, deregulation, a cap on social spending, and an increase in defense spending of 7 percent per year through 1986, despite budget deficits that would range from $100 to $200 billion for seven years in a row. The national debt, which had tripled during the seventies bust, tripled again during the eighties boom, reaching almost $3 trillion. To Americans of earlier eras that peacetime binge would have been the civil religious equivalent of burning incense to Baal, but Reagan got away with it because globalization came to the rescue. Cash-rich Japanese and Arabs were happy to purchase U.S. Treasury bonds and thus subsidize American consumption. By 1983 the economy rebounded, inflation plummeted to 3.2 percent, and the stock market took off on a run that tripled the Dow Jones index by 1988. Unfortunately, it was "trickle down" economics, highly profitable to investment bankers (author Tom Wolfe's masters of the universe) but of marginal benefit to wage earners. Income inequalities sharply increased. Private-sector unions gave up the ghost. Finally, Reagan just swept off the table the Third World's campaign for a new international economic order. In a gracious but firm address to the World Trade Organization's Cancun summit in September 1981 he vetoed suggestions that developing nations be given more leverage over the World Bank and International Monetary Fund in the interest of debt relief and development. Instead, he joined with British prime minister Margaret Thatcher in promoting "a revolutionary idea born more than 200 years ago . . . called freedom and it works." The United States thus surrendered to neo-liberalism and in so doing left the rest of the non-Communist world little choice but to surrender as well. During Reagan's second term the GATT inaugurated the Uruguay Round, during which delegations from 123 countries expanded the global Open Door to include capital, services, and intellectual property, as well as manufactures, produce, and commodities.

Reagan's foreign policy process seemed chaotic since the Defense and State Departments, uniformed services, NSC, and CIA waged a constant war of all against all. That served the president poorly, especially in Third World crises like Lebanon, where a terrorist bomb killed 241 U.S. Marines, and Central America, where the CIA helped to prolong civil wars that claimed more than one hundred thousand Nicaraguan and Salvadoran lives and spawned the Iran-Contra affair. But in the central front of the

Cold War Reagan knew what he wanted to do, and his agencies mostly helped him to do it. His initiatives added up to a coherent and comprehensive strategy with military, economic, rhetorical, and covert components.

The Pentagon accelerated Carter's conventional rearmament in order to deter or prevail in an Air-Land Battle against the Warsaw Pact and pursue a New Maritime Strategy of naval supremacy. It also accelerated Carter's nuclear programs, including deployment of Pershing missiles in Europe to counter Soviet SS-20s. That Cold War recidivism sparked a transnational nuclear freeze movement and a civil religious hiccup from protesting American Catholic bishops. Meanwhile, the State Department turned cool toward SALT, which signaled the U.S. intention to negotiate from a position of strength or else not at all. Liberal critics cried doomsday but were undercut by Reagan's benign assurances to the effect that a nuclear war could never be won and must never be fought. His administration also waged economic war through the Coordinating Committee for Multilateral Export Controls, a U.S.-led consortium of seventeen nations that shut down the export of advanced technologies begun during détente. Third, Reagan deployed the power of words in a rhetorical war that gave heart to dissidents in the Soviet bloc. He succeeded (at last) in getting Americans to accept a U.S. embassy in Vatican City, and he teamed up with Pope John Paul II to encourage and covertly assist Poland's Solidarity movement. Finally, the so-called Reagan Doctrine justified CIA programs to funnel arms to anti-Communist *jihadis*, paramilitaries, and warlords (Reagan called them all freedom fighters) in Afghanistan, Nicaragua, Angola, and Ethiopia.

The strategic blueprint was codified in NSDD-75 (January 1983), which revived—thirty-three years after NSC-68—a rollback strategy designed to contain and reverse Soviet expansionism. That was a big triumph for conservatives and neo-conservatives, who had likened détente to appeasement. It was a disconcerting defeat for liberals in the media, academy, NGOs, and Wall Street, who took for granted the permanence of the USSR, the inevitability of peaceful coexistence in the nuclear age, and the adhesive power of trade and investment. Yet Reagan was decidedly risk-averse regarding conventional military interventions and fixated on the risk of nuclear war. Reagan denounced mutual assured destruction as a suicide pact, a stance that explains his almost superstitious attachment to the Strategic Defense Initiative (SDI). In fact, that expensive Star Wars program to develop earth-orbiting laser or particle-beam weapons capable of zapping ICBMs on launch was (except in Reagan's mind) a colossal bluff. But the Soviets were sufficiently cowed by American high-tech wizardry that they worried, for a few years at least, that space-strike weapons might render nuclear weapons "impotent and obsolete."

The Soviets had plenty of worries. Their leaders were geriatric, their economy sclerotic, their military overextended, their technology backward, and their satellites restless. Though still a superpower, the USSR was encircled geopolitically (thanks to Nixon) and ideologically (thanks to Carter). But what really exposed Soviet weakness was the loss of billions of dollars of foreign exchange from petroleum exports. Due to the global recession and conservation by consumers oil prices declined from 1981 to 1985, then fell through the floor in 1986. Over those same years the most influential members of the Soviet *nomenklatura*—Marshal Nikolai Ogarkov, chief of the General Staff, and Yuri Andropov, chairman of the KGB—hammered home their belief that the Soviet Union was two generations behind the West in technology, especially in the computers powering the so-called revolution in military affairs. Drastic reforms were imperative, which is why the Politburo turned in 1985 to Andropov's young protégé Mikhail Gorbachev.

Margaret Thatcher was the first Western leader to praise Gorbachev's New Thinking and name him someone with whom one could do business. But Reagan soon came around, much to the dismay of his hawkish advisers, because he wanted to believe—his ACR told him to believe—that the Cold War would end by conversion, not convergence. In 1981 he had sent personal letters to Brezhnev assuring him of America's good intentions, only to receive a cold shoulder. Now he imagined the leaders of the superpowers reaching agreements over the heads of their hostile bureaucracies. He wanted to show Gorbachev how American workers lived "with lawns and backyards, perhaps with a second car or boat in the driveway, not the concrete rabbit warrens I'd seen in Moscow." But Gorbachev believed in the ideals of the Bolshevik Revolution as much as Reagan believed in the ideals of the American Revolution. He meant to save communism, to build socialism with a human face, through his bold *perestroika* and *glasnost* reforms.

The odd couple met four times. At Geneva in 1985 they agreed to work toward a 50 percent reduction in nuclear delivery systems. At Reykjavik in 1986 Gorbachev proposed eliminating all nuclear weapons, but the deal fell through because Reagan refused to confine SDI to the laboratory. At Washington in December 1987 they agreed on a zero-option INF Treaty that abolished theater nuclear weapons. At Moscow in 1988 Gorbachev promised to defuse residual Cold War conflicts and Reagan retracted his evil-empire words. Most trenchantly, he preached Americanism to the students at Moscow State University with the aid of a fingernail-sized silicon chip with "more computing power than a roomful of old-style computers." As historian John Diggins observed, "Had the Russians defended communism on religious grounds, the cold war may have continued far longer than it did." But Reagan knew, no less than Nixon in the 1959 Kitchen Debate, that the Cold War was really a contest between rival materialisms. He also understood, as Carter had not, that in the American civil faith plenty and piety were symbiotic, if not identical. So there was no contradiction between Reagan's belief that a million Sears Roebuck catalogues might suffice to defeat communism and his hope that Gorbachev would display "the wisdom to introduce the beginnings of democracy, individual freedom, and free enterprise."

Gorbachev did exactly that in a dramatic address to the U.N. General Assembly on December 7, 1988. The Soviet leader pledged allegiance to peace, human rights, and self-determination. Then he flew back to Moscow, where he lectured the Politburo on the pressing need for internal reform because its forty-five-year competition with the West had been a disaster. The fall of the Berlin Wall, liberation of Eastern Europe, and collapse of the USSR were still to come. But "psychologically and ideologically," U.S. ambassador Jack Matlock concluded, "the Cold War was over before Ronald Reagan moved out of the White House."

Had Reagan won the Cold War without firing a shot, as Thatcher triumphantly claimed? Did he oversee a secret strategy that brought the Soviets to their knees, as neo-conservatives triumphantly claimed? Matlock and other close observers attest that Reagan did not really win the Cold War so much as help to end it peacefully and never pushed any secret plan for regime change in Moscow. His goal throughout was to encourage changes in Soviet behavior, which is why Reagan's greatest contribution was to engage Gorbachev against his hard-liners' advice. By taking the pressure off the Soviets at the right moment, Reagan realized George Kennan's original prophecy. Were anything to occur "to disrupt the unity and efficacy of the Party as a political instrument," he wrote, "Soviet Russia might be changed overnight from one of the strongest to one of the weakest and most pitiable of national societies."

That measured, prudential interpretation of the Cold War's denoue-ment, though well understood in Europe, is almost unknown in the United States. That is so partly because mythopoeic neo-conservatives and liberal internationalists have imparted their own spins to the dramatic collapse of Soviet communism. But that is so partly because the earnest Reagan himself attributed victory in the Cold War to his favorite ACR vision, America as a shining city on a hill:

> I've spoken of the shining city all my political life, but I don't know if I ever quite communicated what I saw when I said it. But in my mind it was a tall, proud city built on rocks stronger than oceans, wind-swept, God-blessed, and teeming with people of all kinds living in harmony and peace; a city with free ports that hummed with commerce and creativity. And if there had to be city walls, the walls had doors and the doors were open to anyone with the will and the heart to get here. That's how I saw it, and see it still.

The images originally invoked by the city on a hill were the infant church at the Sermon on the Mount and the infant colony on Massachusetts Bay. But Reagan's image became official because, historian Richard Gamble has explained, he "took hold of a meta-phor and reworked it to such a degree that a nation of 300 million people has lost the ability to hear that metaphor in any way other than how he used it."

When seen through the lens of civil religion, it becomes evident Reagan was not in the least a conservative. He revered Tom Paine and a utopian future, not Edmund Burke and an inherited past. He neglected to trim government, balance the budget, or support traditional values, much less inhibit Americans' flight into consumerism and expressive individualism. But neither was Reagan a self-conscious Progressive. His transcendent vision was a mix of optimism, nostalgia, and common sense raised to the level of civil theology. His chosen American heresy was the Hollywood–Disney–*Time* magazine version of the Millennial ACR which, contrary to everyone's expectations but his own, descended to earth right on cue.

Or so it seemed at the time.

Obama's World? The Global Civil Religion Aborts

In 1569 the Flemish cartographer Gheert Schellekens solved a mystery as old as the ancients: how to depict the round globe on a flat surface. His conformal cylindrical map preserved the true shapes and angular relationships of land masses so that rhumb lines as wide as oceans could be drawn between them with minimal distortion. Historian Jerry Brotton explains in *History of the World in 12 Maps* that almost nobody knows Schellekens by that name, but even schoolchildren know his Latin name: Mercator, whose projection transformed navigation during the Age of Exploration and first great era of globalization.

Mercator was a scholarly humanist who lived on the northwestern marches of the Holy Roman Empire. Trapped near the front lines of the religious wars following the Lutheran Reformation and Dutch revolt against Spain, he was in danger of persecution from Catholics and Protestants alike. But at length he found refuge in the realm of a tolerant German duke and hope for humanity in the science, commerce, and international law promoted by the Netherlands. So he inscribed his first Mercator map with a paean anticipating Francis Bacon's *The New Atlantis* by over fifty years:

> Happy countries, happy kingdoms, in which Justice, noble progeny of Jupiter, reigns eternal [in accordance with the

will of an] allgood Father who, residing on the crest of the
world, orders all things by the nod of His head, will never
desert His works or His kingdom. When the citizen is in
this wise governed he fears no ambush, he has no dread of
horrible wars and mournful famine, all pretences are swept
away from the unworthy backbiting of sycophants [and]
dishonesty, despised, lies prone, virtuous deeds everywhere
call forth friendship and mutual treaties bind men solicitous of serving their King and their God.

Can a rhumb line be drawn from Mercator's utopian projection
to Ronald Reagan's shining city on a hill? Did something like the
Millennial ACR always lurk in the back of the minds of Dutch,
British, and American Protestants?

It was verily bred in their bones! What else can the pundits
mean when they claim that Americans' idealism was "hard-wired"
or else "in their DNA"? The North Atlantic peoples—littoral, fed-
erative, Protestant, and fiercely commercial—who forged the
United Provinces, United Kingdom, and United States all enjoyed
eras of maritime hegemony, all incubated potent civil religions, and
all rejected the host of accommodations to local traditions and customs made by the Catholic Church over 1,500 years. Their
Presbyterian, Congregational, Episcopal, and Evangelical churches
encouraged political self-government that implicitly translated *vox
populi* into *vox dei*. But whereas the Dutch in their Golden Age and
the British in their Victorian Age harbored fantasies similar to those
of the American Century, they were shackled by history and geography to the Old World. Only Americans imagined themselves liberated from history, contingency, and limits. To them North America
seemed an Archimedes' fulcrum enabling them to move the world.

How could a continental nation of unmoored free thinkers be
disciplined? The Protestant genius, reinforced by Enlightenment
rationalism, was to apply the mantra *sola scriptura* to politics in the
form of a written Constitution and to economics in the form of
written contracts in order to foster liberty under law. The demographic and economic explosions that resulted from that ordered
liberty would astound Alexis de Tocqueveille and ultimately the
world. But over the generations Americans' power, prosperity, and

material progress combined with their spiritual entropy to draw
them down a long spiral staircase that political scientist James
Kurth has called the Protestant Deformation. Led by increasingly
apostate elites, Americans slipped from Trinitarian faith in salvation by grace to Unitarian belief in the rewards of philanthropy, to
an American Creed that made their nation Messiah, and finally to
universal human rights, which Eleanor Roosevelt imagined the
world's religion. The United States reached the last stage by the
1970s as it turned into a post-industrial empire of consumption
and the elites made their peace with the sixties' counter-culture
turned me-generation. In fact, they struck a grand bargain, according to which big business agreed to support radical social equality,
in exchange for which cultural authorities agreed to tolerate radical
economic inequality. British philosopher John Milbank put it this
way: "We're now at a crossroads. Politics is shadow play. In reality
economic and cultural liberalism go together and increase together. The left has won the cultural war and the right the economic one. But of course they are really both on the same side."
Was that a gross violation of ACR, or was the passage history had
reached in the twenty-first century a vindication of ACR, just as
Robert Bellah had projected?

The end of all nation-states and the triumph of universal markets and universal rights were the very day of the Lord promised by
Millennial ACR. The end of the Cold War, reunification of
Germany, peaceful disintegration of the USSR, rise of the Asian ti-
gers, North American Free Trade Association (NAFTA), European
Union and common currency, absorption of Eastern Europe into
the EU and NATO, worldwide wave of democratization, fourfold
increase in the Dow Jones index, balanced U.S. federal budget, and
global economy riding revolutionary computer and telecommunica-
tions technologies: all those signs and wonders seemed ample proof
that Francis Fukuyama's end of history was at hand. Scholars were
quick to attribute causal connections among those developments on
the grounds that all good things go together. Geoeconomics, it
seemed, was supplanting geopolitical hard power with soft or sticky
power—to use the terms coined by political scientist Joseph Nye
and historian Walter Russell Mead. It seemed that the world
America had built during the Cold War ACR era really did make it

possible for peace, democracy, and free markets to become what Michael Mandelbaum imagined were "the ideas that conquered the world." Presidents assuming the high priestly office after 1991 had no choice, it seemed, but to assume an immanentized eschaton.

To be sure, George H. W. Bush, the last World War II veteran to serve in the White House, was prudent and so self-effacing that he never spoke in the first-person singular. Emulating Eisenhower, he began his inaugural address with a non-denominational prayer that asked the Heavenly Father to "write on our hearts these words: 'Use power to help people.' For we are given power not to advance our own purposes, nor to make a great show in the world, nor a name. There is but one just use of power, and it is to serve people. Help us to remember it, Lord." But it was during the elder Bush's term that the United States tiptoed into the future guided by the Millennial ACR. His 1991 State of the Union address envisioned "a big idea; a new world order, where diverse nations are drawn together in common cause to achieve the universal aspirations of mankind—peace and security, freedom and the rule of law. Such is a world worthy of our struggle and worthy of our children's future." The proof texts for this civil theology were the twelve U.N. resolutions condemning Iraq's invasion of Kuwait and the military commitments made by twenty-eight countries on six continents. "The end of the Cold War has been a victory for all humanity," said Bush, and the First Gulf War neither a "Christian war, a Jewish war, or a Moslem war; it is a just war." Finally, of course, Bush 41 cooperated fully with the international investment banks and multinational corporations by advancing the GATT's ambitious Uruguay Round negotiations and by initiating negotiations for the NAFTA.

Bill Clinton, the first baby boom president, was a child of the romantic sixties who grew up with the "We Are the World" anthems of Millennial ACR. Blessed with a giddy decade of peace and prosperity, Clinton devoted his foreign policy to realizing globalization through Engagement designed to convert authoritarian regimes, Enlargement of multilateral democratic-capitalist institutions, and Assertive Multilateralism (humanitarian interventions) to fix failed states and rogue regimes. Influenced both by his mother's social gospel and the analogical thought (read: triangulation) picked up from a Jesuit professor at Georgetown, Clinton was keen to transcend sectarian disputes between, for instance, Jews and Muslims in the Holy Land, Catholics and Protestants in Northern Ireland, and Orthodox Serbs, Catholic Croats, and Muslim Bosniaks in the former Yugoslavia. But Clinton's principal legacy was economic because he continued to collaborate closely with Wall Street, multinational corporations, and Republicans in Congress to bring both the Uruguay Round and the NAFTA negotiations to fruition in 1994 in order to realize an Open Door world and to deregulate the domestic economy as well. For instance, the 1999 repeal of the Glass-Steagall Act on banking, dating from 1933, enabled just twenty institutions to suck up 70 percent of American financial assets, whereupon they became in effect too big to fail. Clinton's buoyant style and policies were reminiscent of Ronald Reagan, and so was his civil religious vision. "At the dawn of the twenty-first century," Clinton proclaimed in his second inaugural, "a free people must now choose to shape the forces of the information age and the global society, to unleash the limitless potential of all our people, and yes, to form a more perfect Union." In literally scores of speeches Clinton preached the Washington Consensus, which predicted all nations, however recalcitrant, must eventually embrace liberalism, the rule of law, transparency, peaceful arbitration, and international norms of governance if they wanted to prosper in the new world order.

Then history happened again. It exposed Clinton as a pied piper, the 1990s a fantasyland, and Millennial ACR a miscarriage. But it wasn't just 9/11. Even during the Clinton years many white working- and middle-class Americans resisted the transcendence required by a global civil religion. They had stoically endured the military burdens of the Cold War; suffered economic privation from de-industrialization and stagflation; and paid the psychic price for racial integration, open immigration, and female emancipation. They knew Bruce Springsteen's "Born in the U.S.A." expressed bitter irony and wounded pride. They heard Ross Perot's giant sucking sound of American jobs siphoned off to Mexico and overseas. To them "the Cold War is over and Japan won" seemed a truism. A paranoid fringe even suspected an elitist conspiracy of deploying U.N. black helicopters to snuff out American freedoms. But prominent politicians also resisted transcendence. In 1992 paleo-conservative Patrick Buchanan warned of a culture war pitting multi-cultural, transnational Progressivism against traditional national interests, plus international banks and multinationals against traditional American workers. In 1993 neo-conservative Irving Kristol lamented, "So far from having ended, my cold war has increased in intensity, as sector after sector has been ruthlessly corrupted by the liberal ethos. . . . We are far less prepared for this cold war, far more vulnerable to our enemy, than was the case with our victorious war against a global Communist threat."

The younger generation of neo-conservatives also resisted transcendence because they denied the millennial presumption that peace had broken out. The world was still full of monsters America needed to slay; hence the feisty neo-Progressive ACR must be retained. The principal fears of people like William Kristol, Robert and Frederick Kagan, Norman Podhoretz, Richard Perle, Paul Wolfowitz, and their fellow travelers were that the United States would disengage (a sin they called isolationism) or else sink into a pusillanimous multilateralism that stymied a muscular foreign policy. Being mostly secular Jews, they had no quarrel with Wall Street or with expressive individualism, and they even professed to believe in Progressive eschatology. But they hated Russia and feared for Israel because the end of the Cold War had devalued its worth as an ally and delegitimized its protectorate over Palestinians. Finally, neo-conservatives projected the rise of new peer competitors threatening what they called America's benevolent hegemony.

Most obviously, Millennial ACR aborted because many foreigners refused to accept normative prescriptions from what looked to them like a decadent civilization addicted to self-indulgence, the wealth needed to sustain that self-indulgence, and the power needed to sustain that wealth. Revisionist states such as Russia and China challenged the Cold War's verdicts. India, Pakistan, North Korea, and Iran defied global norms for nuclear non-proliferation. Transnational Islamic terrorists declared war on the United States and its allies in the Middle East, and American blunders post-9/11 ensured they would inflict damage out of all proportion to their resources. Even continental Europeans rebelled when the Bush

Doctrine exempted Americans from the rules they imposed on others. By 2006 it was obvious that Millennial ACR had failed as completely as Woodrow Wilson's ACR. But just as the first Progressive Era from 1898 to 1920 had brought radical changes that rendered impossible a reversion to the civil theology of the nineteenth century, so did the post–Cold War era bring radical changes that rendered impossible a reversion to the civil theology of the twentieth century. Therein lies a gigantic conundrum.

Western elites are in complete agreement that if the twentieth century proved anything, it was that nationalism is the incubus of racism, imperialism, militarism, and genocide. National sovereignty is also the precondition for messy, irrational, unpredictable democracy, which Progressives and big business hold in equal contempt. In the words of political theorist Kenneth Minogue, they consider the nation-state doubly reactionary and "a mockery of the term 'world community.'" Accordingly, the Olympians (so Minogue dubbed them) have no use for nations except insofar as they evolve into multicultural "rainbow empires" that are easily ruled from without. Olympians mean to iron out the wrinkles of history—national boundaries, commercial restrictions, religious taboos, local traditions—in favor of universal human rights and a universal marketplace.

Of course, the reverse phenomenon has also occurred: the United States has merged into the world and is fast becoming a rainbow empire. In 2004 political scientist Samuel Huntington asked, "Who Are We?" now that traditional Anglo-Protestant identity defined by race, ethnicity, culture, and ideology no longer existed. U.S. elites in academia, business, politics, and the professions have become transnational as a matter of demographic fact or self-definition. Students in elite universities prepare for careers in global markets linked by instantaneous global communications. Professors teach them that patriotism is morally dangerous and their highest loyalty should be democratic humanism. In short, the neo-cons' New *American* Century was always a pretense, as historian John Lewis Gaddis frankly admitted in 2004. The United States, he wrote, "should not content itself with making the world safe for democracy, or for diversity, or even primarily for the United States. Rather, it should seek to make the world safe for federalism, from which all else would flow."

Of course, a world safe for federalism does not yet exist, which means political fragmentation continues to torment (what Progressive billionaire George Soros calls) the "global open society." The most glaring anomaly is that nation-states, most especially the United States, have continued to monopolize military force in the world. But anomaly has turned to impending crisis because the War on Terror, Great Recession, and out-of-control budgets for defense and social entitlements have priced the policing of world order beyond even America's means. With the chairman of the Joint Chiefs of Staff and the secretary of defense both warning the national debt is now America's worst security threat, how long will taxpayers be willing or able to sacrifice, like the Stakhanovite horse in *Animal Farm,* for the sake of the world collective? The likely answer is only so long as they are persuaded they won't have to sacrifice because their entitlements programs will remain intact. That in turns means it is simply irrelevant for hawks to point out that the United States can afford to spend a good deal more than 3.5 percent of its GDP on defense because no politician will dare to "throw granny over a cliff" in order to develop more trillion-dollar weapons systems like the F-35. The guns and butter federal spending bequeathed by Cold War civil religion has caused the United States to mortgage its future to foreign investors for forty-five years and counting. First the Arabs with their petrodollars and then the Japanese bought up U.S. government securities, while today China owns some $1.3 trillion of American debt. Suffice to say the U.S. Treasury has now reached the point at which the British Exchequer was mired around 1965, when its government was obliged to retreat from its last bastions of empire.

Even assuming the U.S. economy rebounds sufficiently to fund its $20 trillion national debt and still pay for a welfare-warfare state, the millennial visions of universal human rights, democracy promotion, and social engineering in the developing world are pious frauds. First, no mechanism exists for enforcement of the U.N.'s Responsibility to Protect agenda; no two countries agree on where to draw the line between sovereignty and individual or group rights, while all three tiers of human rights—civil and political, economic and social, and environmental—collide with each other. To stress the second or third tier, as many groups on the left desire, would require that global bureaucracies be empowered to carve the hearts out of sovereignty, democracy, and, not incidentally, corporate profit margins. Second, nobody knows how to do nation-building save by tedious, expensive, trial-and-error methods, one country at a time, and even those dogged efforts fail more often than they succeed. American missionary efforts from the Philippines and Vietnam to Kosovo and Iraq have been especially expensive and lethal. Third, development economics are no nearer to becoming a science than when Truman launched the Point Four Plan in 1949. Too many variables are involved, not the least of which are human culture, corruption, and contingency. No wonder historian Mark Mazower stingingly concluded that "the idea of governing the world is becoming yesterday's dream."

Wise students of geopolitics knew the end of the Cold War would neither pacify the world so much as liberal internationalists wanted to believe, nor empower the United States so much as neoconservatives wanted to believe. By 2005 Fukuyama had broken with both. By 2008 even Robert Kagan had to admit that history had returned with a vengeance to end America's unipolar moment. Historic imperial centers have reemerged in China, Persia, and Turkey. No one has watched these trends more closely than Robert Kaplan, who has repeatedly concluded the best the United States can do now is to prepare gracefully for its own empire's demise. It is not surprising that the national mood turned sullen and surly during the second term of George W. Bush. The U.S. government was supposed to foster life, liberty, and the pursuit of happiness; freedom, peace, and prosperity; truth, justice, and the American way. By 2008 all nine of those qualities were in short supply. Had the nation forgotten what made it great when it shucked the Constitution and Washington's Farewell Address (not least "cherish the public credit") in order to wield world power?

Into this mess marched Barack Obama, the anti-Bush who outraged Evangelical voters by suggesting that when working-class voters "get bitter, they cling to guns or religion or antipathy to people who aren't like them or anti-immigrant sentiment or anti-trade sentiment as a way to explain their frustrations." During the presidential campaign opponents challenged Obama's patriotism, religion, and eligibility. He associated with sixties radicals and belonged to a church whose pastor cried, "God damn America!" It was said he did not believe in American exceptionalism and might be a closet Muslim. The truth was more prosaic. Half-Kenyan and half-Kansan, the child (in his own words) of a father "black as pitch, my mother white as milk," he grew up in multicultural Honolulu, where he attended the prestigious Punahou School on a scholarship and went on to graduate from Columbia College and Harvard Law School. When he moved to Chicago to work as a civil rights lawyer and community organizer, Obama joined the Rev. Jeremiah Wright's congregation. Not atypically for black churches in the urban north, the preacher often called down judgment upon the people in the manner of Hebrew prophets. So what most likely offended Evangelical Republicans was the blasphemy Wright committed against the civil religious creed to the effect that God always blesses America.

Being a smart politician, Obama disassociated himself from the embarrassing pastor and proceeded to drench his presidency in civil religion. The 2009 inauguration was suitably subdued because the country was mired in two stalemated wars and a Great Recession. Still, Obama called on Americans to renew "the God-given promise that all are equal, all are free, and all deserve a chance to pursue their full measure of happiness." He paid homage to all the American saints—immigrants, pioneers, and soldiers who had gone before us on "the long, rugged path toward prosperity and freedom"—and quoted the apostle Paul's admonition to put away childish things (I Corinthians 13:11). He broke new ground by welcoming Hindus and atheists into America's church (Bush had already blessed Muslims) and expressed confidence in "the knowledge that God calls on us to shape an uncertain destiny."

Perhaps the first black president wanted to reassure Americans with such comfortable words. But he did not need to do that at his second inaugural in 2013. Would Obama, safely reelected, now reject hoary cant in favor of candor? On the contrary, the civil religious liturgy at his second inaugural was so high-church as to eclipse even Bush's second inaugural!

Brooklyn's senator Charles Schumer, the master of ceremonies, welcomed the national congregation to another "sacred yet cautious entrusting of power." He proclaimed faith in America's future, the theme of the day, and declared 2013 "the perfect moment to renew our faith in America." Myrlie Evers, widow of slain civil rights activist Medgar Evers, delivered the invocation. She asked the Almighty to bless elected and appointed officials, seeded her prayer with biblical images (light of deliverance, great cloud of witnesses), and concluded, "In Jesus' name, and the name of all who are holy and right, we pray." The Brooklyn Tabernacle Choir then sang "The Battle Hymn of the Republic," Justice Sonia Sotomayor administered the vice presidential oath, and James Taylor sang "America the Beautiful," emphasizing the words "God shed His grace on thee." At last, Chief Justice John Roberts swore in Obama, artillery fired a twenty-one-gun salute, and the nation's high priest delivered his sermon.

It began by reclaiming American exceptionalism for the Democratic Party, a task John Kerry had begun in a cutting speech to the Democratic Convention in September. Next he recited a litany of the truths Americans had discovered together about slavery, economics, social welfare, the role of government, and the constant need for change. He exhorted Americans to face today's challenges "together, as one nation, and one people." In all, Obama used the word "we" fifty-nine times; "us," seventeen times; and "our," sixty-six times, eclipsing by far the calls for unity of all his predecessors. Obama then echoed Kennedy when he assured Americans their possibilities were limitless because their capacity for re-invention was endless. He declared it their task to make life, liberty, and the pursuit of happiness real even for the person in poverty because "she is an American, she is free, and she is equal, not just in the eyes of God but also in our own." The president pledged to defend the economy and environment God has commended to our care. He assured people that peace and security did not require perpetual war, yet echoed Bush in pledging support for "democracy from Asia to Africa, from the Americas to the Middle East." Last, he reminded all who served in government that the oath they swore was "to God and country, not party or faction" and exhorted all to "carry into an uncertain future that precious light of freedom. Thank you, God bless you, and may He forever bless these United States of America."

That was a tough act for Kelly Clarkson, the star from *American Idol*, to follow. But she captured the mood Obama had set with an exquisite rendition of "America" that rose to a crescendo in the final verse: "Our fathers' God, to Thee, Author of liberty, to Thee we sing / Long may our land be bright with Freedom's holy light / Protect us by thy might, Great God, our King." Schumer was struck dumb. All he could do was to shake his head and say, "Wow." But the liturgy still was not over. Poet Richard Blanco recited a lyrical ode to the American dream. The Rev. Luis León delivered a non-sectarian benediction (meaning he omitted the J-word). Beyoncé sang the national anthem. Finally, the Marine Corps band struck up "Stars and Stripes Forever," during which the president mounted the Capitol steps, turned back for a lingering look at the throng filling Washington's mall, and disappeared.

Obama, like Clinton, was a Progressive in cahoots with big business, a position that became evident almost at once when his Justice Department let Wall Street off the hook for the Great Recession. In foreign policy his evident purpose was to get the Millennial ACR back on track by repairing the damage Bush's unilateral belligerence had wreaked. So he hit the reset button with great power rivals; made a worldwide apology tour; reached out to the Muslim world; exited Iraq and scheduled an exit from Afghanistan; promoted multilateral responses he called "leading from behind" in crises ranging from Libya, Syria, Egypt, and Iraq to Ukraine and the South China Sea; normalized relations with Cuba; and pursued détente with Iran. Obama hoped to minimize foreign commitments in order to press a Progressive domestic agenda he called nation-building at home. Alas, history happened again. The Arab Spring revolts that began in 2010 advanced the Millennial ACR agenda nowhere except Tunisia. The pacification of Iraq and Afghanistan went into reverse. NATO forces helped rebels overthrow Libya's Muammar Gaddafi in 2011, only to make that artificial state another breeding ground for Islamic terrorists. In 2012 a revolt against Syrian dictator Bashar Hafez al-Assad quickly degenerated into a war of all against all that enabled Daesh (ISIS or Islamic State) terrorists to turn swaths of Syria and Iraq into a self-styled caliphate and to launch sporadic attacks at soft targets in Europe and America. The Obama administration, acutely conscious of the limitations of U.S. power, tried to fight terrorism from the air, especially with UAVs (drones) and announced a pivot to Asia that amounted mostly to pretense. Compared to its predecessor, the Obama administration did appear to adhere to his informal doctrine—"Don't do stupid sh-t"—but as of 2016 its only major accomplishments were the (dubious) nuclear deal with Iran and two more denationalizing free trade proposals, the Trans-Pacific Partnership and the Transatlantic Trade and Investment Partnership.

The American economy had not recovered from the Great Recession to judge by post–World War II standards of growth, employment, and wages. But Obama won reelection comfortably, thanks in good part to evolved civil religious rhetoric designed to appeal to changing American demographics revealed by statistics, polls, and big data. In terms of age, the Greatest Generation was all but dead and baby boomers geriatric, whereas Gen X and the Millennials had arrived. In terms of ethnicity, Hispanic and Asian Americans were steadily displacing Caucasian and African Americans. In terms of religion, young people who claimed a Christian affiliation had fallen to 55 percent (and Jewish affiliation to 2 percent) even as unchurched youth insisted they were, in some manner, spiritual. So Obama exploited his high priestly office to invite all Americans—not just Protestants, Catholics, and Jews—to join the human pilgrimage toward "community, prosperity, mutual care, stewardship of the Earth, peacemaking, and human rights." Those six ideals formed the core of what historian of religion Diane Butler Bass has named a "pluralistic, post-religious discourse" designed to move the country toward a civil spirituality potentially appealing to all humankind.

Yet Barack Obama failed to establish Millennial ACR as the nation's new orthodoxy, as was made painfully clear by the anti-establishmentarian mood of so many voters in 2016. Despite his eloquence and inspiring persona Obama was no more able than his three predecessors to escape a second long cusp during which Americans came nowhere near a consensus over what role Providence intended their nation to play in the world of the twenty-first century. How will the cusp come to an end? One possibility is a retrograde movement back to the neo-Progressive ACR, perhaps triggered by another Cold War against a new peer competitor such as China. But it is difficult to imagine how the United States could afford another such protracted conflict without going bankrupt or cracking up under the pressure. Even less likely is the wistful vision of a retrograde movement back to neo-Classical ACR, which bade the United States zealously to defend its own national interests but otherwise to mind its own business, cherish the public credit, and pursue peace and reciprocity with all nations. It is more likely that the pattern of history will repeat, only in dialectical fashion with twenty-first century characteristics. That is, the next generation may coalesce around a neo-Millennial ACR that will most likely double as the first operational global civil religion (GCR).

The characteristics of that GCR can only be guessed, but the famous dystopias of the twentieth century, such as Aldous Huxley's *Brave New World*, George Orwell's *1984*, and C. S. Lewis's *That Hideous Strength*, offer some clues. Most likely the coming GCR will federalize the governments and citizens, now reduced to consumers, of what used to be sovereign nations. The federation will likely mandate collective coercion of all dissenters, be they recalcitrant states, groups, or individuals who remain defiantly on the wrong side of history. The federation will likely be billed as a league of democracies devoted to human rights and free markets. In fact, it will likely be run by authoritarian transnational directorates in control of defense, information, and commerce. The federation will likely be grounded on the manipulation of fear. Indeed, the trigger that inspires the movement for a new American, now Global, Civil Religion may be one or another of defense analyst Andrew Krepinevich's deadly scenarios: nuclear terror, a global pandemic, all-out war in the Middle East or Western Pacific, or a worldwide environmental or economic crisis. There are certainly plenty of plausible fears to be soothed or else stoked.

What may be the theology of a neo-Millennial GCR? The faith will not be an expression of American exceptionalism because it will transcend national borders, institutions, and laws. It will not be grounded in any particular race, ethnicity, or language because Western civilization—the United States, the Anglosphere, the European Union—will have shed its Caucasian and Judaeo-Christian identities. It will not be democratic except in residual pretense because global governance cannot tolerate the exercise of popular sovereignty. But the new civil religion will be spiritual inasmuch as it pays lip service to a godhead with no qualities whatsoever except to be ecumenical, androgynous, nurturing, and affirming. It will be humanitarian to the point that it even suppresses freedoms of speech, assembly, and religion in the name of therapeutic equality. It will be transnational, administrative, and egalitarian in every corner of life except the ones that count most—namely, power and wealth. It will become heavily corporate because, as nation-states wither away, the federal directorates will contract out to the private and semi-private sectors such important functions as military defense, counter-terrorism, and intelligence gathering. There just won't be any need for national armies in an era of "fourth-generation warfare" dominated by drones, robotics, cyberattacks, and total surveillance.

Finally, this world government in beta mode—this global equivalent of the national security state spawned by the neo-Progressive ACR in the mid-twentieth century—will likely be marketed to its docile populations as the enlightened realization of the divine blueprint for humanity. It will pose as friendly fascism, compassionate conservatism, socialism with a human face. In fact, it may have a good deal in common with The Village of Patrick McGoohan's chilling imagination in his 1967 television series *The Prisoner*. In The Village everyone's name is replaced by a number, everyone's movements monitored, all conversations bugged, all elections rigged, all rhetoric phony, all reality virtual, all escapes thwarted by the prisoners' own fears, all the people their own jailors . . . but all material needs are generously met. Such soft authoritarianism was not exactly what the wizened Cold Warrior Strausz-Hupé had in mind when he exulted in 1995 that "the United States has, once more, the chance to sublimate a wartime alliance into a confederal and then—*Deo volente*—a federal state." But it is hard to imagine Europe, North America, Australasia, and the rimlands of Asia uniting around any ethic other than what Philip Bobbitt has called the Market State.

Way back in the last century world historian William H. McNeill told his profession and even the eastern establishment (in the pages of *Foreign Affairs*) that public myths need care, repair, and sometimes replacement. What historians fashion, he said, is really mythistory because truth is inexact and one person's truth is another's myth, especially at the national or imperial levels, where mythistories are invoked to bind populations and justify wars. McNeill declared the time had come to bury American exceptionalism as an outdated mythistory because the United States could only be understood as part of the pattern of world history, and there was no use pretending otherwise: "What we need is an intelligible world." In 2003 McNeill and his son published a "bird's-eye view" of the worldwide web of human interactions that have steadily accelerated since the dawn of civilization. The book ends with some chilling observations. The demographic explosion (from 2 billion people in 1930 to 7 billion today), technological explosion (from 80 exajoules of energy consumed in 1930 to 600 today), and the IT revolution (7 billion cell phones and 3 billion Internet users in 2014) have not only created inequalities unimaginable in past eras, but have also made even the poorest villagers aware of those inequalities. How can this century fail to be plagued by violent political and religious rebellions? How will the world's patricians tame its plebeians? Those questions will likely become first-order business for post-industrial societies, especially if they have confided their governance to an elite, transnational consortium under the auspices of a GCR.

The most obvious strategy is to suppress violent insurgencies while enticing the young, crowded, and poor human populations (especially the males) with the postmodern equivalent of bread and circuses. Recognition of cheap food and drink, cheap drugs, cheap entertainment, and cheap sex as fundamental human rights might indeed drain the swamp of terrorism, assuming that they could be provided. That materialist strategy presupposes organizational feats currently beyond the imaginations of "Build a Smarter Planet" IBM, plus technological breakthroughs ranging from bioengineering to nuclear fusion. But that, after all, was the very world advertised at the 1964 New York World's Fair, so the elite, transnational consortium legitimized by the GCR might devote its immense power to the realization of that world. But how "human" would the "beings" of that world really be if their global church also requires the denizens of our "small-world-after-all" to abandon the symbols and loyalties that give their lives meaning—in effect, their cultures—offering nothing in return except ownership of the means of consumption.

No wonder so many people—and not only radicalized Muslims—rebel against the devolved Protestant project long ago skewered by Herman Melville's harpoon in *Clarel: A Poem and Pilgrimage in the Holy Land*:

The Anglo-Saxons—lacking grace
To win the love of any race;
Hated by myriads dispossessed
Of rights—the Indians East and West.
These pirates of the sphere! grave looters—
Grave, canting, Mammonite freebooters,
Who in the name of Christ and Trade
(Oh, bucklered forehead of the brass!)
Deflower the world's last sylvan glade!

Jacob Burkhardt in *Reflections on History* once argued that revealed religions, unlike classical paganism, preserved their idealism only in protest against the claims of the state and that among them Christianity was the least adaptable to civil religion because of its universality. "How did it happen, then, that Christianity entered into the closest possible union with the state?" The answer is it did not happen everywhere, or anywhere completely, for an astonishing fifteen hundred years. What brought on the subjection of churches by governments were the Renaissance monarchies, the Protestant Reformation, and the rise of the power state. But what engendered Renaissance humanism? Could it be that the sublime Dante Alighieri was partly responsible? His political treatises favoring the secular authority of the Holy Roman Emperor, *Convivio* and *De Monarchia*, in effect denied St. Augustine's ancient distinction between the City of God and the City of Man. "Here for the first time in Christian thought," wrote the English historian Christopher Dawson, "we find the earthly and temporal city regarded as an autonomous order with its own supreme end, which is not the service of the Church but the realization of all the natural potentialities of human culture." The ultimate natural potentiality of the earthly and temporal city is to baptize all nations into a universal society governed by a universal state. Dante anticipated both the Machiavellian republic and Hobbesian Leviathan posing as "the vice-regent of God on earth" and "instrument of divine providence" that was "gradually leading mankind onwards towards perfection."

The Reformation, by splitting Christendom, made modern civil religions inevitable because the secular authority was now the guarantor of ecclesiastical authority rather than its rival. But that posed Burkhardt's dilemma: how to bring Christianity into the closest possible union with the state. Political scientist Ronald Beiner explains that Europe's monarchies and republics tried one or another of three main solutions. The first, or Machiavellian, civil religion, born in the sixteenth century, re-paganized the church and laity by reviving the ancient Greek virtues (and vices) rather than Christian ones. The second, or Hobbesian, civil religion, born in the seventeenth century, re-Judaicized the church by reviving the classical Hebrew virtues (and vices) and promising to build the kingdom of heaven on earth. The third, or Rousseauian, civil religion, born in the eighteenth century, re-secularized the church by reviving the ancient Roman virtues (and vices), including a ferocious intolerance of intolerance. American Civil Religion has, throughout its successive stages, assimilated features of all three solutions and never more so than in the twenty-first century. Thus did J. G. A. Pocock conclude, "It is notorious that American culture is haunted by myths, many of which arise out of the attempt to escape history and then regenerate it."

In 2007 the famed computer science professor David Gelernter dared publish an essay arguing that "America is no secular republic; it's a biblical republic. Americanism is no civic religion; it's a biblical religion." Did he mean the United States was a theocracy or a nation ruled by biblical laws? On the contrary, he meant that Americanism was a real religion, a fourth great Western religion derived from Judaism, Catholicism, and Puritanism. Gelernter's claim is absurd. The godlike presidency and Supreme Court have systematically severed all ties between the American Creed and the Bible, while most churches and synagogues long ago embraced what Jacques Maritain called democratic secular faith. Hence, for most mainstream denominations in the so-called West, Progressive politics and religion have, for all practical purposes, become one and the same.

What American Civil Religion retained from Christianity is universality, which in secular form can only mean world government, which can only reinforce the Machiavellian, Hobbesian, and Rousseauian manifestations of the will to power. Reinhold Niebuhr explained as much over and over again, so it should not come as any surprise. But Americans forget lots of stuff, often on purpose, rather than confront the collateral damage of wielding great power. In *The Four Loves* C. S. Lewis warned against the unhealthy patriotism that imagines "we are superior and therefore we crush lesser peoples" or else "we are superior, therefore we are obligated to help lesser peoples by ruling them." Lewis called both fantasies fatal and observed that "only by being terrible do they avoid being comic." No doubt healthy civil religion has great survival value. Civil religion can provide the emotional glue binding diverse groups to each other and to shared institutions and national interests. Civil religion can encourage citizens (at least those with sufficient republican virtue) to sacrifice for those shared national interests in times of depression, disaster, and war. But civil religion turns toxic when twisted into a Jacobin creed peddled to people at home through mythical history and forced down foreign throats at gunpoint. Perhaps Thomas Pynchon's heterodox charlatan, the Rev. Wicks Cherrycoke, said it best in the 1997 novel *Mason & Dixon:* "Who claims Truth, Truth abandons. History is hir'd, or coerc'd, only in Interests that must ever prove base." The deformation of American Civil Religion has ended by devouring America itself.

Bibliographical Essay

The principal primary sources for a book on American Civil Religion and foreign affairs are inevitably the oral and written words of the presidents and more generally the nation's political, clerical, intellectual, and commercial elites. Sources for presidential rhetoric include comprehensive collections such as Worthington C. Ford, ed., *The Writings of John Quincy Adams*, 7 vols. (1913–17); Roy P. Basler, ed., *The Collected Works of Abraham Lincoln*, 9 vols. (1953–55); Arthur S. Link, ed., *The Papers of Woodrow Wilson*, 69 vols. (1966–94); and the *Public Papers of the Presidents* series. Sources for elite opinion include contemporary newspapers, journals, speeches, sermons, books, the *Congressional Record* and its antecedents, the *Foreign Relations of the United States* series, and myriad online Internet sources.

Some Categories of Secondary Sources

This study falls into several historical categories, yet also falls through them into a basket all its own. That is because it represents the first effort to trace the deformation of American Civil Religion over the nation's entire history, examine the role it has played as both motivation and justification for U.S. foreign policies, and combine that civil theology with strategy and economics in a sort of unified field theory. The broadest category into which *The Tragedy of U.S. Foreign Policy* fits is what used to be U.S. diplomatic history but is now styled "transnational history" or "America and the world." This field was for a long time characterized by the tensions historians discerned between isolationism and internationalism, realism and idealism, and ideology and national interest. Walter A. McDougall, *Promised Land, Crusader State: The American Encounter in the World Since 1776* (1997), suspected those dichotomies were simplistic and organized the history of U.S. foreign relations around eight abiding traditions that reinforced or else clashed with each other.

Political scientist David C. Hendrickson, *Union, Nation, or Empire: The American Debate over International Relations, 1789–1941* (2009), developed in impressive detail a similar argument. But other subsets of historians have challenged those hoary dichotomies by asserting a continuity based on some primacy. The Open Door school, which explains U.S. foreign policy in terms of capitalist expansion, has now spanned four generations, from Charles A. Beard, *The Idea of National Interest: An Analytical Study in American Foreign Policy* (1934), to William Appleman Williams, *The Tragedy of American Diplomacy*, rev. ed. (1959); Gabriel Kolko, *The Roots of American Foreign Policy: An Analysis of Power and Purpose* (1969); Walter LaFeber, *The American Age: United States Foreign Policy at Home and Abroad 1750 to the Present*, 2d ed. (1994); Andrew J. Bacevich, *The Limits of Power: The End of American Exceptionalism* (2008); and Morris Berman, *Why America Failed: The Roots of Imperial Decline* (2012). Their emphasis has great merit insofar as agricultural, commercial, industrial, and/or financial elites have exerted powerful influences on U.S. foreign policy. But they cannot always prove agency on the part of business elites, struggle to explain why U.S. foreign policy has often been harmful to the economy, or else have little to say about the ubiquitous civil religious rhetoric by which presidents and their advisers sell foreign policies to the Congress and public.

Something similar confronts historians of the Realist school because an atmosphere of unreality so often surrounds U.S. foreign policy. Realists focus on power, emphasize geopolitics, and expect nation-states to pursue *raison d'état*, however imperfectly their statesmen respond to threats and opportunities emanating from abroad. Thus did Norman A. Graebner, *Foundations of American Foreign Policy: A Realist Appraisal from Franklin to McKinley* (1985), and *America as a World Power: A Realist Appraisal from Wilson to Reagan* (1984), and Norman A. Graebner, Richard Dean Burns, and Joseph M. Siracusa, *America and the Cold War, 1941–91: A Realist Interpretation* (2010), treat American moralism mostly as window dressing. But as valuable as such books remain, the fact is window dressing matters in a democracy, especially one in which politicians are inclined to believe their own propaganda.

Still other historians imagine that twentieth-century U.S. diplomacy, at least, reflected an ideological continuity based on liberal internationalism. To authors like Thomas Knock, *To End All Wars: Woodrow Wilson and the Quest for a New World Order* (1995); Frank Ninkovich, *The Wilsonian Century: U.S. Foreign Policy Since 1900* (1999); and Elizabeth Cobbs Hoffman, *American Umpire* (2013), the default position of U.S. foreign policy has never been European-style Realpolitik but moralistic and legalistic exceptionalism. As a result, their fine scholarship sometimes verges on teleology and tends to distort American history prior to Wilson. Among the books that argue for a deep continuity in U.S. foreign policy the best are probably Walter Russell Mead's *Special Providence: American Foreign Policy and How It Changed the World* (2001) and *God and Gold: Britain, America, and the Making of the Modern World* (2007), because they establish the unity of the spiritual and material in the Anglo-American worldview that was forged by the English Reformation and rise of the commercial Whig establishment. Among the books that argue for a deep continuity the worst is probably Robert Kagan's *Dangerous Nation* (2006), a case study in the fallacy of prolepsis.

A second category into which *The Tragedy of U.S. Foreign Policy* falls is the fertile field of U.S. religious history, whose excellent recent works include Mark Noll, *America's God: From Jonathan Edwards to Abraham Lincoln* (2002); Harry Stout, *Upon the Altar of the Nation: A Moral History of the Civil War* (2006); William Inboden, *Religion and American Foreign Policy, 1945–1960: The Soul of Containment* (2008); Darryl G. Hart, *From Billy Graham to Sarah Palin: Evangelicals and the Betrayal of American Conservatism* (2011); and Andrew Preston's magnificent and encyclopedic *Sword of the Spirit, Shield of Faith: Religion in American War and Diplomacy* (2012). These historians all flirt with the concept of civil as opposed to sectarian faith, but only Inboden directly links civil faith to foreign policy and only in the context of the Truman and Eisenhower administrations. Political scientist James Kurth has written articles directly pertinent to the subject, including "The Protestant Deformation and American Foreign Policy," *Orbis*, Spring 1998; "The Protestant Deformation," *The American Interest*, December 2005; and "The Crisis of American Conservatism: Inherent Contradictions and the End of the Road," *FPRI E-Note*, December 2012.

The third and most obvious category into which *The Tragedy of U.S. Foreign Policy* falls is the one created in 1967 by University of California sociologist Robert Bellah with "American Civil Religion" in *Daedalus*. That seminal article spawned two decades of scholarship on the definition, origins, and impact of civil religion, including Ernest Lee Tuveson, *Redeemer Nation: The Idea of America's Millennial Role* (1968); Richard W. Van Alstyne, *Genesis of American Nationalism* (1970); Conrad Cherry, ed., *God's New Israel: Religious Interpretations of American Destiny* (1971); Robert N. Bellah, *The Broken Covenant: American Civil Religion in a Time of Trial* (1975); Catherine L. Albanese, *Sons of the Fathers: The Civil Religion of the American Revolution* (1976); Robert N. Bellah and Phillip E. Hammond, eds., *Varieties of Civil Religion* (1980); Ellis M. West, "A Proposed Neutral Definition of Civil Religion," *Journal of Church and State*, Winter 1980; Michael W. Hughey, *Civil Religion and Moral Order: Theoretical and Historical Dimensions* (1983); and Ruth H. Bloch, *Visionary Republic: Millennial Themes in American Thought, 1756–1800* (1985). Nor should one exclude from this category such classics as J. G. A. Pocock, *The Machiavellian Moment: Florentine Political Thought and the Atlantic Republican Tradition* (1975); Michael G. Kammen, *A Season of Youth: The American Revolution and the Historical Imagination* (1988); Conor Cruise O'Brien, *God Land: Reflections on Religion and Nationalism* (1988); Hiram

Caton, *The Politics of Progress: The Origins and Development of the Commercial Republic, 1600–1835* (1988); Garry Wills, *Under God: Religion and American Politics* (1990); Harold Bloom, *The American Religion: The Emergence of the Post-Christian Nation* (1992); Michael Walzer, *What It Means to Be an American* (1992); Gordon S. Wood, *The Radicalism of the American Revolution* (1993); J. C. D. Clark, *The Language of Liberty, 1660–1832: Political Discourse and Social Dynamics in the Anglo-American World* (1994); Rogers M. Smith, *Civic Ideals: Conflicting Visions of Citizenship in U.S. History* (1997); and Pauline Maier, *American Scripture: Making the Declaration of Independence* (1997).

By contrast, however, the list of works linking civil religion to foreign policy is relatively short (albeit getting longer of late). They include Robert Jewett, *The Captain America Complex: The Dilemma of Zealous Nationalism* (1973); Claes G. Ryn, *The New Jacobinism: America as a Revolutionary State* (1991); Tom Engelhardt, *The End of Victory Culture: Cold War America and the Disillusioning of a Generation* (1995); Carolyn Marvin and David W. Ingle, *Blood Sacrifice and the Nation: Totem Rituals and the American Flag* (1999); Cecilia E. O'Leary, *To Die For: The Paradox of American Patriotism* (1999); T. Jeremy Gunn, *Spiritual Weapons: The Cold War and the Forging of an American National Religion* (2009); Susan A. Brewer, *Why America Fights: Patriotism and War Propaganda from the Philippines to Iraq* (2009); Jason W. Stevens, *God-Fearing and Free: A Spiritual History of America's Cold War* (2010); and Raymond Haberski, Jr., *God and War: American Civil Religion since 1945* (2012). A principal theme in these books is that American culture is a cult in which sacramental violence (periodic holy war) in the name of its shibboleths serves to sustain the unity and identity of a diverse citizenry. That may sound mad. But does it really diverge from Lincoln's view of the Civil War as blood sacrifice for the expiation of national sin, or Wilson's celebration of the Great War as a moment when America was privileged to spend her blood, or the veneration of World War II's "greatest generation," or the totemic tributes paid to today's wounded warriors as described by Andrew Bacevich, *The New American Militarism: How Americans Are Seduced by War* (2005)?

The recent flood of monographs and edited volumes examining the religious faith of American presidents constitutes a fourth relevant genre. Indeed, it is hard to see how *The Tragedy of U.S. Foreign Policy* could have been written without the insights and anecdotes in Frank Lambert, *The Founding Fathers and the Place of Religion in America* (2003); Daniel L. Dreisach, ed., *The Founders on God and Government* (2004); John Eidsmore, *Christianity and the Constitution: The Faith of our Founding Fathers* (2004); Michael and Jana Novak, *Washington's God: Religion, Liberty, and the Father of Our Country* (2006); Gary Scott Smith: *Faith and the Presidency* (2006) and *Religion in the Oval Office: The Religious Lives of American Presidents* (2015); Randall Balmer, *God in the White House: How Faith Shaped the Presidency from John F. Kennedy to George W. Bush* (2008); Gastón Espinosa, ed., *Religion, Race, and the American Presidency* (2008) and *Religion and the American Presidency: From George Washington to George W. Bush* (2009); and David L. Holmes, *The Faiths of the Postwar Presidents: From Truman to Obama* (2012). Older treatments of the president's explicitly civil religious role include James David Fairbanks, "The Priestly Functions of the Presidency: A Discussion of the Literature on Civil Religion and Its Implications for the Study of Presidential Leadership," *Presidential Studies Quarterly*, Spring 1981, and Richard V. Pierard and Robert D. Linder, *Civil Religion and the Presidency* (1988).

All the sources above have contributed primary-source quotations, in some cases several of them and in a few cases (e.g., Preston) many references throughout this book.

Introduction: 9/11 in Parallax Vision

The often conflicting and incomplete memoirs of post-9/11 officials include L. Paul Bremer III, *My Year in Iraq: The Struggle to Build a Future of Hope* (2006); George Tenet, *At the Center of the Storm: My Years at the CIA* (2007); Douglas J. Feith, *War and Decision: Inside the Pentagon at the Dawn of the War on Terrorism* (2008); Scott McClellan, *What Happened: Inside the Bush White House and Washington's Culture of Deception* (2008); Karl Rove, *Courage and Consequence: My Life as a Conservative in the Fight* (2010); George W. Bush, *Decision Points* (2010); Donald Rumsfeld, *Known and Unknown: A Memoir* (2011); and Stanley McChrystal, *My Share of the Task: A Memoir* (2012). Richard A. Clarke, *Against All Enemies: Inside America's War on Terror* (2004), and Richard N. Haass, *War of Necessity, War of Choice: A Memoir of the Two Iraq Wars* (2009), are by contrast candid and insightful.

Good journalistic accounts include Bob Woodward: *Bush At War* (2002), *Plan of Attack* (2004), *State of Denial* (2006), and *War Within* (2008); George Packer, *The Assassins' Gate: America in Iraq* (2005); Thomas E. Ricks, *Fiasco: The American Military Adventure in Iraq* (2006); Michael R. Gordon and Bernard E. Trainor, *Cobra II: The Inside Story of the Invasion and Occupation of Iraq* (2009); Peter L. Bergen, *The Longest War: The Enduring Conflict between America and al-Qaeda* (2011); and any of the books by Robert D. Kaplan. First-cut interpretations by scholars include Terry H. Anderson, *Bush's Wars* (2011); Michael C. Desch, "America's Liberal Illiberalism: The Ideological Origins of Overreaction in U.S. Foreign Policy," *International Security*, Winter 2007/08; Jane K. Cramer and A. Trevor Thrall, eds., *Why Did the United States Invade Iraq?* (2012); Peter Rodman, *Presidential Command: Power, Leadership, and the Making of Foreign Policy from Richard Nixon to George W. Bush* (2009); and Michael R. Gordon and Bernard E. Trainor, *The Endgame: The Inside Story of the Struggle for Iraq from George W. Bush to Barack Obama* (2012).

On the fiasco of nation-building in Afghanistan and Iraq, see Rory Stewart and Gerald Knaus, *Can Interventions Work?* (2011); Tim Bird and Alex

Marshall, *Afghanistan: How the West Lost Its Way* (2011); Brian Glyn Williams, *Afghanistan Declassified: A Guide to America's Longest War* (2012); and Gordon W. Rudd, *Reconstructing Iraq: Regime Change, Jay Garner, and the ORHA Story* (2011). On the neo-conservative persuasion, see Anne Norton, *Leo Strauss and the Politics of American Empire* (2004), and Justin Vaïsse, *Neoconservatism: The Biography of a Movement* (2010).

Excellent surveys of the post–Cold War era include George Bush and Brent Scowcroft, *A World Transformed* (1998); William G. Hyland, *Clinton's World: Remaking American Foreign Policy* (1999); David Halberstam, *War in a Time of Peace: Bush, Clinton, and the Generals* (2001); P. Edward Haley, *Strategies of Dominance: The Misdirection of U.S. Foreign Policy* (2006); Zbigniew Brzezinski, *Second Chance: Three Presidents and the Crisis of American Superpower* (2007); Derek Chollet and James Goldgeier, *America between the Wars, from 11/9 to 9/11: The Misunderstood Years between the Fall of the Berlin Wall and the Start of the War on Terror* (2008); Hal Brands, *From Berlin to Baghdad: America's Search for Purpose in the Post–Cold War World* (2008); Richard Sale, *Clinton's Secret Wars: The Evolution of a Commander in Chief* (2009); and Oz Hassan, *Constructing America's Freedom Agenda for the Middle East: Democracy and Domination* (2013).

Washington's World

With regard to the historical eras of U.S. foreign relations this essay is necessarily confined (for the most part) to recent literature. For the founding era that includes Gary L. Gregg II and Matthew Spalding, eds., *Patriot Sage: George Washington and the American Political Tradition* (1999); Robert A. Ferguson, "The Commonalities of Common Sense," *William and Mary Quarterly*, July 2000; Robert D. Sayre, *Britain and France at the Birth of America: The European Powers and the Peace Negotiations of 1782–1783* (2001); Frank W. Brecher, *Securing American Independence: John Jay and the French Alliance* (2003); David C. Hendrickson, *Peace Pact: The Lost World of the American Founding* (2003); George H. Nash, *Books and the Founding Fathers* (2008); Conor Cruise O'Brien, *First in Peace: How George Washington Set the Course for America* (2009); and James P. Byrd, *Sacred Scripture, Sacred War: The Bible and the American Revolution* (2013). On the Constitutional Convention, see Forrest McDonald, *Novus Ordo Seclorum: The Intellectual Origins of the Constitution* (1985); Louis Henkin, *Foreign Affairs and the United States Constitution*, 2d ed. (1996); Jack N. Rakove, *Original Meanings: Politics and Ideas in the Making of the Constitution* (1996); David Gray Adler and Larry N. George, eds., *The Constitution and the Conduct of American Foreign Policy* (1996); Gordon S. Wood, *The Creation of the American Republic, 1776–1787* (1998); Walter A. McDougall, *Freedom Just around the Corner: A New American History 1585–1828* (2004); and Richard R. Beeman, *Plain, Honest Men: The Making of the American Constitution* (2009).

The origins of U.S. foreign relations are the subject of Peter Onuf and Nicholas Onuf, *Federal Union, Modern World: The Law of Nations in an Age of Revolutions, 1776–1814* (1993); Lawrence S. Kaplan, *Alexander Hamilton: Ambivalent Anglophile* (2002); Ron Chernow, *Alexander Hamilton* (2004); Robert W. Smith, *Keeping the Republic: Ideology and Early American Diplomacy* (2004); Scott A. Silverstone, *Divided Union: The Politics of War in the Early American Republic* (2004); Eliga H. Gould and Peter S. Onuf, eds., *Empire and Nation: The American Revolution in the Atlantic World* (2005); Eliga H. Gould, *Among the Powers of the Earth: The American Revolution and the Making of a New World Empire* (2012); and Leonard J. Sadosky, *Revolutionary Negotiations: Indians, Empires, and Diplomats in the Founding of America* (2010). On Washington's diplomacy, see Stanley Elkins and Eric McKitrick, *The Age of Federalism* (1993), and the classic by Felix Gilbert, *To the Farewell Address: Ideas of Early American Foreign Policy* (1961).

On the split-minded diplomacy and civil religion of Thomas Jefferson, see Conor Cruise O'Brien, *The Long Affair: Thomas Jefferson and the French Revolution, 1785–1800* (1996); Robert W. Tucker and David C. Hendrickson, *Empire of Liberty: The Statecraft of Thomas Jefferson* (1990); Arthur Scherr, *Thomas Jefferson's Haitian Policy: Myths and Realities* (2011); Peter J. Kaiser, *The Nation's Crucible: The Louisiana Purchase and the Creation of America* (2004); and J. C. A. Stagg, *Mr. Madison's War: Politics, Diplomacy, and Warfare in the Early American Republic, 1783–1830* (1983). Outstanding scholarship on the incomparable John Quincy Adams continues to appear, as evidenced by Greg Russell, *John Quincy Adams and the Public Virtues of Diplomacy* (1995); Paul C. Nagel, *John Quincy Adams: A Public Life, A Private Life* (1997); Robert V. Remini, *John Quincy Adams* (2002); and Charles N. Edel, *Nation Builder: John Quincy Adams and the Grand Strategy of the Republic* (2014). On U.S.-Latin American relations and the Monroe Doctrine, see William Earl Weeks, *John Quincy Adams and American Global Empire* (1992); Lester D. Langley, *The Americas in the Age of Revolution, 1750–1850* (1996); Frank L. Owsley, Jr., and Gene A. Smith, *Filibusters and Expansionists: Jeffersonian Manifest Destiny, 1800–1821* (1997); James E. Lewis, *The American Union and the Problem of Neighborhood: The United States and the Collapse of the Spanish Empire, 1783–1829* (1998); Lars Schoultz, *Beneath the United States: A History of U.S. Policy toward Latin America* (1998); and Jay Sexton, *The Monroe Doctrine: Empire and Nation in Nineteenth-Century America* (2011).

Recent works on the Jacksonian era include Thomas R. Hietala, *Manifest Design: American Exceptionalism and Empire* (2003); H. W. Brands, *Andrew Jackson: His Life and Times* (2005); Daniel Walker Howe, *What Hath God Wrought: The Transformation of America 1815–1848* (2007); David S. Reynolds, *Waking Giant: America in the Age of Jackson* (2008); Jon Meacham, *American Lion: Andrew Jackson in the White House* (2008); and Walter A. McDougall, *Throes of Democracy: The American Civil War Era, 1829–1877* (2008). On the

Mexican War, see Thomas M. Leonard, *James K. Polk: A Clear and Unquestionable Destiny* (2001); William Dusinberre, *Slavemaster President: The Double Career of James K. Polk* (2003); and Robert W. Merry, *A Country of Vast Designs: James K. Polk, the Mexican War, and the Conquest of the American Continent* (2009). On western expansion the books referred to in the text are Jeremi Suri, *Liberty's Surest Guardian: American Nation-Building from the Founders to Obama* (2011); Carroll P. Kakel III, *The American West and the Nazi East: A Comparative and Interpretive Perspective* (2011); and Anne F. Hyde, *Empires, Nations, and Families: A History of the North American West, 1800–1860* (2011). Timothy Mason Roberts, *Distant Revolutions: 1848 and the Challenge to American Exceptionalism* (2009); Robert E. May, *Manifest Destiny's Underworld: Filibustering in Antebellum America* (2002); and Sam W. Haynes, *Unfinished Revolution: The Early American Republic in a British World* (2010) round out the sources for the chapter on the antebellum era.

No bibliography can do more than scratch the surface of scholarship on Abraham Lincoln. But some of the best recent works include Howard Jones, *Abraham Lincoln and a New Birth of Freedom: The Union and Slavery in the Diplomacy of the Civil War* (1999); John Diggins, *On Hallowed Ground: Abraham Lincoln and the Foundations of American History* (2000); Joseph R. Fornieri, *Abraham Lincoln's Political Faith* (2003); Douglas L. Wilson, *Lincoln's Sword: The Presidency and the Power of Words* (2006); Gabor Boritt, *The Gettysburg Gospel: The Speech That Nobody Knows* (2006); Michael Burlingame: *Abraham Lincoln: A Life* (2008) and *Lincoln and the Civil War* (2011); Ronald C. White, Jr., *A. Lincoln: A Biography* (2009); and Allen Guelzo: *Abraham Lincoln as a Man of Ideas* (2009) and *Fateful Lightning: A New History of the Civil War and Reconstruction* (2012).

On the Republican Party's "second American revolution," see Heather Cox Richardson, *The Greatest Nation on Earth: Republican Economic Policies during the Civil War* (1997), and Mark E. Neely, Jr., *The Last Best Hope of Earth: Abraham Lincoln and the Promise of America* (1993). Some principal sources for U.S. foreign policy during the Gilded Age include Anders Stephanson, *Manifest Destiny: American Expansionism and the Empire of Right* (1995); Fareed Zakaria, *From Wealth to Power: The Unusual Origins of America's World Role* (1998); David M. Pletcher: *The Diplomacy of Trade and Investment: American Economic Expansion in the Hemisphere, 1865–1900* (1998) and *The Diplomacy of Involvement: American Economic Expansion across the Pacific, 1784–1900* (2001); Edward P. Crapol, *James G. Blaine: Architect of Empire* (2000); T. L. Love, *Race over Empire: Racism and U.S. Imperialism, 1865–1900* (2004); Edward J. Blum, *Reforging the White Republic: Race, Religion, and American Nationalism, 1865–1898* (2005); Amy Kaplan, *The Anarchy of Empire in the Making of U.S. Culture* (2005); Frank Ninkovich, *Global Dawn: The Cultural Foundation of American Internationalism, 1865–1890* (2009); and David S. Foglesong, *The American Mission and the "Evil Empire": The Crusade for a Free Russia since 1881* (2007).

The concluding vignette is based on Charles W. Calhoun, "Civil Religion and the Gilded Age Presidency: The Case of Benjamin Harrison," *Presidential Studies Quarterly*, Fall 1993.

Wilson's World

The introductory section on Brownson owes everything to Michael Federici, ed., *Orestes A. Brownson: Works of Political Philosophy* (2007). The powerful trends of the late nineteenth century are the subject of H. W. Brands: *Bound to Empire: The United States and the Philippines* (1992) and *The Reckless Decade: America in the 1890s* (1995), and Jackson Lears, *Rebirth of a Nation: The Making of Modern America 1877–1920* (2009). For the origins of the Spanish-American War, contrast the celebratory interpretation of Warren Zimmermann, *First Great Triumph: How Five Americans Made Their Country a World Power* (2002), with the skeptical Richard F. Hamilton, *President McKinley, War and Empire* (2006), and Evan Thomas, *The War Lovers: Roosevelt, Hearst, and the Rush to Empire, 1898* (2010). The definitive scholar on U.S. intervention in Cuba, however, is Louis A. Pérez, Jr., *The War of 1898: The United States and Cuba in History and Historiography* (1998).

The classic article defining Progressivism is William Leuchtenburg, "Progressivism and Imperialism: The Progressive Movement and American Foreign Policy, 1898–1916," *Mississippi Valley Historical Review*, 1952. For contemporary perspectives, see Sidney M. Milkis and Jerome M. Mileur, eds., *Progressivism and the New Democracy* (1999). But no one explains the movement more succinctly than Bruce Kuklick in the relevant chapter of *A Political History of the USA: One Nation under God* (2009). On Progressive religion, see Charles Howard Hopkins, *The Rise of the Social Gospel in American Protestantism, 1865–1915* (1967). On the implications of the Social Gospel movement for U.S. intervention in Cuba, see Paul T. McCartney, *Power and Progress: American National Identity, the War of 1898, and the Rise of American Imperialism* (2006); Ian Tyrrell, *Reforming the World: The Creation of America's Moral Empire* (2010); and Paul T. McCartney, "Religion, the Spanish-American War, and the Idea of American Mission," *Journal of Church and State*, online, July 2011.

The Filipino insurrection is the ugly subject of Glenn Anthony May, *Social Engineering in the Philippines: The Aims, Execution, and Impacts of American Cultural Policy, 1900–1913* (1980); Stuart Creighton Miller, *"Benevolent Assimilation": The American Conquest of the Philippines, 1899–1903* (1982); Stanley Karnow, *In Our Image: America's Empire in the Philippines* (1989); Paul A. Kramer, *The Blood of Government: Race, Empire, the United States and the Philippines* (2006); and Gregg Jones, *Honor in the Dust: Theodore Roosevelt, War in the Philippines, and the Rise and Fall of America's Imperial Dream* (2011). For U.S. expansion in the Pacific generally, see the precocious transnational history by Walter A. McDougall, *Let the Sea Make a Noise: A History of the North Pacific from Magellan to MacArthur* (1994). The Anti-Imperialist movement is treated in David Mayers, *Dissenting Voices in America's Rise to Power* (2007); Fabian Hilfrich, *Debating American Exceptionalism: Empire and Democracy in the Wake of the Spanish-American War* (2012); and Robert Beisner's classic, *Twelve against Empire: The Anti-Imperialists, 1898–1900* (1968). The soldier's poem is printed in Bill Kaufman, *Ain't My America* (2008).

Sources for the chapter on twentieth-century trends include Avner Offer, *The First World War: An Agrarian Interpretation* (1989); Geoffrey Till, *The Development of British Naval Thinking* (2006); Niall Ferguson, *The Pity of War* (1999); W. Sydney Robinson, *Muckraker: The Scandalous Life and Times of W. T. Stead* (2012); G. K. Chesterton: *What I Saw in America* (1922) and *Heretics* (1905); and Edward McNall Burns, *The American Idea of Mission: Concepts of National Purpose and Destiny* (1957). Recent works on Theodore Roosevelt include the classic John Milton Cooper, Jr., *The Warrior and the Priest: Woodrow Wilson and Theodore Roosevelt* (1983); H. W. Brands, *T. R.: The Last Romantic* (1997); Greg Russell, *The Statecraft of Theodore Roosevelt: The Duties of Nations and World Order* (2009); James Bradley, *The Imperial Cruise: A Secret History of Empire and War* (2009); and Hans Krabbendam and John M. Thompson, eds., *America's Transatlantic Turn: Theodore Roosevelt and the "Discovery" of Europe* (2012). Recent works on Wilson include the excellent books by Lloyd E. Ambrosius, *Wilsonianism: Woodrow Wilson and His Legacy in American Foreign Relations* (2002); Thomas Fleming, *The Illusion of Victory: America in World War I* (2003); Malcolm D. Magee, *What the World Should Be: Woodrow Wilson and the Crafting of a Faith-Based Foreign Policy* (2008); and John Milton Cooper, Jr., *Woodrow Wilson: A Biography* (2009).

By far the most important source for a civil religious interpretation of U.S. intervention in the Great War is Richard M. Gamble, *The War for Righteousness: Progressive Christianity, the Great War, and the Rise of the Messianic Nation* (2003). Wilson's foreign policies leading up to his request for a declaration of war continue to be a fertile field. See Robert W. Tucker, *Woodrow Wilson and the Great War: Reconsidering America's Neutrality, 1914–1917* (2007); Ross A. Kennedy, *The Will to Believe: Woodrow Wilson, World War I, and America's Strategy for Peace and Security* (2009); Justus D. Doenicke, *Nothing Less Than War: A New History of America's Entry into World War I* (2011); and Thomas Boghardt, *The Zimmermann Telegram: Intelligence, Diplomacy, and America's Entry into World War I* (2012). Variations on McDougall's 1997 theme of America as a crusader state include Orrin Schwab, *Redeemer Nation: America and the World in the Technocratic Age, 1914 to the Present* (2004); David Traxell, *Crusader Nation: The United States in Peace and the Great War, 1898–1920* (2006); and Philip Jenkins, *The Great and Holy War: How World War I Became a Religious Crusade* (2014).

A whole library exists on the United States in the world war and Paris Peace Conference, but a few sources of special relevance to Wilson's civil religious crusade are John A. Thompson, *Reformers and War: American Progressive Publicists and the First World War* (1987); Ronald Schaffer, *America in the Great War: The Rise of the War Welfare State* (1991); Anders Stephanson, *Manifest Destiny: American Expansionism and the Empire of Right* (1995); John Milton Cooper, Jr., *Breaking the Heart of the World: Woodrow Wilson and the Fight for the League of Nations* (2001);, Robert W. Merry, *Sands of Empire: Missionary Zeal, American Foreign Policy, and the Hazards of Global Ambition* (2005); Erez Manela, *The Wilsonian Moment: Self-Determination and the International Origins of Anticolonial Nationalism* (2007); and Jonathan H. Ebel, *Faith in the Fight: Religion and the American Soldier in the Great War* (2010). The memoir on propaganda is George Creel, *How We Advertised America: The First Telling of the Amazing Story of the Committee on Public Information That Carried the Gospel of Americanism to Every Corner of the Globe* (1920). The classic study of Protestant opinion is Ray H. Abrams, *Preachers Present Arms: The Role of American Churches and Clergy* (1933).

Roosevelt's World

For the opening vignettes, see Peter J. Kuznick, "Losing the World of Tomorrow: The Battle over the Presentation of Science at the 1939 New York World's Fair," *American Quarterly*, September 1994; Larry Zim, *The World of Tomorrow: The 1939 New York World's Fair* (1988); Jane Holts Kay, *Asphalt Nation: How the Automobile Took Over America* (1997); and Robert Descharnes, *Salvador Dali: The Work, The Man* (1984).

John Lukacs, *The New Republic: A History of the United States in the Twentieth Century* (2004), describes trends in American life throughout the century, but his passage on the 1920s is simply exquisite. Postwar violence is the subject of Ann Hagedorn, *Savage Peace: Hope and Fear in America* (2007), and Beverly Gage, *The Day Wall Street Exploded: A Story of America in Its First Age of Terror* (2009). The organization of a formal foreign policy establishment is the subject of Peter Grose, *Continuing the Inquiry: The Council on Foreign Relations from 1921 to 1996* (2006), and Godfrey Hodgson, "The Foreign Policy Establishment," in *Ruling America: A History of Wealth and Power in a Democracy*, ed. Steve Fraser and Gary Gerstle (2005). The rise of American banks to global prominence and increasing influence on U.S. foreign policy is treated by Emily S. Rosenberg, *Financial Missionaries to the World: The Politics and Culture of Dollar Diplomacy, 1900–1930* (1999). Paul A. C. Koistinen, *Planning War, Pursuing Peace: The Political Economy of American Warfare, 1920–1939* (1998), and Manley R. Irwin, *Silent Strategists: Harding, Denby, and the U.S. Navy's Trans-Pacific Offensive* (2013), describe the military-industrial complex in the interwar years. Serious historians have long since ceased to refer to the 1920s as an isolationist decade. See, for example, Frank Costigliola, *Awkward Dominion: American Political, Economic, and Cultural Relations with Europe, 1919–1933* (1984).

The mood of war veterans in the wake of Wilson's disillusioning crusade is the subject of William Pencak, *For God and Country: The American Legion, 1919–1941* (1989). The opinions of Protestant factions are the subject of Robert T. Handy, *Undermined Establishment: Church-State Relations in America, 1880–1920* (1991); Marku Ruotsila, *The Origins of Christian Anti-Internationalism: Conservative Evangelicals and the League of Nations* (2008); Elesha J. Coffman, *The Christian Century and the Rise of the Protestant Mainline* (2013); and Richard M. Fried, *The Man Everybody Knew: Bruce Barton and the Making of Modern America* (2005).

That nothing reveals American culture during Franklin Roosevelt's isolationist 1930s better than film has recently been demonstrated by Peter C. Rollins, *Hollywood's White House: The American Presidency in Film and History* (2005); Thomas Doherty, *Hollywood and Hitler, 1933–1939* (2013); and Ben Urwand, *The Collaboration: Hollywood's Pact with Hitler* (2013). Michaela Hoenicke Moore, *Know Your Enemy: The American Debate on Nazism, 1933–1945* (2010), chronicles public confusion over the nature of the Nazi regime. The growing prominence of Catholics in the Roosevelt administration and American society is described in Anthony Burke Smith, *The Look of Catholics: Portrayals in Popular Culture from the Great Depression to the Cold War* (2010); Peter D'Agostino, *Rome in America: Transnational Catholic Ideology from the Risorgimento to Fascism* (2004); and Dominic Tierney, *FDR and the Spanish Civil War: Neutrality and Commitment in the Struggle That Divided America* (2007).

The gradual rise of self-styled isolationists to self-consciousness, then prominence, is the subject of Christopher McKnight Nichols's outstanding *Promise and Peril: America at the Dawn of a Global Age* (2011). Hans Schmidt, *Maverick Marine: General Smedley D. Butler and the Contradictions of American Military History* (1998), portrays the military hero who rebelled against U.S. interventionism. Roosevelt's own flirtations with isolationists are described in Robert David Johnson, *The Peace Progressives and American Foreign Relations* (1995), and Robert E. Jenner, *FDR's Republicans: Domestic Political Realignment and American Foreign Policy* (2010). The drama and mystery of Roosevelt's pivot toward interventionism continues to intrigue historians and their readers. Excellent recent works include Waldo H. Heinrichs, *Threshold of War: Franklin D. Roosevelt and the American Entry into World War II* (1988); Justus D. Doenecke: *In Danger Undaunted: The Anti-Interventionist Movement of 1940–1941* (1990) and *Storm on the Horizon: The Challenge to American Intervention, 1939–1941* (2000); David Reynolds, *From Munich to Pearl Harbor: Roosevelt's America and the Origins of the Second World War* (2001); Alan Brinkley, *The Publisher: Henry Luce and His American Century* (2010); Lynne Olson, *Those*

Angry Days: Roosevelt, Lindbergh, and America's Fight over World War II, 1939–1941 (2013); Susan Dunn, *1940: FDR, Willkie, Hitler—The Election amid the Storm* (2013); Andrew Johnstone, *Against Immediate Evil: American Internationalists and the Four Freedoms on the Eve of World War II* (2014); and David Kaiser, *No End Save Victory: How FDR Led the Nation into War* (2014). On the religious turn in the late 1930s, see Heather A. Warren, *Theologians of a New World Order: Reinhold Niebuhr and the Christian Realists, 1920–1948* (1997), and Gary B. Bullert, "Reinhold Niebuhr and the Christian Century: World War II and the Eclipse of the Social Gospel," *Journal of Church and State,* 2002.

Roosevelt presided over the sudden rise of the United States to unprecedented world power, yet he remains an enigma, a sphinx, perhaps even a failure. Recent important books on Dr. Win-the-War's dubious strategy and diplomacy but magnificent economic mobilization include Warren F. Kimball, *The Juggler: Franklin Roosevelt as Wartime Statesman* (1991); Thomas Fleming, *The New Dealers' War: Franklin D. Roosevelt and the War within World War II* (2001); Paul A. C. Koistinen, *Arsenal of World War II: The Political Economy of American Warfare, 1940–1945* (2004); Paul Kennedy, *Engineers of Victory: The Problem Solvers Who Turned the Tide in the Second World War* (2012); Arthur Herman, *Freedom's Forge: How American Business Produced Victory in World War II* (2012); and Maury Klein, *A Call to Arms: Mobilizing America for World War II* (2013).

That the Grand Alliance in general and Anglo-American special relationship in particular were in fact a grand pretense was suggested long ago by Christopher Thorne: *Allies of a Kind: The United States, Britain, and the War against Japan, 1941–1945* (1979) and *The Issue of War: States, Societies, and the Far Eastern Conflict of 1941–1945* (1985), and it has been amply demonstrated by subsequent scholars, including William Roger Louis, *Imperialism at Bay 1941–1945: The United States and the Decolonization of the British Empire* (1986); Randall Bennett Woods, *A Changing of the Guard: Anglo-American Relations, 1941–1946* (1990); Thomas E. Mahl, *Dangerous Deception: British Covert Operations in the United States, 1939–1944* (1998); Mark A. Stoler, *Allies in War: Britain and America against the Axis Powers, 1940–1945* (2005); and Stewart Patrick, *Best Laid Plans: The Origins of American Multilateralism and the Dawn of the Cold War* (2009). On FDR's use of maps, see Susan Schulten, "World War II Led to Revolution in Cartography," *New Republic,* May 2014.

The Roosevelt administration's planning for a postwar new world order is especially controversial—was it wise and generous, shrewd and aggressive, or merely incompetent? Contrast Elizabeth Borgwardt, *A New Deal for the World: America's Vision for Human Rights* (2005); Victoria de Grazia, *Irresistible Empire: America's Advance through Twentieth-Century Europe* (2005); Christopher Layne, *The Peace of Illusions: American Grand Strategy from 1940 to the Present* (2006); Michael Adas, *Dominance by Design: Technological Imperatives and America's Civilizing Mission* (2006); Wendy Wall, *Inventing the "American Way": The Politics of Consensus from the New Deal to the Civil Rights Movement* (2008); David B. Woolner, Warren F. Kimball, and David Reynolds, eds., *FDR's World: War, Peace, and Legacies* (2008); David Ekbladh, *The Great American Mission: Modernization and the Construction of an American World Order* (2010); Frank Costigliola, *Roosevelt's Lost Alliances: How Personal Politics Helped Start the Cold War* (2012); and Eric Helleiner, *Forgotten Foundations of Bretton Woods: International Development and the Making of the Postwar Order* (2014).

The sociological study exposing the low GI morale during the war was Samuel Stouffer et al., *Studies in Social Psychology in World War II: The American Soldier*, vol. 1: *Adjustment during Army Life*, and vol. 2: *Combat and Its Aftermath* (1949). Sources exposing how unlikely it was that the American people would embrace the Soviets as partners after the war include Ralph B. Levering, *American Opinion and the Russian Alliance 1939–1945* (1976); William L. O'Neill, *A Better World: The Great Schism: Stalinism and the American Intellectuals* (1982); John Earl Haynes and Harvey Klehr, *Venona: Decoding Soviet Espionage in America* (1999); Allen Weinstein and Alexander Vassiliev, *The Haunted Wood: Soviet Espionage in America—The Stalin Era* (1999); Mary E. Glantz, *FDR and the Soviet Union: The President's Battles over Foreign Policy* (2005); John Earl Haynes, Harvey Klehr, and Alexander Vassiliev, *Spies: The Rise and Fall of the KGB in America* (2009); G. Kurt Piehler and Sidney Pash, eds., *The United States and the Second World War: New Perspectives on Diplomacy, War, and the Home Front* (2010); and M. Stanton Evans, *Stalin's Secret Agents: The Subversion of Roosevelt's Government* (2012).

The atomic denouement of World War II has been expertly retold by Wilson D. Miscamble: *From Roosevelt to Truman: Potsdam, Hiroshima, and the Cold War* (2007) and *The Most Controversial Decision: Truman, the Atomic Bombs, and the Defeat of Japan* (2011).

Kennedy's World

Sources for the opening vignette include Daniel Yergin, *Shattered Peace: The Origins of the Cold War and National Security State* (1977); Arthur M. Schlesinger, Jr., *A Thousand Days: John F. Kennedy in the White House* (1965); Lewis Mumford, *The Myth of the Machine: The Pentagon of Power* (1964); Murray Morgan, *Century 21: The Story of the Seattle World's Fair, 1962* (1963); Lawrence R. Samuel, *The End of the Innocence: The 1964–1965 New York World's Fair* (2007); and Judith Barad, *The Ethics of Star Trek* (2000).

Ronald A. Knox, *God and the Atom* (1945), introduces the section describing the religious, political, and military reactions to the shock of the atomic bomb. The rich secondary literature includes Gregg Herken, *The Winning*

Weapon: The Atomic Bomb in the Cold War 1945–1950 (1980); Spencer R. Weart, *Nuclear Fear: A History of Images* (1988); Paul Boyer: *By the Bomb's Early Light: American Thought and Culture at the Dawn of the Atomic Age* (1994) and *Fallout: A Historian Reflects on America's Half-Century Encounter with Nuclear Weapons* (1998); Campbell Craig and Sergey Radchenko, *The Atomic Bomb and the Cold War* (2008); Michael Phayer, *Pius XII, the Holocaust, and the Cold War* (2008); Eric Patterson, ed., *Christianity and Power Politics Today: Christian Realism and Contemporary Political Dilemmas* (2008); Robert Dallek, *The Lost Peace: Leadership in a Time of Horror and Hope, 1945–1953* (2010); and Mark Edwards, "'God Has Chosen Us': Re-Membering Christian Realism, Rescuing Christendom, and the Contest of Responsibilities during the Cold War," *Diplomatic History*, January 2009.

For the origins of the United Nations and its human rights declaration, see Paul Gordon Lauren, *The Evolution of International Human Rights* (1998); Mary Ann Glendon, *A World Made New: Eleanor Roosevelt and the Universal Declaration of Human Rights* (2001); Paul Kennedy, *The Parliament of Man: The Past, Present, and Future of the United Nations* (2006); and Michael H. Hunt, *The American Ascendency: How the United States Gained and Wielded Global Dominance* (2007). Sources on the civil religious mobilization of support for containment include Anthony Burke Smith, *The Look of Catholics: Portrayals in Popular Culture from the Great Depression to the Cold War* (2010); Jonathan Herzog, *The Spiritual-Industrial Complex: America's Religious Battle against Communism in the Early Cold War* (2011); and Matthew W. Dunne, *A Cold War State of Mind: Brainwashing and Postwar American Society* (2013).

The passage on the origins of the Truman Doctrine and Marshall Plan drew on the memoir of Joseph M. Jones, *The Fifteen Weeks* (1955). Otherwise, the discussion of containment drew mostly from Michael J. Hogan, *A Cross of Iron: Harry S. Truman and the Origins of the National Security State 1945–54* (1998); Robert R. Bowie and Richard H. Immerman, *Waging Peace: How Eisenhower Shaped an Enduring Cold War Strategy* (1998); Melvyn P. Leffler, "The Cold War: What Do 'We Now Know?'" *American Historical Review*, 1999; Aaron L. Friedberg, *In the Shadow of the Garrison State: America's Anti-Statism and Its Cold War Grand Strategy* (2000); Geir Lundestad, *The United States and Western Europe since 1945: From "Empire" by Invitation to Transatlantic Drift* (2003); John Lewis Gaddis: *Strategies of Containment: A Critical Appraisal of American National Security Policy during the Cold War*, rev. ed. (2005), and *George F. Kennan: An American Life* (2011); Elizabeth Edwards Spalding, *The First Cold Warrior: Harry Truman, Containment, and the Remaking of Liberal Internationalism* (2006); Robert J. McMahon, *Dean Acheson and the Creation of an American World Order* (2009); Campbell Craig and Fredrik Logevall, *America's Cold War: The Politics of Insecurity* (2009); Curt Cardwell, *NSC 68 and the Political Economy of the Early Cold War* (2011); and Marc Trachtenberg, *The Cold War and After: History, Theory, and the Logic of International Politics* (2012).

On Korea, see Bruce Cumings, *The Origins of the Korean War,* vol. 2: *The Roaring of the Cataract 1947–1950* (1990); William W. Stueck, Jr., *Rethinking the Korean War: A New Diplomatic and Strategic History* (2002); Robert Beisner, *Dean Acheson: A Life in the Cold War* (2006); Steven Casey, *Selling the Korean War: Propaganda, Politics, and Public Opinion in the United States, 1950–1953* (2008); and Robert Dallek, *The Lost Peace: Leadership in a Time of Horror and Hope, 1945–1953* (2010). The constitutional issues raised by Cold War mobilization are described in Walter A. McDougall, "The Constitutional History of U.S. Foreign Policy: 222 Years of Tension in the Twilight Zone," FPRI E-Book on-line (2010). John Woo, *Crisis and Command: The History of Executive Power from George Washington to George W. Bush* (2009), applauds the huge increase in presidential war powers. Garry Wills, *The Modern Presidency and the National Security State* (2010), does not.

The Eisenhower administration's neo-Progressive civil religion was implicit in Reinhold Niebuhr, *The Irony of American History* (1952); Will Herberg, *Protestant, Catholic, Jew: An Essay in American Religious Sociology* (1955); and William Lee Miller, *Piety Along the Potomac: Notes on Politics and Morals in the Fifties* (1964). Aspects of it were made explicit by Patrick Henry, "'And I Don't Care What It Is': The Tradition-History of a Civil Religious Proof Text," *Journal of the American Academy of Religion,* 1981; Robert Griffith, "Dwight D. Eisenhower and the Corporate Commonwealth," *American Historical Review,* 1982; Martin E. Marty, "Reinhold Niebuhr and the Irony of American History: A Retrospective," *History Teacher,* 1993; H. W. Brands, *What America Owes the World: The Struggle for the Soul of Foreign Policy* (1998); Lizabeth Cohen, *A Consumers' Republic: The Politics of Mass Consumption in Postwar America* (2003); Eric Patterson, ed., *Christianity and Power Politics Today: Christian Realism and Contemporary Political Dilemmas* (2008); John Diggins, *Why Niebuhr Now?* (2011); Eugene McCarraher, "The Heavenly City of Business," in *The Short American Century: A Postmortem,* ed. Andrew J. Bacevich (2012); and Kevin M. Kruse, *One Nation under God: How Corporate America Invented Christian America* (2015), in addition to the general books on Cold War civil religion listed in the first section of this bibliographical essay.

On the myth of exceptionalism, see Ian Tyrrell, "American Exceptionalism in an Age of International History," *American Historical Review,* October 1991; Michael Kammen, "The Problem of American Exceptionalism: A Reconsideration," *American Quarterly,* 1993; Seymour Martin Lipset, *American Exceptionalism: A Doubled-Edged Sword* (1996); David W. Noble, *The Death of the Nation: American Culture and the End of Exceptionalism* (2002); Walter A. McDougall "The Unlikely History of American Exceptionalism," *American Interest,* 2013; and the masterpiece by Richard M. Gamble, *In Search of the City on a Hill: The Making and Unmaking of an American Myth* (2012). On the military-industrial complex and Cold War strategy in the 1950s, see Ira Chernus, *Apocalypse Management: Eisenhower and the Discourse of National Insecurity* (2008); James Ledbetter, *Unwarranted Influence: Dwight D. Eisenhower and the Military-Industrial Complex* (2011); and Paul A. C. Koistinen, *State of War: The Political Economy of American Warfare, 1945–2011* (2012).

The passages on Broadway shows in the chapter on the 1960s drew upon Alan Jay Lerner, *The Street Where I Live* (1978), and Dale Wasserman, *The Impossible Musical* (2003). The discussion of defense intellectuals was inspired by Karl Mannheim, *Ideology and Utopia: An Introduction to the Sociology of Knowledge* (1936), and is based upon Bruce Cumings, "Boundary Displacement: Area Studies and International Studies during and after the Cold War," *Bulletin of Concerned Asian Scholars*, 1997; Michael E. Latham, *Modernization as Ideology: American Social Science and "Nation Building" in the Kennedy Era* (2000); Christian G. Appy, ed., *Cold War Constructions: The Political Culture of United States Imperialism, 1945–1966* (2000); Alex Roland, *The Military-Industrial Complex* (2001); William Easterly, *The Elusive Quest for Growth: Economists' Adventures and Misadventures in the Tropics* (2002); Bruce Kuklick, *Blind Oracles: Intellectuals and War from Kennan to Kissinger* (2006); Derek Leebaert: *The Fifty-Year Wound: The True Price of America's Cold War Victory* (2002) and *Magic and Mayhem: The Delusions of American Foreign Policy from Korea to Afghanistan* (2010); Inderjeet Parmar, *Foundations of the American Century: The Ford, Carnegie, and Rockefeller Foundations in the Rise of American Powers* (2012); and Michael J. Glennan, *National Security and Double Government* (2014). The shock of Sputnik and origins of the Apollo moon program are the subject of Walter A. McDougall, . . . *the Heavens and the Earth: A Political History of the Space Age* (1985).

Cold War relations with Cuba have recently been treated by Alice L. George, *Awaiting Armageddon: How Americans Faced the Cuban Missile Crisis* (2003); Michael Dobbs, *One Minute to Midnight: Kennedy, Khrushchev and Castro on the Brink of Nuclear War* (2008); Jim Rasenberger, *The Brilliant Disaster: JFK, Castro, and America's Doomed Invasion of Cuba's Bay of Pigs* (2011); and David Barrett and Max Holland, *Blind over Cuba: The Photo Gap and the Missile Crisis* (2012). Insightful books on the Cold War in the Third World generally include Peter W. Rodman, *More Precious Than Peace: The Cold War and the Struggle for the Third World* (1994); Odd Arne Westad, *The Global Cold War: Third World Interventions and the Making of Our Times* (2005); Melvyn P. Leffler, *For the Soul of Mankind: The United States, the Soviet Union, and the Cold War* (2007); Campbell Craig and Fredrik Logevall, *America's Cold War: The Politics of Insecurity* (2009); and Jeffrey D. Sachs, *To Move the World: JFK's Quest for Peace* (2013).

On Vietnam, see Patrick Lloyd Hatcher, *The Suicide of an Elite: American Internationalists and Vietnam* (1990); Edwin Moise, *Tonkin Gulf and the Escalation of the Vietnam War* (1996); Frederick Logevall, *Choosing War: The Lost Chance for Peace and the Escalation of War in Vietnam* (1999); David Kaiser,

American Tragedy: Kennedy, Johnson, and the Origins of the Vietnam War (2000); Mark Moyar, *Triumph Forsaken: The Vietnam War, 1954–1965* (2006); William S. Turley, *The Second Indochina War: A Concise Political and Military History* (2009); and Lien-Hang T. Nguyen, *Hanoi's War* (2012). The fantasy that Kennedy would have pulled out of South Vietnam after his reelection was challenged by Diane Kunz, "Camelot Continued: What If John F. Kennedy Had Lived?" in *Virtual History: Alternatives and Counterfactuals*, ed. Niall Ferguson (1997), and dispelled by Christian G. Appy, *American Reckoning: The Vietnam War and Our National Identity* (2015).

The Cold War as incubator of civil rights legislation is the subject of Mary L. Dudziak, *Cold War Civil Rights: Race and the Image of American Democracy* (2000); Thomas Borstelmann, *The Cold War and the Color Line: American Race Relations in the Global Arena* (2001); and Francis M. Bator, "No Good Choices: LBJ and the Vietnam/Great Society Connection," *Diplomatic History*, 2008. The manipulation of domestic opinion has been examined by Marilyn B. Young, *The Vietnam Wars 1945–1990* (1991); Clarence Wyatt, *Paper Soldiers: The American Press and the Vietnam War* (1993); William M. Hammond, *Reporting Vietnam: Media and Military at War* (1998); Andrew L. Johns, *Vietnam's Second Front: Domestic Politics, the Republican Party, and the War* (2010); and Kenneth Osgood and Andrew K. Frank, eds., *Selling War in a Media Age: The Presidency and Public Opinion in the American Century* (2010).

P. J. O'Rourke, "The Awful Power of Make Believe," is in *Second Thoughts: Former Radicals Look Back at the Sixties*, ed. Peter Collier and David Horowitz (1989). On the beginning of globalization, see James A. Bill, *George Ball: Behind the Scenes in U.S. Foreign Policy* (1997), and Alfred E. Eckes, Jr., and Thomas W. Zeiler, *Globalization and the American Economy* (2003). Baby boomers are the subject of Neil Howe and William Strauss, *Generations: The History of America's Future, 1584 to 2069* (1991), and Steve Gillon, *Boomer Nation: The Largest and Richest Generation Ever, and How It Changed America* (2004). Mark Oppenheimer, *Knocking on Heaven's Door: American Religion in the Age of Counterculture* (2003), describes their spirituality. On the antiwar movement, see Godfrey Hodgson, *America in Our Time* (1978); Todd Gitlin: *The Sixties: Years of Hope, Days of Rage* (1987), *The Twilight of Common Dreams: Why America Is Wracked by Culture Wars* (1995), and *The Intellectuals and the Flag* (2005); Adam Garfinkle, *Telltale Hearts: The Origins and Impact of the Vietnam Antiwar Movement* (1995); Alexander Bloom and Wini Brienes, eds., *Takin' It to the Streets: A Sixties Reader* (1995); Christian G. Appy, *Patriots: The Vietnam War Remembered from All Sides* (2003); Tom Hayden, *The Port Huron Statement: The Visionary Call of the 1960s Revolution* (2005); and David E. Settje, *Faith and War: How Christians Debated the Cold and Vietnam Wars* (2011).

The Nixon administration, globalization, and the oil crises are the subjects of Charles S. Maier, Erez Manela, and Daniel J. Sargent, eds., *The Shock of the Global: The 1970s in Perspective* (2010). Although suppressed for a decade, then ignored by the American left and right alike, Franz Schurmann's *The Foreign Politics of Richard Nixon: The Grand Design* (1987) is still one of the shrewdest accounts of its controversial subject. Other important books on the Nixon era include Herbert S. Parmet, *Richard Nixon and His America* (1990); Joan Hoff, *Nixon Reconsidered* (1994); Melvin Small, *The Presidency of Richard Nixon* (1999); Jeremi Suri, *Power and Protest: Global Revolution and the Rise of Detente* (2003); Fredrik Logevall and Andrew Preston, eds., *Nixon in the World: American Foreign Relations, 1969–1977* (2008); and Daniel J. Sargent, *A Superpower Transformed: The Remaking of American Foreign Relations in the 1970s* (2015).

Globalization, which appeared by the 1970s to threaten both sovereignty and democracy, was the concern of Raymond Vernon, *Sovereignty at Bay* (1971); U.S. Senate Finance Committee, *Multinational Corporations and the World Economy* (1973); Karl Kaiser, "Transnational Relations as a Threat to the Democratic Process," in *Transnational Relations and World Politics*, ed. Robert Keohane and Joseph P. Nye (1973); Myra Wilkins, *The Maturing of Multinational Enterprise* (1974); Robert Gilpin, *U.S. Power and the Multinational Corporation: The Political Economy of Foreign Direct Investment* (1975); Alan Wolfe, *The Limits of Legitimacy: Political Contradictions of Contemporary Capitalism* (1977); and Fred I. Block, *The Origins of International Economic Disorder* (1977). Historical perspectives on the end of the Bretton Woods era and the OPEC oil crises include Daniel Yergin, *The Prize: The Epic Quest for Oil, Money, and Power* (1991); Diane B. Kunz, *Butter and Guns: America's Cold War Economic Diplomacy* (1997); David E. Spiro, *The Hidden Hand of American Hegemony: Petrodollar Recycling and International Markets* (1999); Alfred E. Eckes, Jr., and Thomas W. Zeiler, *Globalization and the American Economy* (2003); Francis J. Gavin, *Gold, Dollars, and Power: The Politics of International Monetary Relations, 1958–1971* (2004); Francesco Parra, *Oil Politics: A Modern History of Petroleum* (2004); F. William Engdahl, *A Century of War: Anglo-American Oil Politics and the New World Order* (2004); Judith Stein, *Pivotal Decade: How the United States Traded Factories for Finance in the Seventies* (2010); Jefferson Cowie, *Stayin' Alive: The 1970s and the Last Days of the Working Class* (2010); and Rohan Alvandi, *Nixon, Kissinger, and the Shah: The United States and Iran in the Cold War* (2014).

Nixon's vocal threats around the time of his landslide reelection are documented by William Safire, *Before the Fall: An Inside View of the Pre-Watergate White House* (1975); Stephen E. Ambrose, *Nixon: The Triumph of a Politician, 1962–1972* (1987); Richard Reeves, *President Nixon: Alone in the White House* (2001); and Conrad Black, *The Invincible Quest: The Life of Richard Milhous Nixon* (2007).

The international human rights movement, which also matured during the 1970s and inspired the Helsinki Accords, appeared to redeem in retrospect the otherwise bleak diplomacy of the Gerald Ford and Jimmy Carter administrations. See Glenn Mower, Jr., *Human Rights and American Foreign Policy: The Carter and Reagan Experiences* (1987); Samuel Moyn, *The Last Utopia: Human Rights in History* (2000); Richard A. Melanson, *American Foreign Policy since the Vietnam War: The Search for Consensus from Nixon to Clinton* (2000); Daniel C. Thomas, *The Helsinki Effect: International Norms, Human Rights, and the Demise of Communism* (2001); David F. Schmitz and Vanessa Walker, "Jimmy Carter and the Foreign Policy of Human Rights: The Development of a Post Cold War Foreign Policy," *Diplomatic History*, January 2004; Burton Kaufman and Scott Kaufman, *The Presidency of James Earl Carter* (2006); and Sarah B. Snyder, *Human Rights Activism and the End of the Cold War: A Transnational History of the Helsinki Network* (2011).

Carter's mostly unsuccessful efforts to promote democracy and development in the Third World are the subjects of Gaddis Smith, *Morality, Reason, and Power: American Diplomacy in the Carter Years* (1986); James A. Bill, *The Eagle and the Lion: The Tragedy of American-Iranian Relations* (1988); Douglas J. Macdonald, *Adventures in Chaos: American Intervention for Reform in the Third World* (1992); James C. Scott, *Seeing like a State: How Certain Schemes to Improve the Human Condition Have Failed* (1999); William Russell Easterly, *The Elusive Quest for Growth: Economists' Adventures and Misadventures in the Tropics* (2001); Kenneth M. Pollack, *The Persian Puzzle: The Conflict between Iran and America* (2005); and David Farber, *Taken Hostage: The Iran Hostage Crisis and America's First Encounter with Radical Islam* (2005).

The mystery of Ronald Reagan's religiosity is the subject of Paul Kengor, *God and Ronald Reagan: A Spiritual Life* (2004); John Patrick Diggins, *Ronald Reagan: Fate, Freedom, and the Making of History* (2007); Sean Wilentz, *The Age of Reagan: A History, 1978–2008* (2008); Walter L. Hixson, *The Myth of American Diplomacy: National Identity and U.S. Foreign Policy* (2008); and William Steding, *Presidential Faith and Foreign Policy* (2014). Clues to his political philosophies (really civil religious articles of faith) can be found in Kirron K. Skinner, Martin Anderson, and Annelise Anderson, *Reagan in His Own Hand: The Writings of Ronald Reagan That Reveal His Revolutionary Vision for America* (2001), and Kirron K. Skinner and Annelise Anderson, eds., *Reagan: A Life in Letters* (2003).

Anthony S. Campagna, *The Economy in the Reagan Years: The Economic Consequences of the Reagan Administration* (1994), describes the neo-liberal Reagan Revolution. Jim Castelli, *The Bishops and the Bomb: Waging Peace in a Nuclear Age* (1983), and Kevin Carnahan, *Reinhold Niebuhr and Paul Ramsey: Idealist and Pragmatic Christians on Politics, Philosophy, Religion, and War* (2010), interpret Reagan's defeat of the nuclear freeze movement. Good studies of his overall foreign policy include Raymond L. Garthoff, *The Great Transition: American-Soviet Relations and the End of the Cold War* (1994); Beth A. Fischer, *The Reagan Reversal: Foreign Policy and the End of the Cold War* (1997); Siobhan

McEvoy-Levy, *American Exceptionalism and US Foreign Policy: Public Diplomacy at the End of the Cold War* (2001); Colin Dueck, *Hard Line: The Republican Party and U.S. Foreign Policy since World War II* (2010); Jack F. Matlock, Jr., *Reagan and Gorbachev: How the Cold War Ended* (2004); Peter J. Westwick, "'Space-Strike Weapons' and the Soviet Response to SDI," *Diplomatic History*, November 2008; Ken Adelman, *Reagan at Reykjavik: Forty-Eight Hours That Ended the Cold War* (2014); James Graham Wilson, *The Triumph of Improvisation: Gorbachev's Adaptability, Reagan's Engagement, and the End of the Cold War* (2014), and Douglas E. Streusand, Norman A. Bailey, and Francis H. Marlo, eds., *The Grand Strategy That Won the Cold War: Architecture of Triumph* (2016).

Obama's World

The opening vignette was inspired by Jerry Brotton, *A History of the World in 12 Maps* (2014). The overall posture of the United States in the post–Cold War world has been elegantly traced by Charles S. Maier, *Among Empires: American Ascendancy and Its Predecessors* (2006). The Milbank quotation is from Richard Bishirjian, *The Conservative Rebellion* (2015).

Prognoses of what the post–Cold War world would look like included such euphoric books as Francis Fukuyama, *The End of History and the Last Man* (1992); Thomas L. Friedman, *The Lexus and the Olive Tree* (2000); Michael Mandelbaum, *The Ideas That Conquered the World: Peace, Democracy, and Free Markets in the Twenty-first Century* (2002); and Joseph P. Nye, *Soft Power: The Means to Success in World Politics* (2004), but also such dire prognoses as Samuel P. Huntington, *The Clash of Civilizations and the Remaking of World Order* (1996); Robert D. Kaplan, *The Coming Anarchy: Shattering the Dreams of the Post Cold War* (2000); Donald Kagan and Frederick W. Kagan, *While America Sleeps: Self-Delusion, Military Weakness, and the Threat to Peace Today* (2000); and Chalmers A. Johnson, *Blowback: The Costs and Consequences of American Empire* (2000), all of which preceded the terrorist attacks of September 11, 2001.

After 9/11 and especially after the Iraqi invasion it became clear how thoroughly the Millennial ACR had failed. A flood tide of books proclaiming the crisis of American empire then appeared, including Francis Fukuyama, *America at the Crossroads: Democracy, Power, and the Neoconservative Legacy* (2006); Robert Kagan, *The Return of History and the End of Dreams* (2008); Fareed Zakaria, *The Post-American World and the Rise of the Rest* (2008); Andrew F. Krepinevich, *Seven Deadly Scenarios: A Militant Futurist Explores War in the 21st Century* (2009); Jack F. Matlock, Jr., *Superpower Illusions: How Myths and False Ideologies Led America Astray—and How to Return to Reality* (2010); Robert D. Kaplan, *The Revenge of Geography: What the Map Tells Us about Coming Conflicts and the Battle against Fate* (2012); Zbigniew Brzezinski,

Strategic Vision: America and the Crisis of Global Power (2012); and Geir Lundestad, *The Rise and Decline of the American "Empire": Power and Its Limits in Comparative Perspective* (2012).

Two early efforts to assess the Obama administration's foreign policies are Colin Dueck, *The Obama Doctrine: American Grand Strategy Today* (2015), and Mark Moyar, *Strategic Failure: How President Obama's Drone Warfare, Defense Cuts, and Military Amateurism Have Imperiled America* (2015). The quotations from Kenneth Minogue are from "Christophobia and the West," *New Criterion*, June 2003; the Huntington quotes are from *Who Are We? The Challenges to America's National Identity* (2004); the Soros reference is from *Open Society* (2000). Political scientist and State Department official Anne-Marie Slaughter, *A New World Order* (2004), advocates multi-multilateralism, meaning transnational governance through overlapping national and international institutions. But it is impossible to imagine sovereignty or democracy surviving in such a regime. Philip Bobbitt, *The Shield of Achilles: War, Peace, and the Course of History* (2002) and *Terror and Consent: The Wars for the Twenty-first Century* (2008), depicts a more ominous future.

So far universal human rights, nation-building, foreign aid, and global governance have everywhere failed. See Simon Chesterton, *You the People: The United Nations, Transitional Administration, and State-Building* (2004); James Dobbins: *America's Role in Nation-Building: From Germany to Iraq* (2003), and *The UN's Role in Nation-Building: The Congo to Iraq* (2005); Francis Fukuyama, ed., *Nation-Building: Beyond Afghanistan and Iraq* (2006); Christopher J. Coyne, *After War: The Political Economy of Exporting Democracy* (2008); Mark Mazower, *Governing the World: The History of an Idea* (2012); and Eric A. Posner, *The Twilight of Human Rights Law* (2014).

Sources for this book's final thoughts include William H. McNeill, "Mythistory, or Truth, Myth, History, and Historians," *American Historical Review*, February 1986; J. R. McNeill and William H. McNeill, *The Human Web: A Bird's-Eye View of World History* (2003); Carl Jacob Burkhardt, *Reflections on History* (1943); Christopher Dawson, "The Christian View of History," in *God, History, and Historians: An Anthology*, ed. C. D. McIntire (1977); Ronald Beiner, *Civil Religion: A Dialogue in the History of Political Philosophy* (2011); David Gelernter, *Americanism: The Fourth Great Western Religion* (2007); Oliver O'Donovan, *The Desire of the Nations: Rediscovering the Roots of Political Theology* (1996); Claes G. Ryn, *A Common Human Ground: Universality and Particularity in a Multicultural World* (2003); and Thomas Pynchon, *Mason & Dixon*, cited by David Dark, *The Gospel According to America: A Meditation on a God-Blessed, Christ-Haunted Idea* (2005).

Supplementary documentation for this book is available on the Foreign Policy Research Institute website at www.fpri.org.

Acknowledgments

I HAVE ALWAYS LABORED alone without so much as a research assistant. Nevertheless, several individuals helped this project along with financial, material, intellectual, or emotional succor. Thanks to the University of Pennsylvania and the Smith Richardson Foundation, especially Senior Program Officer Nadia Schadlow, whose combined grants allowed me a year's sabbatical from teaching. Thanks to Frank Plantan, co-director of the International Relations Program at Penn, who relieved me of administrative duties even more than usual to free time for research and writing. Thanks to Martin Alloy, the surviving donor of my chair in international relations at Penn. Thanks to the trustees of the Foreign Policy Research Institute and especially FPRI President Alan Luxenberg for their generous and gracious support over twenty-five years and counting. Thanks to executive editor-at-large Steve Wasserman of Yale University Press and to agent Don Fehr for their faith that I had at least one more provocative book in me. Thanks to Bojana Ristich, the gifted and gracious copy editor to whom my manuscript was assigned. Thanks to Richard Gamble, Steven Fraser, David Hendrickson, and Alex Roland, who read the manuscript, corrected errors, and gave much needed encouragement. Thanks to Harvey Sicherman, the late president of the FPRI, from whom I learned a great deal about how American government (dys)functions. Thanks to my friend David Eisenhower, who teaches presidential communications in the Annenberg School at

Penn and tutored me, at this late stage of life, in the subtle arts of Aristotelian rhetoric. Special thanks to James Kurth, my personal Owl of Minerva whose criticism, counsel, and stoic wisdom sustained me throughout this anxious process. Thanks most of all to my Wonder Wife Jonna, whose faith and forbearance far exceed my deserts.

Walter A. McDougall
Bryn Mawr, Pennsylvania
June 2016

Index

France, 23, 35, 185, 248, 272; Bourbon
    dynasty in, 41, 60, 68; Britain vs.,
    41; canal project of, 92; CIA
    support for, 257, 261; as colonial
    power, 26, 69, 126, 276; imports
    restricted by, 293; nationalism in,
    139; navy of, 95, 135; reform
    movements in, 65; Second Republic
    in, 82, 83–84; Spain invaded by, 68;
    Spanish civil war avoided by, 193;
    Third Republic in, 130; war debts
    of, 184, 187, 190; in World War I,
    141, 148, 155, 159, 160; in World
    War II, 202–3, 220. See also French
    Revolution
Franco, Francisco, 193
Franklin, Benjamin, 27, 29, 40, 41
Franks, Tommy, 7
Freedom House, 323
freedom of the seas, 55, 58, 139
Freemasons, 27, 29
Free Soilers, 83, 91
Free Speech Movement, 299
French Revolution, 33–34, 37, 46–48,
    54, 56
Frost, Robert, 240
Fukuyama, Francis, 341, 347
Fulbright, J. William, 219
fundamentalism, 121, 177, 178

Gabriel over the White House (film),
    191–92
Gaddafi, Muammar, 313, 350
Gaddis, John Lewis, 345
Gagarin, Yuri, 241, 280
Gallatin, Albert, 81
Gamble, Richard, 97, 336
Garfinkle, Adam, 16, 296, 301
gas prices, 238
Gast, John, 73
Gelernter, David, 356
General Agreement on Tariffs and
    Trade (GATT), 250, 292, 314, 332,
    342

General Electric, 104, 169, 242
General Motors, 169, 170, 206, 238,
    242
Genêt, Edmund, 48, 83
Geneva Accords (1954), 272, 283
Geography of the Peace, The (Spykman),
    221
"Geopoliticus Child Watching the
    Birth of the New Man" (Dalí),
    171–72, 252
George III, king of Great Britain, 27,
    44, 65
Georgia, 63
Geremek, Bronisław, 323
Germany, 23, 126, 139, 250, 261;
    Britain threatened by, 140, 200;
    Catholics in, 193; communists in,
    184, 189; economic turmoil in, 189,
    191; FDR's denunciations of, 207;
    Fourteen Points opposed by, 141;
    Jews persecuted in, 196; navy of,
    95, 135; partition of, 231; Poland
    invaded by, 201–2; propaganda
    war lost by, 148; rearmament of,
    263; Red Army in, 256; reform
    movements in, 65; reparations due
    from, 184, 185, 231; reunification
    of, 341; revolutions in, 81; social
    programs in, 130; Soviet pact with,
    196, 201, 202; Soviet Union invaded
    by, 207, 210; Spanish Nationalists
    backed by, 193; submarine warfare
    by, 150, 151, 152; as world power,
    131, 134, 135; in World War I,
    141–65, 195; in World War II, 200,
    201–2, 207, 212–23
Gettysburg Address, 86
Ghost Dance movement, 105
Gilded Age, 90–99
Ginsberg, Allen, 302
Gitlin, Todd, 296, 300, 302–3, 304
Gladden, Washington, 123, 147
glasnost, 335
Glass-Steagall Act (1933), 343